Management Techniques
for Librarians

Second Edition

LIBRARY AND INFORMATION SCIENCE

CONSULTING EDITORS: *Harold Borko and G. Edward Evans*
GRADUATE SCHOOL OF LIBRARY SCIENCE
UNIVERSITY OF CALIFORNIA, LOS ANGELES

Management Techniques for Librarians

Second Edition

G. EDWARD EVANS

Graduate School of Librarianship and Information Management
University of Denver
Denver, Colorado

1983

ACADEMIC PRESS

A Subsidiary of Harcourt Brace Jovanovich, Publishers
New York   London
Paris   San Diego   San Francisco   São Paulo   Sydney   Tokyo   Toronto

ACADEMIC PRESS, INC.
111 Fifth Avenue, New York, New York 10003

United Kingdom Edition published by
ACADEMIC PRESS, INC. (LONDON) LTD.
24/28 Oval Road, London NW1 7DX

Library of Congress Cataloging in Publication Data

Evans, G. Edward, Date
    Management techniques for librarians.

    (Library and information science)
    Includes bibliographies and index.
    1. Library administration.   I. Title.   II. Series.
Z678.E9 1982   025.1   82-6875
ISBN 0-12-243856-6   AACR2

PRINTED IN THE UNITED STATES OF AMERICA

83 84 85 86   9 8 7 6 5 4 3 2 1

Contents

Preface

Management Techniques for Librarians is intended to serve as a textbook in introductory courses in library and information-center management courses. It emphasizes the basic issues and concepts of management that are especially important for persons starting out in the field. Although not a review of the latest trends in management, this new edition places more emphasis on current management trends than did the first. The discussion of collective bargaining (a much more common practice than in 1974 and 1975 when the first edition was written) and the merit (civil service) system has been expanded to a full chapter (13) in this edition. The subject of leadership appeared in several chapters of the first edition; in this edition Chapter 11 is devoted entirely to this topic. Two chapters on the history of management and approaches to management from the first edition have been combined to form Chapter 3.

Feedback from teachers and students indicated that more library examples were needed to illustrate the important concepts and ideas. To this end the number of examples has been greatly expanded. In a number of cases they are working documents (memos, letters, and position papers) with the names of the library and person(s) involved deleted. This publication of a second edition also allowed me to rewrite in what I hope is a less formal style. Also included are unusual and sometimes painful, and even comic, examples of the foibles of library managers.

Updated suggestions for further reading and study have been included in each chapter. The items were selected on the basis of availability and timeliness (although some of the older classics also appear); it is hoped that the material chosen adds to the depth of knowledge about the topic.

In my philosophy of management, people are more important than things; hence, almost all the chapters have a "people" orientation. The book begins with four general chapters on libraries and management, general management concepts, a brief history of management and managerial styles, and creativity and change in the library. The next 11 chapters cover what are generally considered to be the basic issues of management: the importance of authority and responsibility (including accountability); delegation of the authority and responsibility; decision making; planning; communication; motivation and leadership; personnel work in terms of both individuals and systems (civil service and collective bargaining); budgeting; and analysis of the work. The final chapter deals with some trends in the field.

Library is used to mean library, information center, resource center, or similar phrases that denote an organization that exists to provide information services such as information science, information management, documentation, and so forth. Likewise *librarian* is used in a "generic" sense to cover individuals, both male and female, who work in such organizations. I also use the word *professional* to mean librarian.

An offshoot of the library–information-center usage necessitated the selection of a term to employ for people who use the services of these organizations. Again there seems to be no single generally accepted term in current use. Therefore, I employed the terms *patron* (perhaps the most widely used term), *client* (a more recent entry into library and information science writing), and *user* (perhaps the least widely accepted term) interchangeably.

I wish to thank all of those people who have assisted in the preparation of this edition. Naturally, I would appreciate receiving further feedback from readers on how to improve this book. Finally, I wish all students the best of fortunes as they pursue their careers in the field and assume the responsibility of being supervisors and managers.

1. Libraries, Librarians, and Management

Managing a library requires the same basic skills as managing any other type of organization. Experienced people who possess a fundamental knowledge of management concepts, theories, and principles can manage almost any organization, regardless of its setting. If that is true, why write a textbook on library management?

Libraries and information centers have a combination of features and functions that makes them unlike any other organization. It is the relationship of these features and functions to basic management theories, principles, and practices that is the concern of this book.

This book is designed primarily for the *beginning* librarian who has had no formal exposure to management concepts. It focuses on basic management theory rather than on the newest or most popular current management ideas. There are three reasons for this: (1) as with any skill or subject specialty, one needs to understand the basics first; (2) many new ideas and popular concepts last only a few years before they fall from favor; and (3) a person who lacks knowledge of the basics is in a poor position to judge the advantages and disadvantages of new management concepts as they arise.

In this chapter we will explore the features that combine in a unique way to create the institution we call a library. Part of that exploration will be an examination of Max Weber's description of the characteristics of a bureaucracy and a look at how libraries fit the description of a "model" bureaucracy. Bureaucratic structure has implications for the people staffing and managing it. This chapter contains a brief discussion of the

1

question of whether an organization should be operated by professionals (as is true of most libraries) or by professional managers (as is true of most hospitals). Ultimately management is a matter of accomplishing work through people; therefore the last part of the chapter provides some ideas on how to be a more effective beginning employee and also a beginning supervisor.

SPECIAL ASPECTS OF LIBRARIES

One of the features of a library* that distinguishes it from may other organizations is that it is a not-for-profit (NFP) organization. This fact has a number of important implications, but two of the most important are (1) the financial resources used to operate a NFP organization generally come from an annual allocation of monies derived from sources outside the organization (such as patron donations, grants, government allocations, and private benefactors) and (2) most NPF organizations are considered to be public rather than private (a great many being either governmental agencies or totally dependent on governmental funds) and are thereby more susceptible to public scrutiny.

Profit-making organizations have an advantage over NPF organizations in that profit can indicate efficiency of functioning. When a profit-making organization fails to show a profit, this clearly indicates that a problem exists (although it does not indicate *where* the problem exists). In NFP organizations, however, there is no such indicator. Failure to secure adequate operating funds could point to a problem, but a value judgment of what is adequate is involved here. Generally, there is a long, slow build-up to a budget crisis in NFP organizations—a build-up that can span many years. In the profit sector, the year-end reports and the quarterly reports on profits provide an early warning.

With the exception of private libraries and libraries in profit-making organizations, libraries are dependent upon tax monies derived from governmental jurisdiction (community, county, state, or federal) and, in many instances, a combination of governmental agencies. When tax monies and the politicians who decide when and where those monies are to be spent become involved, the allocation process inevitably becomes political. Failure to recognize this fact has caused many libraries, over the years, to be inadequately funded and thereby not able to provide the needed level of service to the community that is to be served.

---

*The word *library* is used in a generic sense throughout this volume; it should be thought of as meaning libraries, learning centers, media centers, instructional materials centers, documentation centers, and information centers.

Because libraries are part of the political process and of a governmental system (local, state, regional, or federal), many management activities have boundaries of action that do not exist in the private sector (personnel practices, methods of budgeting, manner of decision making, and so forth). Although you will work in one specific situation, you can try to change your system if you know of alternative modes of operation that may be more effective than those used in your system. In order to do this, you need to have a general background in the variations that exist, and a knowledge of basic management principles and practices.

Politics and the political process must be considered as part of maintaining a publicly funded library system—not the politics of party partisanship, but the politics of decision making. The word *politics* has many definitions and connotations, most of which cover the following: (1) the acquisition and maintenance of power; (2) competition and conflict over scarce resources; (3) allocation of resources; and (4) determination of who gets what, when, why, and how. Aside from the first point, libraries constantly find themselves involved in these "political" areas. Certainly, the past few years of taxpayer revolts have demonstrated the fact that libraries can be dramatically affected by politics.

As part of a governmental system that does involve politics, library managers need to understand politics and public administration. Public administration is the process of carrying out the laws, rules, regulations, and policies that have been adopted by a relevant legislative body. Because of the rules and regulations, the director and supervisors have less freedom of action than do managers in the private sector. This is not to say that managers in the private sector have carte blanche. Many factors limit their choices of courses of action—government regulations (at all levels), union contracts, competition, and so forth. However, the private sector does have fewer constraints than are found in a governmental agency. For example, a library cannot set up its own salary scale. Although a library manager may recommend and lobby for a certain pay scale, that scale must fit into the overall system used in the jurisdiction. A private organization is free to set its salaries at any level as long as the minimum wage is paid—and even that restriction does not always apply.

Another special feature of libraries is their service and educational orientation. Until very recently, a basic tenet of librarianship has been that the services provided by a library are free; in other words, the patron was not expected to pay directly for services rendered. Today, as the world economic situation changes, this concept is being questioned with regard to certain types of services for certain classes of patrons. Perhaps in time, libraries will be required to provide services "at cost." This would move the library closer to the profit-making sector, but, until that occurs, most libraries and librarians are going to try to provide the best possible free service given the level of funding they receive.

Part of the service provided by libraries (and in the case of schools, colleges, and universities, the primary service) revolves around an educational function. Therefore, an educational library is tied to a larger organization—the institution that it serves. That institution's curriculum, educational philosophy, and policies have major implications for the way in which the library may be operated. Public libraries are normally expected to provide some self-education materials to the public. Although they are not directly tied to an educational institution, those who are responsible for the education function in a public library must have some knowledge of basic learning and education theories and concepts of the country in which their library is located.

Every library (with the exception of a few private libraries) is part of a larger organization. A school library is part of a particular school, a school district, and a governmental jurisdiction. Although some college and university libraries are part of privately funded institutions, many are also part of both a system and a governmental jurisdiction (University of California, for example). Public libraries are part of a community and a governmental jurisdiction. Even the special library is part of a company, business, or organization. Being part of a part means that the manager of a library must be aware of what the "whole" does and recognize that the whole must have some say in what the library does.

An effective library manager recognizes the part-of-a-part feature of library work and is vitally concerned about the library's environment, both internal (the physical atmosphere encountered by the patron) and external. Naturally, the local (immediate) environment would be most important among the possible external environments, but, as libraries develop networks and cooperative efforts, national, and even international, environments must be taken into account. In point of fact, the environment in which one library is located distinguishes it from all other libraries. A public library serves the general population of a town, city, county, or state; a school library serves the student population of an elementary or secondary school; an academic library serves an institution of higher education; and a special library serves the needs of a specific group or organization.

An excellent, brief article by Beverly Lynch describes four very important factors to consider when studying a library's environment: "(1) The nature of the environment itself; (2) The relationship among the libraries within a set of organizations (also it is useful to study the relationships among the other organizations making up the environment); (3) the characteristics of the exchanges that take place among libraries (again it is also of use to study the exchanges between the other organizations both among themselves and the library); (4) the impact that the environment has upon the libraries' internal structure and operations."[1] Because a library manager today has very little published material upon which to draw that is specifically library related, he or she should also investigate relationships and exchanges between other organizations.

THE LIBRARY AS A BUREAUCRACY

Not-for-profit organizations, especially governmental agencies or those dependent upon government funds, tend to exhibit the characteristics that Max Weber labeled bureaucratic. For many persons, the words *bureaucracy* and *bureaucratic* have only a negative connotation suggesting red tape and delay—no one person or office ever seems to have the entire answer, and no matter what is needed or has to be done, forms must be filled out. It always seems as if it takes forever to get the approvals needed to do (or change) even simple things. However, this aspect of an organization is *not* what Weber was describing. Rather, such features seem to be a function of size. In general, as an organization becomes larger, it becomes more and more difficult to know what its various units are doing and to achieve a high degree of coordination and effectiveness. Forms, reports, memos, etc., and the time factor are a result of attempts to maintain a degree of communication and coordination among a number of units; they do not necessarily indicate that an organization is a bureaucracy in the true sense of the word.

Weber identified the following traits as characteristic of a bureaucracy:

[1.] A continuous organization of official functions bound by rules. . . .

[2.] A specific sphere of competence. This involves (a) a sphere of obligations to perform functions which have been marked off as part of a systematic division of labour. (b) The provision of the incumbent with the necessary authority to carry out these functions. (c) That the necessary means of compulsion are clearly defined and their use is subject to definite conditions. . . .

[3.] The organization of offices follows the principle of hierarchy; that is, each lower office is under the control and supervision of a higher one. . . .

[4.] The rules which regulate the conduct of an office may be technical rules or norms. In both cases, if their application is to be fully rational, specialized training is necessary. It is thus normally true that only a person who has demonstrated an adequate technical training is qualified to be a member of the administrative staff. . . .

[5.] it is a matter of principle that the members of the administrative staff should be completely separated from ownership of the means of production or administration. . . .

[6.] a complete absence of appropriation of his official position by the incumbent. . . .

[7.] Administrative acts, decisions, and rules are formulated and recorded in writing. . . .[2]

Naturally, you ought to read Weber's entire book on this subject in order to fully understand his "ideal" bureaucracy, because it has become a classic in the study of organizations and how they function. The preceding is, however, an adequate base for determining how most libraries fit Weber's model. We shall now consider each point.

Libraries around the world are certainly bound by rules, both internal and external. On the technical side (librarianship), there are rules regarding cataloging and classification; there also are generally accepted practices—at least within one country, if not always on the international level—for example, how interlibrary loan requests are to be formulated and transmitted. Many library practices are standardized by actual work routines rather than rules formulated by a national or international library organization and based on a detailed and systematic study. Libraries formulate rules and regulations regarding who may use the facility, in what manner, and even for how long. There are even books available that provide summaries of libraries' rules and regulations.[3] Finally, the organization or government jurisdiction of which the library is a part will have its own rules, regulations, and laws that govern the way in which that specific library functions.

Most of these rules and regulations are not the result of arbitrary decisions or someone's desire to make more work; they have been developed to save time, provide consistent service, achieve a degree of standardization, and make the best use of scarce resources (people, time, and money). Rules, if administered fairly and applied rationally, ensure equal treatment for everyone. Rules also reduce the amount of ad hoc decision making that can cause inconsistencies and, in time, lead to a reputation for undependability and erratic service.

Certainly, the library has a specific sphere in which to work (Weber's second point), and, in many cases, it has a legal obligation to provide services to a specified group of people. Libraries seldom lack adequate authority to perform basic services. Occasionally, when a library attempts to expand its services (in some cases, expand its sphere of activity), problems arise. For example, if a public library began to expand its collection of theatrical films and to offer film programs once or twice a week, it might find local cinema owners claiming that the library had no right to offer free entertainment. The issue might then have to be resolved by the local municipal officials. Finally, very few, if any, libraries have had problems with the compulsion aspect mentioned by Weber. The major question in this area is how sanctions should be employed (if at all) to ensure patron compliance with rules and regulations.

Despite a great deal of discussion over the past few years about team management, participative management, collegial management, task force methods, etc.—all of which are presumably designed to eliminate or reduce hierarchical environments—most libraries are still good examples of an organizational hierarchy, which fits Weber's third trait of bureaucracy. A few libraries have tried some of the other approaches, but with limited success. You will still find, in any library, a group of persons (top management) who have the final say on almost everything that comes to their attention. Also, there is still a large group of persons "in the middle" who have a certain amount of decision-making responsibility. And finally, there is the largest number of staff members, the "troops." With a top, a middle, and a bottom, the library still resembles a hierarchy, no matter what labels are applied to the levels. The numbers of persons at the various levels may be nearly equal, so the classic pyramid structure no longer exists; however, I know of no library that does not have a director (regardless of the actual title given the position). In some countries, such as the Nordic countries, the top person is often referred to as the library leader, which reflects the fact that the management style is democratic, or group oriented.

As already noted, some of the rules governing the operation of a library are technical, dealing with library or information science and, certainly, there are many professional norms (Weber's fourth point). The application of these rules and norms, if it is to be done rationally, requires formal (specialized) training regarding them. This is one major reason that so few individuals who lack library training succeed in becoming effective librarians or directors of libraries: active involvement in planning and coordinating professional activities demands professional training. It is very difficult to gain the respect and confidence of professionals in a particular field when you do not share their technical background.

As to Weber's fifth trait, there is no question but that library administrative staff members have no "ownership" of the means of production and administration. The ultimate means of production are the monies used to operate the library. These monies come from agencies outside the control of the administrative staff; in fact, the staff is accountable to the funding body. Of course, for most libraries, there is both an annual budget and, theoretically, an annual accounting. The rigor of the accounting varies from slight to extreme, with most libraries finding the process to be light to moderate.

On a day-to-day basis, most libraries are free from outside influences in terms of their operations, so long as they remain within their defined sphere of responsibility and rules (Weber's sixth trait). It is unusual when a governing body or outside group attempts to influence the way in which a library actually *operates*. Cases of censorship or attempts to control what is in a library are all too common, but this is not a matter of how the library functions, but rather, the content of its collection. Very rarely will you hear of cases of a governing board or agency attempting to run a library by going around its director. Normally, when cases in which a governing board or agency with the authority to govern the library feels that it must work around the director, that director is dismissed, and a new person, usually one who shares the board's viewpoint, is hired to fill the position.

Very few libraries have a director who is free to hire and fire staff members at will. In fact, most libraries operate under rather tight controls in this area and are subject to many government regulations. Usually, a person who attempts to operate the library by using intimidation and fear is unable to remain director over a long period of time. In the very few cases of which I am aware, problems of this type were quickly solved by library staff as a group or by a government agency.

Finally, libraries are prime examples of organizations that record in writing their acts, decisions, plans, procedures, rules, and regulations (Weber's seventh point). This tendency, no doubt, arises in part from the nature of the field—dealing with the preservation and distribution of information. It is only natural that libraries are prone to creating and keeping a written record of their own activities. To some degree, a major percentage of the negative feelings concerning bureaucracies is derived from paperwork, forms, and books of rules and regulations that seem to overwhelm persons who seek something simple. However, any organization, bureaucratic or otherwise, can overuse or misuse written records of its past and present. It is not the records themselves that are a problem, but rather their use that generates problems.

Having now reviewed all seven of Weber's characteristics of bureaucracy in terms of libraries, we see that the "typical" library fits all of them. We might conclude, therefore, that libraries are "ideal" bureaucracies. Whether or not an individual library fits the positive or negative image of a bureaucracy depends upon its managers and staff. When run properly, a classic bureaucratic organization provides effective, efficient, rational, and humane service. Because of its characteristics, it provides a stable organization even in troubled times. No organization is good or bad in itself. The people who run an organization determine its positive and negative characteristics. Later chapters discuss some of the basic methods of management that can help you run your library properly.

PROFESSIONALS AND SEMIPROFESSIONALS: ROLE IN MANAGEMENT

One of the characteristics of a bureaucracy, as identified by Weber, is that the administrator (manager) be technically competent in the service being provided, that is, a "professional," whether it be in education, social welfare, or library science. Indeed, this is what we find in many NFP and government organizations, whether a school, social service group, or library. However, this arrangement creates some special problems for the organization.

One of these problems relates to the word *professional*. This word has taken on many connotations and has been defined in many ways. Originally, the word seems to have been applied only to the fields of law and medicine. Today, almost every field uses the term *professional* in some relationship to its work. A major reason for this desire to have the professional label is the prestige that has accrued to the fields of law and medicine over the years.

Librarians have been very concerned about professional status for many years. Many librarians feel that the phrase "professional librarian" is unnecessary, inappropriate, and certainly redundant, because they feel that the term *librarian* automatically carries with it a connotation of professionalism. If that is indeed the case, then many librarians have been wasting time, energy, space, and effort discussing the matter over the past 30 years.

Amitai Etzioni describes two categories of professions: full professions and semiprofessions. He sees a full profession as one that requires 5 or more years of *professional* (as opposed to general) education. Semiprofessional fields require less than five years of professional training.[4] Using his definition, then, there are very few full professions other than law and medicine. Librarianship does not qualify under this definition, as no librarianship program anywhere in the world requires more than 4 years to complete.

Etzioni and others who have studied professionalism[5, 6, 7] contend that a full professional must be allowed autonomy of action based on a responsible conscience in order to perform effective professional work. Without that, there would be no innovative methods or approaches to problems, experiments would seldom be carried out, and a general un-willingness to risk failure in an attempt to solve a difficult or previously insoluble problem would prevail. Naturally, autonomy leads to a very individualized approach to one's work; such an approach is not very compatible with the need for control, coordination, and supervision found in a bureaucratic organization. One needs little imagination to envision what would happen in a library if each librarian employed his or her own system. In order to be effective, libraries need more than occasional cooperation, coordination, standardization, and consistency. If that is true, and librarianship does not fit the educational definition of professionalism, then perhaps we are better off considering ourselves to be semiprofessionals.*

According to Etzioni, semiprofessional organizations "are more concerned with the communication and, to a lesser extent, the application of knowledge [this as opposed to the creation and application of knowledge in a full profession]. Their professionals are less likely to be granted the right of privileged communications, and they are rarely directly concerned with matters of life and death."[8] Again, libraries fit the definition of a semiprofessional organization, but even in a semiprofessional organization, there are always problems relating to management and the semiprofessionals.

One of the first problems is that of autonomy. Failure to recognize the differences between full professional and semiprofessional organizations can create staff conflicts. Persons who view themselves as fully professional often expect full autonomy in their work. Yet, by the nature of its function, a semiprofessional organization must have more control over the activities of its personnel than does a fully professional organization. This control is effected by means of a series of levels of supervision. The work day (schedule) is rather tightly regulated by the organization, and, although there may be flexibility in this area, ultimately, the needs of the organization must be met before those of the individual staff member can be taken into account. When direct supervision does not occur, a common requirement is that detailed written reports be submitted to a supervisor. Even units within an organization are expected to furnish both oral and written progress reports to the person responsible for the overall functioning of that organization.

On the positive side, many of the skills and attitudes required in a semiprofession are needed to manage an organization. As a result, more often than not, managers are drawn from the semiprofessional staff. Such

---

*Despite this, the word *professional* will be used interchangeably with *librarian* in this volume.

managers have the technical knowledge necessary to most effectively plan and operate the desired programs.

In some semiprofessional fields, such as librarianship, the fact that managers are drawn from the field leads to some deprofessionalization. More often than not in librarianship, career and financial advancement come about as the result of managerial rather than professional skills. Because of your success as a reference librarian, you might be asked to take the position of assistant head of reference. You would continue to work the reference desk, but you would spend a percentage of your normal working hours helping to plan work schedules, prepare budget requests, supervise part-time assistants, and probably aid in the assessment of other reference librarians' performance. Should you succeed as an assistant head, you might be offered the position of head of reference. If that occurred you would spend even less time working at the reference desk, not necessarily because you would not want to be there, but because your management responsibilities would take up most of your available work time. After that, higher positions, such as head of public services or assistant director, almost always mean full-time duties in management, with no time left for first-hand work with library clients. Thus, a person's orientation is slowly shifted from the client to the organizational point of view. This is not to say that it is an anti-client orientation. Rather, it is the view that what is good for the organization must be good for the client.

Another problem that has been identified in one way or another in hundreds of books and articles is that, unlike full professionals, most semiprofessionals are female. Until relatively recently, the assumption seems to have been that women are more "manageable" in an organizational sense, that women are less conscious of status, and that they generally have less education than men. In the past, perhaps the last factor was true on the average, but even that is no longer the case. One can question whether semiprofessional organizations have taken their form because of the number of women in the field or whether they have recruited women for organizational reasons.

Whatever the case, an attitudinal problem, as well as an employment problem, still exists in librarianship as far as management is concerned. Figures vary, but it is safe to say that in most countries, the ratio of men to women librarians is somewhere between 1:3 and 1:4. However, the ratio of men to women directors and assistant directors is almost the complete reverse. Occasionally, one will find situations (for example, the United States 10–15 years ago) wherein 90% or more of "top" management positions in libraries were filled by men. Moreover, as in other fields, there are significant differences in the salaries paid to men and women librarians. Male librarians' salaries, even at the beginning level, tend to be higher than those of females, despite the fact that they do the same work. This is shifting to an equal pay for equal work situation; however, differences do exist, and higher pay for males is still found.

Tracing the cause(s) of this situation and others like it has been the life's work of many persons. Undoubtedly, the ultimate sources could be traced back beyond the beginning of recorded history. Male dominance, conscious and unconscious, was no doubt the primary factor. Today, at least as far as viewing who does (or should) hold the position of library director, there is some indication that men and women maintain a stereotyped view. For 2 years (1975–1976) with 203 students, I used a library management case in which there were no personal names, just position titles—director of the library, head of reference, reference librarian, two clerks, and several student assistants. When the written case analyses were turned in, I checked to determine what, if any, personal pronouns were associated with the positions. One hundred seventy-nine students used personal pronouns: 72% used "he" to refer to the director, and 83% used "she" to refer to the reference librarian and the head of reference.

Although the number of students was small and the time frame was limited, these results indicate an image problem. It seems that, even when reading or hearing a term relating to persons in management—a term that should be sexually neutral—men and women tend to view top management as a male domain. As more and more women come to hold top library positions, this stereotype will be less prominent. However, until that happens we need to be more aware of this problem. Thus, an effort has been made to avoid the use of *he* or *she* in this book unless a specific person is involved. When you read the words *manager, director, supervisor, department head,* or *librarian,* remember they should be considered sexually neutral.

HUMAN RELATIONS SKILLS AND MANAGEMENT

Teachers in library schools are in a special position in that they usually have a number of friends in all levels of librarianship. If they have taught for many years after having been practicing librarians, they have friends ranging from long-time directors of major research libraries to recent graduates. This situation is special, because a teacher is exposed to a wide range of thoughts, feelings, rumors, and facts about the ways in which libraries operate and the perceptions of the persons responsible for the work being done. For a teacher of library management, it is depressing to realize how divergent the points of view may be between the "top" and the "bottom" levels of the same library. There is a great deal of "them-and-us" thinking on both sides.

In this section, we shall explore some things that the beginning librarian can do and should remember about management and upon becoming one of "them" (i.e., a supervisor). It is prepared from the point of view of the nonmanager, or at least the lowest level of management, although the remainder of the book deals with the issues contributing to the making of a good manager. This section is designed to help make you both a better employee and a first time supervisor and the emphasis is on the human relations skills you will need to employ and remember.

Beginning librarians cannot be expected to know, with a very few exceptions, what it is like to be responsible for a fairly large and complex organization. They often do, however, have fresh ideas and viewpoints, and occasionally knowledge of a new method of doing something. Managers, both middle and top, too often forget what it was like to be an eager, ambitious new librarian. They feel the pressures of time and the myriad of daily demands, and they seldom have as much time as they would like to get to know beginners or to work with patrons and gain first hand experience with the problems and demands that the staff faces every day.

As with most organizations today, libraries face a problem of staff confidence and, to some extent, trust. All too often, the staff views management's decisions and moves with suspicion. "What do they *really* mean by that?" is heard far too often. Managers, on the other hand, frequently feel that there is little or no staff loyalty to the institution. Loyalty is something that most managers hope to find in their staff members, but managers tend to forget that loyalty is something that is earned, not gained by demand, and that it is fragile. Indeed, it is something that can be destroyed by one act. Yet, what the library staff often fails to remember is that the library is part of a part in most instances and that the director and administrative staff members are not able to go beyond the limited authority available to them. Higher levels of decision making outside the library can and do override decisions made by library administrators. A common staff complaint when something like this happens is that the top managers "did not really want X, so they did not *really* work to get it." This is not true 90% of the time. The statement merely reflects an unwillingness to admit, if not an unawareness of, the fact that the library is only part of a part.

One of the first things to remember about the "boss" is that that person is a human being with the same needs as any other person. These include the need to be liked (despite what you might think), to be respected, to have friends, to do a good job, and to succeed. Bosses do care, and they suffer the same frustrations that you do when things do not go the way they should. Remember that, when you succeed, your boss also succeeds, just as your failure is also a failure for your boss. Therefore, your supervisor really *does* want you to succeed.

Telling the boss that you care about the success of the unit is fine. Showing the boss that you are not only interested but also willing and able to do something to contribute to that success is even better. Your efforts will make the unit and the supervisor look good. They also will gain support for the unit and its supervisor from the units above, which should mean that your supervisor will be more supportive of you. All of this is a means of gaining mutual trust and confidence, and a sense of sharing.

Sharing is important, and must frequently begin with the employee. Supervisors have a great many demands on their time and attention, both from above and from below. It may not seem like it, but you do have more free time than your supervisor does. Passing along a bit of good news is always welcome, and if you do this quickly, realizing that the boss is busy, it is even better. Remember that both the good and the bad need to be shared. Discussing a problem when it is small is much better than waiting and hoping that it will go away. Usually, when you start this sharing, your supervisor also will start sharing. In essence, you both will have improved the communication process. A word of caution is in order, however. If sharing is done privately or secretly, you can expect a very negative response from your peers. Sharing should be done openly and for the unit, *not* in secret or for personal gain.

Opening communication lines is vital, as we shall see in Chapter 9. Lack of (or poor) communication is the most frequently identified organizational problem. You can blame almost anything on it. Frequently, lack of communication is the real problem, but it is the scapegoat complaint on occasion. Numerous studies have shown (and my own consulting work has demonstrated) that, at at every level of the library staff, people feel that they do not have enough of the *right* information. Communication is present—both written and oral—but what is there is not what is needed or wanted.

You can help in this regard by identifying for your boss what you think you need to know in order to perform your job effectively. At the same time, you and your boss may find it useful to review your duties. Do not be surprised if there is a significant difference of opinion; this is one of the most common sources of misunderstanding in any organization. Only when there is frequent discussion of problems and successes in job performance will there be mutual understanding of duties. Again, if you start the process of sharing, you can help encourage the process of effective communication.

When you have a "great" new idea for something, take some time to think it through carefully. Do some checking, collect some data, and then prepare a brief proposal with some evidence for your boss. Again, your boss has a time problem, and throwing a half-thought-through idea to a very busy person usually is like throwing something to the wind. You should not be surprised if such an idea is rejected on the spot. On the other hand, an idea presented in such a manner as to show that it has been developed and that evidence to support it has been gathered will undoubtedly be given consideration. By putting information in writing so that your boss can study it during a quiet period, you improve the chances of securing a serious review of your idea.

When you do present a written proposal, or a request of any kind, do not become a nag about it. Nagging is one of the best ways to ensure a negative answer. There is nothing wrong with asking your supervisor when you might expect an answer at the time you present an idea, or even asking whether you might be told the decision by a certain date. If you do not do one of those two things at the time of presentation, though, it is not usually considered nagging to inquire after 2 or 3 weeks as to whether the boss has had an opportunity to look at your proposal.

If you become frustrated with your boss, there is a natural tendency to think that it would be a good idea to talk to your boss' boss. Do not do it at that point. At times, going over someone's head is appropriate and necessary; but those circumstances are not nearly as common as the desire to do so. The fact that your boss has turned down your twentieth "great idea" or your repeated requests is no excuse for breaking the chain of authority. When there is a unit-wide problem *and* there have been repeated requests to discuss the situation with the immediate supervisor (without satisfactory results), then the time has come to seriously consider "going around" that person. Even in that circumstance, though, it is better to ask the supervisor in question whether you could all meet with a third party to air the problem rather than go behind a person's back. By going around someone, you create an atmosphere of suspicion and distrust—generally, one in which very little productive work gets done. If you remember and do the things in the preceding paragraphs, as well as those that follow, you probably will never get to the point of even considering going over someone's head.

The following summarizes the preceding paragraphs in terms of positive actions that you can take to help generate more and better understanding between yourself and your boss. Additional suggestions also are included.

As an Employee

Take responsibility for good communication; do not wait for others to do it.

Be considerate of the time pressures that your boss must face daily.

Remember that you are an assistant to the boss, no matter what your title may be; you both succeed when you succeed.

Accept delegated responsibilities with good grace; remember that if you have been given more responsibility, so has your boss.

Whenever necessary, take the initiative, and remember to balance this against any image of being overly ambitious, aggressive, or "power hungry."

Share ideas and library news without being a gossip or demanding more than your share of the boss's time. Also, when presenting new ideas, do not be a nag or a "boat rocker."

Provide an opportunity for the boss to learn something about you beyond your professional skills and interests; be friendly without over-doing it.

Remember that you do not have to agree with everything the boss does and says, but do your disagreeing in private rather than in public.

Tell the boss when something has happened that you like; bosses enjoy compliments just as everyone else does.

Trust and understanding work both ways: If you trust the boss, then the boss will probably trust you.

Remember that bosses are human; treat them the way you want to be treated.

As a Supervisor

Be the first to admit your mistakes. Demonstrate that you have learned from them.

Be willing to accept responsibility; do not "pass the buck."

Be certain to seek the causes of a work problem, not merely its symptoms.

Be positive in emphasizing the future over the past and the present; this helps people to handle change more easily.

Be willing to see both short-term and long-term implications of your acts and decisions.

Be active in involving people in decisions that affect them, as it makes acceptance of new ideas much easier.

Be willing to use only ethical means to gain supervisory or institutional goals.

Be an example setter at all times; show, not demand, what you want.

Be certain that you attempt to understand the staff, and be certain that you actually do understand them.

Be willing to treat everyone with dignity and respect. (If you do, you will be treated in the same way.)

The rest of this book is concerned with the things that go into creating a well-managed library. Even if you do not become a manager, learning something about management will help you to understand what is being done to you and why. Such an understanding will make you a better employee, and it will help you to feel more satisfied with your work environment.

The next chapter explores some of the background material on management and libraries. This is followed by a chapter on the history of management and managerial styles. A chapter on innovation and creativity has been included because these are the means by which organizations remain viable in a changing society. The following 10 chapters cover the basics of management, authority and power, decision making, delegation, communication, motivation, personnel, finance and budgeting, and work analysis. The final chapter focuses on the future of library management. Each chapter includes a list of suggested further reading. These are designed to provide more depth on a particular topic, and to help students to gain a fuller understanding of the subject matter.

BIBLIOGRAPHY

1. B. Lynch, "The Academic Library and Its Environment," *College and Research Libraries* 35 (Mar. 1974): 126–132, p. 127.
2. M. Weber, *The Theory of Social and Economic Organizations.* Translated by A. M. Henderson and Talcott H. Parsons (New York: Free Press of Glencoe, 1947), pp. 330–332. Copyright © 1947, renewed 1975 by Talcott Parsons.
3. M. Murphy and Johns, C. J. *Handbook of Library Regulations* (New York: Dekker, 1977).
4. A. Etzioni, *Modern Organizations* (Englewood Cliffs, N.J.: Prentice-Hall, 1964).
5. P. M. Blau, *Dynamics of a Bureaucracy* (Chicago: Univ. of Chicago Press, 1955).
6. A. W. Gouldner, *Patterns of Industrial Bureaucracy* (Glencoe, Ill.: The Free Press, 1954).

7. M. Haine, *Psychology in Management* (New York: McGraw-Hill, 1956).
8. Etzioni, p. 78.

FURTHER READING

Libraries and Management

Abell, M. D. "Changing Role of the Academic Librarian." *College and Research Libraries* 40 (1979): 154–164.

Aston, B. R., and Brodie, M. B. "Management: The Intellectual Challenge." *ASLIB Proceedings* 19 (1967): 7–18.

Bailey, M. J. "Requirements For Middle Managerial Positions." *Special Libraries* 69 (1978): 323–331.

Baldwin, D. R. "Managerial Competence and Librarians." *Pennsylvania Library Association Bulletin* 26 (1971): 17–24.

Beckman, M., and Brown, N. A. "The Role of the Librarian in Management." *Special Libraries* 66 (1975): 19–26.

"Bibliothécaire et Administrateur." *Argus* 6 (1977): 75–93.

Booz, Allen, and Hamilton, Inc. *Problems in University Library Management.* New York: Booz, Allen, and Hamilton, 1970.

Bowler, R., ed. *Local Public Library Administration.* Washington, D.C.: International City Managers Association, 1964.

Brose, F. K. H. "Allen's Principles of Management Applied to Library Administration." *California Librarian* 30 (1969): 30–34.

Bryson, J. M., and Kelley, G. "Using Maxims in Library Administration, Planning and Research." *Minnesota Libraries* 25 (1977): 247–251.

Burlingame, D. F., Fields, D. C., and Schulzetenberg, A. C. *The College Learning Resource Center.* Littleton, Colo.: Libraries Unlimited, 1978.

Castagna, E. "Public Librarian and the City Manager." *Public Management* 43 (1961): 32–35.

Conant, R. W. "Sociological and Institutional Changes in American Life: Their Implications for the Library." *ALA Bulletin* 61 (1967): 528–536.

Corbett, E. V. *Fundamentals of Library Organisation and Administration: A Practical Guide.* London: Library Association, 1978.

Corfield, B. "Public Library Management By Results." *Ontario Library Review* 62 (1978): 99–104.

DeGennaro, R. "Library Administration and New Management Systems." *Library Journal* 103 (1978): 2477–2482.

D'Elia, G. P. "The Determinants of Job Satisfaction Among Beginning Librarians." *Library Quarterly* 49 (1979): 283–302.

Dougherty, R. M. "Impacts of Networking on Library Management." *College and Research Libraries* 39 (1978): 15–19.

Drake, M. A. "The Management of Libraries as Professional Organizations." *Special Libraries* 68 (1977): 181–186.

DuMont, R. R. "The Management of Public Libraries." *Southeastern Librarian* 28 (1978): 25–30.

Edwards, R. M. "The Management of Libraries and the Professional Function of Librarians." *Library Quarterly* 45 (1975): 150–160.

Ellison, J. M. "Coping With Administrative Problems: A Survival Kit for Librarians." *Unabashed Librarian* 17 (1975): 9–10.

Elman, S. A. "Politics, the Public Library and the National Commission on Libraries and Information Science." *Californian Librarian* 38 (1977): 22–26.

Fisher, E. L. *Checklist for the Organization, Operation and Evaluation of A Company Library.* 2d rev. ed. New York: Special Library Association, 1966.

Gardner, J. J., and Webster, D. E. "Management, Library." In *American Library Association Yearbook.* Chicago: American Library Association, 1976.

Gore, D. "Mismanagement of College Libraries: A View from the Inside." *AAUP Bulletin* 52 (1966): 46–51.

Gore, D. "Things Your Boss Never Told You about Library Management." *Library Journal* 102 (1977): 765–770.

Green, D. M. "The Structure and Functions of Management." *Special Libraries* 55 (1964): 550–554.

Hausdorfer, W. "Guidance for Administration." *Library Trends* 7 (1959): 481–491.

Heintz, I. *Organization of the Small Public Library.* Paris: UNESCO, 1963.

Holbrook, A. "Librarian as Manager." *New Library World* 77 (1976): 95–97.

Holley, E. G. "Magic of Library Administration." *Texas Library Journal* 52 (1976): 58–63.

Holley, E. G. "Who Runs Libraries?" *Wilson Library Bulletin* 47 (1973): 42–50.

Houser, L. J., and Sweaney, W. "Library Administration Literature: A Bibliometric Measure of Subject Dispersion." *Library Research* 1 (1979): 359–376.

Howard, E. N. *Local Power and the Community Library.* Chicago: American Library Association, 1978.

"Increasing Managerial and Organizational Effectiveness In Libraries: A Workshop for Senior and Middle Management: A Report." *BCLA Reporter* 21 (1977): 1–3.

Kaiser, J. B., ed. "Legal Aspects of Library Administration." *Library Trends* 6 (1958): 387–510.

Kemp, S. D. "Management Tools: Their Use In the Design, Development and Operation of Information Services." *ASLib Proceedings* 28 (1976): 364–369.

Kemper, R. E., and Ostrander, R. E. *Directorship by Objectives.* Littleton, Colo.: Libraries Unlimited, 1977.

Koepp, D. W. *Public Library Government: Seven Case Studies.* Berkeley, Calif.: Univ. of California Press, 1968.

Kok, J., and Strable, E. G. "Moving Up: Librarians Who Have Become Officers of Their Organizations." *Special Libraries* 71 (1980): 5–12.

Lewis, M. "Sociology, Management and Libraries." *Library Review* 26 (1977): 3–9.

"Library Administrators: Time to Show Them the Door?" *Wilson Library Bulletin* 51 (1977): 636–638.

Lock, R. N. *Library Administration.* 3rd ed. Brooklyn Heights, New York: Beekman Publishers, 1973.

Lyle, G. R. *The Administration of the College Library.* 4th ed. New York: McGraw-Hill, 1974.

Lynch, B. P. "Libraries as Bureaucracies." *Library Trends* 27 (1979): 259–267.

Lynch, B. P. "Role of Middle Managers in Libraries." In *Advances in Librarianship* (Vol. 6). New York: Academic Press, 1976.

McAnally, A. M., and Downs, R. B. "The Changing Role of Directors of University Libraries." *Colleges and Research Libraries* 34 (1973): 103–125.

Matthews, V. *Libraries for Today and Tomorrow.* New York: Doubleday, 1976.

Meyers, G. E. *Insurance Manual for Libraries.* Chicago: American Library Association, 1977.

Morein, G. "The Academic Library Development Program." *College and Research Libraries* 38 (1977): 37–45.

Mount, E. *University Science and Engineering Libraries.* Westport, Conn.: Greenwood Press, 1975.

Murphy, M., and Johns, C. J., Jr. *Handbook of Library Regulations.* New York: Dekker, 1977.

Palmer, J. W. "Changes in Medical Librarianship: A Content Analysis of Job Advertisements." *Medical Library Association Bulletin* 66 (1978): 464–466.

Plate, K. *Management Personnel in Librarians: A Theoretical Model for Analysis.* Rockway, N.J.: American Faculty Press, 1970.

Presthus, R. *Technological Change and Occupational Response: A Study of Librarians.* Toronto: York University, Dept. of Political Science, 1970.

Rayward, W. B. "Bureaucratic Organization of Libraries." *Australian Library Journal* 19 (1970): 245–253.

Rettig, J. "Suggestions for Job Seekers." In *Library Literature, 8—The Best of 1977,* edited by W. A. Katz. Metuchen, N.J.: Scarecrow, 1978.

Rizzo, J. R. *Management for Librarians: Fundamentals and Issues.* Westport, Conn.: Greenwood Press, 1980.

Rogers, R. D., and Weber, D. C. *University Library Administration.* New York: H. W. Wilson, 1970

Rohlf, R. H. "Library Management." In *ALA Yearbook.* Chicago: American Libary Association, 1979.

Schellenberg, T. R. *The Management of Archives.* New York: Columbia Univ. Press, 1965.

Shaffer, K. R. "Library Administrator as Negotiator: Exit the Boss." *Library Journal* 100 (1975): 1475–1480.

Shapiro, L. L. "Bureaucracy and the School Library." *Library Journal* 98 (1973): 1346–1351.

Shaughnessy, T. W. "Participative Management, Collective Bargaining and Professionalism." *College and Research Libraries* 38 (1977): 147–152.

Simon, B. V. "Need for Administrative Know-how in Libraries." *Medical Libraries Association Bulletin* 57 (1969): 160–170.

Smith, E. R. "Do Libraries Need Managers?" *Library Journal* 94 (1969): 502–506.

Sparks, R. "Library Management: Consideration and Structure." *Journal of Academic Librarianship* 2 (1976): 66–71.

Stibitz, M., and Hamlin, A. "Accent on Administration." *ALA Bulletin* 55 (1969): 32–61.

Stone, E. W. "Administrators Fiddle While Employees Burn or Flee." *ALA Bulletin* 63 (1969): 181–187.

Strable, E. G. *Special Libraries: A Guide for Management.* Rev. ed. New York: Special Libraries Association, 1975.

Steuart, R. D., and Eastlick, J. T. *Library Management.* 2d. ed. Littleton, Colo.: Libraries Unlimited, 1980.

Summers, F. W., ed. "Trends In the Governance of Libraries." *Library Trends* 26 (Fall 1977): entire issue.

Veit, Fritz *The Community College Library.* Westport, Conn.: Greenwood Press, 1975.

Waller, S. B. "Libraries, Managers, and People." *Special Libraries* 66 (1975): 411–415.

Wasserman, P., and Bundy, M. L. *Reader in Library Administration.* Washington, D.C.: Microcard Editions, 1968.

Weber, A. R. "The Transferability of Management Skills." *Library Quarterly* 43 (1973): 385–393.

White, H. S. Management: A Strategy for Change." *Canadian Library Journal* (1978) 329–334.

Willard, D. D. "Seven Realities of Library Administration: Fear, Blame, the Productivity

Obsession, Expediency, Management by Crises, Bureaucracy, Management by Platitude." *Library Journal* 101 (1976): 311–317.

Yates, E. G. "Sexism in the Library Profession." *Library Journal* 104 (1979): 2615–2619.

Young, R. "Young Adult Librarian As An Administrator." *Drexel Library Quarterly* 14 (1978): 19–28.

Not For Profit

Bowman, James S., and Hajjar, Sami G. "English-Language Journals In Public Administration: An Analysis." *Public Administration* 56 (1978): 203–226.

Brakeley, G. A. *Tested Ways to Successful Fund Raising.* New York: AMACOM, 1980.

Brechner, J. C., and Koprowski, E. J. *Public Administration.* 2d. ed. Encino, Calif.: Dickenson Publishing Co., 1976.

Crane, E. G. *State Government Productivity: The Environment for Improvement.* New York: Praeger, 1976.

Drucker, P. F. "Managing the Public Service Institution." *College and Research Libraries* 37 (1976): 4–14.

Einsenstadt, S. N. "Bureaucracy, Bureaucratization and Debureaucratization." *Administrative Science Quarterly* 4 (1959): 302–320.

Fried, R. C. *Performance in American Bureaucracy.* Boston: Little, Brown, 1976.

Golembiewski, R. T. *Public Administration: Readings In Institutions, Processes, Behavior, Policy.* 3rd ed. Chicago: Rand McNally, 1976.

Golembiewski, R. T. *Perspectives On Public Management; Case and Learning Designs.* 2d. ed. Itasca, Ill.: F. E. Peacock Publishers, 1976.

Gordon, G. J. *Public Administration in America.* New York: St. Martin's, 1978.

Henry, N. *Public Administration and Public Affairs.* Englewood Cliffs, N.J.: Prentice-Hall, 1975.

Herbert, T. T., and Yost, E. B. *Management Education and Development: An Annotated Resource Book.* Westport, Conn.: Greenwood Press, 1978.

Hummel, R. *The Bureaucratic Experience.* New York: St. Martin's, 1977.

Lane, F. S. *Current Issues in Public Administration.* New York: St. Martin's, 1978.

Lynn, L. E., Jr., and Seidl, J. M. "'Bottom-Line' Management for Public Agencies." *Harvard Business Review* 55 (1977): 144–153.

Management Handbook for Public Administration. New York: Van Nostrand-Reinhold, 1978.

Managing Nonprofit Organizations. New York: AMACOM, 1977.

Mercer, J. L., and Koester, E. H. *Public Management Systems,* New York: AMACOM, 1978.

Miewald, R. D. *Public Administration: A Critical Perspective.* New York: McGraw-Hill, 1978.

Nachmias, D., and Rosenbloom, H. *Bureaucratic Government, USA.* New York: St. Martin's, 1980.

Nigro, F. A., and Nigro, L. G. *Modern Public Administration.* 4th ed. New York: Harper, 1977.

Nutt, P. C. "Calling Out and Calling Off the Dogs: Managerial Diagnosis in Public Service Organizations." *Academy of Management Review* 4 (1979): 203–204.

Presthus, R. *Public Administration.* 6th ed. New York: Ronald Press, 1975.

Richardson, I. L., and Baldwin, S. *Public Administration: Government In Action.* Columbus, Ohio: Chas. E. Merrill Publishing Co., 1976.

Starling, G. *Managing the Public Sector.* Homewood, Ill.: Dorsey Press, 1977.

U.S. Civil Service Commision Bureau of Training. *Basic Management Functions.* Washington, D.C.: Government Printing Office, 1977.

Uveges, J. A., Jr. *The Dimensions of Public Administration.* 3rd ed. Boston: Allyn & Bacon, 1978.

Preparing Résumés and Job Interviews

Berliner, D. *Want a Job? Get Some Experience. Want Experience? Get a Job.* New York: AMACOM, 1978.

Corwen, L. *Your Résumé: Key to a Better Job.* New York: Arco Publishers, 1976.

Dickhut, H. W. *Professional Résumé/Job Search Guide.* Chicago: Management Counselors, 1978.

Galassi, J. P., and Galassi, M. D. "Preparing Individuals for Job Interviews: Suggestions from More Than 60 Years of Research." *Personnel & Guidance Journal* 57 (1978): 188–192.

Gaughan, T. M. "Résumé Essentials for the Academic Librarian." *College and Research Libraries* 41, 1 (1980): 122–127.

McDaniels, C. *Developing a Professional Vita or Resume.* Garrett Park, MD: Garrett Park Press, 1978.

Wanous, J. P. "Job Survival of New Employees." *Personnel Psychology* 32 (1980): 651–662.

Wyant, J. F., and Vise, R. "Résumé Writing: Form and Function." *Special Libraries* 70 (1979): 328–332.

Women In Management

Baron, A. S. "New Data On Women Managers." *Training and Development Journal* 32 (1978): 12–13.

"Beyond Awareness: Women In Libraries Organize for Change." *School Librarian Journal* 23 (1977): 31–36.

Blau, F. D. *Equal Pay In The Office.* Lexington, Mass.: Lexington Books, 1977.

"Bringing Women Into Computing Management." *EDP Analyzer* 14 (August 1976): entire issue.

Burrow, M. G. *Developing Women Managers: What Needs to Be Done?* New York: AMACOM, 1978.

Cannie, J. K. *The Woman's Guide to Management Success: How to Win Power In The Real Organizational World.* Englewood Cliffs, N.J.: Prentice-Hall, 1979.

Farley, J. *Affirmative Action and The Woman Worker: Guidelines For Personnel Management.* New York: AMACOM, 1979.

Fenn, M. *Making It In Management: A Behavioral Approach For Women Executives.* Englewood Cliffs, N.J.: Prentice-Hall, 1978.

Fox, H. W., and Renas, S. R. "Stereotypes of Women In the Media and Their Impact on Women's Careers." *Human Resource Management* 16 (1977): 28–31.

Foxley, C. H. *Locating, Recruiting and Employing Women: An Equal Opportunity Approach.* Garrett Park, MD: Garrett Park Press, 1976.

Frank, H. H. *Women In the Organization.* Philadelphia: Univ. of Pennsylvania Press, 1977.

Greenlaw, P. S., and Foderaro. "Some Further Implications of the Pregnancy Discrimination Act." *Personnel Journal* 59 (1980): 36–43.

Hart, L. B. *Moving Up! Women and Leadership.* New York: AMACOM, 1980.

Heim, K. M., and Kacena, C. "Sex, Salaries, and Library Support." *Library Journal* 104 (1979): 675–680.

Herbert, T. T., and Yost, E. B. "Women as Effective Managers . . . A Strategic Model For Overcoming the Barriers." *Human Resource Management* 17 (1978): 18–25.

Inglehart, A. P. *Married Women and Work, 1957 and 1976.* Lexington, Mass.: D. C. Heath, 1979.

"Loses in Directorships For Women Pegged." *Library Journal* 101 (1976): 573.

Meyer, M. *Women and Employee Benefits.* New York: The Conference Board, 1978.

Neuse, S. M. "Professionalism and Authority: Women In Public Service." *Public Administration Review* 38 (1978): 436–441.

Organization for Economic Co-operation and Development. Equal Opportunities for Women. Paris: OECD, 1979.

Putnam, L., and Heinen, J. "Women in Management: The Fallacy of the Trait Approach." *MSU Business Topics* 24 (1976): 47–53.

Schaeffer, D. "Suggestions for the New Woman Supervisor." *Supervision* 40 (Nov. 1977): 3.

Schwartz, E. B., and Mackenzie, R. A. "Time-Management Strategy for Women." *Management Review* 66 (1977): 19–25.

"Sex Discrimination Complaint: Professional Librarians at Temple University Have Filed a Class Action Complaint." *Herald of Library Science* (1977): 448.

Stead, B. A. *Women In Management.* Englewood Cliffs, N.J.. Prentice-Hall, 1978.

Stewart, N. *The Effective Woman Manager: Seven Vital Skills for Upward Mobility.* New York: Wiley, 1978.

U.S. Dept. of Labor. Office of the Secretary Women's Bureau. *A Working Woman's Guide to Her Job Rights.* Washington, D.C.: Government Printing Office, 1978.

"Woman In Public Administration: A Symposium." *Public Administration Review* 36 (1976): 347–389.

Women, Minorities, and Employment Discrimination. Lexington, Mass.: Lexington Books, 1977.

Women Working: Theories and Facts In Perspective. Palo Alto, Calif.: Mayfield, 1978.

2. Management Training and Background

Every organization must have someone who makes things go well, which is what management is all about. Human beings have kept things going for thousands of years, of course, but schools of management and business administration are recent phenomena. These schools have developed and prospered, though, only because persons educated in them seem to succeed at keeping things going better than those who have not been exposed to principles of management.

Some years ago, Yale economist Charles Lindbloom described "the science of 'muddling' through."[1] You will probably always have to muddle through as a manager, regardless of your training, but the amount of muddling generally goes down as the amount of training goes up. Unfortunately, libraries and other NFP and governmental organizations have been rather slow to see the need for formal training in management.

Formal training for management in the profit sector places heavy emphasis on fiscal control. Because money and materials are more predictable variables than human beings, a person can effectively use formulas, models, and theories to successfully solve a problem (for example, increasing profits or changing a loss to a profit). Libraries deal in rather imprecisely defined services to what is most often a very heterogeneous population. Lacking precise goals and measures of achievement, then, they and a great many other service organizations have, in the past, seen little need for formal training in management.

Over the past 20 years, though, the notion that any librarian can be a manager has shifted to the recognition that a need exists for some formal background in management. Formal training can provide some under-standing of the basic elements of managerial activities, since, over the years, managers have accumulated a large body of literature about their activities, both successful and unsuccessful.

The remainder of this chapter explores what some writers have had to say about management, management theory, people and organizations, and what roles managers play.

WHAT DO MANAGERS DO?

Before answering the question of what mangers do, we need to dis-tinguish between *management* and *administration*. A widely accepted distinction, and the one that this book employs, is that administrators establish fundamental patterns of operation and goals for an organiza-tion, while managers primarily carry out the directions of the administra-tors. In the profit sector, the board of directors is empowered to establish the overall direction of an organization (as administrators), while the officers of the company (from the president down) are the managers. Very often the top/senior officials of the company also are members of the board of directors; hence, outsiders and lower-level employees often have difficulty making a distinction between management and adminis-tration.

Practically all librarians, including library directors when they are in their librarian role, are managers rather than administrators. Since al-most all libraries are part of a larger organizational unit (corporation, educational institution, or government unit), libraries must operate with-in a body of guidelines, goals, objectives, rules, regulations, policies, pro-cedures, etc. that are formulated by others. Managers are not, however, without influence and a void in the establishment of these directions. Quite often a manager or a director sees the need for a change, formu-lates specific suggestions for that change, and passes these suggestions on to the person(s) empowered to make decisions. A properly function-ing situation includes cooperation between manager(s) and an admin-istrative body that is based on mutual respect.

Now, just what do managers do? Many answers to that question occur; however, the question can be seen from two points of view—function and behavior. Some examples of functions are planning, directing, budget-ing, etc.; behavior is defined in the sense of roles filled, such as leader. Writers tend to take one side or the other. Most basic management text-books seem to take a functional approach. Advanced level books seem to favor the behavioral approach. This book, while organized according to functions, explores behavioral aspects as well. In the next few pages I explore a few of the approaches that have been employed by some important writers in the field of management.

To gain an idea of what managers do, try this experiment. Approach a person you know to be a manager, director, or unit head, or someone who is responsible for overseeing the work of someone else (the scope of the individual's duties is not important in this context). Simply ask the person to tell you what he or she does. Do not be surprised if the response is something like "Well, I'm head of the reference department," or "I'm assistant director for technical services," or "I'm the director of the library." You must then probe further by saying "Fine, but tell me what you actually *do* during a typical work day." You will seldom get the answer "Oh, I direct, plan, control, delegate, budget, and hire and fire people." More often, the answer will be "I attend lots of boring meetings, write letters, reports, and memos, and listen to complaints. It seems like I never get anything done."

Presumably a manager who says something like "I never get my real work done" is referring to some of the classical concepts of the functions of a manager. One set of labels for these functions was set forth in a classic paper by Gulick and Urwick (1937). In it, they coined the acronym POSDCORB, which stands for the following functions:

Planning
Organizing
Staffing
Directing
Coordinating
Reporting
Budgeting

These seven functions (for which labels may vary) are assumed to underlie, in one form or another, all management activities. They do *not* describe the work of a manager; they merely identify the objectives of a manager's work. At least one writer claims that, because the labels fail to describe what is actually done, they are of little use.[2] This seems to be too harsh a judgment, for if we do not know where we are going (that is, if we do not have objectives), how shall we know when we get there? By studying the concepts covered by labels such as POSDCORB, a student can gain an understanding of what good management attempts to accomplish.

Various writers use slightly differing labels, but all of them draw directly or indirectly from a set of concepts described by the French industrialist, Henri Fayol. After many years of profitably managing several unrelated industrial organizations, Fayol set down principles that he had found valuable in his work. All of his principles reflect the thinking of a practical person, not of someone concerned with developing a grand philosophy or a great theory. Fayol's concepts may seem to reflect common sense, but no management text in the United States identified them until the late 1940s (although he published his observations in 1916). Today his views fit extremely well into most contemporary thinking.

Fayol divided the activities of organizations into six fundamental groups: (1) technical, or production, aspects; (2) commercial aspects (buying, selling, and exchanging goods); (3) financial aspects (the search for, securing of, and efficient use of money); (4) security (protecting the safety of employees and property alike); (5) accounting (including statistics and record keeping); and (6) managerial activities (planning, organization, and control). At the time Fayol wrote his book, the sixth group had not been adequately defined; he devoted most of his attention to the question of defining managerial activities.

Fayol reasoned that a worker's most important attribute is the technical ability to carry out a prescribed function properly. As a worker rises in the hierarchy of an organization, the importance of managerial ability increases, until, at the top level, it becomes the basic requirement. Fayol thought that managerial skill could be acquired and that the best way to acquire it was through a combination of education and practical experience. In many ways, this view reflects my philosophy. Education in the fundamentals of management must be seasoned with experience in situations entailing real responsibilities and duties. When a solid background is lacking, learning on the job can be tedious and frustrating, because the manager-in-training needs a great deal of time to become a productive staff member. As libraries have come to recognize this problem, some larger systems have attempted to provide special management training. An example of on-the-job training is the trainee fellowships offered by the Council on Library Resources for a year-long work-study management program. The program is needed, because, until very recently, library schools did not offer courses in general management, and practitioners found themselves at times lacking basic information about management.

Fayol's entire list of activities is useful in the library situation. *Production* is obviously an aspect in the processes of cataloging books and making them ready for use. Buying, selling, and exchanging library materials certainly represent *commercial* activities. There is a clear *financial* aspect, in that administrators, and frequently the entire staff, are concerned with locating sources of funds to support library programs. *Security* is an important library concern whether it involves protection of material against theft and physical deterioration or the consideration of the safety of personnel and patrons. Anyone who has had experience with an acquisitions department recognizes the significance of the *accounting* function. And, finally, although a profit–loss statement does not exist for the library, good *managerial* skills are just as critical to the library as they are to a profit-making organization.

FAYOL'S GENERAL PRINCIPLES

Fayol identified 14 principles of management.

Division of Work or Specialization   It is best to assign workers to jobs fairly limited in scope, so that they can develop a high degree of skill. This promotes efficiency for the organization. Moreover, the superior has control, because only a small range of activities must be dealt with for any one person. Since division of work is necessary for efficiency; the only real question is how to handle the division. In a library, this can be by type of service or by type of material. Regardless of the method, it is important to consider a unit's direction and objectives. (See Chapter 6 for further details.)

Authority and Responsibility   Authority and responsibility *must* go together. This may seem obvious, but very often, only responsibility is delegated, not authority. The frequency with which this principle is violated is surprising, yet the reason for this is quite evident. The person delegating authority always retains some responsibility for the accomplishment of a task; many managers are reluctant to delegate authority to subordinates, because they doubt that their subordinates can do the job. (This will be explored in more depth in Chapter 5.)

Discipline   Clearly defined limits of acceptable behavior are absolutely necessary, so that everyone in an organization knows what can and cannot be done. When a rule is violated, it should be enforced equally and fairly by someone who is competent, understanding, and able to apply discipline. Often this principle is difficult for a supervisor to apply impartially, because a tendency exists, especially within the human-relations managerial style, to modify discipline in terms of non-work-related factors—a practice that may or may not benefit an organization as a whole. (See Chapter 12 for details.)

Unity of Command   An employee should receive orders from only one supervisor. Yet, because of a number of interacting variables in any job situation, line and staff as authority become opposed to line and staff as function (see Chapter 6). For example, to whom should subject specialists report? Possibly to the head of technical services, because they are concerned with both the selection and the processing of acquired materials. However, subject specialists also answer specialized reference questions. Thus, their assignment to public services might seem logical. Yet most libraries with personnel of this type divide their duties between technical services and public services, which clearly violates the principle of unity of command. Therefore, the specialist must satisfy the expectations and requirements of both departments. Frustration under such circumstances is easily understandable. Almost all readers have, at one time, found themselves working under two bosses simultaneously. I have experienced this situation as a nonprofessional in public and academic libraries and as a professional in academic and special libraries.

Unity of Direction   There should be only one plan, and the person should be responsible for supervising it; all activities have the same objective should be supervised by one person. For example, bibliographic checking units should have one supervisor and one plan of operation, yet libraries frequently violate this principle by having a bibliographic checking unit in both the acquisitions and catalog departments. A plan to combine the units and satisfy both acquisitions and cataloging needs should be formulated. (See Chapters 7 and 8.)

Subordination of Individual to General Interest   Fayol believed that the individual should subordinate self-interest to the general good. This is difficult, though, in a work situation in which employees perceive no managerial concern for individual well-being. It is incumbent upon management to reduce conflict between the individual and the general well-being wherever possible. (See Chapters 10 and 11.)

Remuneration   Remuneration for work must be fair and accurate, affording maximum satisfaction for both employee and employer. Some libraries pay the minimum amount necessary to hire an individual, but these systems obviously have no standards for hiring or promotion. The library manager must examine tasks, identify responsibilities, and decide upon a just level of compensation. The next step is to find someone to carry out the defined duties for the established salaries. (See Chapter 13.)

Centralization   Fayol thought centralization of authority to be desirable, at least for overall control. Certainly, both formulation of policy and the generation of basic rules and procedures ought to be centralizaed. Managerial decisions may be made at a lower level, but only within the framework established by the central administrative authority. Many libraries adhere rather strongly to this principle, embracing the idea of centralization of authority, physical facilities, and services. (See Chapter 6.)

Lines of Command or Scalar Chain   Organizations need a formalized hierarchy that reflects the flow of authority and responsibility. Fayol suggested that a chain of command is necessary most of the time, but, at times, it is best ignored. When the organization obviously will be harmed significantly by adherence to a hierarchical arrangement, the rule must be violated. (See Chapter 5.)

Order   Relationships between various units must be established in a logical, rational manner, so that these units work in harmony.

Equity   Managers/supervisors elicit loyalty from employees only when they deal with them as individual persons. Employees must be seen as persons, not things to be manipulated. If managers hope to create a good working environment, they must treat everyone fairly and with equity. (See Chapters 9, 10, and 11.)

Stability of Tenure   A high turnover rate is expensive for an organization. Turnover of a high degree is both a cause and an effect of bad management, and one way of evaluating a manager/supervisor is to examine the turnover and absenteeism rate of persons working under that manager. A low turnover and absenteeism rate may or may not indicate a good manager, but a high rate indicates the existence of a problem that the manager/supervisor has failed to correct. Naturally, every time an employee leaves, the organization incurs significant costs in time and money spent recruiting, selecting, and training a new employee. Furthermore, the new employee will require time to become an integrated member of the staff. A person who is often absent can create bottlenecks in the flow of material, hindering the entire organization's efficiency (and often costing the organization far more than his or her salary). (See Chapters 12 and 13.)

Another form of absenteeism not usually reflected in statistics is that of employees who are "present but absent." These people arrive at the last possible moment, take longer than necessary to set up for work, begin coffee breaks early and drag them out, extend lunches beyond the normal schedule, and push cleanup further and further into the working period. The equivalent of one workday per week may be lost by such persons; if this happens, the supervisor (and the supervisor's supervisor) must examine the situation.

Initiative   Initiative should be encouraged at all levels, and subordinates should be asked to submit plans and new ideas. All of these should be carefully reviewed, and each person who makes a suggestion should be informed as to its status. Although this principle is given lip service by many libraries, in actuality, it is often not practiced. For example, when personnel-evaluation forms enquire about an employee's initiative, often the only true interest is in conformity (that is, lack of initiative). This was not Fayol's intention, and it should not be the intention of a good manager. (See Chapter 4.)

Esprit de Corps   As a good Frenchman, Fayol believed in esprit de corps. He felt that all successful organizations survive only when a feeling of unity pervades the group and that viable organizations deal with crises as a team. (See Chapters 9, 10, and 11.)

I emphasize Fayol's work because his ideas have served at the basis of most management writers since he published his book—as they do for this book.

Frequently, you will encounter articles discussing the question of whether management is an art or a science. Generally, these articles conclude that, despite many elements of science present, management is, in the final analysis, an art. Although you can learn basic concepts, principles, functions, and techniques as described by Fayol and others, each management situation is unique. Even when certain situations appear to be similar, the individuals involved will be different, whether in fact or just with the passage of time. Thus, what worked yesterday may or may not work today. Your ability to assess degrees of change is the real art of management.

As a manager, you will have to fill a number of roles in varying situations. The statement "I have to wear a number of hats" is truer than most people realize. In discussing what managers do, Henry Mintzberg identified 10 basic roles[2]: (1) figurehead, (2) leader, (3) liaison, (4) monitor, (5) disseminator, (6) spokesman, (7) entrepeneur, (8) disturbance handler, (9) resource allocator, and (10) negotiator.

Although several of these roles have elements of the political process in them, the librarian in a publicly supported library needs to add a role to Mintzberg's list—politician. With all these roles to fill, it is not surprising to find most managers agreeing that management is an art form, not a scientific exercise. For this reason, throughout this book the behavioral aspect is tied to the functional activities.

THE NATURE OF FORMAL ORGANIZATIONS

A few words about the nature of formal organizations will help set the context in which behavioral and functional activities occur. Formal organizations are social units formed in order to accomplish certain objectives. Individuals join the organization because its objectives represent to some degree objectives that they wish to achieve personally or professionally (or both). As an organization grows and changes, its original objectives will be modified, and they may well change to such an extent that the founders might have trouble recognizing "their" old organization. Formal organizations, then, have two basic characteristics: (1) they are formed to accomplish a specific objective, and (2) that objective may well change many times during the lifetime of the organization.

As an organization becomes more complex, one objective may come into conflict with another. Society itself is composed of thousands of organizations, many of which have objectives in conflict with the objectives or other organizations. Furthermore, the personal goals of the members of organizations rarely are in total harmony with organizational objectives, especially as each person belongs to hundreds of organizations (formal and informal, voluntary and involuntary membership). As is readily apparent, another major characteristic of organizations is the widespread existence of conflict.

A number of management articles in the 1960s and early 1970s dealt with conflict control, which some people view as the central issue for management. Granted, conflict is a fact of life, but it is as naive to pretend that conflict is the only element of life as it is to assume that there is no conflict at all. What we must recognize is that a series of interactions constantly takes place:

Individuals interact with the environment
Individuals interact with one another
Individuals interact with organizations
Organizations interact with other organizations
Organizations interact with the environment

Because people and organizations are interdependent, and because every action does produce a reaction, management is clearly a complex problem.

Conflict has a great many sources; the ability to recognize the major sources can help a manager to perform more effectively. Perhaps the major source of conflict is competition for resources, as all organizational resources are limited in quantity. During any given period, some resources are more available than others, but the pattern of availability and demand fluctuates. In the 1950s, libraries were concerned about material resources, physical facilities, and funds to support intellectual freedom. In the 1960s, the big resource problem was personnel, and in the 1970s, it was financial support. The 1980s cannot be predicted.

Competition for scarce resources takes place both inside and outside an organization, and competition between similar organizations can be very strong. Because most libraries are governmental agencies, they find themselves in a yearly struggle to secure a larger portion of the tax dollar (or to hold onto their present allotment). Because each agency's request justifies the full amount of tax money that it could use, and because each request will have active supporters, the library has competition for every dollar that it seeks. The total monies requested by all agencies usually exceed the amount available; therefore, conflict (and often ill will) can arise as each agency tries to prove that it is worthy of its requests.

Competition for resources takes place within the organization as well, among the units that compose it. Perhaps the library secured only one of six new positions that it requested, and all department heads are trying to justify their receiving the new staff member. Just as with interagency conflict, the manager (decision maker) must realize that any decision may result in tension and conflict that may last for some time. Obviously, competition for resources forces the issue. The manager must try to avoid the long-term effects of such conflicts.

Another form of conflict, line-versus-staff, is built into the organization and is sometimes deliberately encouraged. In a library, this type of conflict often arises between systems personnel and other staffers. Trying to improve the library as a whole, systems people tend to have a broader perspective than the operations staff. When a systems person recommends a change in one department, and when both the systems person and the department personnel know that it would mean less efficiency in the department (even if it would mean more efficiency for the library), vigorous objections from the department are only natural. The department staff members do not want the library to be less efficient, but they also do not want their own work to be less efficiently performed. The manager's task is to make certain that the department realizes that it will not be penalized when a decrease in efficiency does occur. The conflict that arises is encouraged here, though, because department members have forgotten the question of overall organizational performance. Yet, that overall performance and operation must remain the top priority of everyone working in the system.

Sometimes, several staff members make conflicting demands on a unit head. Because each unit has its own purpose and responsibilities, the unit head often assigns a level of importance to each request. Yet this should never be allowed to happen. Top management must assign all priorities, allowing the entire organization to benefit from staff and line specializations.

Other types of conflict arise from differences in work orientation and needs. In a library, one of the clearest examples of this can be seen in bibliographic searching. Acquisitions departments can secure books without the detailed bibliographic searching that catalog departments often need. Frequently, discussions arise concerning when, where, and how such searching should be done. If acquisitions does a complete search, it takes more time than necessary to meet that department's needs. If cataloging does the search, the cataloging work flow will be improved, but the actual acquisitions process may be slowed down. In either case, one department is doing the work of the other, which almost inevitably leads to tension and conflict.

Whatever its source, conflict must be controlled if organizations are to operate efficiently. Persons holding management positions *must* have a tolerance for conflict situations. A manager must recognize the sources and nature of each conflict, must not be afraid to tackle problems and must be comfortable in dealing with problems. Methods of dealing with conflict situations range from using personal judgment to attempting bargaining to the all too popular muddling through.

PEOPLE IN ORGANIZATIONS

Accomplishing goals with and through other people is a basic human activity, and most persons are involved in working with others in some fashion. If we define an organization as two or more persons acting together to achieve a specified goal, then we can say that everyone is a member of a number of organizations. Members of organizations must interact in a structured, interdependent manner to achieve their desired objective. While the degree of structure and interdependence vary constantly, whenever two people seek a common goal, some structure and interdependence must be present in their organization.

Anthropology, archaeology, and history supply ample evidence that organization is necessary. Indeed, the findings of these disciplines reinforce the contention that both formal and informal membership in organizations marks all stages of an individual's life. As Etzioni (1964) and others have noted, an individual is not really dead until the state officially certifies the fact. A brief discussion of just a few of the many types of organizations one belongs to will illustrate the complexity and the pervasive nature of organizations.

Economic groups include not only a person's place of employment, but banks, savings and loan associations, and credit unions, among others. Owning a credit card implies membership in an economic group. In these instances, each group represents a structure created to fulfill some specific economic objective(s) that each member desires to accomplish (service or product). The organization itself desires a profit for providing the desired service or product.

Religious groups affect the individual even when a person does not belong to a formal group. Religious holidays and their observance influence the behavior of both organizations and individuals; as a result, even the nonreligious person comes under the influence of formal religious bodies.

Governmental agencies of all types (including military) constantly affect the individual. Membership in such organizations is not always voluntary; one becomes a member simply by living or working in a specific area. Other organizational groups are *educational, social,* and *political.*

In several of his books, Peter Drucker has described four principles of production—unique product, rigid mass, flexible mass, and "flow" production.[3] Although the principles were originally established through the study of industrial production, they apply equally well to producing and handling information and to what can be labeled "knowledge work." Libraries and most service organizations fall into the "unique product" category. If librarians keep the definition of this category in mind, they will be able to relate their activities to most other activities in a manner that managers and politicians *outside* the field of librarianship will understand.

Drucker characterized unique product work as labor intensive:

> Even when highly mechanized—and it does not lend itself to automation—capital investment will be comparatively low compared to labor cost. But it has great flexibility. Costs of individual products are high, but break-even points are low. Unique product production can operate at a low volume of output or with considerable fluctuation in output. It makes high demands on skill, but little or no judgment.[4]

With the exception of the last phrase in the last sentence, this is an accurate picture of library work. Libraries devote well over 50% of their budgets to salaries and staff benefits. Capital investments, compared to labor costs, are low, and (when they are actually calculated) unit costs for services to individuals are high. Generally, the degree of skill and judgment required are high, contrary to Drucker in this case.

As a labor-intensive activity, even without considering the clients, the management of libraries places emphasis on people and interpersonal relations. Because of the increasing complexity and growing numbers of organizations, though, we must be concerned with the question of whether organizations control individuals. This brings us back to the two basic aspects of management: activities and people. As long as the manager remains fully aware of the ramifications inherent in organizations and people, and as long as the manager tries to maintain a balance between the needs of the two, people are in control of organizations. When the balance tips in favor of activities, people are no longer in control. An organizational threat to individual freedom and dignity cannot exist in a balanced situation.

Saul Gellerman summed up the situation with the following:

> Thus we return to the dilemma that organizations have always faced, and always will, as long as they are comprised of individuals. The organization exists, thrives, and survives by harnessing the talents of individuals. Its problem is to do so without hobbling those talents or turning them against itself. This perpetual balancing act is the responsibility of management, especially those members of management in the lower echelons, whose influence upon employees is most direct.[5]

I agree with Robert Townsend's statement about people and organizations in the preface to his book, *Up the Organizations:* "Solution two is non-violent guerilla warfare: start dismantling our organizations where we're serving them, leaving only the parts where they're serving us."[6] Very few people deny that every formal organization has anti-people elements. Nevertheless, when someone threatens the entire organizational structure, many others rush to the defense of the status quo. If, however, energy is directed toward correcting the anti-people elements and developing a balance between people and things, then almost everyone in an organization will help with the process. Libraries and librarians are people-oriented, and a little more awareness of management techniques is all that is needed for libraries to become *effective* people-oriented organizations.

BIBLIOGRAPHY

1. C. Lindbolm, "The Science of Muddling Through," *Public Administration Review* 19 (1959): 79–88.
2. H. Mintzberg, *The Nature of Managerial Work* (New York: Harper, 1973), p. 11.
3. P. Drucker, *Management* (New York: Harper, 1974), pp. 203–216.
4. Drucker, p. 213.
5. S. Gellerman, *Management of Human Resources* (Hinsdale, Ill.: Dryden Press, 1976), p. 13.
6. R. Townsend, *Up the Organization* (New York: Knopf, 1970), p. 11.

FURTHER READING

Alter, S., and Ginzberg, M. "Managing Uncertainty in MIS Implementation." *Sloan Management Review* 20 (1978): 23–31.
Anderson, R. C., and Dobyns, L. R. *Time: The Irretrievable Asset.* Los Gatos, Calif.: Correlan Publications, 1973.
Anthony, W. P. "Living with Managerial Incompetence." *Business Horizons* 21 (1978): 57–64.

Anthony, W. P. "Management for More Effective Meetings." *Personnel Journal* 58 (1979): 547–550.

Bartolome, F., and Evans, A. L. "Professional Lives versus Private Lives—Shifting Patterns of Managerial Commitment." *Organizational Dynamics* 7 (1979): 3–29.

Batten, J. D. *Tough-Minded Management*. 3rd ed. New York: AMACOM, 1978.

Becker, S. W., and Neuhauser, D. *The Efficient Organization*. New York: Elsevier, 1975.

Beiswinger, G. L. "10 Books Every Public Relations Person Should Read." *Public Relations Journal* 34 (1978): 38–40.

Belker, L. B. *The First-Time Manager*. New York: AMACOM, 1979.

Brinckloe, W. D., and Coughlin, M. T. *Managing Organizations*. Encino, Calif.: Glencoe Press, 1977.

Brown, R. *The Practical Manager's Guide to Excellence in Management*. New York: AMACOM, 1979.

California Department of Finance. *Program Management: Achieving Purpose in Public Programs*. Sacramento, Calif.: Department of Finance, 1977.

Carlisle, H. M. *Management Essentials: Concepts and Applications*. Chicago: Science Research Associates, Inc., 1979.

Child, J. *Organization: A Guide to Problems and Practice*. New York: Harper, 1977.

Cummings, P. W. *Open Management*. New York: AMACOM, 1980.

Dale Carnegie and Associates. *Managing through People*. New York: Simon and Schuster, 1979.

Dale, E. *Management: Theory and Practice*. 4th ed. New York: McGraw-Hill, 1978.

Davis, K. *Organizational Behavior: A Book of Readings*. 5th ed. New York: McGraw-Hill, 1977.

Douglass, H. E., and Donne, N. *Manage Your Time, Manage Your Work, Manage Your Self*. New York: AMACOM, 1980.

Drucker, P. F. *Management*. New York: Harper, 1974.

Drucker, P. F. *Management: Tasks, Responsibilities, Practices*. New York: Harper, 1974.

Effective Management and the Behavioral Sciences. New York: AMACOM, 1978.

Etzioni, A. *Modern Organizations*. Englewood Cliffs, N.J.: Prentice-Hall, 1964.

Fayol, H. *General and Industrial Administration*. London: Pittman, 1949.

Flippo, B., and Munsinger, M. *Management*. 4th ed. Boston: Allyn & Bacon, 1978.

Francis, D., and Woodcock, M. *Unblocking Your Organization*. Rev. ed. La Jolla, Calif.: Univ. Associates, 1979.

Fulner, M. *The New Management*. 2nd ed. New York: Macmillan, 1978.

Gendron, B. *Technology and the Human Condition*. New York: St. Martin's, 1977.

Glueck, W. F. *Management*. Hinsdale, Ill.: Dryden Press, 1977.

Gulick, L., and Urwick, L. *Papers on the Science of Administration*. New York: Columbia Univ. Press, 1937.

Haimann, T. *Managing the Modern Organization*. 3rd ed. Boston: Houghton, 1978.

Handy, C. B. *Understanding Organizations*. Baltimore, MD: Penguin Books. 1976.

Hecht, M. R. *What Happens in Management*. New York: AMACOM, 1980.

Huse, E. F. *The Modern Manager*. St. Paul, MN: West Publishing Co., 1979.

Johnson, T. W., and Stinson, J. E. *Managing Today and Tomorrow*. Reading, Mass.: Addison-Wesley, 1978.

Kantrow, A. M. "Why Read Peter Drucker?" *Harvard Business Review* 80, 1 (1980): 74–82.

Kiev, A. N., and Kohn, V. *Executive Stress*. New York: AMACOM, 1979.

Koontz, H., and O'Donnell, C. *Management: A Systems and Contingency Analysis of Managerial Functions*. 6th ed. New York: McGraw-Hill, 1976.

Lawless, David J. *Organizational Behavior: The Psychology of Effective Management*. 2nd ed. Englewood Cliffs, N.J.: Prentice-Hall, 1979.

Leach, J. "The Notion and Nature of Careers." *Personnel Administrator* 22 (1977): 49–55.

Levin, R. I., and Kirkpatrick, C. A. *Quantitative Approaches to Management.* 3rd ed. New York: McGraw-Hill, 1975.

Life In Organizations: Work Places as People Experience Them. New York: Basic Books, Inc., 1979.

Lindbloom, C. E. "The Science of 'Muddling Through.'" *Public Administration Review* 19 (1959): 79–88.

Luthans, F., and Kreitner, R. *Organizational Behavior Modification.* Glenview, Ill.: Scott, Foresman & Co., 1975.

McCarthy, J. *Why Managers Fail and What to Do About It.* 2nd ed. New York: McGraw-Hill, 1978.

Mackintosh, D. P. *Management by Exception; A Handbook with Forms.* Englewood Cliffs, N.J.: Prentice-Hall, 1978.

Mahoney, T. A. "Organizational Hierarchy and Position Worth." *Academy of Management Journal* 22 (1979): 726–737.

Marshall W. Meyer and Associates. *Environments and Organizations.* San Francisco, Calif.: Jossey-Bass, 1978.

Marston, J. E. *Modern Public Relations.* New York: McGraw-Hill, 1979.

Miller, N. "Career Choice, Job Satisfaction and the Truth Behind the Peter Principle." *Personnel* 53 (1976): 58–65.

Mintzberg, H. *The Nature of Managerial Work.* New York: Harper, 1973.

Mitchell, R. *People in Organizations: Understanding Their Behavior.* New York: McGraw-Hill, 1978.

Nirenburg, J. "Managing Failure." *Supervisory Managment* 24 (1979): 17–22.

Perrow, C. *Complex Organizations: A Critical Essay.* 2nd ed. Glenview, Ill.: Scott, Foresman & Co., 1979.

Quick, T. L. *Understanding People at Work: A Manager's Guide to the Behavioral Sciences.* New York: Executive Enterprises Publications, 1976.

Rausch, E. *Balancing Needs of People and Organizations: The Linking Elements Concept.* Washington, D.C.: Bureau of National Affairs, 1978.

Robbins, P. "Reconciling Management Theory with Management Practice." *Business Horizons* 20 (1977): 38–47.

Scanlan, and Keys, J. *Management and Organizational Behavior.* New York: Wiley, 1979.

Shemetulskis, R. P. "Coming to Grips With Conflict." *Management World* 8 (1979): 14–16.

Stewart, R. "The Jobs of the Manager." *Management Today* 11 (1976): 64–67.

Terry, G. R. *Principles of Management.* 7th ed. Homewood, Ill.: Richard D. Irwin, 1977.

Young, G. A. *Effective Management: Basic Principles and Practices.* Philadelphia: Dorrance, 1977.

3. History and Styles of Management

If you accept the concept of management as an art, it goes without saying that you will need to develop your own style. Furthermore, as you move from one management role to another, slight variations will emerge in that style. If you share the basic approach of this book—that is, that people are the most important resource of an organization—you recognize that each person is unique. And, because each person is unique, you do not respond to everyone in the same way. In essence, you change your style as situations and the persons involved in them change. A corollary of the statement that management is an art is that there is no such thing as a "correct" style. You may have had an opportunity to observe two persons of differing personalities and styles of management effectively manage the same organization. Such experience is the clearest demonstration that a variety of styles can be effective in the same work situation.

The beginning manager needs to start by assessing his or her own personal strengths and weaknesses. Ask yourself such questions as: What don't I like done to me? What type of direction or supervision do I like? What type of directions am I comfortable giving? Can I (and how do I) tell someone that they have done a good or a bad job? As you develop answers to such questions, you will be developing your own style of management. Yet, this style will change as you change; by the time you retire, you might not recognize the style with which you started.

Changes in personal style will be based on existing ideas about how one can approach management. In this chapter, you will find a number of approaches discussed that may provide you with some ideas regarding your individual approach or style to management. The word *approach* has been used throughout the chapter as a "generic label" for ideas, concepts, philosophies, schools, and styles. One problem in the management literature is that writers tend to use terms such as *school*, *style*, and *philosophy* in various ways. Thus, you may find one writer using the term *school*, while another uses the word *philosophy* when both are discussing the same concept or approach. I use the word *approach* because all the ideas discussed in this chapter represent a way of viewing and approaching the field of management.

Not all the approaches to management have been outlined in this chapter. Such a review would require a book twice as long as this. Before discussing some of the approaches to management, I briefly review the history of the development of management thought is in order. All of the approaches that will be discussed were developed within the context and due to the influences of the historical development of the field.

HISTORY OF MANAGEMENT THOUGHT

The development of management history can be divided into four periods: prescientific, scientific-management, human-relations, and synthesis. The labels and dates for these periods vary slightly when discussed in management textbooks, but the general features of each of the four are fairly well agreed upon. Library management practice has followed the same pattern of development (several years behind practices in business and industry, but along the same basic lines). As yet, little evidence would appear available to support the notion of a synthesis period in library science, although a few libraries do seem to be moving in that direction.

Prescientific Period, Pre-1880

The prescientific period might be depicted by a long line of sweating slaves painfully dragging a limestone block toward a pyramid. Along the slave line would be the "managers" cracking their whips. The word for this period is *autocratic*. To become a manager, one needed only authority. Exceptions existed, of course, but heavy reliance on unchallenged authority is representative of this period.

During this vast period, many remarkable feats of organization and joint human efforts to modify the environment were performed. Works such as Middle Eastern ziggurats, Egyptian and Middle American pyramids, the Great Wall of China, and Peruvian roads and buildings attest to this fact. They reflect an extraordinary expenditure of human labor, and each could probably have been constructed through the use of management techniques that depended heavily on coercion. We also know that slaves were used for such labor in the Old World (although it is uncertain whether that was the case in the New World). However, it is likely that these early major building efforts were largely dependent on authority and force. The results are often spectacular, but the limited number of such sites indicates one of the weaknesses of the approach—there was seldom any cooperation between the manager and the managed.

The rise of industrialism and the factory system brought with it the first glimmer of thinking in terms of management skill. A study by Eric Roll (1930) indicates that in 1805, at least one factory in Birmingham, England, employed the "modern" measures of assembly-line operations, a costing system equal to almost any presently in use, and "an organization on the management side which was not excelled ever by the technical skill of the craftsman it produced."[1]

Inevitably, certain characteristics of the factory system led to the development of some managerial concepts. Because of the magnitude of the problems confronting owner–managers of factories, a great deal of effort went into coordinating activities, planning, and decision making. Replacing the traditional owner–worker relationship, a system of formal methods of dealing with each group arose (eventually to give rise to unionism). Conflict became a basic feature of the employer–employee relationship, control became the issue for successful factory operation, and profit became a primary concern. Since capital investments in all phases of operation increased sharply, control of expenditures, output, and income had to be closely coordinated. Thus, power and authority were still important, as the owner–manager held the economic whip and laborers were well aware of this fact. Nevertheless, very few companies that relied solely on authority succeeded during this period. Elements such as planning, the ability to select good workers, and the ability to retain services also were important. It was, then, only a matter of time before some of the repeatedly successful methods were combined in a unified form.

Scientific-Management Period, 1880–1927

If a line of sweating slaves characterized the prescientific period, a representation of the second period, the Industrial Revolution, would be a montage of machines, assembly-line operations, gears turning, steam rising, and huge piles of goods—the key word here is *mechanistic*. Most of the managerial concepts of the time emphasized organization aspects of work, especially those related to the production of goods.

What was the *second* industrial revolution? Some authors suggest that it was the development of data processing and automation, while others hold that it was the advent of scientific management. No matter what position one takes, though, the work of such people as Frederick Winslow Taylor, Frank and Lillian Gilbreth, and Henry Gantt is undeniably basic to the development of scientific-management theory and practice. Exactly when the period began is open to question, as is the matter of who did what first, but, generally, Taylor is thought to be the person who founded the scientific approach to management.

Taylor and His Followers

Frederick Winslow Taylor began his career in 1874 in a machine shop in Philadelphia as an apprentice machinist. In 1878 he started working at the Midvale Steel Company as a laborer, but, within a short time, he was working as a machinist. He successively became gang boss, foreman of the machine shop, master mechanic, and chief draftsman. Within 6 years, he had become chief engineer. Also, while working for the company, he took correspondence courses in the sciences. He moved up the ranks quickly because he emphasized production and knew what could be done under the best conditions. Consequently, because he was concerned with maximum production, Taylor gained the reputation of being anti-worker, but his basic attitude toward the job situation can be seen in the following:

> When a naturally energetic man works for a few days beside a lazy one, the logic of the situation is unanswerable: "Why should I work hard when that lazy fellow gets the same pay that I do and does only half as much work?[2]

In Taylor's view, the difficulty between labor and management was rooted in the definition of a fair day's work, even though both groups made their estimates based only on general impressions. Making random observations of the work area, having briefly performed the job, or knowing the figures on a high-output situation all gave managers a biased point of view. Workers, on the other hand, "knew" that management expected too much. With objective standards, managers would be satisfied and workers would strive to achieve a given production level (because they would receive more pay). Toward this end, Taylor made time-and-motion studies to define a fair day's work for a given task. Today, many of his basic techniques are still used (see Chapter 15 for a discussion of their application to library problems).

The second element in Taylor's system was a new salary payment plan, one using incentive pay. Since workers obviously would not be willing to do more work for the same amount of money, Taylor created what he called *differential piecework*. Thus, workers received one rate when they met the established standard, but a higher rate when they surpassed the standard (owners could afford this because of increased productivity). There were, however, two problems with the plan. One was the assumption that the standard was reasonable and acceptable to the workers. The other was the failure to anticipate what could happen when the standard was not met. Real breakdowns of equipment, delays in getting necessary supplies, illnesses, and the like were all factors that could cause a worker to fail to meet the standard. Such inequities, if allowed to continue, could create real economic hardships and morale problems. Henry Gantt solved some of these problems with his *task-and-bonus* plan. Under this concept, workers would receive a basic salary for doing a certain task, whether they accomplished the "standard" amount of work or not. When they exceeded the standard, they received a bonus.

To my knowledge, no library makes use of the piece-rate system, although I see a number of areas in which it might be tried. While the library may not be able to provide additional monetary compensation for extra work, time is available, and time off could be used as an incentive, especially for some of the more routine tasks.

Many people contributed to the field of scientific management. Gantt also developed some charting techniques that still carry his name (see Chapter 15 for a discussion of Gantt charts). Perhaps the best-known innovators, however, were the Gilbreths (of *Cheaper by the Dozen* fame). Other major figures in the field include C. Bertrand Thompson, H. Emerson, and A. P. Sloan. Today, much of the work in systems analysis and work flow depends on techniques developed by these and other persons. Certainly, the utility of scientific management should not be overlooked simply because it tends to emphasize tasks rather than people.

The basic objective of scientific management is to carry out more work in an effective manner. Attention is focused on production, efficiency, and the prevention of waste. Because of this focus, there seems to be no concern with the people involved. To some extent, the "anti-people" charge is valid, but only in the light of more knowledge and the recognition that people are motivated by more than economic factors.

This discussion points out one of the flaws in the scientific-management approach—the underlying assumption that people are primarily economically oriented. Taylor assumed that both labor and management would respond favorably to his concept because they both would benefit from the results. Other factors, however, influence performance. Working

conditions, interpersonal relationships, social pressure, group acceptance, and union views also play a critical role in the amount of work
produced.

Human-Relations Period, 1927–1950

The human-relations period could well be represented by a series of
rapidly changing pictures: the company bowling team or softball team,
people playing cards during their lunch hour, company cafeterias, and
spirited coffee-break discussions. The background would be out of focus
a bit, but it would clearly be a work environment. This period was a
reaction against the overemphasis on productivity during the scientific-
management period. The worker was not seen as an unfeeling, uniden-
tified unit to be fit into the organizational pattern like a piece in a set of
Tinker Toys.® *Humanism* would be the term best characterizing this
period, and Elton Mayo was perhaps the most influential figure.

Mayo belonged to a research team from the Harvard Graduate School
of Business Administration that undertook a long-term study of worker
fatigue and productivity at Western Electric's Hawthorne, Illinois, plant.
The purpose of the study was to determine the validity of a suggestion
(by the Gilbreths) that brief rest periods would improve production.
Western Electric gave the team a relatively free hand to investigate worker
fatigue and the influence of rest periods on production. As a result of the
5-year study, Mayo has been credited with being the founder of industrial
sociology–psychology and of the human-relations theories of management.

A number of experiments involving relay-assembly and bank-wiring
work were undertaken. The relay-assembly work was done by a group of
women, while the bank wiring was done by a group of men, and both
groups showed great improvement in production. Having observed the
workers beforehand and having kept careful production records on each
one (without the knowledge of the workers), the team then requested
workers to participate. The volunteers were moved to a separate work
area that was identical to the area in which the work was previously performed (as far as arrangement of work equipment was concerned). Because even this change could affect production, no other changes took
place for some time.

Then began the famous series of experiments: short rest periods; longer, less frequent rests; a light lunch in the morning and afternoon—all
these were tried. The series was concluded by a return to the original
system. Yet, no matter what was done, production continued to improve.
Sick time and tardiness were reduced to about one-third the level of the

rest of the work staff, and supervision was reduced to a minimum because the experimental group could be depended on.

Hawthorne Effect

What happened at Western Electric's Hawthorne plant is now widely known, but, at that time, no one realized what was going on. The "Hawthorne effect," as it is now known, is common in all studies of human behavior; because of it, a manager must be very cautious in employing the results of short work-study projects. In essence, the effect is a result of an observer's presence and the subject's awareness of it. The person being observed will not perform in a typical manner for some time, if ever, because of the presence of the observer. Also, there is no way to know exactly what the effect will be: workers may become nervous and do very badly; they may work harder than they normally do; or the observer may be viewed as a threat, and the subjects will respond with the type of performance felt to be most likely to cancel the perceived danger. Obviously, work analysis is necessary to effectively manage any work unit, but the supervisor or manager must be fully aware of the potential problems that may be hidden in the results of a short-term study.

Mayo's real contribution to management theory was a sociological perspective of the work situation. When they realized what had happened, the experimenters changed their focus and concentrated on the sociological aspects. The results at Hawthorne, as well as other studies, convinced Mayo that the long-held notion of the "rabble hypothesis" had to be rejected. This hypothesis held that workers were a disorganized group of individuals, each of whom acted only out of self-interest. If managers accept the hypothesis, they seek to appeal to that self-interest to increase production. Mayo's work, though, demonstrated the importance of the group and proved the fallacy of the rabble hypothesis.

Work groups frequently become the center of a worker's social life, especially in an urban society. In libraries, both the clerical and professional staff find much of their social life in some way connected with individuals from or related to their work environment. Whether this is good or bad for society is not the issue here; it is important to know that the situation exists. Thus, when changes are projected for the work situation, a strong sense of threat exists not only in terms of job security but also in terms of social security. A manager who is concerned with people will always bear this fact in mind.

Synthesis Period, 1950–Present

Graphically, this period could be represented by a complex series of images of people and machines superimposed on one another. There would be a problem in determining which image was dominant because of the constant change back and forth, and no image would ever completely fade out. This also would represent the orientation of this book; the term that might be most appropriate is *balance.*

Who was correct, Taylor or Mayo? The response must be that they both were correct. Not as far apart in philosophy as some people suggest, both were concerned with people to some degree as well as with production. Taylor recognized individual needs and differences as well as peer pressure, just as Mayo recognized the need for high production. The major difference lies in their views of what most motivates people: for Taylor, it was economic consideration; for Mayo, it was group togetherness.

However, both Taylor and Mayo overlooked one important element: individual ego needs. Ego needs may override both economic and social needs for an individual. Just as the work situation is composed of three elements—people, organization, and environment—work motivation for an individual seems to be composed of three types of elements: economic, social, and personal. Taking into account these six variables alone, one can begin to understand why the work situation is full of conflict. All six factors must be in balance before a semblance of harmony may be achieved, and, even then, undertones of conflict will be present.

To be a good manager, then, one must know not only a great deal about the organization's "product" and pertinent management theory but also something about economics, statistics, sociology, political science, and many other social and natural sciences. Almost every field provides aids for the manager, making the work easier and the employees' work situation more pleasant. No one can be expert in all fields, but one ought to have a knowledge of some of the more significant findings if one intends to become a manager. For the librarian, the career path is still one of moving up the organizational hierarchy in the library. Even if one does not become a manager, such knowledge can be helpful by making day-to-day work easier and more efficient.

Since the early 1950s, management thought has been directed toward refining the concepts originated by Taylor and Mayo and toward combining elements of both schools with ideas from other fields. As new concepts and theories from the behavioral sciences are added to the older management theory, many persons have started talking about management as a *process of synthesis.*

DEVELOPMENT OF LIBRARY MANAGEMENT

The preceding pages seldom mentioned libraries. The development of library management follows basically the same pattern evident in business (but not the same chronology). There are three basic periods in the development of library management: pre-1937, scientific (1937–1955), and human relations (1955–present). It also should be noted that these divisions are even more arbitrary than those in general-management theory and that the overlap between periods is very great. Although it may be premature to speak of the development of library-management theories or to begin to identify periods, some evidence suggests that the periods identified do represent an effort on the part of library administrators to pick up ideas from other disciplines, particularly from management and public administration. One of the hazards involved in picking and choosing from other disciplines is, of course, that many administrators and librarians lack sufficient background to be able to evaluate the full impact of some of the concepts being selected and tried out in libraries. As with most individuals or groups, the tendency is to pick up the idea or concept getting the greatest publicity.

Library Management, Pre-1937

Until the middle of the 1930s, most libraries were operated under an authoritarian or at least conservative approach to management. Changes came slowly. The head librarian was expected to make decisions in almost all phases of operation. As libraries tended to be small, this was usually possible. Even in libraries in which the staff and collections were extremely large (such as the Library of Congress, New York Public, Harvard, Yale, Columbia, Cleveland, and Chicago) and directors had to delegate some authority, emphasis was still pretty much on following past practice and comparing what other libraries were doing. (Library B did what Library A had found successful; Library E would examine Libraries A, B, C, and D, and adopt whatever looked best.)

Although the practice of observing other libraries is still evident today, it may not be the best approach. Perhaps more time might be spent thinking about the unique needs of each library's community and how to meet them in a special, if not unique, manner. In this way, perhaps, we can progress a bit more rapidly toward fulfilling the library's purpose.

Scientific Management, 1937–1955

A number of doctoral dissertations produced in the late 1930s began the period of scientific management for libraries. Studies on cost analysis, technical services, cataloging, and the use of edge-notched cards appeared at this time. Librarians began investigating scientific management to see whether some techniques were applicable to library situations.

Following World War II, librarians applied a combination of scientific-management ideas and some of the mathematical/operations-research techniques developed during World War II. Dougherty and Heinritz's *Scientific Management of Library Operations* (1966) is representative of the concern during this period with efficient operation and is highly recommended for anyone interested in library management.

Most library-related work during this period tended to focus on activities and things rather than on people, in contrast to Taylor, who definitely did consider people in his work. Rather than determine what each job should be and then find workers with the qualifications for them, as Taylor would have done, scientific library managers usually determined work flow without regard for personnel. This is not to say that library management had become anti-people but simply that the concern was not with matching people and tasks.

Human Relations, 1955–Present

We are now beginning to see what is perhaps the development of synthesis in library-management theory rather than a strict human-relations phase of operations. Only a few of Mayo's and his followers' concepts have been adopted during this period, and these have not really been applied as Mayo might have expected. "Human relations" in libraries usually means democratic administration, participative administration, great use of committees, and involvement (or apparent involvement) by staff in decision making. However, the way in which many library administrators have used human relations in democratic administration has resulted in an emphasis on some of the more difficult aspects of human relations. For example, real involvement in the decision-making process by the people affected will unquestionably make the decisions more palatable to them; all too often, however, outside factors limit the scope of real involvement. This in turn can cause the staff to view the process as a sham; managers must be careful when and how they use this process.

APPROACHES TO MANAGEMENT

Since the mid-1950s, a number of approaches to management have appeared. Proponents of one particular point of view combine various aspects of management theory and techniques into what is held to be a unique system. In this section, I discuss some of the more popular approaches, examining the basic subdivisions that usually are presented.

Traditional

The traditional approach to management is the one most commonly followed, and many of the principles set forth by Henri Fayol underlie its basic philosophy. There are four fundamental characteristics: (1) the functions of management, such as planning, organizing, motivating, and communicating, can be defined, emphasized, and studied; (2) principles or fundamental truths exist concerning organization and management, and they are very important in clarifying the study of management and in improving managerial practice; (3) principles derived from the study of management should be the starting point for research and should produce even more useful managerial theory; and (4) management is to a great degree an art concerned with the application of certain principles that are only to a certain degree susceptible to scientific study. Although not always so identified, much of the material in management texts is based on these concepts.

The traditional approach analyzes management processes in order to establish a theoretical, philosophical framework; principles are identified and used to build a unified theory of management. Management is seen as a universal activity, but environmental factors that create special problems also are recognized. A body of knowledge universal in applicability is held to exist, all special environmental questions aside. Also, persons using this approach, whether in practice or in theory, often do not recognize disciplines such as sociology, biology, psychology, and economics as having relevance to their activities. The fact remains, however, that these factors do influence all organized activity, and the manager should be aware that the study of them can contribute to daily managerial activities.

Empirical

Experience is the basic element in the empirical. With little emphasis on theory, practitioners maintain that examination of past experience can be useful but that general principles may not be readily derived from such study. The best way to learn management skills is through experience under the tutelage of someone who is recognized as a successful manager. This might be considered an operational approach, because it is shaped by practice—thus leading to the label of the "past practice approach." The manager asks questions such as: How would my predecessors have dealt with this situation? How have managers in organizations like mine handled such problems in the past? This approach includes looking into the history and development of organizations, into memoirs, and into biographies of managers; the goal is to improve by absorbing the lessons of history.

The empirical approach relies heavily on the case study—certainly a useful technique. Rather than pose a question and rely on students to propose solutions, the empirical teacher uses real cases and the actual attempts at solution that were made by managers—all to reveal basic truths. Certainly, however, in some libraries, custom has almost become a sacred cow, and such libraries respond very, very slowly to their changing environments. Their objective is to maintain the status quo, which would seen in this view to have allowed the organization to survive. From the managers' point of view, this seems to ensure a stable, successful organization; however, the patron/client may not be so sanguine about the success ratio and may see the organization as slightly moribund.

The empirical and traditional approaches share a number of basic premises. Both stress the necessity of knowing certain fundamental truths of successful management, and many of Mayo's generalizations are equally applicable to both approaches. The difference is that the traditional approach holds that these principles can be taught, studied, and examined in an abstract manner. Empiricists maintain that such knowledge can be gained only through actually working under a manager of some reputation and experience.

Decision Theory

The decision-theory approach focuses attention on logic and the rational process involved in decision making, as well as on the process of analyzing situations and problems in order to make decision. Its basic tenet is that decisions must be made before any plans or actions can take place, that management functions—planning, organizing, actuating, and controlling—only operate so long as decisions are being made, and that the more rational the decision, the more efficient and effective the organization will be. Economics, value analysis, and information-transmission process provide some of the input for this method. Herbert Simon created and developed this approach, drawing on the work of Chester Barnard. Others who are well known for their work in this area include James March and Richard Cyert.

Decision theory concentrates on the rational decision—the weighing of alternatives and consequences. It deals with the actual decision, the people or groups involved, and the analysis of the decision process itself. The primary problem lies in the area of values and ethics, where decision making becomes highly subjective. However, when the approach is limited to the economic area, it is highly effective. In its early phase, decision theory was geared primarily toward evaluating economic alternatives, but now almost every human activity is considered legitimate for a decision-making study.

Problems facing libraries—for instance, new facilities, special services, development of children's services—all require careful analysis. Decision theory provides some methods whereby decisions can be approached in a more consistent, if not completely rational, manner. The decision-theory approach has provided managers—library managers—with a very useful means of developing techniques that allow problems to be identified and attacked systematically.

Mathematical

The primary difference between decision theory and the mathematical approach is that the latter sees mathematical models (illustrating programs and attempted solutions) as the best way by which to determine results without having to actually implement a decision. The logical aspect of mathematics easily fits within the framework of decision theory, but the primary thrust of the mathematical approach is not decision making but model building. Persons using this approach consider themselves to be operations analysts or researchers, and often call themselves management scientists. To their way of thinking, their approach is the one most likely to provide a scientific theory of management.

Clearly, a mathematical approach can be useful in any inquiry: it causes the manager or researcher to define problems accurately and carefully; it allows for the use of mathematical symbols for both known and unknown quantities; and it can be understood by people who are unfamiliar with management principles but who are familiar with mathematics. The fact that a mathematical model is logical, consistent, and easily comprehended makes it a very valuable tool, especially in solving complex problems or logically arranging information sources and data for easier quantification.

Naturally, this approach has been most successful in areas where measurement is easy, such as technical processing, where there is no ambiguity as to the nature of an item. In assessing human behavior, though, precise identification becomes more difficult. This is especially true in libraries, which are service oriented rather than profit oriented. For instance, in public services, most of what takes place is not easily quantifiable. (How do you determine a value for answers to questions such as the height of Mount Everest as opposed to possible sources for Agatha Christie's Jane Marple? Is value a function of time spent finding an answer? the use made of the answer?) Thus, when the mathematical model is applied in areas where measurement becomes judgmental rather than scientific, major problems emerge. It is that limitation that makes it difficult to consider this as the sole approach, as the mathematical model presents only one aspect of the total problem.

Human Relations

The human-relations approach to management, based on the work of Elton Mayo, maintains that the manager's role is to keep the organization as conflict-free as possible in order to accomplish its objectives. The manager's role naturally leads to a dependence on social and individual psychology as sources for developing new concepts of management. Since practitioners of this approach consider every individual to be a sociopsychological being, they view psychology as central to all aspects of management; this moves them toward the art side of management, with every problem being unique and defying generalizations.

Thus, the manager must understand and satisfy the psychological needs of each individual employee as well as utilize a wide variety of group psychology factors. This approach has contributed to a general managerial theory in two ways: (1) it emphasizes individual participation and involvement at all levels in the organization, and (2) it suggests ways of handling conflict within the organization. A lesser contribution is a recognition that environment will influence an organization as well as individuals; this has been helpful in understanding ways in which people and organizations interact.

Much debate has taken place over the question of whether human relations is just an approach to management or whether it is really a theory. Perhaps it simply studies group dynamics, interpersonal relationships, and sociopsychological relationships. The concepts of motivation factors and the manager-as-leader are important, as the considerable literature published concerning leadership characteristics testifies. Undoubtedly, running organizations and accomplishing tasks involve human behavior, and a manager who ignores person-to-person and person-to-organization relationships will probably have serious problems within a short period of time. Yet, those who say that human behavior is a manager's total field of concern ignore the areas of planning and organizing, where behavior is much less important than it is in actuating and controlling various activities.

Social Systems

Closely related to and often confused with the human-relation approach is the social-systems approach. Here the emphasis is on formal organizations and the interplay between them and human beings. One might even say that the social-systems approach is concerned with cultural interrelationships that result from the interaction between formal organizations and individuals; thus, the study of miniature social systems, with heavy dependence on the behavioral sciences, becomes the goal.

A characteristic of this approach is its emphasis on cooperation within a social unit, the ideal being one in which people communicate effectively and work toward a common goal in harmony. But note that the ideal is rarely attained, if ever. As a result, the problem becomes one of resolving tensions and conflicts among members of the unit, who will vary in ability and desire to cooperate. Mention also must be made of the importance of the informal relationships among unit members, which may not coincide with their individual roles in the formal organization. This can either help or hinder the organization, but it must be accounted for under the social-systems theory. Finally, managers must consider the general social context within which the organization functions, both in terms of general social trends and each organization's relationships with other organizations.

The founder of the social-systems approach is Chester I. Barnard, who developed it in the belief that individuals must cooperate in order to offset personal, biological, physiological, and sociological limitations. The approach has contributed to general-management theory the view of the organization as a social organism, subject to exactly the same problems and pressures to which the individual is subject. Thus, it offers a balance to the mathematical approach. Perhaps a blend of the two approaches can offer a viable alternative to the extremes.

Formalistic

The formalistic approach to management assumes that members of an organization perform best when their jobs and duties are clearly defined and highly structured. They know exactly what is expected and what to strive for in order to achieve the level of performance required. The primary concern, then, is with a hierarchy of objectives, formalized authority and responsibility, unity of command, and span of control (defined in an organizational chart). To a great extent, the bureaucratic system (as identified by Max Weber) relies on this approach, which draws heavily on "classical" management thought.

The criticism has been made that this approach is anti-human, placing greater emphasis on office and duty than on people. However, the approach does recognize the relationship between the office and the person in it, so the charge is not completely accurate.

The great strength of this approach is that it creates highly stable organizations despite radical environmental changes, so continuity is assured. The French government after World War II was a perfect example of an organization providing stability despite numerous external changes over the years. As to charges that such institutions become rigid and actually kill initiative and creativity, this may be true in some instances. A good manager, however, will maintain an awareness of the balance between the job description for an office and the person holding the office, so rigidity need not be inevitable.

Spontaneity

Followers of the spontaneity approach to management hold that group coordination and effective behavior automatically emerge around a group's "natural leader." The approach draws a great deal from social psychology, group dynamics, and psychological disciplines for its concepts. The primary drawback is that there is little middle ground between spectacular success and spectacular failure if one adopts this approach. The danger lies in the fact that very few people can operate in an unstructured environment, and this approach demands as little structure as possible. Thus, when the question arises as to how people know what to do in order to achieve the organization's goals, the answer often becomes, no one knows.

Some people find it difficult to function in an unstructured environment, because of lack of direction, while others find it challenging and rewarding, if only for a short time in some cases. To some extent, then, this approach is the opposite of the formalistic approach, although both recognize the interaction between individual and organization. The main contribution of the spontaneity approach is that it accentuates the creative abilities of the human being.

Participative

The participative approach attempts to balance the formalistic and spontaneity approaches in the belief that individuals perform best when given a chance to participate in decision making, especially regarding matters that affect them. It de-emphasizes the power of one person, often using the committee as the decision-making tool. Many libraries have used this approach, and it is a reasonable one to try in such a setting. All the elements of the formal organization remain intact, but structure, hierarchy, and job descriptions are decided on by committees, not individuals.

The major advantage is that the talents, ideas, and skills of a great many people can be tapped, whereas they might well go unused under another approach. "Several heads are better than one" might sum this up. Yet, committees can be inefficient, time-wasting groups that produce watered down results that no one can enthusiastically embrace. On the other hand, absence of participation can result in straightforward opposition to one-person decrees.

Perhaps the greatest damage occurs when participation is not employed meaningfully and when the person employing the method does not believe in it or intend to implement the results. Individuals must know that their participation will have consequences and that the administration will actually follow through on what the group has decided. Nevertheless, this is a valuable approach, and it has been discussed frequently in library literature.

Challenge–Response

This approach is akin to the participative approach in that it allows for freedom of movement and decision making by individuals; however, it retains a formalized structure. Decision making is basically individual rather than committee oriented, but the individual has formalized objectives and boundaries within which to exercise initiative in approaching a task. Challenge–response might well be suited to more libraries than use it, especially in technical-services areas, where individuals are free to improve their performance by any method that achieves the unit's objectives.

The point is that the freedom of an individual to achieve a given goal (say, catalog 800 books per month) is precisely the element that stimulates that person to respond positively to the challenge presented. This may not always work, especially with people whose culture does not emphasize competition or with people who actually require that a routine be established for them. In such cases, the manager may well present one person with step-by-step directions, emphasizing that this is *one* way to accomplish a task and that improvements and variations are acceptable. Thus, security is provided for the hesitant, but freedom of action is maintained for those more adventuresome or innovative persons doing the same work.

Directive

The directive approach is the opposite of challenge–response in that its adherents contend that people both want and need to be told what to do, often in minute detail. Thus, it can be seen as taking the form of time-

and-motion studies one step further—there is a *best* way, and people want and need to be told what it is. This approach emphasizes the rights, powers, and authority of management, contending that only the people on top know what is good and what will work. Moreover, it tends to equate power with knowledge, as was the case in the prescientific historic period of management. However, the idea did not always work then, and it does not always work now. Indeed, today it would probably fail more often than it did in the past if it were applied consistently and over an extended period of time.

The directive approach differs from the formalistic in that the directive emphasizes the powerful individual, while the formalistic emphasizes the organization's hierarchy—that is, the office. Thus, in the directive view, the power of a certain office stems from the person holding it, and the same position might carry much different influence when occupied by different persons. Also, the formalistic approach recognizes and relies on two-way communication, while the directive approach tends to ignore it.

Remember that a directive method is sometimes the only one that will work with some individuals. Also, understanding the theory of the directive approach can help you in recognizing the problems involved in power struggles, in understanding the seeking and control of power, and in identifying the effects of power struggles on the success or failure of an organization.

Checks and Balances

"Power corrupts" is the basic tenet of the checks-and-balances approach, reflecting the idea that an individual in power inevitably becomes corrupted by it. Thus, the organization must be structured in such a way that no one person or group can entirely control it; that is, seats of power must be multiple and balanced against one another (as in the United States government, with its three branches in balance).

One frequent problem, however, is that so much energy goes into developing these checks and balances that the organization's objectives get lost in the process. Also, the manager must cope with both individual and group psychology. Hence, management in such a situation may entail extra duties and activities that have little to do with organizational objectives.

The primary contribution to this approach is that a need exists for some check on the unrestricted growth of power in a particular unit, or even within a single individual. The techniques of checks and balances are useful, and the manager should be aware of them. However, the approach does seem to be overly concerned with the corruptive nature of power and with some of the less desirable aspects of human behavior.

Management Process

Some managers hold that management process is the essential and central core of management. In this approach, four elements are common: planning, organizing, actuating, and controlling. These fundamental functions are interwoven to such an extent that, in most cases, one cannot really determine exactly when any single function is taking place. About the only time this is possible is when an organization is being set up. Thus, the individual who starts a library from scratch has a unique opportunity to define objectives, lay out plans to accomplish them, determine the organization's structure and how best to set it up, select personnel to fit the plan, and see that the work is carried out.

The person given the task of reorganizing an existing organization or setting up a new unit within an organization *must* understand the process of management, because objectives are already set, and it is more difficult to modify old objectives than it is to create new ones. Should certain skills be lacking in the staff, the manager is then faced with this human-relations problem: To what extent does the manager modify plans and the organization to fit the capabilities of the personnel available? How long can the organization operate at a low level before changes must be forced on it? How much inefficiency and expense can be tolerated before making a change in personnel?

A manager who is not comfortable carrying out a wide variety of functions and activities simultaneously will not be too successful. Those who demand absolute peace and quiet to plan and create will find themselves working long hours outside the normal work day; if they try to isolate themselves during the work day, staff morale problems will result. Rarely is a manager responsible for only one plan, and, although the sequence of planning, organizing, actuating, and controlling remains constant, the stage of each plan will probably not coincide with the stage of any other plan being undertaken. Thus, a manager may be planning one program, controlling several others, and organizing even more.

The individual who must have everything happen in a neat, linear format may find it inadvisable to accept a management position in a dynamic organization. Libraries, however, tend to change slowly, and they do not require quite the high tolerance for ambiguity and change in a manager that some other organizations might require.

Other Approaches

As noted earlier, approaches to management have many labels. Effective managers create individual styles, drawing on existing ideas, the literature, and, of greatest importance, their experiences as managers. Therefore, when a person writes about her or his own style, there is a strong tendency to create a unique label for it rather than to use an existing label—which leads to a form of "management alphabet soup." Depending on the individual's stature in the field, the label gains greater or lesser popularity. Simply check the titles of articles for one year in a leading management journal (say, the *Harvard Business Review*) or the titles of management books published within a year to see the variety available. Careful analysis can usually easily place the "new" approach under one of those described here.

Some ideas have a very limited life span, primarily because the persons who created them were the only ones who could make them work. Others last longer, then drop by the wayside because they were valid only for a limited period of time. Sometimes it takes several years for adverse effects to be seen. However, by having a clear understanding of the fundamentals of management and of the basic approaches to management, the manager is able to personally assess the value of new ideas as they come along.

Two approaches that gained some popularity in libraries (and, naturally, in business and other service organizations) during the 1970s were MBO (Management by Objectives) and OD (Organizational Development).

George Odiorne's *Management by Objectives* (1965) provided an early impetus to the MBO approach. Although originally intended as a means of coordinating individual and organizational objectives, the technique as applied usually results in major shifts in the operation of an organization. The basic concept in this approach is straightforward: based on knowledge of the organization's overall objectives, each supervisor and employee develops a set of goals for each person. These goals then guide daily work and are used to assess accomplishments.

Yet, what sounds simple and appears to be an ideal method in the abstract often proves to be very complex in the real world. Considerable time must be devoted to preparing overall organizational goals, communicating them to all levels of personnel, developing individual goals, ensuring that the individual goals cover the whole, and assessing the results. My first-hand experience with MBO indicates that approximately 46% of normal work time is lost to these activities during the 8 to 10 months required to institute the concept. After a year or two, the time commitment decreases significantly; however, reaching that point can cause considerable trauma for both staff and patrons. Certainly, there is *no* hope of successfully instituting this approach without the *complete* cooperation of the entire staff—from head librarian to part-time clerks.

Specific MBO applications do reveal major advantages, though: improved communication, an increase in mutual understanding of mutual problems, better coordination of plans, improvement in attitude regarding the evaluation process, better use of all managerial abilities, and, to some degree, an increase in innovation and creativity. These are all certainly worthwhile changes. The question is, can you afford the time to get there?

Organizational development (OD) has had a number of proponents; a good overview is found in J. K. Fordyce and R. Weil's *Managing with People* (1971). W. G. Bennis' *Organization Development: Its Nature, Origins, and Prospects* (1969) contains a brief definition of the concept: "O.D. is a response to change, a complex educational strategy intended to change the beliefs, attitudes, values, and structure of organizations so that they can better adapt to new technologies, markets and challenges and the dizzying rate of change itself."[3] This is usually accomplished by means of a "third" party—an outside consultant who reviews what is taking place and sets up some situation(s) in which the staff must confront problems head on.

Practitioners of OD have developed a number of methods for achieving the goals of their programs. Generally, one can divide these methods into four categories: (1) bringing about change; (2) determining exactly what is happening; (3) improving meetings; and (4) changing the quality of interpersonal relationships. Such methods require skilled application and considerable experience in order to achieve positive results, and an inexperienced person who tries to apply these methods runs great risks. I know of several supervisors who ran into trouble when they attempted to implement OD methods after taking just one academic course in their use. (In fact, one supervisor was demoted because of the difficulties that arose with the staff as a direct result of the application of OD methods.)

Your Style

Cases of demotion or dismissal as a result of trying a new technique or a popular idea are rare. Nonetheless, they do occur often enough to clearly illustrate why a person needs to know a great deal about any new idea before applying it. Usually, I have found that, in such cases, the person attempting to use the idea has little or no knowledge of the basics of management (much less the "new" idea) beyond knowing a few catch words and phrases. I also have found a strong correlation between cases of demotion, transfer, and dismissal and individuals who are in trouble trying something that they are not comfortable doing.

If there are any fundamental rules (old as well as new) for managers, they are: (1) know yourself and how you work with people; (2) know the fundamentals of management before you explore new ideas in the field; and (3) think twice before trying something, and then think again. The major point about any new idea or different approach is that it needs to be thought through very carefully before it is applied.

BIBLIOGRAPHY

1. E. Roll, *An Early Experiment in Industrial Organization* (London: Longman, Green, 1930), p. xv.
2. F. W. Taylor, *Principles of Scientific Management* (New York: Harper, 1947), p. 31.
3. W. G. Bennis, *Organization Development: Its Nature, Origins, and Prospects* (Reading, Mass.: Addison-Wesley, 1969), p. 17.

FURTHER READING

Adizes, I. "Mismanagement Styles." *California Management Review* 19 (Winter 1976): 5–20.
Albrecht, K. G. *Successful Management by Objectives: An Action Manual.* Englewood Cliffs, N.J.: Prentice-Hall, 1978.
Anthony, W. P. *Participative Management.* Reading Mass.: Addison-Wesley, 1978.
Beck, R. J. "Your Turn: Opinion: Say It with Flowers." *Idaho Librarian* 28 (1976): 30–33.
Blake, R. R., and Mouton, J. S. "Principles of Behavior for Sound Management." *Training and Development Journal* 33 (1979): 26–28.
Campbell, R. "A History of Administrative Thought." *Administrator's Notebook* 26 (1977–78): entire issue.
Castagna, E. "Democratic Administration." *Library Journal* 82 (Dec. 15, 1957): 3138–3144.
Classics of Organization Theory. Oak Park, Ill.: Moore Pub. Co., 1978.
Copley, F. B. *Frederick W. Taylor: Father of Scientific Management.* Vol. 2. New York: Harper, 1923.
Delang, W. "The Development and Decline of Patrimonial and Bureaucratic Administrators." *Administrative Science Quarterly* 8 (1963): 458–501.
Dougherty, R. M., and Heinritz, F. J. *Scientific Management of Library Operations.* Metuchen, N.J.: Scarecrow, 1966.
Fischer, R. G. "Worker's Self-Management & Libraries." *Canadian Library Journal* 34 (1977): 165.
Flipps, G. M. "Participative Management In Libraries." *Illinois Libraries* 60 (1978): 538–540.
Frame, R. M., and Luthans, F. "Merging Personnel and OD: A Not So Good Couple." *Personnel* 54 (1977): 12–22.
Futas, E. "Management by Objectives: The History of An Idea." *LACUNY* 4 (1975): 9–12.
Giblin, E. J., and Sanfilippo, F. "MBO: A Misunderstood Tool for Creative Planning." *Managerial Planning* 26 (1978): 4–10.
Golightly, H. O. *Managing with Style and Making It Work for You.* New York: AMACOM, 1977.

Harsha, K. K. "And Now, Theory Z." *Management World* 7 (1978): 24–26.

Hoffman, R. R. "MJS: Management by Job Standards." *Personnel Journal* 58 (1979): 536–540.

Kaplan, L. "Literature of Participation: From Optimism to Realism." *College and Research Libraries* 36 (1975): 473–479.

Kemper, R. E., and Ostrander, R. E. *Directorship by Objectives.* Littleton, Colo.: Libraries Unlimited, 1977.

Koontz, H. "Making MBO Effective." *California Management Review* 20 (1977): 5–13.

Koontz H. "Making Sense of Management Theory." *Harvard Business Review* 40 (1962): 24–48.

Lyder, R. A. "Results Oriented Management through MBO." *Medical Library Association Bulletin* 67 (1979): 287–296.

Lynch, B. "Participative Management." *College and Research Libraries* 33 (1972): 382–390.

McDonnell, J. "Participative Management: Can Its Acceptance Be Predicted?" *Human Resource Management* 15 (1976): 2–4.

March, J. G., and Simon, H. A. *Organizations.* New York: Wiley, 1958.

Marchant, M. P. "Literature of Participation." *College and Research Libraries* 37 (1976): 369–371.

Marchant, M. P. "Participative Management." *Library Trends* 20 (1971): 49–58.

Marchant, M. P. *Participative Management in Academic Libraries.* Westport, Conn.: Greenwood Press, 1977.

Martell, C. "Administration Which Way—Traditional Practice of Modern Theory." *College and Research Libraries* 33 (1972): 104–111.

Mayer, R. J. "The Secret Life of MBO." *Human Resource Management* 17 (1978): 6–11.

Mayo, E. *The Human Problems of an Industrial Civilization.* New York: Viking, 1960.

Michalko, J. "Management by Objectives and the Academic Library." *Library Quarterly* 45 (1975): 235–252.

Morgenstern, O., and von Neumann, J. *Theory of Games and Economic Behavior.* Princeton, N.J.: Princeton Univ. Press, 1944.

Morse, G. E. "Pendulum of Management." *Harvard Business Review* 43 (1965): 158–164.

Murray, S., and Kuffel, T. "MBO and Performance Linked Compensation in the Public Sector." *Public Personnel Management* 3 (1978): 171–176.

Ochs, M. "Holistic View of Modern Management Theory." *Southeastern Librarian* 26 (1976): 138–141.

Odiorne, G. S. "MBO in the 1980's: Will It Survive?" *Management Review* 66 (1977): 39–42.

Odiorne, G. S. "How to Succeed in MBO Goal Setting." *Personnel Journal* 58 (1978): 427–429.

Odiorne, G. S. "MBO: A Backward Glance." *Business Horizons* 21 (1978): 14–24.

Oh, T. K. "New Dimensions of Management Theory." *College and Research Libraries* 27 (1966): 431–438.

Nyren, K. E. "Participatory Management in Libraries: What Is Its Future?" *Library Journal* 101 (1976): 1186–1187.

Parent, R. "Experience with Participatory Management." *LACUNY* 4 (1975): 2–8.

Roethlisberger, F. J., and Dickson, W. J. *Management and the Worker.* Cambridge, Mass.: Harvard Univ. Press, 1947.

Roll, E. *An Early Experiment in Industrial Organization.* London: Longmans, Green, 1930.

Shaughnessy, T. W. "Participative Management, Collective Bargaining and Professionalism." *College and Research Libraries* 38 (1977): 140–146.

Simon, H. A. "Comments on the Theory of Organizations." *American Political Science Review* 46 (1952): 1130–1139.

Sokolik, S. L. "Feedback and Control—The Hollow in MBO Practice." *Human Resource Management* 17 (1978): 23–28.

Swanson, R. W. "Organization Theory Related to Library Management." *Canadian Library Journal* 30 (1973): 356–364.

Taylor, F. W. *Principles of Scientific Management.* New York: Harper, 1947.

Terry, G. R. *Principles of Management.* 7th ed. Homewood, Ill.: Irwin, 1977.

U.S. Civil Service Commission Bureau of Policies and Standards. *Management by Objectives: Guidelines for Managerial Decision Making.* Washington, D.C.: March 1978.

Weber, M. *Theory of Social and Economic Organization.* Oxford: Oxford Univ. Press, 1947.

Wood, M. B. "Organization of Successful Participative Management in a Health Sciences Library." *Bulletin of the Medical Library Association* 65 (1977): 216–223.

Wren, D. A. *The Evolution of Management Thought.* New York: Ronald Press, 1972.

4. Change, Creativity, and the Library

Creativity and change go hand in hand: when implemented, a creative idea leads to change, and creative ideas very often result from changing circumstances. How organizations can and do handle change and "creativity" is the focus of this chapter.

Perhaps no other topic has generated more heated student response during the years that I have taught management than has creativity. One student turned in a term paper entitled "The Organizational Rape of the Creative Personality." Others have stated either in person or in a paper something to the effect that "my attitude toward creativity has been nurtured in my course work in music (or art, or literature, or dance)." The often hostile response to a limited definition of the term *creativity* indicates to me that the subject causes students to think and to read more on the subject. Yet, they continue to ignore, even after periodic restatement, the point that creativity aids in the generation of new organizational ideas and in the handling of change. Part of the difficulty, then, seems to reside in defining creativity.

CREATIVITY AND MANAGEMENT

Every writer who tries to deal with the concept of creativity seems to arrive at a unique definition. A few examples will illustrate the wide range in the definitions and also show why everyone seems to have trouble understanding what is meant by the term. Donald MacKinnon claims that creativity "is a process extended in time and characterized by originality, adaptiveness, and realization."[1] David Green defined it as "the employment of imagination in getting the job done."[2] But, according to G. K. Bennett, creativity is "the mental activity in problem-stating, problem-solving situations where artistic or technical innovations are the result."[3] And J. W. Haefele simply defined it as "the ability to formulate new combinations from two or more concepts already in mind."[4] Some of these definitions indicate a process, while others are concerned with a product. From an organizational point of view, Haefele's definition is the best, even though it does not completely solve the problem of "raping" the artistically creative person.

Viewing creativity through Haefele's definition ("new combination"), one can see why it is important to an organization. Certainly any organization is heavily influenced by its environment, and, in addition to the inevitable death and taxes, one other thing in life can be counted on—change. On the one hand, almost everyone, at some time or other, feels that society (the environment) is changing too rapidly. On the other hand, organizations tend to become static and less responsive with time. Libraries in the United States illustrate this well, as they are usually highly structured, traditional organizations. Most of them appear to be managed by persons using the formalistic managerial style combined with bits and pieces of various social-systems approaches. Stable, relatively viable organizations have been the result.

Unfortunately, this approach is not as responsive to a changing environment as is desirable for a social-service organization. The spontaneity style is very responsive, but it does not generate stable, long-lasting organizations. Here we shall look at some ways of generating creativity in a structured organization. Perhaps the application of a few of these ideas will result in a more dynamic library system, one that is responsive to the rapid pace of change in our society.

CREATIVITY IN THE ORGANIZATION

Creativity allows organizations, including libraries, to make productive changes vital to their existence, rather than merely react to change after it occurs. But how does a manager go about getting new, imaginative ideas for a library? One of the best ways is to recognize that everyone has some creative ability and to allow staff members to frequently exercise their creativity. Certain techniques apparently help to increase the individual's capacity to use this ability and to produce a large number of new ideas in a brief period of time. These operational techniques help people to overcome their fear of using their imaginations by enabling them to move back to the childhood pattern of asking *why, what if,* and *how.* They then explore their environment to find the answers.

Several factors must be borne in mind about these operational techniques, however. First, their use should be an ongoing project, not a short-term activity following a one-day or two-day creativity workshop (after which things revert quickly to their original state). Also, because of the nature of the techniques, the first-time effort is unlikely to produce very many useful results. Neophytes tend to see few useful ideas the first time around; as a result, usually they decide not to try again. Actually it takes a great deal of experience and frequent repetition to come up consistently with productive ideas.

Management must intend to employ the ideas that have been generated. Nothing is more discouraging than to be asked for a number of new ideas, to produce them, and then to see them disappear into limbo. After a few such experiences, the ideas generated will diminish both in quality and quantity. Obviously, many suggestions will be silly or impossible, but workable ideas deserve an explanation of why they were rejected.

A manager, therefore, must plan for and encourage creativity on the part of all employees, with the goal of a positive mutual benefit for both the individual and the organization. In order to plan for the creative employee, though, a manager must be aware of the results of studies of the creative personality. Basically, these studies indicate that such personalities tend to be introspective, rather critical of the status quo, and strong willed after reaching a decision. Moreover, it is difficult for the creative individual to work in and with large groups.

TYPES OF CREATIVE THINKING

The literature on the process of creative thinking provides four basic types. (Bear in mind that *creative* here means an original pattern formed and expressed.) The four types clearly conform to this definition of *creative,* and all four can be used in the library setting, *if* the manager is willing to accept the creative process as an integral element in the organization.

The first type of creative thinking involves a *logical,* pragmatic approach. A problem is viewed as a situation in which some imbalance exists. To correct that situation, a hypothesis is formulated and then tested through a series of carefully planned experiments. Originality enters to the extent that the individuals involved in the process link dissimilar concepts and formulate a hypothesis regarding the relationship. The emphasis is on a planned, logical approach: $A = X, B = X, A = B$. Although in many ways this approach may be seen as the least creative (especially from an artistic perspective), new concepts, new approaches, and new patterns may nonetheless be developed by this means.

The second category of creative thinking, closely related to the logical approach is labeled *problem solving*. The difference between the logical approach and the problem-solving approach is that problem solving places great emphasis on a careful definition of the problem. Obviously, these two types of creative thinking are related. In fact, all four types are related to one another, and to say that one is used to the exclusion of the others is simply not valid.

Idea linking is the third type of creative thinking. A wide variety of ideas, experiences, observed situations, and the results of the situations are gathered, then linked together in various ways. Some of the techniques used to increase creativity depend to a large degree on idea linking. One takes dissimilar concepts, products, and ideas, and then places them next to one another and attempts to answer the questions: What if? What would happen? What are the relationships? Could this be used? What would happen if these were combined? Through this technique, one can come up with new concepts.

Free association, one of the most popular concepts in the last few years, is an attempt to bring to the conscious level a great many more ideas than are normally at this level. The idea is that only a narrow opening exists between the unconscious and the conscious levels in the human personality, and that the unconscious level suppresses a great many ideas for a variety of reasons. Because people tend to think in tightly structured patterns, they have difficulty seeing the relevance, purpose, or relationships among many ideas—sometimes even to the point of not seeing the total picture. Free association shakes the ideas loose from the normal pattern in which they are held so as to form new patterns. Also, it allows some unconscious ideas to mingle with the conscious ones, further expanding the range of possible patterns. The results of free association are often extremely original (sometimes to the point that no one can understand what is meant).

It is now time to consider the second element of the definition—the *expression* of the patterns that have resulted from creative thinking. Only when one can communicate or express a new concept in a way that others will understand can it be said that the true creative process is taking place. The line between the creative and the noncreative process depends on the way in which, or the degree to which, an idea is communicated to others. A person may have many original ideas, but, if they are not expressed understandably, then that person is not creative. However, creative geniuses may not be understood in their own time, through no fault of their own, but they can come to be understood and appreciated later. This is perhaps one of the dangers in being creative—one may not be understood; and the understanding and recognition of creative ideas are important to every individual.

Any library administrator may make use of all four types of creative thinking. If all four types were to be combined, two things might be achieved: (1) a great many innovative ideas and methods for handling library operations might be developed, and (2) these ideas could fit into the organizational pattern with the least disruption. In some ways, the use of participatory management draws on the same concepts. The disruption or *disturbance factor* arising from the implementation of new ideas is often the cause of most resistance on the part of managers to employing creative thinking techniques.

ENCOURAGING CREATIVE THINKING

Assuming that you as a manager are interested in encouraging original thinking on the part of your library staff, what organizational and supervisory steps can you take? Research has confirmed what many individuals have claimed and felt for a long time—that a conformist, tightly structured, and stratified organization (bureaucracy) frustrates creativity and encourages mediocrity. One way of encouraging original thinking is to increase decentralization of decision making and delegation of authority (see Chapter 6 on delegation). (Note, too, that the existence of branch libraries may mean nothing more than decentralization of services.) Even if original thinking does not increase as a result of this move, feedback from all levels and peer recognition will increase, which will enhance the sense of purpose for the staff.

Decentralization should be accompanied by a loosening of departmental lines and jurisdiction, which causes more interdepartmental contact and communication. For example, bibliographic checking can be done by almost any unit in a library. Suppose the process had been centralized but the results were not satisfactory. All units could try out new approaches. In order to maintain some control, interdepartmental communication would need to be increased. The increase in communication and perhaps a little competition can produce innovative ideas. Greater communication provides a slightly stressful situation, which stimulates the creative mind. It creates naturally the type of situation that is simulated in certain idea-generation techniques. Such interdepartmental communication may result in the discovery of a new angle on a task to be performed or a problem to be resolved. The more speicalized a job is, the less likely the person doing it is to encounter a variety of information with which to synthesize and create or to come to a problem from a fresh viewpoint. Instead, that person is likely to fall into patterns of task performance that become an inescapable rut.

Both England and Mars[5, 6] point out that large organizations may provide greater challenge and require less conformity than do small ones. Large organizations generally put more money into research and innovation activities than do small ones. Moreover, large organizations generally exhibit less centralization then do small organizations. Due to a broader selection of personalities and viewpoints, large organizations tend toward less conformity as well as toward less close supervision.

What can the small organization do to encourage creative thinking? The typical small public or school library is staffed by one librarian, with perhaps a paraprofessional or volunteer to help. Sometimes the librarian is completely alone. Certainly such a situation can encourage stagnation, because the stimulation of working with professional peers is lacking. In this situation, reading material on creativity and its managerial applications is of utmost importance. Keeping up with the profession through journals and conferences is the least that one should do to avoid settling into a dull and unimaginative routine. It takes all the mental stimulation possible in such a situation to keep up with professional standards and to continue personal creative growth. Outside hobbies broaden a person's scope and provide a wide selection of idea sources, and the interaction of two or more interests may spark a synthesis (idea linking) that is a creative idea.

In some respects, the librarian in a small library is in an ideal environment for creative management. There is a built-in high amount of independence in task choice and in approaches to problem solving, program building, and decision making. Also, although on-the-job professional peer interaction may be lacking, librarians who work alone do not become stuck in a highly specialized groove, because they are responsible for acquisitions, cataloging, reference, and circulation. If the librarian is lucky enough to have assistance with routine tasks, then there is more time for creative planning. The creative personality has been characterized as one that likes working independently and dislikes following orders; both traits fit well into the small library situation.

Within the library itself (regardless of size), management will need to make special efforts to encourage creativity on the part of subordinates. In any unit of an organization, it is easy to be heavy-handed in control and delegation; such an approach tends to provide the stable environment and "economies of scale" so often sought by directors. Yet, the best method for generating new ideas is to encourage independent thinking and responsibility in subordinates. The more they feel a part of the unit's decisions and functions, the better the quality of their production—a result of increased feelings of commitment and accomplishment. This applies to student aides as well, no matter what level of complexity or importance it may have. By utilizing student aides, the librarian decentralizes (for example, if they are included in policy making). Student input is nothing to smile at patronizingly, as their fresh viewpoint is a rich source of ideas. Because user input also helps in shaping a library and in maintaining a program that meets user needs over a period of time, it should be sought, too.

TECHNIQUES FOR GENERATING NEW IDEAS

Several group techniques for generating ideas are discussed in this section, but the success of each technique depends on two rules:

1. *No evaluation or judgment, verbal or nonverbal, may be made of any idea or suggestion during the idea-producing stage.* Once everyone understands this, verbal judgment is relatively easy to control, although an occasional gasp may be heard when a bizarre idea comes up. More significant, and more difficult to control, is the constant nonverbal evaluation expressed through body language. Rolling eyes, raised eyebrows, sudden turning away, looking out the window or at the ceiling—all are physical projections of mental evaluations, and one only needs to watch the people in a group discussion to see how frequently such behavior takes place. But any such evaluations at this stage will prevent persons whose ideas are being so criticized from continuing.

2. *All ideas produced during the first phase of the session must be considered as serious proposals and must be discussed during the evaluation phase.* This is difficult, for, inevitably, someone will maintain that a certain idea is so stupid that to discuss it would be a waste of time. Yet, as soon as such a view is expressed (verbally or nonverbally), the session is likely to fail. Only when everyone agrees to discuss every suggestion seriously is there any hope of succeeding.

Three basic categories of techniques are employed to stimulate new ideas and thinking: analytical techniques, free-association techniques, and forced-relationship techniques.

Analytical Techniques

The analytical approach relies very heavily on logical problem solving for generating ideas. The following three analytical techniques seem to have the greatest potential in a library situation: attribute listing, input-output, and grid analysis.

Attribute Listing

Attribute listing consists of two processes: (1) the major features of a particular problem are carefully isolated and listed, and (2) discussion takes place regarding changes that could be made in each attribute on the list in order to solve the problem, and these solutions are listed. Further, each change in each attribute is listed to determine whether that change will affect the other attributes listed. The point of the session is to generate a large number of ideas for change and to evaluate them.

For instance, the problem might be to reduce a cataloging backlog. The group assembled to solve the problem begins by listing all of the problem's attributes—flow of information, storage of uncataloged materials, descriptive cataloging, subject cataloging, professional staff, nonprofessional staff, equipment, space, filing, processing, and so on. This list goes into as much detail as appears appropriate. The group then discusses each item on the list, suggesting changes to speed up the cataloging at all stages. Finally, they consider whether the proposed changes in one area (say, descriptive cataloging) would affect other areas (say, staffing patterns, subject cataloging, filing, processing, and so on).

This method works reasonably well, except that individuals tend to assume too quickly that they have listed all problems and all possible solutions. They may fail to explore a problem in sufficient depth because they have come to the meeting with preconceived ideas as to how things should be. This is another reason that one-time or infrequent use of this technique may produce unsatisfactory results; practice is the only way to get people to abandon preconceived ideas and to truly explore alternatives.

Input-Output

Although the input-output technique seems quite similar to attribute listing, there are several fundamental differences. First, this approach specifies what the desired result should be (output). Second, the output is specified by someone who does not belong to the discussion group. Thus, the group is confronted with a problem for which a specified solution has been determined; its task is to figure out how to restructure the situation so as to generate that result. This forces the group to consider a great many more alternatives than they might consider in attribute listing, because obvious alternatives will not be compatible with the desired end in many cases.

Again, the cataloging backlog example is useful. Say that the library director specifies an end to the backlog in English-language materials—that current materials in English must be processed in 5 days or less. The group must consider all the factors contributing to the backlog. Then, all available resources (input) that can help to eliminate the backlog must be examined. The primary advantage here is that, while the discussion is more sharply focused than it is in attribute listing, the group must consider a broader range of possible solutions than they might otherwise consider.

Grid Analysis

Grid analysis is simply attribute listing carried to a finer degree. All the items that normally would be listed as attributes are instead placed on a two-dimensional grid. The grid ensures that all possible combinations

Attributes	1	2	3	4	5
1					
2					
3					
4					
5					

will be considered. To some extent, then, this is a forced-relationship technique as well as an analytical technique in that each square on the grid must be examined. In this way, new ideas and relationships that might otherwise be overlooked may well be seen.

Free-Association Techniques

Brainstorming

Several free-association techniques have been highly publicized as means of developing new ideas and products in business and industry. *Brainstorming*, the basic technique, uses the rules previously discussed, with two important differences. First, although a general topic is to be considered for discussion, no strict definition of a problem is presented. Second, any comment, idea, or suggestion—no matter how "harebrained" or "free wheeling"—is welcome; indeed, they are actively encouraged and sought. Also, there should be no negative reactions, either verbally or through body language. The session should last as long as ideas flow, and partipants are encouraged to present improvements or modifications of ideas previously presented. The idea is to gain the maximum possible number of approaches to a topic or problem.

Used judiciously, and with a small number of individuals (6 to 8), brainstorming can provide a great many new approaches to a library's problems. If new people are brought into the group periodically, the type of ideas concerning the same problem will vary considerably. This helps to avoid stagnation when people become overly familiar with one another's patterns of thinking. The idea behind the technique is to gain fresh insights whenever possible.

Gordon Technique

This is a method developed by an employee of the Arthur D. Little Company (Cambridge, Massachusetts), a consulting firm that has done some library work. This firm has a rather unusual service: an invention-design group that claims never to have failed in developing a new product at the request of any company. The Gordon technique resembles brainstorming, except that only the group leader knows the exact problem to be solved. The actual group is given only a vague indication, as it is thought that, when the group knows exactly what the problem that they are approaching is, they will fix on one or two ideas immediately and feel that they have solved the problem. This notion stops the flow of ideas as soon as the most obvious solutions have been proposed. The Gordon approach of a general statement of the problem (for example, "how to move things" rather than "how to move a library collection") helps to avoid the situation in which an individual becomes highly critical or defensive of a proposed solution, in which case more broad-ranging thought could be stifled.

As a method of obtaining creative ideas for the library, the Gordon technique is not as easily implemented as, for instance, brainstorming or grid analysis. A Gordon group demands a great deal of skill on the part of the leader (who must relate free-flowing general discussion to a specific problem), and it requires a lot of practice by group members to develop the technique to a high level. Library staffs simply do not have the time necessary to develop a group that could successfully utilize the Gordon technique.

Phillips 66 Buzz Session

Another variation of brainstorming is the Phillips 66 buzz session. A large group (perhaps 50 people) is divided into small discussion groups of 5 or 6 persons. These groups then brainstorm, with one person acting as leader and recorder. When the small groups have finished their work, they reassemble, and the leader of each group presents that group's ideas. The large group then discusses the ideas put forth and comes to a point at which a number of recommendations can be made.

This type of technique could probably be used in libraries when the entire staff's participation is desired. One problem with this method is that it tends to force critical evaluation of ideas at an early stage, which can reduce the number of options presented. For libraries, another problem is the difficulty of closing the library for an entire day for such sessions. And, as with the Gordon technique, the buzz session requires practice by the group members. These problems illustrate that the costs of learning would probably outweigh the benefits to the library.

Forced-Relationship Techniques

The difference between forced-relationship techniques and the previous two is that relationships are established before the discussion takes place, and the discussion group is small. The method relies heavily on probability, random occurrence, and serendipity to stimulate new points of view and to get people to ask "what if?" The three major forced-relationship techniques (catalog, listing, and focused object) all depend on a mechanical or arbitrary association being forced on two dissimilar ideas, solutions, or problems.

Catalog Technique

The catalog technique is a method that helps generate new ideas rather than solving a particular problem. With the catalog technique, the group comes together, and a handbook (such as a library handbook) is opened to a page at random. A paragraph is selected from that page, and the idea or concept discussed in that paragraph is then recorded. The book is closed, reopened at random, and another paragraph is chosen and its content recorded. Then, the two ideas that have been recorded are discussed in relation to each other. What pattern, what ideas are generated by considering these two things together? The process of selection and comparison continues for several hours.

Listing Technique

This approach uses a list of concepts, ideas, services, etc. that is drawn up by someone who does not know the exact purpose of the list. The compiler is given several items to include and is instructed to add more items. Each item on the list is then considered by the group in relation to all other items on the list in the same manner as in the catalog method. The difference is that the list of items for discussion has been generated by one person instead of being chosen at random.

Focused-Object Technique

Using the focused-object technique, a list of preplanned ideas or concepts is prepared by a person who wants a specific problem solved. The list would be similar to an attribute list. Each item on that list is then paired with a series of items selected randomly from a dictionary or handbook in the same field of inquiry. The resulting pairs are then discussed by the group, again, in the search for new ideas derived from forced comparison.

All three forced-relationship techniques might be useful in the library if they are used judiciously, most probably in terms of public service activities. They might generate new concepts for dealing with patrons and new services that might be closer to what patrons actually want and need. However, it is worth reiterating that the techniques must be used regularly if they are expected to yield useful ideas. Only with practice will people become more comfortable with these methods and allow their imaginations to roam freely.

ANALYTIC AND CREATIVE THINKING

Two basic types of thought processes are required to maintain an effective, dynamic organization: analytic and creative. Analytic, scientific thought that is oriented to problem solving is essential. It brings order to chaotic situations. It values conformity, or at least consistency. It approaches problems in terms of logic, careful experimentation, and study. Tied in with the scientific techniques developed by Taylor and others, analytic thought is concerned with job analysis, job descriptions, costs, cost benefits, standardization, theory, accounting methods, and research in general. All of these topics are approached from a very logical, rational point of view. This type of thinking provides continuity and the ability to keep moving forward—perhaps slowly, but moving forward nonetheless. Analytic thought is essential in day-to-day operations.

Creative thought is relatively unstructured and unpredictable, and it often appears to be illogical. It is necessary for quantum jumps—real breaks with the past. This type of thinking is required to keep an organization dynamic and in motion. Any manager who thinks that this is unimportant is likely to produce a stagnant service organization that quickly finds itself out of step with the community's needs. It is disappointing that many managers feel no need for creative abilities in their organizations—especially in libraries—and that more attention is not devoted to the concept of creativity and its place in organizations and management.

During the academic year 1978–1979 Dr. C. Metoyer-Duran of the Graduate School of Library and Information Science, University of California, Los Angeles, undertook a study of attitudes of directors of large public libraries in the United States regarding current issues in library administration. Several of her questions concerned innovation and creativity and the efforts being made to foster such activities in the library system. She found that very few directors understood the role of creativity in the organization. Those that did understand had systems that seemed to suffer less from budgetary and staff problems (specifically, personnel communication). Although her analysis is not yet complete and follow-up work needs to be done, these data support the idea that creativity in an organization may help it to become more viable.

When a deliberate effort is made to encourage new ideas and to combine them with analytic thinking, the library stimulates its users and staff alike and has relevance to their lives. It is an entity with a future in a world where changes take place more rapidly than ever before. Since a library is a storehouse of information, innovation is essential, because information becomes obsolete much more quickly than it did in the past. The focus now is on *using* information rather than merely having it, and the library occupies a pivotal position in the stimulation of creative thinking. Creative management is necessary if a library is to grow in the future as an institution with continuing relevance to the society that produced it.

BIBLIOGRAPHY

1. D. MacKinnon, "The Nature and Nurture of Creative Talent," in *Creativity and Innovation in Organizations*, ed. by D. C. Dauw and A. J. Freidan (Dubuque, Iowa: Kendall/Hunt Publishing, 1971), p. 97.
2. D. Green, "Creative Organization: The Librarian as Manager," *Special Libraries* 55 (Oct. 1964): 549.
3. G. K. Bennett, "What Is Creativity?," *Transactions of the New York Academy of Science* 26 (May 1964): 789.
4. J. W. Haefele, *Creativity and Innovation* (New York: Reinhold, 1962), p. 5.
5. A. O. England, "Creativity: An Unwelcome Talent?," *Personnel Management* 49 (Sept. 1964): 458–464.
6. D. Mars, "Developing a Climate for Creativity," *Public Management* 49 (Mar. 1967): 59–62; "Creativity and Organizational Leadership," *News Notes of California Libraries* 64 (Spring 1969): 281–290.

FURTHER READING

Anderson, L. R. "The Effect of Participatory and Supervisory Leadership on Group Creativity." *Journal of Applied Psychology* 48 (1964): 227–236.
Baeckler, V., and Larson, L. *GO, PEP, and POP! 250 Tested Ideas for Lively Librarians.* New York: Unabashed Librarian, 1976.

Bennett, G. K. "What is Creativity?" *Transactions of the New York Academy of Science* 26 (1964): 779–794.

Bryand, D. "The Psychology of Resistance to Change." *Management Services* 23 (1979): 10–14.

Changement; Understanding and Managing Business Change. Lexington, Mass.: D.C. Heath & Co., 1979.

"Creative Organization: The Librarian as a Manager: A Symposium." *Special Libraries* 55 (1964): 548–558.

England, A. O. "Creativity: An Unwelcome Talent?" *Personnel Journal* 43 (1964): 458–461.

Francis, D., and Woodcock, M. *People At Work: A Practical Guide to Organizational Change.* La Jolla, Calif.: University Associates, 1975.

"Getting the Creative Juices Flowing Again." *International Management* 35 (1980): 23–24.

Golann, S. E. "The Creativity Motive." *Journal of Personality* 30 (1962): 588–600.

Hoffman, L. R. "Differences and Disagreement as Factors in Creative Group Problem Solving." *Journal of Abnormal and Social Psychology* 64 (1962): 206–214.

Howard, G. W. "Managing Creative Personnel." *Personnel Administration* 30 (1967): 31–37.

Kleiner, B. H. "A Manager's Guide to Organizational Change." *Personnel* 56 (1979): 31–38.

Lockwood, J. D. "Involving Consultants in Library Change." *College and Research Libraries* 38 (1977): 498–508.

McCollum, L. F. "Challenging Horizons for Creative Managers." *Advanced Management Journal* 32 (1967): 3–38.

Mangham, I. *The Politics of Organizational Change.* Westport, Conn.: Greenwood Press, 1979.

Mars, D. "Developing a Climate for Creativity." *Public Management* 49 (1967): 59–62.

Maslow, A. H. "The Need for Creative People." *Personnel Administration* 28 (1956): 3–5.

Messick, W. L. "Creative Management." *Advanced Management Journal* 29 (1964): 54–60.

Organization Development: Managing Change in the Public Sector. Chicago: International Personnel Management Assoc., 1976.

Porras, J. I., and Berg, P. O. "The Impact of Organization Development." *Academy of Management Review* 3 (1978): 249–266.

Preston, P., and Hawkins, B. L. "Creative Conflict Management." *Supervisory Management* 24 (1979): 7–11.

Reuter, V. G. "Suggestion Systems: Utilization, Evaluation, and Implementation." *California Management Review* 19 (1977): 78–79.

Rickards, T., and Freedman, B. L. "Procedures for Managers in Idea-deficient Situations: An Examination of Brainstorming Approaches." *JMS: Journal of Management Studies* 15 (1978): 43–55.

Sager, D. "The Comfortable Pullman: Administrative Creativity on the Siding." *American Libraries* 1 (1970): 587–592.

Shirk, J. C. "Research in Action—An Introduction to Strategy for Change: The Librarian as Change Agent." *Public Librarian* 17 (1978): 8–10.

Stein, R. T., and Leja, E. "Impact Models as a Method for Planning Change." *Sloan Management Review* 18 (1977): 47–61.

Wagner, G. R. "Enhancing Creativity in Strategic Planning Through Computer Systems." *Managerial Planning* 28 (1979): 10–17.

Watson, C. E. "The Problems of Problem Solving." *Business Horizons* 19 (1976): 88–94.

Watzlawick, P. *Change: Principles of Problem Formation and Problem Resolution.* New York: W.W. Norton & Co., 1974.

Williams, F. E. "A New Perspective on Creativity." *Personnel Administration* 29 (1966): 3–5.

Wismer, J. N. "Organizational Change: How to Understand It and Deal With It." *Training* 16 (1979): 28–32.

5. Power, Authority, and Accountability

Public libraries derive their power and authority from governmental jurisdiction. Special libraries, either in private foundations or in affiliation with commercial firms, derive their power and authority from the parent organization and its governing board. In this chapter I consider basic management concepts and techniques in relation to power, authority, and a reciprocal concept—accountability. I explore the manner in which these concepts relate to the idea of line and staff organizational patterns and their impact on the use of committees.

Libraries, which are normally part of larger organizations, present their managers with some interesting problems regarding power and authority. Certainly one of the first things that a new manager needs to do is to gain a clear understanding of how much power and authority are associated with the position. Many beginning librarians are surprised to learn that there are laws specifically relating to the way in which a library may operate. Generally, these laws are passed by state, county, and municipal governments; however, in some countries, the matter of library service is considered too important to be left to local jurisdictions. Therefore, national laws and regulations are implemented (in the Nordic countries, for example).

In addition, national laws that do not specifically mention libraries may have a surprisingly strong influence on what a library may or may not do. For example, in 1964, the United States Congress passed a Civil Rights Law. Since that act was intended to assure equal treatment for all citizens, one would expect libraries not already providing equal service to do so. And, indeed, most libraries reviewed their programs and made whatever adjustments seemed necessary. But the concept of equal service, from a legal point of view, is more complex than first might be expected.

At least one library system ran into some problems with the local district attorney over the way in which that system's branch libraries were funded. Most American public libraries have employed one of three basic methods of funding branches. One method is simply to divide the available funds by the number of branches, which does not take into account heavier work loads and higher costs for some locations than for others. A second technique is to base funding on the level of use—home use of materials, reference questions answered, or some other measure(s) of use. The most common practice is to combine these two methods so that all branches receive a minimum level of support, with additional funding provided on the basis of some measure of use. This is an attempt to ensure that heavily used (high cost) branches can provide the level of service needed by their communities. At first glance, then, these methods, especially the latter, seem fair and would not be considered to violate the Civil Rights Law. Such was not the case, though, with our example, since the local district attorney's office found several potential violations of both state and federal laws. Although the library had no intention of creating unequal service, the system had in fact created that situation, and the outcome, not the intent, is what the courts are concerned about.

What is not taken into account by funding based on level of use or dividing available funds is the changing composition of a community. Assuming that the library had built a collection designed to meet the needs of the local community (say, a predominantly White middle-class group), problems can arise when the community changes to, say, 60% Hispanic. The collection originally designed for the previous group may have less appeal to the new residents. A slight drop in use will result in a slight decrease in funding. At this point, a cycle starts that is hard to break—less money and increasing prices will make it harder and harder to revamp an entire collection.

The Los Angeles library system encountered this problem with branches serving racially changing communities. The city attorney's report concluded as follows:

> As set forth above, the criterion of circulation, though neutral on its face, appears to function in a manner that is not racially neutral in fact, operation, effect, and consequences. As a result, existing disparities in the allocation of library resources between white and minority communities raises serious legal difficulties under applicable federal and state constitutional and statutory law.[1]

Although no legal action was taken as a result of the report, it did stimulate the library, the library board, and others to completely review the situation. By 1980, some increased funding and reallocation of resources had helped to improve the balance of service.

This example demonstrates how easy it is to do something "by the book" and still find yourself in potential trouble, with possible legal problems. Even when people have the best of intentions, problems can and do arise. If you have a question about the legality of a situation, most libraries have access to legal counsel, and you can ask for an *opinion*. But, remember that an opinion is just that—a best estimate of how the courts *might* construe the point of law in question. If you act on the basis of a legal opinion from a municipal or city attorney's office, you still may be found guilty of violating a law, although you probably will not receive a penalty, because you acted in good faith (that is, you were guided by opinion of counsel). For libraries, such legal opinions can be very important. Consequently, the California State Library, to cite one example, publishes an annual list of the state attorney general's opinions regarding library issues as a guide for local and state practices. However, the majority of issues involving power, authority, and accountability in any one library involve management and staff, so an examination of these concepts in that context is appropriate.

POWER

Power is the ability to do something; authority is the right to do something. The degree of power, then, is determined by the degree to which sanctions are available to the person possessing power, without regard to position or office. Managerial power is often measured by the ability to give, promise, withdraw (or threaten to withdraw) rewards; inflict (or threaten to inflict) punishment; and fire (or threaten to fire) subordinates. Such sanctions are common to all institutions and form the basis of power. In essense, they are penalties for failure to conform to and accept a supervisor's authority.

From a positive point of view, power involves the giving of rewards for the acceptance of authority. One interesting feature common to most contemporary discussions of power is the negative reaction to it. In almost every discussion, the text begins with the punishment (negative) aspect of power, which reflects the idea that power is harmful.

What is frequently overlooked is the subjective nature of power. Opinions differ as to how much power a position or person should have. There is also a reciprocal aspect of power in that sanctions exist for both the supervisor and the subordinate. Subordinates possess one very definite sanction for use against supervisors—their working capacity and their ability to control their own production. Subordinates using this sanction can stage slowdowns and cause equipment breakdowns. Deliberate misinterpretation of instructions or orders is a tactic frequently employed by subordinates as a weapon against the indiscriminate use of power or authority by a supervisor. The weakness of such subordinate sanctions is that they require the cooperation of a large group of subordinates in order to be effective.

Another employee sanction is striking. Although most libraries are agencies of a governmental unit and in the United States are generally forbidden to strike, this sanction does in fact exist. The legal basis against govenment employees' striking has been challenged, and strikes have occurred, despite questions of legality.

Groups outside the organization also can contribute to sanctions available to the subordinate. Unions, professional associations, and special-interest groups can bring pressure to bear on an institution and its administrators. One type of agency that can employ sanctions in many libraries is the Civil Service Commission. Its sanctions can be applied to both management and subordinates, but, usually, subordinates are the ones requesting help. Such commissions are indeed powerful, as they can overrule a management decision regarding promotion, job security, and probation matters. Hearings are usually long and involved, with both winners and losers finding the process frustrating. Because of the possibility of commission intervention, supervisors tend to avoid making decisions that are likely to cause an employee to request a hearing. The existence of such commissions, therefore, acts as a strong sanction against blatantly prejudicial managerial actions.

To some degree, all sanctions act as psychological whips, because their mere existence often generates the desired behavior in both employee and employer. Ultimatums seldom need to be issued, because everyone knows that existing sanctions will be applied if undesirable behavior persists. When a sanction actually is applied, it is in a very real sense an admission of failure, because undesirable behavior has not been prevented. Negative power sanctions (punishments) are generally less effective than positive sanctions (rewards) in maintaining desired behavior.

In 1965, D. Cartwright reviewed the literature on the nature of managerial power.[2] This review still stands as one of the best brief conceptual summaries of the types of managerial power. Cartwright presented five categories of power:

1. *Reward power* is based on a subordinate's belief that the supervisor has the ability to grant rewards.

2. *Coercive power* is based on a subordinate's belief that the supervisor has the ability to impose punishments.
3. *Referent power* is based on a subordinate's desire to be identified with the supervisor and that person's power.
4. *Legitimate power* is based on a subordinate's internalized belief that the supervisor has the right to direct that person's activities.
5. *Expert power* is based on the subordinate's belief that the supervisor has special knowledge and skills that make it reasonable that the supervisor directs the person's activities.

Most managers' power is a combination of these categories, usually with one or two of them dominating. When a manager has strong expert and referent power, there is seldom a question about the others. When expert power is weak, you will usually find a significant question about legitimate power. How often have you heard (or made) the statement that "X shouldn't hold that job. They don't know anything about it"? When a person is appointed unit manager in a library without having a strong background in librarianship, there always seems to be a testing period during which professionals wait to see how much "expert" knowledge the new manager has. Should the professionals find the manager lacking, a power struggle usually results. When power is viewed in terms of the five categories, then, it does not seem nearly as dangerous or threatening as it might otherwise seem.

AUTHORITY

All organizations, including libraries, are concerned with the distribution of power and authority within the organization. As already noted, authority is the right to do something and is associated with a position within an organization. Yet, this definition is really inadequate for discussing managerial authority; a better definition is provided by R. V. Presthus in an excellent article on authority and organizational structure:

> *Authority* can be defined as the capacity to invoke compliance in others on the basis of formal position and any psychological rewards, inducements, or sanctions that may accompany formal position. The capacity to invoke compliance without relying on formal role or sanctions at its disposal may be called *influence*. A formal position is not necessarily involved but when extensive sanctions are available we are concerned with *power*. The definitions turn upon formal position and role because this point of reference best suits the conditions of large-scale organizations. The sanction control of organized resources through formal position is probably the major source of power in modern society. Authority, power, influence, are usually interlaced in operating situations. However, the definitions attempt to focus on the conception of organizing as a system in which interpersonal relations are structured in terms of the prescribed authority of the actors.[3]

In a library, a manager's authority consists of the right to do such things as make decisions, assign work to subordinates, review their work, and recommend their retention or release on the basis of their performance. On occasion, the manager has the formal right but not the capability to enforce actions under that right. This difficulty arises from the reciprocal and subjective nature of authority. Authority is reciprocal because each person in the process uses the *anticipated* reactions of the other persons involved as the basis on which to act. The anticipated behavior may or may not materialize. Authority is subjective in that each person's estimate of how much authority others should or do have is influenced by individual moral and ethical values. It is surprising, in view of the receiprocal/subjective nature of authority, that challenges of authority in an institution do not occur more frequently.

One reason for this lack of challenges is the source from which authority is derived. Most institutional authority resides in the formal position or office rather than in the transient officeholder. Authority is legitimated by the process of socialization. An individual is integrated into a group or institution. If the institution has operated with some offices having a certain degree of authority, and current employees accept this as proper, then new employees are likely to accept the situation. Because people are generally taught from birth to accept a subordinate role, the individual normally accepts institutional definitions and assignments of authority as a matter of course.

Although socialization is basic to the legitimization process, other factors are equally important for the acceptance of authority. There must be a constant *validation process.* A position may carry an accepted amount of authority, but the officeholder must demonstrate an ability to retain that office and exercise its authority, usually through technical–professional skills and/or knowledge. Presthus (1962) calls this *legitimation by expertise.* Whenever subordinates begin to doubt a supervisor's ability or knowledge, that person loses authority and must often resort to the use of sanctions. In so doing, the supervisor is partially admitting to the loss of authority by using whatever power is available. Such wielding of power may enforce conformity, but that conformityy will last only a limited time.

Formal role and rank is another way to legitimate authority: if your position in the library is above mine, then you must have more authority than I have. In libraries, especially large ones, authority is delegated in small amounts to a number of positions, but each level in the structure must have some authority. No level, however, has as much authority as the level above it. A hierarchical pattern of authority results. Bureaucratic organizations depend on this method of legitimating authority. As Presthus points out, however, both expertise and formal role methods of establishing the right for authority lead to conflict at higher levels, where the officeholder cannot be expert in all the fields in which authority is held.

Leadership that depends on personal qualities apart from technical expertise represents another method of legitimating authority. Presthus labeled this as legitimation "by rapport," and it seems to have an element of Weber's charismatic basis of authority. Certainly few individuals in contemporary society, and even fewer in the library world, can be considered charismatic. Nevertheless, for many individuals, their real basis of authority lies not in position or professional skill but in an ability to work with people. Some can hold a great deal of authority in an institution solely on the basis of their being "a real person with a genuine interest in people." Individuals of this type hold their positions because of the affection that subordinates and superiors have for them.

A manager needs to be aware of the forms of legitimation and how they function. Authority is an active process, both subjective and reciprocal. It flows in two directions: downward through an organizational structure of positions, and upward from subordinates to individuals holding superior positions. The bases for validating authority are: traditional acceptance of authority, expertise, position, rank, and personal characteristics.

ACCOUNTABILITY AND RESPONSIBILITY

Although *accountability* and *responsibility* are frequently used interchangeably, there is a significant distinction between them. In essence, responsibility is what one must do, whereas accountability is the being answerable for an action. Thus, accountability is important in the process of enforcing responsibility. Usually, one is accountable to one's immediate supervisor.

Aspects of Accountability

The relation among accountability, power, and authority is direct. The process of accountability includes three basic factors: *legal, legislative,* and *administrative.* Two of these (legal and legislative) are for the most part extrainstitutional. Administrative accountability is basically internal in nature, although it can be external. For example, the university library is accountable to the university administration.

Legal accountability relates both to actions taken and failures to comply with certain legal orders or statutes. Most frequently, issues revolve about federal laws or orders concerning such things as equal employment, affirmative action requirements, and school bussing. Local and state statutes and regulations also have an impact on the library's operations, as courts can and do impose financial or penal sanctions on managers and institutions found guilty of failing to act within the prescribed legal limits. At least one librarian was dismissed and fined for the way in which he handled book fines, even though he used practices commonly used in libraries and acceptable to the library board. Those practices, though, were contrary to city ordinances, and, when a complaint was filed, legal action resulted.

Legislative accountability is enforced in two main ways—through the courts and through hearings. Because the cost of the judicial process mitigates its frequent use, the lawmaking body can (and often does) call for hearings to determine whether the manager or agency has carried out the wishes and/or orders of the legislative body. Investigative hearings, budgetary hearings, and new legislation hearings are some types frequently encountered. Lawmaking bodies also have the ability to reduce or to increase an agency's authority and appropriations. Libraries are especially vulnerable to the last-mentioned type of control, as has become increasingly evident in some parts of the United States.

However, the legislative control process operates within limits. No legislative body has the time to oversee all details of all agencies accountable to it. Since such details are left to the agencies, interpretation of what a legislative order means and what can be done will vary. Usually, the legislative body checks back with an agency only during budget hearings, when an agency makes a request, or when a complaint is made against an agency. Although legislative values are imposed during the accountability process, the manager usually finds a wide range of activities not determined by the legislative body; decisions or activities within that range will not be inferfered with.

Administrative accountability is common to all libraries. For governmental agencies, including libraries, the matter is somewhat more complex than it is for private institutions. Political factors must be taken into account. For instance, a campaign to limit or reduce taxes may mean that the library will not be allowed to request an increase, even up to the existing legal limit.

Because the library is accountable to the government, it naturally must comply with government regulations controlling accounting and purchasing. Yet these regulations can cause a great deal of extra work for the library if they are faithfully followed, because they seldom are drawn up with the problems of purchasing library materials in mind. In order to gain an exception for library materials, the library can become involved in a long, drawn-out legislative process.

Administrative accountability in government is complex, political, and confused, because different units may issue conflicting orders, each based on a legislative mandate. Also, there frequently are doubts as to where real accountability lies, especially when legislative and administrative units clash over a issue in which political gain seems to be the dominant factor.

Aspects of Responsibility

As previously indicated, accountability and responsibility are not identical. One is always completely accountable, and one can make someone else completely accountable, but responsibility does not work in the same way. Responsibility is *always* shared. An individual or unit has the responsibility or obligation to do something, but the individual or unit assigning that responsibility always retains a portion of it. In a sense, delegating responsibility increases the responsibility of the delegator, because that person must then supervise the assigned responsibility.

Responsibility is really created within a person when an assigned task is accepted. Someone who is unwilling to accept a certain responsibility usually refuses the job, but sometimes an individual feels no responsibility after accepting a task because he or she knows that someone else will do it. Everyone has worked at some time with persons who do not accept responsibility for their work but do it just well enough to keep from being fired. No amount of talking or delegating responsibility will change their attitudes. Acceptance must come from within the individual. Responsibility is a person's obligation to himself or herself to perform given tasks.

Successful managers are those who are comfortable delegating responsibility *and* authority; also, they do not become unduly concerned about residual responsibility.

STATUS

Changes in authority or responsibility usually bring about changes in status; therefore, a manager should look at any proposed change in procedure or policy in terms of how existing delegation of authority and responsibility might be affected. What may appear to the manager to be a very minor change is often viewed by subordinates as significant.

The status that subordinates assign to an individual is not entirely the result of formal authority and rank. Most persons dislike taking orders from persons they consider equal to themselves unless this "right" has been established by custom or performance. For example, a clerk may take "orders" from a peer in areas where the latter is considered more expert or skilled. In general, however, a person must be given an order-giving rank by a superior if the peer group is to accept the orders. Authority and status are, then, closely related.

The use of titles and other status symbols can be useful, but they also can be detrimental. A manager should never attempt to use titles or status symbols as a substitute for real rewards for work performance, especially in place of promotions or salary increases. When titles are used, they should be used for clearly defined activities and abilities. Yet, in many libraries, there is no clear distinction between the abilities, skills, and training required for top-grade clerical personnel and beginning-grade librarians. Some job descriptions are so confusing that one cannot readily determine whether the position should be filled by a clerk, para-professional, or librarian. Confusion as to role, status, and authority results in poor work flow, communication, and morale. There should be a clear-cut distinction in titles, and the application of these titles should be consistent throughout the library.

LINE AND STAFF

One method for handling authority, responsibility, and decision making is to use the concept of line and staff. Military organizations have used it for some time, as it makes possible a unity of command without a loss of specialization along functional lines. Moreover, it allows a great deal of influential informal interaction to take place. Yet, although the concept is widely used, it is widely misunderstood. Actually, there are two distinct points of view from which line and staff can be understood: in terms of *function* and in terms of authority *relationships.*

From a function standpoint, line and staff denote the different functions that can be carried out within an organization. A line official is directly responsible for accomplishing the organization's objectives. All others are staff. To determine whether a person is line or staff, one must objectively determine whether that person has responsibility for accomplishing organizational objectives.

In a library, where the basic function is to secure and disseminate information, the line units are the acquisitions department, the catalog department, the circulation department, the reference department, and the director of the library. Staff members would be those individuals in personnel, accounting, systems, public relations, and photoduplication. Although the individuals within the library might disagree with these divisions, an objective view will support this division according to function.

From the point of view of authority relationships, a line official is one who has relatively unlimited authority over subordinates. A staff official's authority is limited to a functional area. To determine whether a person is line or staff, take the viewpoint of the person receiving orders. Only a line officer has unlimited authority over you and your work; everyone else is staff. In a library, for instance, the head of the systems department would be held to be a line officer by any of the systems staff insofar as systems analysis work was concerned. That same department head would be considered, from an authority viewpoint, to be staff by anyone else in any other department (circulation, reference, acquisitions, and so forth).

As for problems with employing the line and staff concept, the biggest problem is status conflict. In some situations, line members are thought to be the first-class members in the organization, whereas staff are considered "overhead." The opposite situation also can develop. This happens in libraries quite often, because librarians are concerned with and somewhat insecure about their status. In libraries, the staff (which tends to be composed of people with training in systems analysis, personnel, or public relations—all nonlibrary areas) often become the elite. Library systems people often are viewed as members of a superclass—sometimes because librarians themselves do not understand systems analysis, computers, or computer programming. In a few cases, systems personnel have been placed in librarian positions, but regular librarians resent and have even fought this practice. To add to the difficulties, systems people are sometimes paid a higher salary than are librarians.

Other types of staff also can exist. Personal staff, usually found only in top management, are those people who serve as assistants to the manager, performing the more routine duties of the manager's office as well as special assignments. They also may be advisors. The usual label for such people is *executive assistant* or *administrative assistant* (or AA). In many of the larger public and academic libraries, AAs are common, and their use has been increasing. Usually, the AA has special skills in either technical areas (for example, computer technology or research) or administrative areas (such as personnel or budget). A good AA can reduce the manager's burden by handling routine functions and being responsible for the office staff. However, definitions of routine matters and job responsibility must be carefully worked out at the beginning; otherwise, the manager's nonroutine functions could be absorbed by the AA without the manager's specific authorization. It is easier to expand from a narrow job definition to a larger one than it is to do the reverse, and it is less frustrating for everyone involved.

Although some businesses allow staff personnel to issue direct orders to line departments, this is not recommended, especially in libraries. The major problem is related to the status issue mentioned earlier, and to the question of who runs the library—line or staff. Only when all line and staff members have total confidence in one another's ability could this work well.

One major problem with the line and staff concept is the degree to which line officials will accept (or even consider) staff recommendations. Certainly, line officials need to have full decision-making power concerning activities and personnel in their own departments. And the line official may very well choose to ignore all staff advice. But anyone who chooses such a position should be aware that a blanket refusal to consider expert advice harms the institution as well as everyone who is trying to serve to the best of their ability. The challenge, then, is to strike a balance between unity of command and the staff specializations in order to take advantage of constant changes both in the profession and in society.

COMMITTEES

Committees can be important to an organization in a number of ways. They can serve in an advisory/informational capacity (gathering material and making recommendations), promote coordination and cooperation (especially among disparate areas), improve communication (but this can backfire), and make decisions. Although the rhetoric about committees is often negative, everyone continues to use them. Actually, committees are the best *and* the worst means of accomplishing a specific goal.

The structure of committees ranges from such informal gatherings as a lunch group to a formal standing committee that has a long list of responsibilities and powers. The manager who is aware of committees (especially informal ones) and knows how and when to use them best can be highly effective. Because the informal gathering differs from a committee meeting only in purpose, alert supervisors often encourage informal gatherings of committee people (or supervisors). Once they are gathered for social activities, it is only natural for co-workers to "talk shop" and make decisions.

Permanent committees can be set up at any and all levels of the hierarchy. Their purpose is clearly related to important institutional activities. Libraries have employed permanent committees for a long time, a prime example being the promotion committee (which arose with the concept of peer evaluation). Although the membership of such committees must rotate, the committees themselves play a permanent, vital role in the library's operations.

Library governing boards operate much like committees, because they are just that. Top management uses committees for special problems or problems that cut across functional lines. Middle management can use them to coordinate existing operations, plan new programs and service, and evaluate work. For lower-level management, committees can be useful with special operational problems, unit decision making, and procedural change recommendations.

When forming a committee, you need to devote some time to formulating an accurate statement of what you want the committee to do (its "charge"). A charge should clearly indicate which of the possible roles the committee should fill. Perhaps the greatest area of confusion, almost always due to a poorly prepared charge, is between an advisory and a decision-making role. It is not uncommon to read or hear about an "advisory" committee being angered when their advice is not taken. The time used to write out a formal charge can save a lot of time and, not infrequently, emotional energy.

There are several advantages of using committees. Committees bring several people to decision making, coordinate work among departments, stimulate client interest through involvement, and are helpful in training managers and supervisors. Perhaps the most important of these advantages is that the committee allows a number of people, many of whom might otherwise have no voice but do have something to contribute, to enter the decision-making process. This not only helps to protect against the rule of a single point of view, which can become a danger in an institution, but it also allows people to feel more comfortable with a decision that they helped to formulate. (Chapter 4 presented methods of stimulating thinking in a group assembled to attack a problem.) To an extent, this overlaps with the specific library situation noted previously—stimulating client interest. User input can help to keep a library in touch with its community, and one good way of obtaining that input is to have community members on committees that plan new services and programs.

To an extent, the functions of coordinating activities that involve more than one department and of being helpful in training management/supervisory personnel do interact. For instance, while a committee might have as its primary task the coordination of work between technical services and public services, or between acquisitions and cataloging, it may produce a secondary benefit: inexperienced personnel can serve with experienced members, thereby broadening their perspective on the library and gaining practice in working with peers and superiors on a common problem. This can be invaluable.

Several disadvantages of using committees also exist: high cost, stalemate, inordinate delay, compromise, domination of the group by a single viewpoint, and no true accountability. The high cost (in salary, time, and lost production) can be mitigated by a close watch on the use of committees; if they are proving wasteful and unproductive, they should be abolished.

Another disadvantage involves the quality of the decision reached by a committee. If a committee patches together a compromise that can only worsen a situation if implemented, or if its decision is the product of a dedicated minority that has forced the group to adopt its special views, then the committee has failed in its function. If an unworkable compromise forces a manager to create his or her own solution, then feelings may be hurt and future cooperation endangered. If a minority recommendation is overturned by a manager, then that minority will probably be especially vocal in opposing any proposed solutions.

The shared responsibility of the committee for its decisions means that no one person, not even the committee head, can be held accountable for a poor decision. Even if an idea began with one person, the group's acceptance of it makes it their recommendation. Of course, committees that do badly can be disbanded, or new members can be appointed. It would be unfair to apply sanctions (such as firing, demotion, or no promotion) against individual committee members for a committee's failures. *If accountability for decisions is required, the manager should not use a committee.*

SUMMARY

As we shall see in the following chapter, there are several methods of structuring an organization. However, no matter which method(s) you choose, the amount of power, authority, and accountability that you allow to each unit is your starting point. As has been discussed, these concepts are reciprocal. It is not, as some persons feel, a matter of top management (supervisor) holding all the power, or even all the authority. Subordinates do have the power and ability to withhold recognition of the skills and knowledge of their supervisors, which effectively reduces that person's power and authority. Subordinates also have the power to control the level and quality of their production, which places a control on the supervisor's actions. When you recognize that these concepts are reciprocal, and if you act in a positive manner on that knowledge, then the work environment should have a strong element of mutual respect and, perhaps, understanding.

BIBLIOGRAPHY

1. *Report on Legality of Branch Library Funding Disparities* (Los Angeles, Calif.: City Attorney of Los Angeles, 1975), p. 76.
2. Cartwright, "Influence, Leadership and Control," in *The Handbook of Organizations*, ed. J. G. March (Chicago: Rand/McNally, 1965), pp. 28–30.
3. R. V. Presthus, "Authority in Organization," in *Concepts and Issues in Administrative Behavior*, ed. S. Mailick and E. H. Van Ness (Englewood Cliffs, N.J.: Prentice-Hall, 1962), p. 123.

FURTHER READING

Dickenson, D. W. "Some Reflections on Participative Management in Libraries." *College and Research Libraries* 39 (1978): 253–262.

Ellison, J. W., and Lazeration, D. B. "Personnel Accountability for Academic Reference Librarians: A Model." *Reference Quarterly* 16 (1976): 142–148.

Fenn, D. H. "Finding Where the Power Lies in Government." *Harvard Business Review* 57 (1979): 144–153.

Golembiewski, R. T. "Authority as a Problem in Overlays." *Administrative Science Quarterly* 9 (1964): 23–49.

Govan, J. F. "The Better Mousetrap: External Accountability and Staff Participation." *Library Trends* 26 (1977): 255–267.

Gray, B. V. "Professional Accountability and Credibility for Public Library Administrators: A Personal View." *Michigan Librarian* 43 (1977): 10–11.

Gusfield, J. R. "Authority and Democracy: Conflicts in Organizational Principles." *Illinois Libraries* 43 (1961): 742–749.

Kaiser, J. B. "Legal Aspects of Library Administration." *Library Trends* 6 (1958): 389–391.

Kilpela, R. "University Library Committee." *Library World* 57 (1956): 189–190.

Harrigan, J. *Library Accountability.* Denver, CO: Univ. of Denver, 1971.

Howard, E. N. *Local Power and the Community Library.* Chicago: ALA, 1978.

Ladenson, A. *American Library Laws.* 4th ed. Chicago: ALA, 1973. *1st Supplement, 1973–1974.* 1975. *2nd Supplement, 1975–1976.* 1977.

Lane, R. P. "Governance and Financing of Libraries in New York." *Bookmark* 38 (1978): 34–43.

Shields, G. R., and Burke, J. G. *Budgeting for Accountability in Libraries: A Selection of Readings.* Metuchen, N.J.: Scarecrow, 1974.

Vogt, W. "Die Rechtsstellung der Bibliotheken," in *Beiträge zum Bibliotheksrecht* (Berlin: Deutscher Bibliotheksverband, 1978), pp. 5–25.

Weeks, R. C. "Types of Governing Library Boards." *News Notes of California Libraries* 72 (1977): 3–5.

Young, V. G. *Library Trustee.* 3rd ed. New York: Bowker, 1978.

6. Delegation

Delegation can take in any of several forms: delegation of authority and responsibility, delegation of decision making (which is strongly influenced by a person's authority), and delegation of actual duties. Certainly, libraries have drawn from just about every type of delegation that has been tried in other institutions. Some libraries and information centers have been effectively managed by one or two persons in authority, while others have been effectively managed by an entire professional staff in authority. The same pattern is apparent in the other forms of delegation. Thus, there may be several "right" methods for a library, other than the one that works for it at present. Effective delegation depends on a number of factors, which will be discussed in this chapter.

The word *organization* was previously defined as a social unit formed to achieve a specific objective. In this chapter, the term *organization* still relates to the unit, but it refers to a method of arranging work units and resources to accomplish an objective. Thus, either *institution* or *library* will be used to refer to the social unit.

PURPOSES AND NATURE OF DELEGATION

Delegation of authority involves the establishment of authority relationships that provide both horizontal and vertical coordination between working units in an institution. In the library, its purpose is to help units work together to achieve the library's overall objectives. Delegation, then, is a means of organizing or structuring the library to achieve its institutional goals. Organizing brings together necessary resources and arranges personnel so that work can be accomplished most efficiently. It must be clearly understood that the process of organizing combines people and resources. George Terry's definition of organizing emphasizes this point: "Organizing is the establishing of effective behavioral relationships among persons so they may work together efficiently and gain personal satisfaction in doing selected tasks under given environmental conditions for the purpose of achieving some goal or objective."[1]

Proper organizing lets everyone know what they are supposed to do. When duties are made clear, performance is greatly improved, and confusion and uncertainty are reduced. Lines of authority and responsibility also become clear, leaving no doubt as to who is responsible for what and who is accountable when accountability is required. Lines of communication (which normally follow those of authority and responsibility) become known, so that everyone knows where to send official communications and from whom to expect such communications.

Human nature being what it is, cooperation sometimes does not come easily. But delegating authority and structuring work flow make cooperative efforts much easier to achieve. They constitute one of the easiest ways in which to bring about people's *willing* cooperation.

Anyone who attempts to organize a library must bear in mind that it is a social system within which an informal organizational structure exists. Job-related experiences give rise to informal groups such as the morning coffee regulars, the bowling group, the lunch bunch, the water cooler clique, the technical-services crowd, the Young Turks, and so on. And whatever common denominators brought these groups together, all the groups share a common, usually dominant, conversational theme—the job. News, complaints, rumors, and ideas may be exchanged with a fair degree of regularity; there is always "the news and the rumors behind the news." Because the informal groups usually cut across departmental or unit lines, information will quickly spread through the entire library. This informal communications system carries a few facts, some half-facts, and a lot of rumor. If the formal communications lines are basically inadequate, however, the grapevine, over which a manager has no control, will soon take over as chief information source.

A manager must remember that nothing will eliminate the informal organization. An able manager can even use this informal structure to achieve organizational objectives, in much the same way the formal organization is used. This is *not* to say that a manager should try to manipulate informal groups. Rather, the manager should observe the groups; it may well be possible to put together more productive work teams by grouping together like-minded people. Observing informal groups will give any person more knowledge of the people in them; therefore, a manager should do this and apply that knowledge in a way that will increase everyone's satisfaction and productivity.

Departmentation

Departmentation is the process of dividing work into semi-independent units. Each level in an organizational chart (discussed later in this chapter) represents a unit of departmentation. Most libraries feature a wide range of activities, differing in the complexity and skill required to carry them out. Activities should be organized for the purpose of accomplishing library objectives, *not* for one person's convenience or because of tradition.

There are five basic departmentation techniques in common use, all of which have been used in libraries at one time or another. The five techniques are

1. Functional departmentation
2. Territorial departmentation
3. Product departmentation
4. Customer service departmentation
5. Equipment or process departmentation

Functional departmentation is the oldest method of organizing. It utilizes three universal functions: production, sales, and finance. If one is willing to stretch a few points, libraries can be included in this framework. *Production* is defined as adding to the utility of a good or service. Technical services work certainly contributes to the utility of library materials. *Sales* is defined as finding the customer who is willing to accept the goods or service at the price set by the institution. Public service units do this now, and this function will increase as libraries are forced to charge a fee for some of their services. *Finance* is defined as securing and controlling the expenditure of funds. This certainly is a function of library administration.

In general, libraries have used this method, at least in talking about their organizational patterns. Most librarians would divide library work into three broad areas: technical, public, and administrative services. Many undoubtedly make finer distinctions and use additional methods of organizing services. However, almost every library makes some use, usually at the higher levels, of the functional method. A few libraries use this method to the exclusion of all others, which is probably unsound, especially at the lower levels.

The functional method has been employed successfully for a long time. It has the advantage of being logical, and it ensures that proper

attention is given to basic functions. It can even provide for more specialization and efficient use of manpower. The major problem is that it is
hard to employ in an institution having units in different and sometimes
distant locations. The method can, on occasion, end up de-emphasiz-
ing institutional goals and objectives. This could be a serious problem in
service organizations, if the functional method is used to the exclusion of
all approaches.

Territorial departmentation is sometimes employed when a library's
activities cover a wide geographic area. In theory, all activities within a
geographic area are handled by one unit (such as a branch of a public
library, a departmental library within an academic setting, and so on).
But the fact that units are widely separated does not mean that the
territorial approach *must* be employed. Only when location is the primary factor in determining responsibilities should territorial departmentation be used.

Most territorial departments are small, self-sufficient units. They can
be used to create smaller units within a library that is already departmentalized on a higher level (function or product). For instance, a central
financial and production unit may be logical for a library; sales (serving
patrons), however, may benefit from being divided territorially. Very few
branch libraries do technical processing, and seldom are they responsible for securing their own funding.

There are several situations in which territorial departmentation
should *not* be used. First, it cannot improve communication. Indeed, if
there are a number of small units in an organization, further compart-
mentalization will increase the communication only *within* units. And
they, in turn, will become more isolated from one another. Second, the
territorial approach cannot be used to increase the rate of service. Because delays usually are due to ineffective handling or routing services,
and because adding new service locations will only increase handling
and add time to procedures, isolated units do not appear to be the
answer. And, as for better library–patron communication, the danger lies
in various units not being fully aware of exactly what the whole system is
doing or has to offer. Sometimes, misinformation can lead to a lack of
confidence in the institution.

The territorial approach is a good method, though, for providing more
personal service for the client. Although service might be a bit slower as a
result of this method of distribution, the personal impact of more thorough and attentive service usually results in increased client satisfaction.
Increased client satisfaction can often be very valuable to the library
when it attempts to secure funds. Moreover, the existence of branches
serves as a constant reminder of the system's own existence. People will

be likely to use something that is relatively convenient and familiar. And remember, people do not *have* to use the library; as a result, the library must be close to the people it wishes to serve.

From the viewpoint of management, there is another reason to use branch units (including bookmobiles). Since branch managers and supervisors are on their own as far as making spot decisions is concerned, they either develop or fail much more quickly than might ordinarily happen. People become more confident in their decision-making ability as they are forced to settle matters for themselves. Also, using branch units provides more training opportunities than might exist with a central operation, because each unit requires some degree of supervision.

As a means of organizing work at the lower levels of an institution, the territorial method has much to offer. When used in the proper way, it can be one of the most effective methods of organizing at the community level.

Product departmentation is frequently used to create little "institutions" out of larger ones; in libraries, it is known as form division. In this approach, the unit takes on all the activities of the parent institution, but only for one product (serials, maps, government documents, etc.). When using the territorial method, staff members usually deal with all forms of materials but only one function (such as reference); in products/form departmentation, the staff specializes in one form (for instance, records and tapes). They then perform all activities regarding that form (selection, acquisition, cataloging, etc.). This specialization allows workers to develop a high level of competence with one form, gaining skills and knowledge that someone working with several forms would have little opportunity to acquire. Another advantage is that this high degree of specialization allows an equally high degree of public service. Patron confidence in the institution increases, as does patron satisfaction. My own experience shows that, even when materials cannot be provided, the staff in a form unit is able to provide convincing explanations as to why the materials are unavailable. Patrons are given knowledgeable explanations, not excuses that place blame on someone who is not present.

When product/form departmentation is employed, the budget in each unit will require close continuous scrutiny. Branch libraries have a budget, of course, but they can only rely on the central library and other branches for a common pool of materials and services. Thus, a branch's budget does not truly reflect its potential for service. A form unit, on the other hand, has a precise budget and precise goals, and it must match them. For instance, a specific amount of money will be allotted to serials, but persons working with serials must plan for rising subscription costs and postal rates when they apportion the monies available to them.

Customer service departmentation may well be a useful tool for libraries, the most obvious example being children's services. Other examples include young adult services, undergraduate libraries, services for the blind and shut-ins, institutional services (for hospital wards, prisons, and nursing homes), and special populations. As may be evident, this type of orientation is usually confined to the sales/service activities; production and finance are usually handled by the larger unit. Another feature of this departmentation is that a wide variety of factors can come into play when designing such a unit—age, sex, income, health, educational level, etc. Special skills (such as storytelling) and special equipment (such as special children's furniture) might well be necessary if this approach is used; however, under the right circumstances, it can provide a very high level of customer satisfaction. Customer-oriented service can also increase staff skills, because staff members work in depth in one area. Customer service departmentation should be used as often as possible in the library, because it is a reflection of a basic element in the philosophy of librarianship—service.

Equipment/process departmentation, yet another method, is not often used in libraries, except in the areas of photoduplication and data processing. Use of this method hinges on two factors: money and space. For instance, it would be entirely too expensive to provide photoduplication equipment for each unit in a library, and few units would be able to provide the space even if the equipment were available. Yet, since a need exists, many libraries acquire one set of equipment for the use of all departments. Also, the skills needed to run such equipment will be concentrated in one place, and departments will not spend time squabbling over access to the equipment, because it will be out of their hands. Savings in time alone can be considerable if such debating is obviated. However, the primary advantage is that, with skilled operators, the equipment will last longer and produce better products.

Each form of departmentation has some advantages and some disadvantages; only by careful analysis of an institution's special situation can we determine which form(s) should be employed. What works in one situation may not work in what appears to be an identical situation, even within the same institution. Functional and product/form approaches are most common at the higher levels of the library, while the lower levels normally use territorial, customer, and equipment methods to divide their work.

Work Assignment

Through careful analysis and organization, it is possible to reduce the tedium of many jobs; this is done by setting up work situations that involve a variety of activities. Thus, although each task in itself may be boring, the combination of tasks may make the entire function reasonably interesting, at least in the short term. Also, a number of people can be assigned to the combined sets of activities so that no one person has to do one dreary job all day. This, in turn, should improve both morale and performance.

The manager's primary task, of course, is to assign workers, or groups of workers, to specific tasks in order to accomplish the organization's objectives. To do this, the manager must consider the ideal structure and the structure as it exists, and then find a common ground. One should remember, though, that a variety of possible structures exists; therefore, the ways in which work can be assigned will not be limited to one or two variations. The factors to consider when choosing a structure include: commonality, intimate association, frequency of use, managerial interest, competition, and policy control.

Commonality appears to be the simplest approach. In this method, people who perform the same tasks work in one specific area. However, determining the basis of commonality can be a problem. Consider typing skills in the library. Commonality might seem to dictate a typing pool, but one must consider the variety of typing skills needed in that setting. Would increased production result from combining the work of typing administrative materials with the work of typing cataloging cards or order forms? In some libraries, it might; in others, it might not. Even with a unit, that problem can arise. In cataloging, for instance, a common typing pool might be used for processing original cataloging copy or one typist might be assigned to one or two catalogers. The first mehod might be more flexible, while the second might yield greater efficiency as work habits meshed. The point to remember is that the application of commonality is more complex than it first appears.

The method most typical to libraries is *intimate association:* all activities required to carry out a particular objective are placed within one unit. Almost all units have clerical staff, paraprofessionals, and professionals, and the staff is assigned on the basis of need. This may be somewhat inefficient, because several units may have somewhat similar functions but not at a level at which anyone develops a great degree of skill. The danger here is duplication of effort. The manager should always be aware of benefits relative to costs.

Frequency of use comes into play when one department accounts for the major share of the use of a function. For example, cataloging might be responsible for and house all the terminals for access to OCLC or RLN, if cataloging activities represent the major use. However, if two or more departments make equal use of a service, then a separate unit might well be considered (as in product/form departmentation).

Strong *managerial interest* might lead to the assignment of an activity to a supervisor who has an especially strong interest in that area. There are two problems with this approach, however. First, the person who has a strong interest in an area might not have the ability required to succeed. Second, space and location problems may make it impossible to handle an assignment in this manner.

Competition can come into the picture when one unit is not performing its functions as well as it might and another unit is created to take over those functions. If a reclassification project, for instance, is not going very speedily in cataloging, a separate reclassification unit might be created. The resulting competitive situation can lead to higher performance in both units, but a potential danger (due to personnel factors) should be borne in mind when employing this method.

Work can also be assigned on the basis of policy control—the interpretation of general library policy. The assumption is that work that does not clearly belong to any one unit will be assigned to that unit most likely to give the interpretation of the task sought by top management. For instance, assessment of fines could be handled by circulation, readers' services, or the reserve book room. In an academic library, though, circulation and reserve may have very different views of the matter. The top management would probably assign the task of policy determination to that unit whose philosophy is closest to its own and whose solution would be closest to that desired. By knowing the personnel in a unit, the manager may need or wish to assign a task on the basis of how general policy will be specifically interpreted. This can be a matter of assignment within a unit as well as being institution-wide.

The preceding discussion points out that assigning work may not be as simple as a person might first think. Creating a new unit to perform a task previously done by several units may appear to be a good idea on paper, but the full ramifications of a new unit must be explored before the plan is initiated. Assigning work takes a great deal of time and thought, and, with changing personnel, the manager must constantly reexamine assignments to ensure efficient work performance and a reasonable distribution of tasks to capable personnel.

Span of Control

One important element of the organizing process is brought out in a verse from Exodus regarding the number of persons that an individual can supervise. As Moses was told, "This thing is too heavy for thee. Thou are not able to perform it thyself all alone." (18:17–18). Organizing is a *sharing* of responsibility and authority. No one is capable of making all the decisions required in our present complex social and industrial environment; those who try usually fail. Some who succeed in finding the time might make the right decisions for a while, but often they destroy their health and fail for that reason: "Thou wilt surely wear away" (Exodus 18:17). Span of control, then, denotes the *degree* of delegation and sharing.

One of the first factors to note about span of control is that the width of the span (the number of subordinates) does not correlate with success. And, even though a great variety of widths have proven successful, people still tend to think in terms of the classical span of between four and eight subordinates. Lawrence Hill (1963) proposed an even more rigid definition; he maintained that the ideal span of control was six subordinates. George Terry (1972) has summarized it as follows:

> The preferred span of authority is six subordinates to one superior under the conditions of (1) the time spent by the supervisor with the subordinate is one-half hour (called service time), (2) the time between such conferences (called service sessions) is seven and one-half hours, and (3) the number of supervisors is one. If the service time is reduced to one-fourth hour, the span increases to nine or ten employees to one supervisor.[2]

This formula would leave 5 hours per day for nonsupervisory activity— a rather unrealistic picture, at least in libraries.

The rate of change in a situation must be considered when determining how many subordinates constitute a workable span of control. Quickly changing situations usually call for a narrow span of control, during World War II; Eisenhower had only three subordinates. Libraries tend to be more classical (having four to six), but, given the rate of change in libraries, that number could be increased in many situations.

Haphazard organizational growth is another factor to consider. As in many institutions, library units often simply grow and become more complex without any true plan controlling the process. After a few years, relationships both between and within units can become confused, and supervisory control can expand in the same indistinct way. Sometimes 12 subordinates for one supervisor becomes the norm rather than the exception, especially in the circulation units and technical service units in larger libraries. In a situation involving 12 subordinates, there are, according to one formula,* 4708 potential supervisory relationships.

A span of control problem not often discussed concerns full-time ver-

---

*A formula that has been used to calculate the maximum number of subordinate–superior relationships that *may* develop is $N = n (2^{n-1} - 1)$. This formula indicates the maximum number of potential relationships. Not all the relationships will develop, and those that do are not equally important, nor do they occur all the time.

sus part-time employees. Formulas deal with the number of positions, not with the type, and most managers tend to think in terms of full-time equivalents (FTE). Although two part-time employees may be one FTE, those two people require more supervisory time than would one individual. Both persons will have individual problems as well as problems in common, and all these must be attended to if the unit is to function efficiently. In libraries in which students are used as part-time help, one task may be done by 15 to 20 persons, and good coordination is required to keep everyone up to date on policies and procedures. Therefore, when thinking about the span of control and using formulas, it is important to think in terms of persons rather than full-time equivalents.

A few things must be remembered about span of control. As the number of supervisors at a given management level increases, narrowing individual supervisors' spans of control, certain problems come up. First, the system costs more in terms of salaries, benefits, and equipment. Second, communication becomes more difficult, and response time is increased. (For example, five supervisors with a common area of concern will pass decisions on and make decisions faster than ten supervisors—but not twice as fast.) Third, coordination becomes more difficult among supervisors as their number increases—the more people, the more difficulty.

There *are* arguments for expanding the span of control. The primary argument maintains that subordinates assume more responsibility under a wide span of control (because they are under less supervision). In this situation, great care must be taken to select workers of better-than-average ability and motivation, because they will be on their own to a large degree. In conjunction with this is the notion that managerial skills among subordinates will be exercised more than they might otherwise be. And people who are allowed to exercise their decision-making ability are more likely to develop a strong but flexible managerial style. Moreover, people respond positively, maintain higher morale, and frequently perform better when they are not supervised closely.

The supervisor also will benefit, because, although thorough instruction will be needed at the outset of assigning a task, that same thoroughness will save time later. Most problems will have been covered, and the subordinates will expect them and know how to deal with them. This will reduce the frequency of manager-subordinate contact and save time for both individuals.

In widening any span of control, the delegation of authority and responsibility is critical. By making this very clear, the supervisor will save time and reduce confusion. When everyone knows when to do what, a great deal of discussion time regarding who is to do what can be eliminated. If supervisors fail to provide complete work plans but still expect subordinates to know what is going on, the only result can be confusion, delay, and increased cost.

As noted earlier, only an institution or unit that is not undergoing rapid change can employ a broad span of control. Rapidly changing situations cannot be handled effectively by using a wide span, because an increase in the number of persons involved means an increase in the time required to accomplish any task. Obviously, when a situation is slow to change, people learn their duties more thoroughly, and when they really understand their duties, less supervisory time is required.

Clearly defined, objective standards for judging work performance are necessary if one person is to effectively supervise a large number of workers. Certainly there is a time savings: no one has to discuss whether they have met the standard, and performance evaluation takes less time, because the evaluation process does not involve prolonged discussion of a subjective report. And, because workers know where they stand, morale is normally higher.

Also, when a large number of subordinates are involved, written presentations of information are far preferable to oral presentations. Written policies leave little room for interpretation, and they constitute a permanent record; this saves time by avoiding needless discussion. Speaking to a group can convey information quickly, but the mechanics of setting up a meeting and the socializing that goes on before and after it often consume more time than is saved.

Finally, if the supervisor makes careful use of personal contact, the span of control can be expanded. By creating an atmosphere of availability, the supervisor lets subordinates know that they can get help when a crisis arises. Knowing that such support is there, the subordinates can work more independently, which is conducive to good morale even if the span of control is narrow. Balance must be maintained, of course, between availability, personal concern, and socializing.

One personal factor enters into the question of the width of control. Even though some people do try to expand it, there are only 24 hours in a day. No one should be allowed to let their job become a 24-hour-a-day, 7-day-a-week affair. Anyone who does this consistently definitely needs to develop other interests. Otherwise, in the long run, the work and the work unit alike will suffer. If a subordinate persists in overextending the workday, the supervisor should do as much as possible to reduce that person's opportunities to work on such an extended basis. If the supervisor has this habit, everyone will suffer, because such people tend to forget that others have a variety of interests and feel little need to work beyond the required time.

Centralization/Decentralization

Another vital aspect of delegation is the degree of centralization established within the organization. How much delegation should take place, and how far down should it extend? The manager should be aware of the fact that little delegation means a great deal of centralization, which may not be an entirely bad situation. Although decentralization has acquired a somewhat hallowed status by virtue of its association with the phrases "more democratic" and "less authoritarian," it can lead to some very real problems, as the following statements indicate:

> I find myself just a little annoyed at the tendency of all of us to adopt certain cliches about decentralization and then glibly announce that we're for it. I've been somewhat amused at some of my colleagues who have been vocal at expounding the virtues of decentralization and yet quite unconsciously are apt to be busily engaged in developing their own personal control over activities for which they are responsible.[3]

> An examination of the total activities of chief executives discloses that they continue to make most or all major decisions, either directly or through an informal framework of strict rules, checks and balances, informal instructions and through mental compulsions on the part of subordinates to act as the boss would act.[4]

In libraries, as in other organizations, the lip service given to the concept of decentralization often belies the reality of day-to-day operations. The decentralization of facilities in the case of libraries might be especially confusing, because it is very rarely accompanied by decentralization of decision-making authority.

Criteria for Decentralization

In 1952, Ernest Dale developed criteria for determining the degree of centralization within an organization. These criteria were developed in order to conduct a management study for the American Management Association, and they remain valid today.

1. The greater the number of decisions made lower down in the management hierarchy, the greater the degree of decentralization.
2. The more important the decisions made lower down the management hierarchy (for example, the greater the sum of capital expenditure that can be approved by a plant manager without consulting anyone else), the greater the degree of decentralization.
3. The more functions affected by decisions made at the lower levels (thus, companies which permit only operational decisions to be made at separate branch plants are less decentralized than those which permit financial and personnel decisions to be made at branch plants).

4. The less checking required on the decision. Decentralization is greatest when no check at all is made, less when the supervisors have to consult before the decision is made. The fewer the people to be consulted and the lower they are in the management hierarchy, the greater the degree of decentralization.[5]

Although such criteria make the examination and analysis of an organization's structure more objective, several subjective elements also are involved. Things are not always what they appear to be, and what is said often differs sharply from what is done. Many of the subtle pressures noted previously cannot be observed, and the entire question of number will always be relative.

Factors Affecting the Degree of Decentralization

Six basic factors affect the degree of decentralization within an organization. The primary factor is probably the *cost* of any decision, because monetary costs are fundamental. The correlation between the cost of a decision and how high up in the structure it is made is very positive: the more kroner/dollars/yen/shekels involved, the higher the position of the person making the decision. For instance, because most library fines are small and involve or affect the library in very minor ways, these assessments are ordinarily left to clerks and part-time help. However, when it comes to determining who may use the library, institute a new service, or plan a new facility, the head librarian or department head actually makes the decision. This is true, not because top-level administrators make fewer mistakes, but because responsibility cannot be delegated along with authority in such cases. Ultimately, the person in the library who will be held responsible for a costly decision will most likely be the person who made it, if only for self-protection.

Uniformity of policy interpretation is a second factor affecting the degree of decentralization. Because policies are guides to thinking, they are subject to varying interpretations; therefore, the variation in construing policies will increase as the number of persons allowed to interpret them increases. Consistency can ultimately be achieved only by a uniform interpretation of existing policy, and the person most likely to have the "last word" will be in the upper levels of the hierarchy.

Size is always significant in establishing the degree of decentralization within a library. In a larger and more complex library, authority is more likely to be delegated. Because large organizations can consume enormous amounts of time to clear decisions, both horizontally and vertically, the tendency is to delegate a great deal of authority to the lower levels of the library in order to facilitate decision making.

A library's *history* often plays a significant role in decentralization, because the library will tend to perpetuate the structure and procedures that have characterized it during its lifetime. Rarely will a library lacking a history of staff participation adopt a decentralized decision-making procedure; even under new leadership, it will take time for the staff to get comfortable with the idea that they should decide.

Closely akin to a library's history is its *managerial philosophy*. Organizations tend to hire people whose philosophy is consistent with that already in practice. And, even if they do not hire such people—that is, even if centralized organizations hire someone in an attempt to decentralize—most attempts to alter a highly centralized structure will fail because of problems in actual operation, abilities of supervisors to handle new authority, and inconsistencies in policy interpretation. Such factors would (or should) give new manager pause before embarking on restructuring an organization.

Finally, *staff abilities* influence the degree of decentralization. Decentralization requires a staff that is comfortable making quick decisions. If they are not, the manager should either postpone decentralization until the proper staff is assembled or undertake staff development activities to improve their skills.

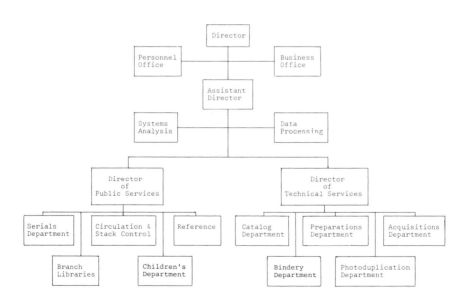

Figure 6.1 Library organization chart.

ORGANIZATIONAL CHARTS

If it is kept up to date, the organizational chart can be a useful management tool. If it reflects all the factors discussed in the preceding pages,
then it should give a clear picture of the formal lines of communication
within the library.

Figure 6.1 illustrates a number of points about delegation within the
library. Even though it is fictitious, it shows functional line and staff

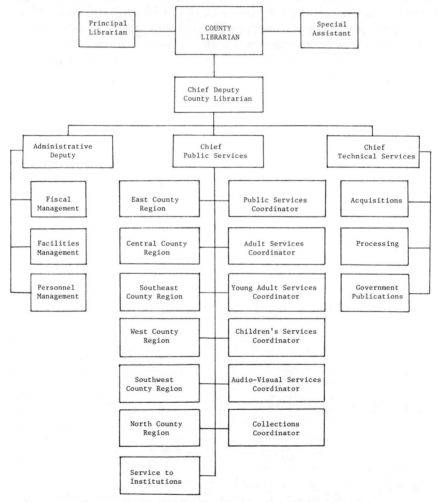

Figure 6.2 The organizational chart of the Los Angeles County public library system.

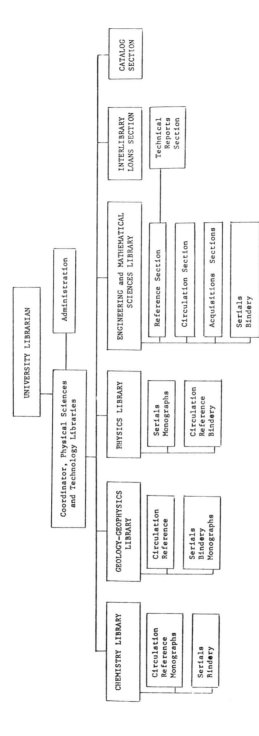

Figure 6.3 Organizational chart of the University of California, Los Angeles, physical science and technology libraries.

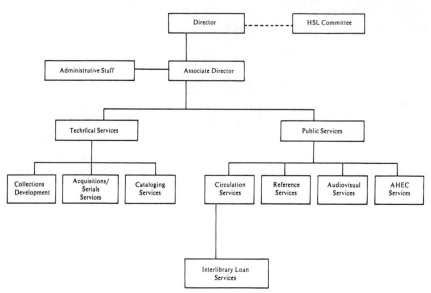

Figure 6.4 Organizational chart of the Health Sciences Library, University of North Carolina, Chapel Hill, North Carolina.

divisions. Personnel, Systems, and Data Processing units are all staff, while the others are all line. The chart also exemplifies all types of departmentation: functional (top-level units—director, assistant director, head of public services and of technical services), territorial (branch libraries), product (serials, circulation, reference, cataloging/classifying, acquisitions, and preparation/bindery), customer (undergraduate library), and equipment (duplication). Other examples (Figures 2, 3, and 4) are from actual situations, and they show the variety of labels that are used in different types of libraries. Despite the variety of labels, however, each unit in each chart can always be assigned to one of the general departmentation categories.

COMMON MISTAKES IN ORGANIZING

An institution, its staff, and its external environment exist in a complex, interwoven relationship. Organizing provides techniques for structuring these relationships in a meaningful manner, that is for establishing relationships that provide the best flow of activities, ideas, authority, and responsibility. Order and clarity should arise from organizing as well as meaning and status for individual activities. Yet a manager's first attempts to organize will often involve a number of common mistakes, among which are

1. Failure to plan properly or in enough detail. This often shows up when a structure is maintained long after the organization's objectives and activities have changed.
2. Failure to take individuals and their skills into account. Recognizing both the abilities and limitations of each staff member is basic to successful organizing.
3. Failure to clarify relationships—both within a unit and between it and other units. This is especially common when restructuring a department or subunit.
4. Failure to delegate authority. Two related errors are giving responsibility for an activity without the required authority, and delegating authority without clearly defining responsibility.
5. Failure to balance delegation among units. This is common when an institution tries to maintain a loose structure.
6. Failure to use lines of authority as lines of communication. Overuse of confidential messages or messages "around" a position defeats the point of establishing lines of communication in the first place.
7. Misuse (or poor use) of the staff system.
8. Reliance on functional authority rather than reorganization.
9. Overorganization; that is, the development of a tight structure in which there are too many levels of control and in which there is no room for discretion.
10. Failure to regard the difficulties experienced by both supervisors and subordinates in handling authority and responsibility.

Yet, the bottom line in delegation will always be how well the individual manager or supervisor is able to deal with the problem of delegating responsibility for an activity while remaining ultimately responsible for it. Psychological difficulties associated with working under such strictures may cause many personnel and morale problems within institutions; the manager should always bear this in mind.

BIBLIOGRAPHY

1. G. Terry, *Principles of Management*, 7th ed. (Homewood, Ill.: Irwin, 1977), p. 298.
2. Terry, p. 389.
3. H. Baker, and R. France, *Centralization and Decentralization in Industrial Relations* (Princeton, N.J.: Princeton Univ. Press, 1954), p. 37.
4. E. Dale, *Planning and Developing the Company Organization Structure* Research Report 20 (New York: AMA, 1952), p. 18.
5. Dale, p. 105.

FURTHER READING

Arthur, D. "Guidelines for Effective Delegation." *Supervisory Management* 24 (1979): 9–13.

Axford, H. W. "The Interrelations of Structure, Governance and Effective Resource Utilization in Academic Libraries." *Library Trends* 23 (1975): 551–571.

Baker, H., and France, R. *Centralization and Decentralization in Industrial Relations.* Princeton, N.J.: Department of Economics and Sociology, Princeton Univer. Press, 1954.

Baumfield, B. H. "Attitudes and Authority: A Personal Examination of the Public Library Scene." *Journal of Librarianship* 2 (1970): 22–32.

Brown, D. W. "Why Delegation Works and Why It Doesn't." *Personnel* 44 (1967): 44–52.

Carlisle, H. H. "Developing the Adaptive Organization." *Management Advisor* 9 (1972): 40–43.

Dale, E. *Planning and Developing the Company Organization Structure.* Research Report No. 20. New York: American Management Association (1952): 126–127.

Durkheim, E. *The Division of Labor in Society.* Glencoe, Ill.: The Free Press, 1952.

English, J. W., and Gottesman, J. I. "Telling Subordinates What to Do and How to Do It." *Supervisory Management* 24 (1979): 21–24.

Fisch, G. G. "Line-Staff is Obsolete." *Harvard Business Review* 39 (1961): 67–69.

Geedes, A. "Current Trends in Branch Libraries." *Library Trends* 14 (1966): 365–367.

Hill, L. "The Application of Queuing Theory to the Span of Control." *Academy of Management Journal* 6 (1963): 79–85.

Himes, G. K. "Multiply Your Effectiveness." *Supervision* 41 (1979): 3–6.

Lynch, B. P. "Organizational Structure and the Academic Library." *Illinois Libraries* 56 (1974): 200–207.

Patton, J. A. "Make and Use an Organization Chart." *Business Management* 24 (1963): 55–62.

Randsepp, E. "Why Supervisors Don't Delegate." *Supervision* 41 (1979): 12–15.

Schleh, E. C. "Handing Off to Subordinates: Delegating for Gain." *Management Review* 67 (1978): 43–47.

Sheldon, A. *Organization Structures.* Arlington Heights, Ill.: Altman Publishing, 1978.

Smith, W. E. "Centralization vs. Decentralization." *Data Management* 15 (1977): 24–25.

Thompson, R. E. "Span of Control: Conceptions and Misconceptions." *Business Horizons* 7 (1964): 49–58.

Weber, M. *The Theory of Social and Economic Organization.* New York: Oxford Univ. Press, 1947.

Wedgwood, H. C. "Where Committees Go Wrong." *Personnel* 44 (1967): 62–67.

White, H. W. "Organizational Placement of the Industrial Special Library. Its Relationship to Success and Survival." *Special Libraries* 64 (1973): 141–144.

7. Decision Making

Management folklore aside, decision making occurs at all levels in an organization, not just at the "top." No matter at what level, an individual in a management position is expected to make decisions. And, because making decisions means taking a stand (often public) on an issue, many persons find it a difficult thing to do—difficult, because one seldom knows everything one would like to know about a situation. Most situations are composed of a large number of variables that interact in unpredictable ways, especially when people are involved. This means that a manager will make the "wrong" decision at times. At the time a decision is made, the choice might seem to be the best, but, after the fact, it may be seen as a lesser, if not a completely inappropriate, choice. Yet, some people do not like to make "mistakes" of this type, so they try to avoid decisions, assign the responsibility to a committee, or blame someone else for supplying poor information. In an effort to help potential managers avoid such unproductive behavior, this chapter addresses the nature and processes of decision making, the types of decisions, and their effects.

Accountability, as noted earlier, is an important factor in the life of any manager. Decision making generally calls for clear-cut accountability, which is one reason that committee decision making may well be dangerous. A few years ago, the *Los Angeles Times* published a news story that neatly summarizes the problem of committee decision-making accountability.

The University of California is a large university system and like many American academic institutions uses the committee format for securing staff input and decision making. For many people within the University and certainly for the general public the university's decision making process is a mystery and often it is difficult to say just what happened during the process.

Several years ago there was concern about the English language entrance requirement for undergraduate admission to the University. A system-wide committee was set up to make a decision regarding what high school classes would meet the entrace requirements. Eventually, letters were sent to California high schools announcing that journalism, speech and drama classes would no longer satisfy the entrance requirement. Naturally, there were a number of objections to the decision, especially from journalism teachers. In an attempt to learn when and how the decision was made the *Los Angeles Times* reporter interviewed members of the committee that presumably made the decision as well as university officials, all of whom could not remember making such a decision. The reporter concluded the article by saying "the result: a circle of accused, bemused and slightly embarrassed designated decision makers in search of an important decision that no one says he made. And yet a decision was made. Minutes of a June 3 committee meeting of the state-wide Academic Senate say so. . .!"[1]

Problems of the type described in the article occur all the time in every large organization. Certainly, they occur most frequently when there is extensive use of committees, but you will also encounter situations in which the only decision maker involved remembers neither how, when, or whether a decision was made. This chapter, then, concerns both the background on decision making and its application to your situation in a library.

THE NATURE OF DECISION MAKING

Every problem, every situation, has one built-in alternative: do nothing. People constantly choose this "solution" by procrastinating until more information is available (or until the problem appears to have "gone away"). A decision maker's task is to provide a better alternative.

Decision making almost invariably involves a problem, a difficult situation, or a conflict. It may be deciding on objectives, or it may be deciding on procedures. Either way, some urgency usually accompanies the decision-making process. Ideally, a decision maker quickly analyzes the problem at hand, develops a list of alternative solutions, and quickly chooses the most effective solution.

A major managerial function is ensuring that the work flow in the organization be as smooth and efficient as possible. Many of the problems that hamper efficiency relate in some way to people. People problems thus become a variable in the work flow and in coordination between units. If a manager dealt strictly with machines, or automatons, or robots, there would be no great difficulty in supervision. When dealing with people, though, the problems are quite different and more subtle than the problems encountered with replacement parts.

In light of this fact, then, methods by which to improve the decision-making process need to be understood. An individual might try to use some of these techniques in day-to-day decision making on a personal level; this would help her or him to begin to think in terms of the decision-making process. Then, when that individual is confronted with an actual organizational decision, the process would be more natural, and it might take place more quickly.

Success as a manager is largely dependent upon success as a decision maker. Sound decisions make for a smoothly working unit, an efficient organization, and a personnel situation in which there is high morale and a pleasant working environment. But sound, successful decisions are the result of several factors.

Adequate, accurate data about the situation are essential. The biggest factor, though, is the environment in which the decision is made. Frequently, decisions must be made under pressures of time, emotion, and people. If an individual cannot deal with this type of pressure, the decision will be poor; but, given an opportunity to sit back, reflect, and analyze a problem, most people will make good decisions. This is one of the reasons for the importance of practice in decision making. The knowledge of what is actually involved in the decision-making environment is also useful to the manager, especially to those who might have difficulty working under pressure.

PROBLEM ANALYSIS

Problem analysis is the first step in making any decision. Once the problem is analyzed, it is possible to examine potential solutions and decide which solution seems best for the existing circumstances. Although this may seem terribly obvious, it is astonishing how many times people attempt to tackle a problem and offer solutions (decisions) before they are certain of the nature of the problem. Kepner and Tregoe,[2] among many writers on decision making, have identified seven factors involved in analyzing a work-related problem (These can be adapted to nonwork problems as well.) The following is a summary of their approach to problem analysis.

1. *Assume that a standard of performance exists against which one may compare real performance.* For libraries, this must read, "There *should* be a standard of performance against which one may compare real performance." Any standard can be established within an institution (such as objective production standards in technical-service units).

2. *Determine whether a deviation from the standards has occurred, and determine the degree of deviation.* Once the standard has been set, it is possible to measure deviation. Without a standard, deviation cannot be identified or measured; one may only have the feeling that deviation exists.

3. *Locate the point of deviation in the sequence of activities or in the situation.* This is often more difficult than it might seem, as the result of the deviation may show up only in the final product. The deviation may have entered the system at the beginning, come into the system with the material itself, entered with a person somewhere along the sequence, or intruded in the final preparation or presentation of the material under consideration. The important thing to remember when dealing with people as possible sources of deviation is that the deviation must be correctly identified. Failure to identify the source correctly can create problems in morale and trust. When a person has been incorrectly blamed for a problem, that person begins to doubt the ability of the individual placing the blame and frequently wonders about the "real" reasons for the accusation.

4. *Ascertain what distinguishes the affected group from the unaffected group.* What makes the deviant? It is very easy to convince oneself that the source of the problem has been found; it is equally easy to identify the incorrect factor when leaping to facile conclusions. Yet, when the affected group has been carefully distinguished from the unaffected group, and when the elements of distinction are very clear, the problem is almost solved.

5. *Affirm that the problem has been caused by a change that has taken place in the system.* The only exception to this is in the case of a new system that is being tested. The change may be very minor, or it may be in a system related to the one experiencing the problem, but change is always the cause of a problem.

6. *Analyze all the possible causes that can be deduced from the relevant changes that have taken place in the system.* First, identify all changes in the system. Then, examine each one to determine whether it could be the cause of the problem, or the actual problem.

7. *Take the cause that most exactly explains the facts, correct that point in the system, and test the system to see whether deviation continues to take place.* If the deviation disappears, the proposed solution was correct;

if not, search must be made for other causes. Too often, this step is ignored, and even more problems within the working situation are created where they need not have occurred.

How could these steps be employed in an actual library situation? The following example will illustrate this and will show at the same time that not all problems require that a manager follow all seven steps. The hypothetical situation involves a problem in reproducing catalog cards by using photoduplicating equipment located in the library. The library had had the equipment for two years, but the problem of unsatisfactory copy had only recently arisen, most notably with the catalog cards. Because the volume of work had increased dramatically, the catalog department had expanded its staff.

On some days, the unit produced clean, clear cards; at other times, the cards would have faint ink spots on them; and at still other times, it looked as though a light gray film had been applied to the cards. Occasionally a card would come out completely black.

Certainly, there was an obvious standard—clean, clear catalog cards. When the problem first arose, a move to change the standard to "readable copy" was begun, but no one could be enthusiastic about this change, because it was too nebulous. The point of deviation also was clear—the duplicating equipment. Moreover, it was clear that the problem usually occurred only with the card stock, not with the regular paper. Thus, one factor in the deviation was identified: paper stock, unaffected; card stock, affected, but not always. Records revealed that a new card stock had been ordered some months previously. This new stock was at first thought to be the cause of the deviation; however, tests of old and new stock revealed this not to be true.

Step five (affirming that the problem was caused by a change) thus proved difficult. The only known change had been identified, and it was not the source of the problem. The equipment, the ink, and the photographic plate material had not been changed, and the equipment operator had been on the job for over 18 months. Even the service representative from the equipment manufacturer was unable to fix the problem—or even identify the cause.

When all internal factors had been considered, it became necessary to look outside the unit. But where? It was like looking for the proverbial needle and not knowing which haystack to search. Finally, the operator could not produce any acceptable copy during an entire week. It was in the middle of August, everyone had had a bad week, and the air conditioning/ventilating system had been turned off in order to complete the remodeling that had been going on. As soon as the equipment service representative learned of this, he suggested both the cause and the cure for the problem. When the temperature and humidity in the equipment reached a certain point, the ink splattered a film over the cards. When the equipment was used with heavy card stock, the addition of a teaspoon of solid vegetable fat to the ink reservoir solved the problem. Finding the solution had taken almost 3 months.

Part of the difficulty was due to the initial lack of a systematic effort to solve the problem. People jumped to conclusions as to the cause and tried to lay blame on someone or something without carefully checking, thereby causing even more problems. Both the equipment operator and the supervising librarian were subjected to more than a little verbal abuse during the early phases of the investigation; this caused a drop in their morale and increased their anxiety. Although it is questionable whether the problem could have been solved earlier (given its nature), careful analysis from the outset could have reduced the personnel problems and made it clear that the source of the difficulty was outside the unit.

The seven steps described here can be very useful in solving problems—both job-related and personal. Practice them on some "simple" problems, and it soon will be second nature to use the technique. Consequently, as a manager (whether at the job or in your own life), you will not create unnecessary people problems by jumping to conclusions as to who or what is the cause of a particular problem.

THE DECISION-MAKING PROCESS

Having analyzed a problem, one must being the decision-making process. Kepner and Tregoe suggest a seven-stage model for making a rational, logical decision. These stages are closely related to the steps used in analyzing a problem.

First, search for and define the important organizational objectives that are relevant to the problem. Keep the most important objectives, and discard the others. If you fail to do this, you will make no decision at all, because there will be too many variables to consider. The decision maker or manager retains perspective and deals with a problem by limiting the number of objectives to be considered in relation to that problem.

Second, classify these objectives according to their relative importance. Some of them must be satisfied; others are important but not essential; and still others have no bearing on this particular decision, and therefore can be ignored. Frequently, without thinking about it, a manager will give priority to less important objectives rather than to more important ones. By classifying them, you can eliminate this problem.

Third, search for and define all the feasible methods of solving the problem. This is frequently more difficult than it appears to be. People have a tendency to define a problem, choose one or two solutions, and declare the problem solved. But, as noted in Chapter 4, it may be better to define a problem less stringently so that the range of ideas relating to that problem will be greater in number and broader in scope. This can help to ensure that the best solution will find its way into the light. (For instance, in teaching management, I have found that individuals may list 7 or 8 possible solutions to a problem, whereas the entire class may list 25 to 30. Obviously, all the proposed solutions will not be of the same caliber, but the field of choice is certainly greater.) During this process, alternatives can be weighed in relation to the classified objectives; and the more objectives met, the better the solution(s).

Fourth, evaluate the solutions one by one in relation to the objectives. This is more formal than proposing alternatives, because the ranked importance of each objective that is met must be weighed. Solutions that meet minor objectives but fail to address major ones must be identified as such.

Fifth, choosing from among the alternatives after they have been fully evaluated, select the one(s) to be implemented.

Sixth, explore the consequences of the tentative choice, particularly the adverse ones. What will the implementation of the decision mean to the system? Can adverse effects be identified? Are they major or minor? Can compensation be made in implementing the decision so as to avoid the adverse effects?

Seventh, determine how to head off adverse effects or at least how to keep them from becoming major problems in themselves. Then, by combining the solution and the modifications, determine the final decision; and then implement that decision.

TYPES OF SOLUTIONS

The manager should be aware that there are several types of solutions. For every decision being sought, you should identify which type of solution is needed or desired. Most people tend to think only as far as the second type (adaptive solutions), but the greatest efficiency will ultimately be gained by going on to the last three types.

The *interim solution* will buy you time while the cause of the problem is being sought. It will also buy time while changes are being made to implement the final decision. However, interim solutions have a way of becoming permanent, or at least bandages that will hold a trouble spot together a while longer.

The *adaptive solution* does not really solve the problem, but it allows the organization to continue to function (or appear to function) some-what normally. If an interim solution is a bandage, an adaptive solution is a plaster cast. It is often chosen in the hope that, with the application of a few cosmetic changes, the problem will take care of itself. However, job situations, unlike broken bones, do not heal themselves. A problem that is glossed over will become even larger later on.

The *corrective solution* actually solves the problem. If requires time, effort, and careful analysis of the problem. It is the ideal, and, if a system is to be healthy, the corrective solution must be sought.

The *preventive solution* goes back to the Kepner/Tregoe idea of explor-ing decisions for adverse consequences. In this way, the problem at hand is solved, and possible problems arising from the solution are anticipated and (one hopes) avoided. This takes even more time than a corrective solution, but it could repay the costs by allowing future time to be spent in ways other than solving problems that could have been prevented if foreseen. An example of the need for preventive solutions is seen in the area of implementing the new cataloging code and its implications for public catalogs.

The *contingency solution* simply involves the establishment of standby or emergency procedures to help offset the effects of a serious problem. In libraries, this type of solution may be most important in technical-services units. This is due to the fact that a major breakdown in one part of technical services will quickly affect other unit. The only problem is that managers usually lack the time needed to prepare contingency plans, even though such plans would be useful.

LONG-RANGE EFFECTS OF DECISION MAKING

As noted previously, one of the most important features of the Kepner/Tregoe model is the evaluation of tentative solutions for possible adverse consequences. At least nine variables need to be examined when one is trying to assess the long-range implications of decisions: people, organi-zational factors, external factors, equipment and facilities, ideas and pro-cesses, material, money or financial factors, output, and personal factors.

In terms of people, consider any decision in light of its effect on staff motivation and morale. Will it be positive or negative? Will it affect atti-tudes toward work or toward the system? Will it enhance either their skills or their abilities? Is it going to be detrimental? Will it affect perfor-mance or productivity? Will the staff be able to grow either as individuals or as a group? Will it somehow affect health or safety? The simple insert-ion of an additional range of bookstacks could cause safety hazards, change ventilation, and create cramped working conditions. Bigger changes would have even greater implications. Because work can only be done through people, most decisions affect people in some way, either positively or negatively. Therefore, I think it is important that a decision's long-term and short-term effects on people be given first consideration.

Organizational factors are important, but, in my opinion, less so than the people factor. If the staff are performing well, then the organizational aspects are quite easily resolved. However, some questions need to be asked: How will the decision affect relationships between work units? Will the functions of units change as a result of the decision? Will the decision improve or hinder communication? Will the decision change the lines of authority and responsibility? Is coordination going to be easier or more difficult under the new setup? Are either the formal or the informal organizations going to change? If so, how?

Environmental factors (part-of-a-part concept) are important in libraries, the external factors address the issue of the organizations' environment. Among the pertinent questions to ask are: Does the decision go against economic or social trends? Is it compatible with events in the library's community? Because the basic management triad is composed of people, organizations, and the environment, the manager's basic task is to control the conflicts and relationships among them. Will a decision affect the library's image or status? Because status does affect a library staff's morale, library managers ought to recognize that status is achieved through comparison and competition. Thus, it is quite reasonable to take the environment of any organization into account when seeking to improve it. Status and success do not exist in vacuums.

Obviously, facilities and equipment are important, even though they might seem a bit mundane. Questions need to be asked along these lines: Is space available? Will space be committed over a long period of time? Will the decision affect the flexibility of the space involved? What about the adaptability of the equipment or the space? Will the decision affect the location (or relocation) of the equipment? Is the facility or the equipment (usually the latter) compatible with other equipment of a similar type? How available is it? What about service and supplies? All these factors need to be considered in a sound evaluation.

Ideas and processes need to be examined from a security/safety viewpoint. This is not a matter of business or product security. It is a concept that involves the following questions: Is the process safe? Will it harm materials (books and other information materials in the library)? Is the process flexible (adaptable), or must it be rigidly followed? How easily and well do the new ideas and processes conform to existing ideas and processes?

Materials often receive primary consideration when new equipment or a new process is considered. How available is the material? How good are its sources? What about service? What is the quality? Are there any special handling or storage problems? Is transportation easy?

Fiscal or monetary considerations will always be extremely important, especially in their long-term implications. Will this decision involve capital outlay, operating expenses, or both? Is it a fixed or a variable cost? Is it a long-term or a short-term investment? Will it be a continuing expense to either the capital outlay or the operating budgets? What are the overall costs for a given period of time? What is the return, the benefit? What is the cost–benefit factor for this particular decision?

Output involves hundreds of potential questions, but the most elementary ones are these: Will the decision affect the quantity of production? Will it affect quality? Will it in some way change the location or the timing of production? Will handling the output be easier or more difficult if the decision is implemented?

Finally, and perhaps almost equal in importance to the consideration of people, are the manager's personal qualities. These cannot be stressed too heavily. It is necessary to understand both oneself and one's own abilities in order to have the makings of a successful manager. Major decisions in the organization will obviously concern a manager, usually along these lines: Will the decision have any implications on personal goals and plans? Will it somehow affect family relationships? Will it affect personal strengths or weaknesses? Does it conform or conflict with personal interests? Will it affect the amount of time and energy needed for the job? If so, to what extent?

A manager may not wish to consider all these factors in every situation, but their consideration on major decisions can act as a final check on the process. Such a check cannot guarantee success, but it can help a manager avoid mistakes. This may appear to be common sense and, therefore, a waste of time. But each individual has a different idea of what common sense is, so it is best not to rely too much on intuition to find solutions for problems. The whole point of the process of decision making is to come up with the best possible solution to a problem (or at least to avoid making no decision). and these techniques can be of help in allowing "common sense" to prevail.

DECISION AIDS

A number of techniques have been developed to aid the decision maker. Some of these are quantitative in nature, allowing a means of measuring input; these methods are helpful in *some* situations. Other methods are qualitative in nature, dealing with the underlying values of the organization and the behavior that those values permit or prohibit. Quantitative methods are often employed in business and industry in production areas; their application in libraries is also most successful in production areas. On the other hand, libraries often find themselves resolving problems in a qualitative manner, even when there has been quantifiable input along the way.

Quantitative Techniques

Although quantitative techniques can be useful, they have several limitations, the chief one being that people can become overly dependent on, and uncritical of, numbers in themselves. Numbers often make people feel secure, whether or not the data are substantial in themselves. Some people even go so far as to suggest that, if a person is not able to quantify a situation, then that person does not really understand it. Yet, it is equally true that one can quantify a problem without understanding it at all. Quantitative techniques are only aids; they are *not* the ultimate cure.

Among the quantitative aids available are *linear programming*, matrix algebra, and linear mathematical equations—all forms of operating research techniques. In order to use linear programming, several conditions must be met. First, there must be a definite objective, and this must be expressed in a quantifiable way: money, time, or quantity. Second, the variables that will have an effect on the outcome must have a straight-line (linear) relationship. Third, restrictions on variables must be present; otherwise, this approach would not be necessary. As is evident from this summary, linear programming is very mechanical, and cannot be used in many library applications. Most library processes are not in a straight-line relationship, and even circulation, the most obvious place, has enough variations in terms of work to make the application of quantifiable methods difficult. Overall, then, libraries tend not to adopt linear programming—and this is due in part to the fact that the librarians who are supposed to make use of it do not understand it.

In the *simulation model* techniques, an attempt is made to carry out a solution in a vacuum. A model representing some aspects of the real world is set up and subjected to the various influences of that world. Of course, all factors must be quantifiable. In this way, their frequency of appearance can be determined either on the basis of past performance or by the use of a random number table, which helps to take chance into account. The simulation model attempts to trace changes in activities as variables come into play—it attempts to quantify the behavioral and non-logical attributes of a situation. (This technique differs from operations research techniques that are totally mathematical.)

The *Monte Carlo technique* is a form of simulation model in which an attempt is made to control chance. Random sampling is used to simulate natural events and to establish the probability of each of several outcomes. This type of model is used to answer such questions as: What are the chances of an event (or events) actually happening? Which of the alternative decisions should be adopted? What are the chances of breakdown in a given unit or in a certain piece of equipment? In the case of libraries, the use of this method would probably be limited to larger institutions that have computers and expensive hardware.

Queuing theory can prove useful to those librarians who have the ability and background to employ it; it is concerned with the length of time it will take to render a certain service. For instance, how long must staff, patrons, and machines remain idle because of an inefficient arrangement of facilities? Combining queuing theory and the Monte Carlo approach, a person can determine expected arrival rates in a facility and the amount of delay that might be expected. This could be quite valuable in a heavily used public-service area (for example, an academic library's reserve room, or a public library's reference room) in determining staffing in a way that will meet demands most efficiently.

Another quantitative decision-making technique is the *game theory* developed by Von Neumann and Morgenstern (*Theory of Games and Economic Behavior*). However, since game theory deals basically with competitive situations, it really is suited more for business adaptations than for library use (library competition is not that of increasing a "share" of the market at the expense of other libraries).

Two excellent books that provide useful models for library decision making are *Book Availability and the Library User* (1975), by M. H. Buckland, and *Library Planning and Decision-Making Systems* (1974), by M. Hamburg, R. C. Clelland, M. R. W. Bommer, L. E. Romist, and R. H. Whitfield. Buckland was concerned with collection development and user needs, and he provides a number of useful models and suggestions. Using such things as Bradford's law of scattering, decision curves, probability analysis, Chi square, queuing theory, the Monte Carlo technique, and other quantitative methods, Buckland demonstrates a number of things: (1) Problems in library service tend to be worldwide, and solutions in one country often work in another. (Work for the book was done in England, and its techniques have been used elsewhere since.) (2) A wide variety of quantitative methods (rather than just one or two) solve a complex problem (such as better user access to materials). (3) The material and ideas that come out of a quantitative approach can be presented, and to some degree applied, to and for persons who are not mathematically inclined.

The book by Hamburg and associates attempts a much broader approach to library decision making. The authors were concerned with planning and decision making in large academic and public libraries, and they, too, used a variety of quantitative methods. At one point, they discuss the value and limitations of this approach.

> Managerial decision making has become much more complex and difficult in both the private and public sectors as the American [or any other country's, for that matter] economic, political and social structures and the corresponding business, governmental, and social organizational units have grown larger and more complicated. Logical apparatuses and frameworks are needed to bring an objective systematic approach to planning and decision making in keeping with the objectives of these organizations. To answer this need, analytical decision models are being increasingly utilized. A model is simply a representation of *some* aspects of the real world and is often mathematical in nature. Such models change complex management problems, which may seem too chaotic or too uncertain to handle except by intuition, to rational structures that can be analyzed by quantitative, objective method. The past can be described, and predictions can be made of changes that would take place in the real-world situations represented by the models. The overall purpose of such models is to seek out the best combination of factors under the control of the decision maker to improve performance of the organization and make its goals more achieveable.
>
> . . A combination of improved management information systems for libraries and the aforementioned decision models could bring about a more systematic approach to decision making in and concerning libraries. These systems and models are clearly *not intended* to replace managerial intuition and experience. Rather they represent attempts to *provide the basic information and alternative to which managerial judgment may be applied* [emphasis added].[3]

Even given the intention stated here, there are several limitations on the use of many mathematical models. Often, the sheer magnitude of the calculations involved requires access to a computer. Because models tend to be very complex, attempts to apply a model without the proper background can be disastrous. Also, many factors cannot be quantified— they are the qualitative factors mentioned earlier (and discussed in the following section). Frequently, cases simply do not yield enough data to be quantified into a model, because the data were not collected with that purpose in mind. Library data bases are just too limited at this time for widescale use in model building. Another significant problem is that most librarians lack the training in mathematics and statistics needed to handle these techniques. At the outset, costs of this type of decision making tend to be very high in terms of both people and computer time. Finally, even when factors are quantified, they may be imprecise and yield a false sense of security, especially to the uninitiated.

Qualitative Techniques

Decision making has been defined as "a conclusion drawn from a set of premises of two kinds, factual and ethical. Since factual statements are empirical proposition, their validity may be determined. However, ethical (value) statements are imperatives; they have to do with the 'ought' and cannot be empirically validated."[4] Because of this inability to objectively validate ethical (value) judgments, one must ask a very basic question concerning the values employed: Whose standard of correctness is to be employed? Another thing to be aware of is that decision making often appears to be an unconscious activity, because it is one that goes on continuously in everyone's life. Yet the steps that have been outlined can help bring this process to a more conscious level and perhaps improve the quality of decisions being made.

Consider the decision (problem) of whether or not to charge a fee for library data base reference services when they are used by persons outside the library's primary service population, as was the case in 1981 in Denver. (It is assumed that no law or rule forbids this.) An unlikely approach would be simply "to decide" to do it out of the blue (but even this would have taken some decision making on an unconscious level). Or one could attempt to use the quantitative methods previously outlined, which might help to identify the major variables and weigh the alternatives. But neither approach will resolve the ethical (value) conflicts that will arise, and ethical considerations often determine the final disposition of a matter. Thus, the hypothetical librarian may have determined demands on the library's resources by "outsiders," the cost of providing the service, and an equitable fee (based on demand and cost); however, the basic question of "Should we?" has not yet been answered.

Among the qualitative questions to be answered are: Would creation of a fee service hurt the library's public relations? Would it hurt the public relations of the institution of which the library is a part? Would continuing free service lead to greater industrial support of the institution and the library? Would a fee service be contrary to public welfare? To whom is the library (publically supported) obligated to provide free service, and under what circumstances: Finally, does the library have any obligation at all to select, process, and house data bases that would be of primary interest to profit-making entities? Every answer involves a value judgment.

The literature on qualitative decision making is not as large as that on quantitative decision making, and most of it is derived from the disciplines of psychology, sociology, and philosophy. Dwight Waldo[5] defined *administration* as a cooperative human action marked by a high degree of rationality. He defines *rational action* as action that is taken to maximize the realization of goals. He also states that, since decisions contain, on the whole, more nonrational than rational factors, there is no way of making totally rational decisions at all times. Fred Rigby[6] suggests three components of input in decision making: (1) facts, opinions, and impressions based upon identifiable sources subject to the decision maker's conscious control; (2) Intuition/knowledge build up on past learning or experience, which cannot be analyzed particularly as to source or quality, and which can be only slightly controlled by the decision maker; and (3) biases composed of emotions and unconsciously assembled attitudes and values that are completely untouchable by the decision maker's conscious control.

Judgments, values, and valuing have always been of interest to philosophers. Most qualitative decisions involve value judgments, which are influenced by both linguistic and unconscious attitudes. Indeed, the words used to describe a situation may well call into play several sets of values and attitudes (words such as *good, bad, desirable, undesirable, likeable,* and *unlikeable,* for instance). Language inevitably calls up such judgemnts within us, even when we are totally unaware of it. We also know full well that no system can contain all the proper solutions for any setting at any one time, no matter how philosophically grand it may appear to be.

The move in the past 100 years has been away from a debate over whether a relativist or an absolutist approach is proper in ethical situations to a new emphasis on a *pluralistic approach,* which I think will produce more usable results. The advantage is that no universal standard is imposed on a situation; as a result, the pluralistic approach allows for a positive frame of reference in dealing with a problem.

Wayne A. R. Leys[7] has attempted to approach value-judgment decision making from a pluralistic nonquantifiable point of view. Leys suggests comparing a decision against several pairs of values in order to review all options and their consequences. The first pair is *harmony versus survival.* By *harmony* Leys means the plan's logic, its relation to the common good, orderliness, justice (Platonic), and its acceptability to the people involved. These concerns are contrasted to the effect on the organization's strength overall, on its various parts, on relationships among individuals and units, and on the system's ability to survive.

A second pair is *integrity versus loyalty.* This brings to the fore questions regarding a decision's impact on the decision maker's personal integrity, self-respect, and rationality (both as perceived by others and by the decision maker). The other side of the coin concerns the individual's relations with social and institutional units. Here the issues involve loyalty to the larger unit, the question of whether the proposed plan will adversely affect the larger unit, and the degree to which a tie-in should exist between institutional and general social goals. The problem of integrity is compounded by whether the decision maker is worried only about self-image and integrity, or whether the individual's self-concept has become inextricably entwined with the institution's image.

The third pair is *happiness versus lawfulness*. Happiness concerns the desirability of a solution overall, its effect on efficiency, its effect on the people involved and their morale, and its contribution to the entire unit as compared with the contribution of other possible solutions. Lawfulness involves precedents for actions, their effects on customs, possible conflict with legal restrictions (contracts, laws and rules), and the possible generation of problems concerning authority and responsibility.

To Leys' pairs, I would add a fourth: *obligation versus duty*. This pair is partly subsumed by both integrity/loyalty and happiness/lawfulness; however, duty is not legally based. As for duty and loyalty, although both imply a degree of voluntary cooperation, one can perform duty without any sense of loyalty. Here, duty implies that one has agreed to perform a series of functions for another group, but this is not legally enforceable. The questions focus on whether discharging a duty will alter the unit, either positively or negatively. The other term in the pair, *obligation*, carries sense of permissiveness, a situation wherein integrity and loyalty come into play. The usual way of incurring obligations is to accept a favor from someone who was under no compulsion to perform the service. The decision maker needs to know whether solutions will discharge obligations or create them, which plans will generate the fewest obligations for all parties concerned, and what kinds of obligations may be created by alternative solutions.

While these pairs may not cover everything, the paired approach can prove fruitful in many situations. The importance of choosing pairs that reflect and are related to the decision-making environment cannot be stressed too heavily, however. And it must be admitted that this approach would not solve the dilemma of whether to charge a fee for data base services to industry. It would, however, provide a safety check by bringing to mind points that may have otherwise been forgotten.

The search for mechanical aids and formulas to ensure consistently optimum decisions belongs in the same class as the search for the philosopher's stone. Methods that help bring unconscious factors to a conscious level should result in increasingly rational value judgments, but we are barely able to handle the problem of conscious and unconscious behavior. We may be able to objectively determine needs and goals, but motives remain another matter entirely. *Satisfaction* has yet to be precisely defined for anyone.

Practice in decision making is important. I have found that there is a significant improvement in the quality of decisions made by students after 3 or 4 weeks of practice with case studies. Improved quality in the sense that they review more alternatives, consider more factors, and see long-range implications more clearly. The main thing to remember is to avoid the "easy" decision—doing nothing. By reviewing and practicing the techniques outlined in this chapter, you will be able to make decisions more easily—decisions that will be better for being based on an analysis rather than on a feeling.

BIBLIOGRAPHY

1. D. Speich, "English Ruling, for Instance, UC Decisions Sometimes Just Seem to Happen," *Los Angeles Times* (Nov. 14, 1976), Pt. 1, p. 34.
2. C. H. Kepner, and B. B. Tregoe, *The Rational Manager* (New York: McGraw-Hill, 1965).
3. M. Hamburg, R. C. Clelland, M. R. W. Bommer, L. E. Romist, and R. H. Whitfield, *Library Planning and Decision-Making Systems* (Cambridge, Mass.: MIT Press, 1974), pp. 6–7.
4. M. Landau, "The Concept of Decision Making in the Field of Public Administration," in *Concepts and Issues in Administrative Behavior,* ed. by S. Mailick and H. Van Ness (Englewood Cliffs, N.J.: Prentice-Hall, 1962), p. 19.
5. D. Waldo, *Study of Public Administration* (New York: Doubleday, 1965), Chapter 1.
6. F. D. Rigby, "Heuristic Analysis of Decision Situations," in *Human Judgment and Optimality,* ed. by W. Shelby and L. Bryan (New York: Wiley, 1964).
7. W. A. R. Leys, "The Value Framework of Decision Making," in *Concepts and Issues in Administrative Behavior,* ed. by S. Mailick and H. VanNess (Englewood Cliffs, N.J.: Prentice-Hall, 1962).

FURTHER READING

Allutto, J. A., and Belasco, J. A. "A Typology of Participation in Organizational Decision-Making." *Administrative Science Quarterly* 17 (1972): 117–125.

AMACOM. *Organizational Dynamics—Managerial Decision-Making.* New York: American Managerial Association, 1973.

Arnold, J. D. *Make Up Your Mind! The Seven Building Blocks to Better Decisions.* New York: AMACOM, 1978.

Berlin, V. N. "Administrative Experimentation: A Methodology for More Rigorous 'Muddling Through'." *Management Science* 24 (1978): 789– 799.

Bernholz, P. "On the Reasons for the Influence of Interest Groups on Political Decision-making." *Zeitschrift für Wirtschafts und Sozial Wissenschaften* 94 (1974): 45–63.

Bobbitt, H. R., and Ford, J. D. "Decision-maker Choice as a Determinant of Organizational Structure." *Academy of Management Review* 5 (1980): 13–23.

Bommer, M. R. W. *Development of a Management System for Effective Decision Making and Planning in a University Library*. Philadelphia: Univ. of Pennsylvania Press, Wharton School of Finance and Commerce, 1972.

Bramson, R., and Parlette, N. "Methods of Data Collection for Decision Making." *Personnel Journal* 57 (1978): 243–249.

Bundy, M. L. "Decision-making in Libraries." *Illinois Libraries* 43 (1961): 780–793.

Burton, G. E., and Pathak, D. S. "Social Character and Group Decision Making." *SAM Advanced Management Journal* 43 (1978): 12–20.

Carnarius, S. E. *Management Problems and Solutions: A Guide to Problem Solving*. Reading, Mass.: Addison-Wesley, 1976.

Cook, K. K., and Greco, C. M. "The Ugly Duckling Acknowledged: Experimental Design for Decision-Making." *Journal of Academic Librarianship* 3 (1977): 23–28; 85–90.

Douglass, M. "How to Conquer Procrastination." *SAM Advanced Management Journal* 43 (1978): 40–50.

DuMont, R. R. "The Management of Public Libraries: The Tension Between Problem Solving and Purpose." *Southeastern Librarian* 28 (1978): 25–30.

Dyer, W. G. "When Is A Problem A Problem?" *Personnel Administration* 23 (1978): 66–71.

Elbing, A. *Behavioral Decisions In Organizations*. 2nd ed. Glenview, Ill.: Scott Foresman, 1978.

Fisher, D. W., and Keith, R. F. "Assessing the Development of the Decision Making Process: A Holistic Framework." *American Journal of Economics and Sociology* 36 (1977): 1–18.

Freeman, M., and Mulkowsky, G. "Implementation of Quantitative Techniques: A Managerial Perspective." *Management Review* 68 (1979): 51–54.

Hansen, J. V., McKell, L. H., and Heitger, L. E. "Decision-oriented Framework for Management Information Systems." *Information Processing and Management* 13 (1977): 214–225.

Heinritz, F. J. "Decision Tables: A Tool for Librarians." *Library Resources and Technical Services* 22 (1978): 42–46.

Heirs, B. J., and Pehrson, G. *The Mind of the Organization*. New York: Harper, 1977.

Heller, F. A., Drenth, P. J. D., Koopman, P., and Rus, V. "A Longitudinal Study in Participative Decision-making." *Human Relations* 30 (1977): 567–587.

Hughes, R. Y. "A Realistic Look at Decision Making." *Supervisory Management* 25 (1980): 2–8.

Kaplan, L. "On Decision Sharing In Libraries: How Much Do We Know?" *College and Research Libraries* 38 (1977): 25–31.

Keeney, R. L., and Raiffa, H. *Decisions With Multiple Objectives: Preferences and Value Tradeoffs*. New York: Wiley, 1976.

Kepner, C. H., and Tregoe, B. B. *The Rational Manager*. New York: McGraw-Hill, 1965.

Lamkin, B. "Decision-making Tools for Improved Libraary Operations." *Special Libraries* 56 (1965): 642–646.

Lloyd, I. "Don't Define the Problem." *Public Administration Review* 38 (1978): 282–286. (1978): 282–286.

Love, S. "Group Decisions Without Conflict." *CA Magazine* 109 (1976): 52–52.

McGiverin, R. "Decision Tree Analysis." *Pennsylvania Library Association Bulletin* 30 (1975): 11–12.

Martin, Merle P. "Decision Making: The Payoff Matrix." *Journal of Systems Management* 30 (1979): 14–18.

Martino, J. P., and Lenz, R. C., Jr. "Barriers to Use of Policy Relevant Information by Decision Makers." *Technological Forecasting and Social Change* 10 (1977): 381–400.

Miner, F. C., Jr. "A Comparative Analysis of Three Diverse Group Decision Making Approaches." *Academy of Management Journal* 22 (1979): 81–93.

Morano, R. A. "Managing Conflict for Problem-solving." *Personnel Journal* 55 (1976): 393–394.

O'Leary, R. *Interviewing for Decision Maker.* Chicago, Ill.: Nelson-Hall, 1976.

Olson, P. D. "The Overburdened Manager and Decision Making." *Business Horizons* 22 (1979): 28–32.

Oxenfeldt, A. R. *A Basic Approach to Executive Decision Making.* New York: AMACOM, 1978.

Radford, K. J. "Decision Making In a Turbulent Environment." *Journal of the Operational Research Society* 29 (1978): 677–682.

Rados, D. L. "Selection and Evaluation of Alternatives in Repetitive Decision-Making." *Administrative Science Quarterly* 17 (1972): 196–206.

Rappaport, A. *Information for Decision-making; Quantitative and Behavioral Dimensions.* 2nd ed. Englewood Cliffs, N.J.: Prentice-Hall, 1975.

Roach, J. M. "Simon Says: Decision Making Is A 'Satisficing' Experience." *Management Review* 68 (1979): 8–17.

Sherwood, J. J., and Hoylman, F. M. "Individual Versus Group Approaches to Decison Making." *Supervisory Management* 23 (1978): 2–9.

Simon, J. A. *The New Science of Management Decision.* Rev. ed. Englewood Cliffs, N.J.: Prentice-Hall, 1977.

Smart, C., and Vertinsky, I. "Designs for Crisis Decision Units." *Administrative Science Quarterly* 22 (1977): 640–657.

Snyder, M. B. "An Examination of Methods Used in a Study of Decision-Making." *ALA Bulletin* 61 (1967): 1319–1323.

Stimac, M. "A Model for Evaluation of Decision Passages: A Facet of Self-Assessment." *Personnel and Guidance Journal* 56 (1977): 158–163.

Thompson, A. A. "Employee Participation in Decision-Making." *Public Personnel Review* 28 (1967): 82–88.

Thompson, K., and Pitts, R. E. "The Supervisor's Survival Guide: Involving Your Staff in the Decision-making Process." *Supervisory Management* 24 (1979): 31–38.

Wheeler, D. H., and Janis, I. L. *A Practical Guide for Decision Making.* New York: Free Press, 1980.

White, D. J. *Fundamentals of Decision Theory.* New York: North Holland Pub., 1976.

Wilks, D. W. "An Introduction to Decision Making." *Management Services* 22 (1978): 54–55.

Wolfson, R. J., and Carroll, T. M. "Ignorance, Error and Information in the Classic Theory of Decision-making." *Behavioral Science* 21 (1976): 107–115.

8. Planning

Planning is a critical element in the success of any person or organization. Certainly luck, fate, chance, and random occurrence play a role at times in the lives of both individuals and organizations; but seldom, if ever, will people claim that their success is the result of pure luck. Plans always play a significant role in anything that is being accomplished. Yet, although few persons question the need for planning, it is surprising how few individuals and organizations really do plan.

Plans and planning obviously can take many forms, but there are, in general, two broad categories: short-range and long-range. Any plan that covers a period of up to 5 years is thought of as a short-range plan. Beyond 5 years, you are in the realm of long-range planning. Sometimes, though, government agencies such as libraries fail to engage in any true long-range planning, usually because they seem assured of a continuing future. Once established, government agencies, like committees of professional associations, seem to acquire a life of their own, and their existence is seldom, if ever, questioned. Recently, with various forms of tax revolts taking a heavy toll on library services, the assumptions of continued support have been proven invalid. Groups lacking realistic long-range plans have found themselves receiving less and less support. Libraries have been forced to make quick decisions regarding which services should be cut or reduced. Not infrequently, these quick decisions have had to be revised or reversed as libraries see the need to plan for long-term reductions in funding. In this chapter, we shall explore the issues and processes of planning that can guide and direct the library over both short-range and long-range planning.

NATURE OF PLANNING

The purpose of planning is to coordinate the library's activities in order to achieve previously established objectives. The only alternative to planning is random movement, which has only a slight chance of leading to unified or coordinated activity. Thus, planning must become pervasive in the library, because random activity is dysfunctional in nature. (Even if one unit's activities were functional on a random basis, they probably would be dysfunctional in relation to another unit's activities.)

Successful planning provides the proper direction for library activities, with the ideal situation being one in which all activities and all units work in a common direction. This ideal is rarely achieved. Normally, libraries (and other organizations) are fortunate when most units and activities move in one general direction specified by objectives. Planning, then, prevents the manager from falling into the trap of reacting to specific situations with long-term goals in mind—it provides a shape for the future.

At the same time, this concern for the future is one of the basic problems in planning. Most managers are either afraid to predict or they feel that data are inadequate, and so they refuse to take the risks involved in planning. But the bottom line remains the same—management must take responsibility for planning and shaping the future, and any manager who refuses to take such risks has abdicated managerial responsibility to the library and its employees.

Planning involves selecting facts and relating them to a number of assumptions concerning the future, all with a view toward visualizing and formulating a proposal outlining the activities necessary to achieve a desired result. There are several aspects involved in effective planning.

Planning includes personal and/or organizational identification. A plan specifies future actions and the individuals who are to undertake them. It identifies what is to be implemented, who is to implement it, and when. If a plan is not set forth in detail, it will become a meaningless abstraction.

Planning relates both to the present (relative certainty) and to the future (probable uncertainty). Because planning is undertaken in an effort to avoid some of the dangers of an uncertain future, the probability of certain events either happening or not happening becomes a critical factor. Using knowledge of both the past and the present, one may be able to predict to some degree what will happen in a similar situation in the future.

Planning is intellectual—it is a mental activity. This may be a primary problem for many libraries in countries that place a high premium on work, which usually is defined in physical terms. When people see no physical product or activity, they question whether work is actually taking place at all. Yet the real work of planning involves reflection, imagination, and foresight; only when a plan is fairly well formulated will it be put on paper, and thereby acquire the "appearance" of work. But always, in order to plan, one needs to visualize proposed patterns of activities, deal with many intangible variables, and combine these into a workable procedure.

Planning always involves the future. It is an attempt to anticipate difficulties and contingencies and to provide a procedure to be followed in the event that activities do indeed take place in the predicted manner.

Planning is a continuous activity that exists at *all* levels of the library. Even the worker who is not responsible for others must engage in some degree of planning. This is equally true for everyone who is above that person in the hierarchy. Even though a library depends on planning, the degree to which plans affect a library can be quite varied. One individual worker's plans may not have a major impact on the library, but the plans of someone who is in charge of public services can be critical to the library's success. Planning cannot be confined to one period of time during a year or simply used as a reaction to specific crises. It must incorporate new data and knowledge as they become available so that any plan will reflect reality as clearly as possible. Plans should *always* be subject to revision.

Planning is of such importance that it should be the first item of business in any new situation. Plans allow for control of a situation and provide a standard from which any deviation can be noted; identifying deviations from the norm is critical to controlling a situation and solving problems that arise. With proper planning, a manager can see the relationships among units, note factors and variables within the organization, and determine how best to use resources. Planning and control, then, are simply opposite sides of the same coin—if there is to be control, there must be planning.

As already noted, all levels within a library must plan to some degree. At the higher levels of management, plans are library-wide, very general, and tied to library objectives. At the lower levels, plans tend to be very narrow and tied specifically to one unit's objectives. Nevertheless, studies have shown that *all* successful supervisors at the lower levels are those who have the ability to plan and implement plans.[1] They are able to schedule their work within the limits set for them, they deal with problems in a logical, straightforward manner, and they use their time well. Because job satisfaction suffers when people cannot plan (when they feel that they are victims of uncontrolled activity), plans help both supervisors and subordinates.

Plans are usually judged on their efficiency in attaining an objective. One must consider not only the cost of implementing a plan but also the cost of developing it. The latter can sometimes be exceedingly high; both should be considered when assessing efficiency. In libraries, the cost of developing a plan may be easier to assess than the cost of implementing it. In technical services, unit costs and variables are easily recognized, but in public services, the definition of a work unit is more tenuous. Costs should, therefore, be calculated roughly rather than precisely, even though this can lead to inaccuracies in evaluating a plan.

If the person evaluating a particular plan had nothing to do with the development or implementation of that plan, and if cost criteria are imprecise, then the evaluator cannot fully understand the situation. The use of outside consultants frequently leads to this type of problem. The consultant may have the theory down but may have little practical experience. Consequently, a worker may be judged inefficient when the knowledge and data available for the evaluation are imprecise. This often leads to hostility toward the evaluator, especially if the plan formulator has given no input in the evaluation. This is not to say that the formulator should evaluate the implementation of the plan, but that person should definitely have input. (The persons who implement a plan should not evaluate it either, but they should have input.)

The evaluator needs a solid working knowledge of the area, as well as work experience in the area being evaluated. Only through careful evaluation of plans as to their efficiency, costs, and benefits can improved performance come about. This evaluation is part of the control process that every manager must undertake.

TYPES OF PLANS

Several types of plans are necessary in the library: (1) objectives, (2) policies, (3) procedures, (4) rules, (5) programs, and (6) budgets. Each of these will be discussed, although budgets will be covered more extensively in Chapter 14. Two additional types of plans—grand and competitive strategies—will be discussed briefly. The question of *change* will also be discussed, because planning implies change and the means by which change can be made more acceptable.

Objectives

Planning objectives is the basis for any library operation. In fact, some
writers, such as Peter Drucker, in *Management* (1974), hold the planning
of objectives to be *the* major factor in successful management. It should
be notes that the terminology regarding this concept is rather confusing.
The words *missions, goals, targets, objectives,* and *purposes* are used by
various writers to mean the same thing. Each term can be and has been
used—sometimes with strictly defined distinctions and sometimes interchangeably—to describe where a library is going and what it is doing
over a period of time. In one publication, the authors proposed a hierarchy of concepts: from mission to goal to objective to activity.[2] This may,
in time, reflect reality, but currently, such a hierarchy can be seen only as
a theoretical construct. The present reality is that terminology is imprecise at best. In this book, then, the word *objective* has been chosen
because of its relative familiarity through the concept of management by
objectives (MBO).

A library's basic objectives must be determined even before it comes
into existence as a corporate body. A library first exists in the minds of a
number of people who feel that it would be a good thing to have. Once
they decide to actually form a library, they must formulate a list of goals
that they hope the library will accomplish. If each person formulates a
list, it is likely that the lists will differ in many respects and that only a few
similarities will emerge, depending on individual value systems. It will be
necessary to resolve the differences so as to arrive at a list of common
desires and accomplishments. At this point, a label can be applied to the
list—*purposes, objectives, goals,* or *missions.* In this text, the label will be
objectives.

A danger during this developmental stage is that of locking the library
into too rigid a structure, thereby making it difficult to modify the objectives. If objectives are spelled out in too much detail, the organization will
be unable to respond to changes in social needs and in its environment.
The objectives and the social needs that are to be met by a library should
be continually examined. Because of this, planners find themselves in the
dilemma of developing objectives that are both general and specific
(without being constricting). For instance, a library objective might be to
"provide community service." This allows for flexibility in response to a
changing environment; however, it is so broad as to potentially include
any and all community services, which is very unrealistic. A better objective might be to supply the community's need for reading material (this
has been a basic goal for many libraries). Even better, though, would be a

commitment to supply the community's information needs, regardless of format. This is radical revision of the concept of the traditional library, but it reflects the reality of information storage and builds flexibility into the library.

Objectives must be prepared at two levels. One level is the library-wide level; the other is the unit or departmental level. Objectives prepared at the former level are more general and long-range in nature; the latter are more specific and deal with the day-to-day realities of the unit's contribution to the achievement of the library's overall objectives. The connection between unit objectives and library objectives must be clear, and, if a conflict arises, the library's objectives must take precedence over what the unit perceives to be its own best interests. Even so, unit objectives occasionally dominate a library.

In an acquisitions department, several objectives that do not conflict with the library's objectives may have been established: consider all media for acquisition, provide a wide coverage of subjects, process an order within 8 working hours, and process invoices within 16 working hours. Even though these are unit objectives, they have been implemented with the overall library objectives in mind. If, however, an objective stated that no book would be ordered until it had been favorably reviewed in three journals, this could well conflict with the overall library goal of providing information as quickly as possible. If such a situation were allowed to persist, it could be very hard to resolve. But such situations do exist when no one is immediately aware of a conflict; the unit may simply not have informed a supervising unit that a specific objective had been established, and the unit may not have examined its decision in terms of the overall objectives of the library.

Many libraries (especially public libraries) and other social service organizations concern themselves with social responsibility, which puts them in a somewhat unusual position—a position not shared by a great many other organizations. Changes will be made in a library's basic objectives as its social environment changes. The problem for the library is knowing how and when to respond to which social changes—a problem that is compounded by great demands being made on limited resources. Once again, we are reminded that the basic concept of management involves the interaction of three often conflicting factors: people, organizations, and the environment.

It thus becomes the library's (and its governing board's) responsibility to assess the various demands and to arrive at a reasonable decision as to the changes that will take place within the library. Libraries have made many false starts and some successful starts in dealing with this problem, but they always face the fact of conflicting demands on limited resources, which limits the number of and the depth to which needs can be satisfied.

General guidelines can be employed in generating objectives; they will give an indication of how to formulate objectives, but they won't give an indication of how to choose from among them. An objective ought to represent hopes and desires, but only those that are attainable. Completely unrealistic objectives will be ignored at best; at worst, they will lead to dissatisfaction, frustration, and perhaps even bitterness on the part of both staff and patrons. Idealism may well be reflected in objectives, so as to give people something to strive for, but not set up impossible demands. For example, no library can hope to supply *all* of a community's information needs—that would entail, among other things, supplying a newspaper, a radio, a T.V. set, books, films, video discs and tapes, etc., to everyone in the community. An announcement that a library will seek to do this will lead to great expectations on the part of patrons, even though those expectations can never be met.

Objectives, in addition to being attainable, should give some indication of how they are to be met. It is somewhat surprising that, even though this is extremely important, it is frequently overlooked. Serving "the public good" or the "community's information needs" sounds good, but how is either one to be done? If an objective is at all quantifiable, planners and those who are to implement the procedure(s) will be able to determine their level of performance. Even if a substitute measure is adopted, the formulation will provide some guidance.

In libraries, because so much of performance evaluation of both organization and staff depends on stated objectives, unclear or imprecise objectives can cause very real problems. Like many other organizations, libraries tend to state their objectives too broadly rather than state them as measurable objectives. One study concluded, "In analyzing recorded objectives of public and university libraries, we found that these objectives were not sufficiently explicit to be of direct assistance to management in planning and decision making for libraries. The sort of finding occurs in management science analysis of virtually every large-scale organization or system."[3]

An example of a very clear library objective would be to provide a service point or an information outlet within 2 miles of every community resident. This would *not* commit the library to meeting all information needs, but only to providing service points (not necessarily buildings, but mobile units, portable kiosks, etc.) that would blanket the community. Another measurable objective might be to provide service to 100% of the English-speaking population, 75% of the Spanish-speaking population,

75% of the Chinese-speaking population, and so forth, by a certain date. The objective could also specify the distance that a patron would have to travel in order to gain access to materials on a citywide basis. This type of formulation would enable everyone to know what the organization's direction is and how it expects to achieve its goals.

Objectives must be compatible with one another. A library often finds itself developing a series of objectives over a period of time, and then modifying them as the community changes or as the library sees the need and opportunity for change. The difficulty is that every time an objective is revised or added, every other objective must be reviewed in order to eliminate incompatibiliites. Strange as it may seem, it is perfectly possible for one unit to operate on the basis of one objective while another unit operates on the basis of a completely different objective. Academic libraries are especially susceptible to this, as many of them have twin objectives: serving undergraduate needs and supplying the research needs of graduate students and faculty. The incompatibility arises from the undergraduates' need for multiple copies of heavily used materials (such as term papers and class research projects) and the advanced researchers' need for specialized, esoteric materials. (In some academic libraries, as much as 50% of the book stock is seldom, if ever, used.) School and public libraries also face this difficulty of conflicting patron claims on resources. Special libraries are perhaps unique, because their clientele are quite specific and homogeneous, and, as a result, there is less likelihood of incompatible objectives being generated.

A library needs both long-range and short-range objectives. This becomes particularly evident when one examines a situation in which only short-range objectives have been developed. As one short-range objective is achieved, a new short-range objective is likely to be formulated. Although short-term objectives may proceed logically from one to another, without long-range planning their net effect is to take the library nowhere.

Long-range objectives are those that cover a period of 5 or more years and give coherence to short-range objectives, which themselves may cover a period of only 6 months to 1 year. Long-range goals are necessarily less specific, because they concern themselves with what will happen toward the end of the time period covered (5–10 years is not uncommon). Short-range objectives are quite specific, but they must always be formulated with long-range objectives in mind, because long-range objectives provide direction.

Obviously, objectives must be communicated to all those who will be affected by them—in the case of libraries, they must be communicated to both staff and patrons. The premises and assumptions on which objectives are based, and the logical processes used to formulate them, also should be explained. It would be reasonable and sensible for everyone affected in the library and community to have some input into the selection of objectives. Certainly, generating them in isolation and presenting them in final form dispels any feelings of participation. A clear understanding of both the objectives and the process by which they were formulated aids in building trust in and enthusiasm for those objectives. As always, there must be a concern for people and for the ways in which managerial actions will affect them.

As noted at the beginning of this section, some management experts believe that formulating objectives is critical to all other management activitis. Management by objectives (MBO), while a specific concept, has become a catch phrase, and many organizations and persons talk about, or even attempt to use, some form of MBO. Unfortunately, such efforts are all too often based on only a partical understanding of the concept. In libraries especially, MBO whould be used very cautiously. An excellent analysis of MBO and libraries, by James Michalko,[4] concludes with a statement about the utility of MBO in the library:

> Having seen that the nature of library objectives does not bar the use of MBO, can this approach be recommended for the library? We think such a blanket recommendation is unwise. Our examination of MBO's foundations and of research into MBO has not yielded a clear-cut decision about the validity of MBO claims. . . . Structural considerations would restrict MBO to certain organizational levels and functional areas of the library. . . . In terms of organizational levels MBO will be restricted to middle management (section and department heads) of the library. . . .
>
> Management by objectives in the library is a limited approach. Improved performance is related to the system only in an uncertain tenuous way. The improvement in planning, control, and flexibility that accrue directly to the formal MBO process may be attainable through less formal examination of the organization's activities.

My own experience as a library management consultant supports this very cautious assessment of the value of MBO. I have also found that the time required for even a modified MBO program is disproportionately large in comparison to the benefits gained. Therefore, although objectives are essenial to the successful operation of a library, MBO cannot, at this time, be considered central to library management.

Policies

Policies are general statements or understandings used to guide and channel the *thinking* of subordinates in making decision. Policies specify the limits within which a decision is to be made. Clearly, a policy must be consistent with library objectives, because policies help to direct actions that are intended to achieve objectives. Policies, then, are a matter of day-to-day routines.

Policy making is not normally confined to top management; it exists at all levels in the library. A supervisor may allow subordinates to implement a policy so long as it does not conflict with overall library policy. For instance, library policy may dictate that no purchase order for more than $100 may be placed without the director's approval, while an acquisitions policy may specify that no book order over $50 may be placed without the approval of the head of acquisitions. Examples of this type occur continually, which illustrates the fact that most major policies produce minor spin-off policies. The larger the organization, the more numerous the minor policies.

Actually, there are several types of policies: originated, appealed, implied, and imposed. Libraries must deal with all four types.

An *originated policy* is the type of policy that libraries should attempt to generate. Such a policy is one that comes from top levels of management and concerns major, basic issues. This is reasonable in that top management is best able to see the overall structure of the library and the direction that the library should be taking. The more policies that can be generated this way, the better off the library will be, because specific direction is established and everyone knows what to do and why. Also, a solid body of originated policy allows subordinates to create minor policies that are consistent both with policies in other units and with the library's objectives as a whole. The chief danger in generating policy is that it can be so tightly written that policy may become the rule rather than the guide to thinking that it should be.

Appealed policy develops in a situation wherein there is no actual policy. This might arise when someone does not know what to do in a particular situation, or when someone interprets existing policy with too much or too little latitude. The need for clarification becomes evident, so the person goes to the next level decision maker. If that person finds the situation to be too nebulous for a firm decision, then the problem is passed around or up the hierarchy. When this happens, time is wasted, differences of opinion become entrenched in the absence of clarity, and the likelihood of reaching a decision that pleases everyone decreases dramatically. In a more successful library, appealed policy does not occur often, but it does arise. Since there exists little hope of stopping appealed policy making completely, the next best thing is to keep it to a minimum. The way to avoid appealed policy is to spend time developing originated policies that are clear enough to preclude the need for appeal and clarification.

Implied policy is the most dangerous way to function. It arises from the staff's or the patron's perception of a policy, regardless of whether or not the perceived policy contradicts the actual policy. Top administrators usually function as though stated policy is being carried out; however, on the operational level, people may well be operating on the basis of implied policy. Libraries are just as susceptible to this as any other organization. For example, the library objective may be to provide the client with materials as quickly as possible, but certain operations in technical services seem to slow down delivery. The policy that is implied operationally is that perfection outweighs speed, even though stated policy is the reverse.

Difficulty with implied policy frequently arises in the area of promotions and advancement. Stated policy may be to promote from within, but if staffers see a number of important positions filled by outsiders, they may (perhaps correctly) assume that the actual policy differs from the stated policy. Morale problems can easily result. In some cases, implied policy comes about when a manager is unwilling or unable to enforce a stated policy. More often than not, however, implied policy comes into play when there is no real policy. People merely operate as if they know what policy is, but they have gained their ideas only by observing the behavior of others, not by asking questions. This can be quite embarrassing, expecially in a large library, when each of several units generates an independent implied policy with regard to the same situation. At such a point, implied policy is likely become appealed policy, because someone will get tired of operating in a vacuum or under contradictory policies. This in turn means little likelihood of a satisfactory resolution, because implied policy has been given legitimacy through custom.

Recently libraries have had to deal with *externally imposed policy*. A certain amount of this pressure has come from the fact that most libraries are part of a governmental unit, and are therefore subject to non-library-imposed policies regarding personnel, promotion, retirement, and other matters.

Other factors have been coming into play recently, however, only to complicate the situation even further. For instance, if a library staff unionizes, this will affect several areas—promotion may be given only on the basis of seniority, not ability, for instance. National governments also can impose policy, especially if they are a primary source of funding for the library. (The library could refuse funds in order to avoid restrictions, but most libraries simply cannot afford to turn down funds, so they comply with national, state, or provincial regulations.)

When a library becomes a government documents depository, certain conditions must be met as to the use and preservation of the materials. If these policies are not entirely in line with existing library policies regarding the remainder of the collection, the two sets of policies must be brought into agreement as much as possible. Sometimes, though, the library must operate with conflicting policies, letting the type of material involved dictate which policy will prevail in a given situation. A similar problem might occur when the donor of a large collection wishes to impose policies regarding the use, housing, and staffing patterns of that collection. This usually occurs only in large public or academic libraries, and they often acquiesce because of the great value of the material being offered, even if conditions are highly restrictive.

A few fundamental rules and suggestions apply to policy making, regardless of the level at which it occurs. You should never delegate authority to a staff member without providing some policy guidelines. Granting authority without providing direction regarding its use can be dangerous, and it simply does not make good sense. An up-to-date policy manual is essential if everyone is to know what is and what is not policy. It is surprising how few libraries have policy manuals, and few manuals are up to date. Policies should clearly reflect objectives, and therefore the rationale behind a policy should always be evident to employees and patrons.

Policies should be consistent. In libraries, service policies can easily become inconsistent within themselves and with the overall policies and objectives of the library. Efforts at coordination in such cases often result in rules; this needs to be avoided. While policies need to be consistent, they also must be flexible. They must allow room for decision making. As environment and needs change, policies must change. This implies that policies need to be controlled and continually reviewed for obsolescence and for areas demanding new or altered policies. If people consistently operate under a policy in ways that seem diametrically opposed to that policy, perhaps it should be eliminated.

Finally, policies must be taught. They cannot simply be disseminated in a policy manual without an explanation. New personnel especially should be acquainted with policies—the goals and the reasons for them—and they should be given a chance to discuss their interpretations of policies. In this way, clear understandings are established at the outset, which should help to reduce potential problems (if not eliminate them).

Procedures

Procedures are guides to *action* rather than thought. They provide a chronological sequence of events that may be used to achieve a specific policy and objective. Procedures are *not* policies, but they occur within the framework of policy. Planning good procedures consists of a number of features.

Keep procedures to a minimum. Long lists of procedures that detail every action stifle initiative and individuality and induce boredom. Failure to limit the number of procedures can lead to a morale problem, which often becomes a staffing problem, which finally develops into a full-blown production problem. Since procedures are rather easy to develop, once one gets the knack of it, some people fall in love with doing just that—they "procedurize" everything in sight. And, in the process, they create a deadly atmosphere for the worker, who must follow steps A, B, C, D, ad nauseam. This is bad management.

Procedures must be designed to serve a useful purpose. Libraries often retain procedures that have outlived their usefulness simply because no one thinks of discarding them. Also, procedures are sometimes developed with no true goal in mind; they seem to have a relation to the job, but this is not always true. The key question to ask is, are procedures planned or do they merely reflect practice? If they reflect actual practice, they may be true plans, but they could be carry-overs from activities involving objectives that no longer exist. Analyzing procedures carefully is the duty of every manager.

Careful examination of existing procedures may result in eliminating some while still being able to carry out the same basic task. Such an examination involves techniques of work analysis. It is not necessary to hire an outside consultant for this. Supervisors generate procedures and know what purposes are being served. Consequently, they can analyze procedures on a day-to-day basis, which can make operations more effective and efficient. When the analysis is done, procedures will be seen as a system, as part of a series of interrelated activities (both within themselves and within other procedures). A change in one procedure may effect changes in other procedures. Recognizing that all procedures are part of a system is essential if one is to analyze them with a view toward creating an effective work atmosphere.

Costs of procedures can be estimated in terms of time (if not in terms of money). Naturally, certain costs cannot be measured—such as patron frustration with a new procedure. But it might be possible to estimate the amount of time saved or lost in gaining requested information once a new procedure is implemented. The precise validity of the cost figure is not the issue. The purpose is to provide the person who is responsible for decision making with a better idea of what a procedure will cost the system.

As with other planning activities, procedures must be controlled. One form of this control is the development of a procedures manual. The procedures manual is one of the first things a new employee should be given. Libraries tend to produce procedures manuals more than policy manuals, because procedures are easier to identify and update than are policies. However, I would be surprised if more than 50% of libraries have good, current procedures manuals available for most of the activities that they carry out. Procedures manuals must be revised on the basis of past performance and in light of the changing needs of a department or an organization. If policies and objectives change, procedures must certainly be reexamined.

If you have clear policies to guide (and promote) good thinking and good procedures to guide actions (yet allow individual initiative), then you have created a favorable work environment. Procedures should be based on an adequate knowledge of the library—its objectives, policies, physical facilities, and personnel—and of the actual work area. The supervisor's problem is to maintain the proper balance of stability, consistency, and flexibility in procedures so that the staff is able to work effectively.

Rules

Rules are precise statements regarding specific and definite actions to be taken (or not to be taken) in a specific situation. Whereas procedures guide actions and policies guide thinking, rules *require* that a specified action be taken in a specified situation. Rules must be written out clearly and taught in the same manner that policies and procedures are taught. (There should be *no* unwritten rules, as they can create only trouble and misunderstandings.)

Most libraries inform new employees of rules only after hiring them. It would be better if these rules were discussed *before* a person decided to accept a position. In that way, the person would know in advance of any rules that might cause personal discomfort (for instance, a library's rules regarding employees' attire).

As Fayol noted, rules must be enforced evenly. A library rule may dictate that an employee who has been absent a certain number of times without notifying the supervisor must be laid off without pay for a certain time period. Such a rule should be enforced for everyone—administrator, clerk, part-time assistant, and librarian. All too often, rules that make no distinction between professional, nonprofessional, administrative, and part-time employees are enforced unevenly; this can cause a drop in morale.

The good supervisor will see to it that rules are kept to a minimum and enforced evenly.

Programs

The term *program* is commonly used to identify a relatively large undertaking, although George Terry has supplied a more extended definition: "A comprehensive plan that includes future use of different resources in an integrated pattern and establishes a sequence of required actions and time schedules for each in order to achieve the stated objectives."[5] Programs are made up of policies, procedures, rules, job allocations, resource requirements, sources of resources, and other elements necessary to carry out a combination of objectives.

A library's program for a new public-service activity would include a set of policies to guide staff thinking regarding the new project, procedures by which to carry out the actions, necessary rules, and personnel requirements (both in terms of special skills and the frequency with which those skills will be called upon). The following would be identified: personnel requirements, the proportion of time and staff (old and new) to be employed in the program, and the types of knowledge and skills the staff must possess. (This is over and above identifying the full-time equivalent staff needed for the project.) Also, the program would include information regarding any special equipment or resources that might be needed.

Not every program necessarily includes all these elements, but anything labeled as a program should include a large number of them. Programs should outline actions to be taken (and when, where, and by whom). They should also indicate why those actions are needed and how they fit into the library's existing set of objectives. Also, programs need not be library-wide; they can be limited to a single department (for example, an acquisitions department program to increase purchases of Spanish-language materials).

Whether it is for a unit or for the library, any large-scale program will require that a number of subprograms be developed in order to accomplish the overall program. This may mean organizing a fund-raising effort to buy special equipment or hiring someone with a strong second-language background to implement second-language acquisitions and programs.

When managers think of policies, procedures, rules, and objectives as part of a system, they are better able to identify and isolate variables that might be affected by a new program or by changes in an old program. This is because the program itself ties together a wide range of things usually thought of as being independent. The manager who fails to consider the entire system and the interrelationships of the parts may well end up calling in an outside consultant to help sort them out.

Budgets

Budgets are simply plans of action expressed in terms of cost. These costs may be expressed in monetary terms, machine-hours, or a combination of these two. Budgets are simply *estimates* of what management thinks it will cost to carry out a plan of operation during a specified period of time, which can vary from a few days to many years. Generally, however, the fiscal budget covers 1 year. Budgets that concern man-hours or machine-hours are used to analyze costs before a plan is implemented; these usually cover a short period of time.

Many people do not think of budgets as plans; however, because they can be used as control devices, they are legitimately called plans. The budget estimate comes before any action occurs, it is the basis upon which money and resources are acquired and personnel are hired to carry out established programs.

Financial budgets are usually concerned with two types of costs: (1) operational expenses (which, in a library, include most general expenses), and (2) capital expenses, or capital outlay (which cover equipment and physical facility costs). In the case of major capital outlay (such as for a new building or data processing equipment), a long-range fiscal plan must be developed, and the librarian must become concerned with securing much of the financing. The fact that the time interval between the decision to build a new facility and the actual beginning of construction may be 5 to 6 years indicates the necessity of advance planning. The discussion of budgets in Chapter 14 will explain why library budgets can be and should be considered plans.

Strategies

The term *strategy* is employed rather loosely in the business world. It has been defined as "the process of deciding on objectives of the organization, on changes in these objectives, on resources used to attain these objectives and on the policies that are to govern the acquisition, the use and disposition of these resources"[6] Strategies tend to be concerned with an organization's viability and its position vis-à-vis other organizations. They provide a framework in which to place objectives.

Grand strategies and competitive strategies are the two types usually discussed (see any general management textbook). Grand strategies are often taken as super-programs, but it is more realistic to think of them as a separate type of plan, because they encompass all the organization's objectives. Thus, a grand strategy is one that ties together all the objectives, policies, procedures, rules, and budgets into a single plan. Competitive strategies are concerned with the organization's position in relation to other organizations of a like kind. In general, a competitive strategy is a plan designed to enhance the position of the organization vis-à-vis other like organizations.

Libraries *do* engage in competitive activities, although few librarians would really want to admit this. Libraries definitely compete as they grow and develop, because they are always in competition for financial resources. Librarians should freely admit this and go on from there. By honestly recognizing that they are in a competitive situation, they can deal much more effectively in a competitive way. Also, this might help bring about recognition of some of the unvoiced (but very real) barriers that are present in cooperative efforts; such recognition may help to dissolve those barriers.

WHY PLAN?

The underlying assumption in the preceding discussion has been that planning is necessary. Some reasons for planning were presented in the section on the nature of planning. Yet, a number of other factors explain why planning is so vital to a library's success.

Planning saves time. Obviously, time is a critical factor in any job, as both developing plans and carrying out activities do take time—often a great deal of time. Librarians often find themselves in the dilemma of not having enough time to both do their job and plan: something always seems to be shortchanged under the pressure to do everything. The key to success in this area is to include in the original plan enough time for further planning along the way.

Planning is the only way to combat uncertainty and to accommodate environmental changes. Many librarians are willing to sit back and wait for lightning to strike before they move; this is a good way to destroy an effective library. When librarians fail to examine their operations and to plan for some of the more obvious problems that can develop, they spend a lot of time fighting management brushfires—imposing adaptive solutions or handling problems of appealed policy, thus contributing to staff uncertainty. An environment in which social, political, economic, and other pressures fluctuate unpredictably requires that libraries plan well in order to maintain themselves as stable organizations.

In the mid- and late-1960s, American libraries were very optimistic about their situation. Money was readily available, and it looked for a while as though everything would continue to expand and improve. No real thought was given to alternative futures, despite the fact that inflation was spiraling, politics were becoming increasingly volatile, and the social situation was becoming increasingly complex. Few librarians thought much about what these factors might mean to libraries. (For example, library schools and librarians continued to use American Library Association manpower need projections long after it was clear that these did not reflect reality.) So, when government funds were cut or kept at the same level year after year, service hours were reduced and staff were laid off or were not replaced. In essence, shock waves reverberated throughout librarianship; yet the shock need not have been so great. Efforts to carry out long-range planning and investigations of alternative futures (good and bad) and social indicators would have saved a great deal of heartache for everyone. When planning, consider *all* environmental factors and consider both good and bad possibilities.

When it is done properly, planning focuses attention on the long run rather than on the short run and requires constant attention to library objectives. As librarians continually examine library objectives, the objectives will probably be revised to reflect current needs (and revised again as those needs change). Without continually reexamining objectives, a library faces the possibility that its "real work"—its day-to-day operations—will come to dominate the organization at the expense of its long-range objectives. Staff members need to be reminded that a reexamination of objectives does not threaten the library's ability to perform its activities; on the contrary, it enhances the library's ability to serve its community and to respond to change.

A TIME SCALE FOR PLANNING

As has been pointed out, time is critical to successful planning. The following paragraphs give a rough indication of how much time might be consumed in various aspects of planning. Sometimes, though, it will be necessary to move more quickly than these estimates would indicate; however, in general, the suggestions represent minimum times. On the basis of my extensive library management consulting and library work experience, I have formulated Evans' Law of Library Planning, which states that "the greater the costs of a plan, the greater the number of approvals required, and the longer the period of time between development and implementation." This is especially true in publicly supported institutions. Failure to recognize this fact and work with it will lead to anger and frustration. (Occasionally, it can lead to the dismissal of a librarian who pushes too hard too soon.) In any event, the suggested times are fairly typical, although they can increase or decrease as the situation requires.

For office supplies, it is wise to plan 6 months ahead. For easily available material, 3 months might be adequate; but remember, the more often you order pens, pencils, paper clips, and rubber bands, the more time is taken from other activities. Monthly orders mean ordering 12 times; ordering every 6 months means only two orders a year (and typing time will not be much more for an order covering 6 months than it would be for an order covering 1 month).

"Special order" items should be ordered in amounts adequate for 6 months or 1 year, preferably the latter. These might include special charge cards, IBM cards, book plates, and any number of things manufactured or printed by commercial sources (and often custom-made for a particular library).

Operating-expense budgets must be planned at least 1 year in advance. Because libraries must go to external bodies for funds, the library staff must first agree on what is needed and how resources are to be allocated. The budget must be approved both by the library's governing board and by the funding agency. And all this takes time.

A capital-outlay budget will probably require 1 year to 18 months, especially if major capital commitments are to be made. It takes longer than the operating-expense budget because there is usually more money involved and because the funding agency may require more detailed information and examine the request more closely.

When requesting a new position, plan 2 years in advance. The library staff needs to agree on what positions are needed, which may take a long time. Then the funding group needs to be convinced of the need, because this involves an increase in the budget as well as a long-term commitment. Once the position is approved, the process of searching for and interviewing candidates must be completed, and this may take several months.

Large capital-outlay items, such as bookmobiles and electronic data processing (EDP), require somewhere between 24 and 30 months. First, the funding agency must be convinced of the need. Then, because such equipment is usually custom-designed for each library that orders it, there will be a time lapse between letting the contract and actually having the equipment available for the library's use.

New service programs take between 36 and 40 months to come into being. Here, the problem involves not only designing the new program but also checking its compatibility with the entire library's operations—its objectives, policies, procedures, rules, and so forth. These activities will take time; they are more complex than they might first appear to be. Next comes the inevitable trip to the funding authority, which has the job of allocating limited resources to seemingly unlimited areas of demand. If funding is made available, then contracts must be let for equipment and staff must be hired (or retrained). To do all this in less than 3 years would place inordinate demands on the time and energy of people whose primary duties probably lie elsewhere; and the program would probably barely function if these activities were done too quickly.

When the library is faced with constructing a new physical facility, at least 5 years will pass before actual construction begins. Remember Evans' Law of Library Planning, because it comes into play here more overtly than it does anywhere else. Monetary amounts are always large in this area, and costs continually rise, so it would be nice to shorten the planning process as much as possible. However, 5 years seems to be the minimum span of time between making the initial request and moving into the facility. A study I did in 1971 of 350 new library building projects showed that the average time from the first request to the date of occupancy of the new building was 8.35 years.

PLANNING MEANS CHANGE

Any plan involves change in the existing situation. Because people prefer the status quo, they often resist change—sometimes passively, sometimes actively. Amitai Etzioni has written an article entitled "Human Beings Are Not Very Easy to Change After All: An Unjoyful Message and Its Implications for Social Programs." In it, he notes two basic approaches to change. One approach is based on the belief that people can be taught to change their habits; the other is based on the belief that people will change only in response to changes in their environment. Almost all programs presently existing in the area of social change operate on the basis of the first assumption—people are seen as pliable and amenable to suggestions to change when they are shown how much better off they will be as a result of the change. Etzioni discussed the ongoing campaign against smoking, which is based on precisely this assumption. A slight decrease in the number of smokers was noted in the late 1960s, but the 1970s saw a reverse in that trend, and numbers are greater than ever:

The moral: If you spend 27 million dollars you may get enough people to switch from Camels to Kools to make an investment worthwhile for the Kools manufacturers. However, if the same $27 million is used to make nonsmokers out of smokers, that is to

try to change a basic habit, no significant effect is to be expected. Advertising teases
appetities, but it does not change basic tastes, values, or preferences. Try to advertise
desegration to racists, world government to chauvinists, temperance to alcoholics, or,
as we will do at the cost of 16 million dollars a year, drug abstention to addicts and see
how far you get.[7]

Etzioni further cites automobile driving safety programs as he tries to
demonstrate that it is easier to change environments than it is to change
people. He contends that an all-out effort to force redesign of auto-
mobiles to make them safer would have been much more effective than
campaigns to promote defensive driving. And it would have been less
expensive. He also describes a study of work behavior in which he concluded that it was difficult, and almost unethical, to change work patterns (that is, attitudes and behavior patterns rather than basic work
procedures).

The outlook for convincing people to freely embrace change, then,
looks rather gloomy, if one accepts Etzioni's analysis. And, unfortunately,
he seems to be correct to a large degree. It is easier to change an environment than it is to change the people in it. But it must be remembered that
those same people will become involved in changes in their environment
as soon as they begin. If they do not want the environment to change,
they will fight any attempts to change that environment just as hard and
effectively as they would fight attempts to change their personal lives.
However, in a work situation, the manager is generally not concerned
with changing staff members' personal habits, unless they adversely affect the work situation (for example, being late or being careless). If the
problem is a personal habit, ultimately the issue is resolved by dismissing
the person from the environment rather than by attempting to change
the habit. Normally, this takes place only after the person has had several
opportunities to "correct" the behavior.

MAKING CHANGE ACCEPTABLE

Despite the rather dark picture painted by Etzioni, you as a manager
can do a number of things to make change more acceptable in the library.
Explain the prospective change to your staff well in advance of implementing it. Give them a complete explanation for the change; if they fully
understand what is involved, they may more readily accept the change
and adapt. Whenever possible, allow those who will be affected by the
change to have input in the planning process. Not only do they have a
right to be consulted but they also have information that could be critical

to the success of the change. Externally imposed change usually takes a long time to be accepted (if it is accepted at all).

If a change will affect job security, say so from the outset; do not try to hide the fact. Rumor is always a factor in any work situation, and, if employees imagine that their jobs are threatened, high anxiety will result. Trying to convince people of their own security in the midst of upheaval may not always work, but once a manager is perceived as being sneaky or dishonest concerning change, that person may never regain the confidence of subordinates. If positions are threatened, make that very clear; if they are not threatened, explain that as well.

If you can demonstrate that a change resulted from the application of previously established principles, data, and decisions—rather than from your personal whim—then the staff is more likely to accept the change.

If a series of changes lies ahead, incorporate the changes into the system gradually. Do not force a myriad of changes on the staff; handling one or two changes simultaneously is more than enough. A frequent temptation when moving into a new work area is to seize the chance to change operations as well (because of either more or less available space). This is a poor idea! Staff members usually need a month or two to adjust to the physical change, and this interferes dramatically with their ability to adjust to operational changes (even if they thought they wanted the change).

Whenever possible, if a new approach has not worked out, wait one or two months before suggesting yet another one. The staff will be skeptical of any new attempt, and they may unconsciously put less effort into implementing another new plan. The more problems there have been with changes, the more breathing time there should be between changes. Never present a change as an experiments. Experiments should be conducted on a small scale with a limited number of people, never on a unitwide basis. If the staff considers a change to be an experiment, they may not take the change seriously, hence the chance of its failure is greater.

When you can clearly demonstrate that a change will benefit the staff, it is more likely to be accepted. A common mistake when identifying the advantages of a change is to confuse library or management gains with staff gains. Staff members know the difference, though, and if understanding or trust of management is poor, they may suspect that an attempt is being made to fool them. Even if relations between staff and management have been good, such a presentation will cause the staff to wonder "what is really going on."

If you establish an environment in which change is welcomed and new ideas are encouraged, then staff will be much more likely and willing to accept change. This means welcoming staff ideas, discussing new approaches to problems found in the literature, asking for reactions, and soliciting new ideas. In essence, this means training the unit's staff to view change as an opportunity rather than a threat.

Planning is designed to help control the uncertainties of the future and to provide concrete directions for the day-to-day operations of the library. Thus, existing plans create a predictable environment, whereas new plans and modifications bring about a change in the status quo. If you use some or all of the ideas presented here to make change more acceptable—especially the idea concerning the creation of an environment that encourages change—then the library staff will view both planning and change in a positive manner.

BIBLIOGRAPHY

1. R. D. Arvey, "A Longitudinal Study of the Impact of Changes in Goal Setting on Employee Satisfaction," *Personnel Psychology* 31 (1978): 595–608.

   R. E. Boynton, "Policies of the Successful Manager," *California Business Review* 73 (1970): 38–44.

   R. J. Mockler, "Theory and Practice of Planning," *Harvard Business Review* 48 (1970): 148–159.

   W. R. Osgood, *Basics of Successful Business Planning* (New York: AMACOM, 1980).
2. R. D. Steuart, and J. T. Eastlick, *Library Management* 2nd ed. (Littleton, Colo.: Libraries Unlimited, 1980).
3. M. Hamburg, R. C. Clelland, H. R. W. Bommer, L. E. Romist, and R. M. Whitfield, *Library Planning and Decision Making Systems* (Cambridge, Mass.: MIT Press, 1974), p. 4.
4. J. Michalko, "Management by Objectives and the Academic Library: A Critical Overview," *Library Quarterly* 45 (July 1975): 248–250.
5. G. R. Terry, *Principles of Management* 6th ed. (Homewood, Ill.: Irwin, 1972), p. 243.
6. R. N. Anthony, *Planning and Central Systems* (Cambridge, Mass.: Harvard Business School, 1965), p. 24.
7. A. Etzioni, "Human Beings Are Not Very Easy to Change After All: An Unjoyful Message and Its Implications for Social Programs," *Saturday Review* 72 (June 3, 1972): 46.

FURTHER READING

Arvey, R. D. "A Longitudinal Study of the Impact of Changes in Goal Setting on Employee Satisfaction." *Personnel Psychology* 31 (1978): 595–608.

Ascher, W. *Forecasting; An Appraisal for Policy-Makers and Planners.* Baltimore, MD: Johns Hopkins Press, 1978.

Association of Research Libraries. *Library Policies.* Occasional Papers, no. 2. Chicago: Association of Research Libraries, 1972.

Bell, J. H., and Keusch, R. B. "Comprehensive Planning for Libraries." *Long Range Planning* 9 (1976): 48–56.

Bewley, L. M. "The Public Library and the Planning Agency." *ALA Bulletin* 61 (1967): 968–974.

Boynton, R. E. "Policies of the Successful Manager." *California Business Review* 73 (1970): 38–44.

Bozeman, B. *Public Management and Policy Analysis.* New York: St. Martin's, 1980.

Brink, V. Z. *Understanding Management Policy and Making It Work.* New York: AMACOM, 1978.

Campbell, H. C. *Metropolitan Public Library Planning throughout the World.* Oxford: Pergamon, 1967.

Carlson, T. S. "Long Range Strategic Planning: Is It for Everyone?" *Long Range Planning* 2 (1978): 54–61.

Corrigan, D. C. "Practical Policy-Making." *Illinois Libraries* 48 (1966): 497–500.

Corrigan, D. D. "Public Library Policies for People." *Illinois Libraries* 51 (1969): 103–105.

Crabill, T. B. "What IF?—Planning Models for Plotting Future Scenarios." *Management Focus* 26 (1979): 32–35.

Durisch, L. L. "Planning Metropolitan Library Service for the Next Twenty-five Years." *Library Quarterly* 38 (1968): 101–105.

Edmunds, S. W. *Basics of Private and Public Management: A Humanistic Approach to Change Management.* Lexington, Mass.: D.C. Heath, 1978.

Etzioni, A. "Humans Beings Are Not Very Easy to Change After All." *Saturday Review* 72 (1972): 45–55.

Fish, J. "Community Analysis: A Planning Tool." *Bay State Librarian* 67 (1978): 17–19.

Hamburg, M. *Library Planning and Decision-Making.* Cambridge, Mass.: MIT Press, 1974.

Heie, B. "Bibliotekenes målsetting og Prioritering." *Bok og Bibliotek* 44 (1977): 411–412.

Highum, D. "Participatory Program Planning and Management for Libraries." *Illinois Libraries* (1978): entire issue.

Holtz, V. H., and Olson, P. E. "Planning a Meaningful Change in Libraries and Library Networks: A First Step." *Medical Library Association Bulletin* 64 (1976): 376–381.

Irwin, P. H. "Changing Organization Behavior Through Strategic Planning." *Managerial Planning* 28 (1979): 3–5.

Irwin, P. H. "Who Really Believes in Strategic Planning?" *Managerial Planning* 27 (1978): 6–9.

Jones, A. "Planning and Policy of Public Library Buildings." *IFLA Journal* 2 (1978): 103–106.

Kahalas, H. "Long Range Planning—An Open Systems View." *Long Range Planning* 10 (1977): 78–82.

Kahalas, H. "A Look at Major Planning Methods: Development, Implementation, Strengths, and Limitations." *Long Range Planning* 11 (1978): 84–90.

Library Management: Quantifying Goals. Terre Haute: Indiana State Univ. Press, Dept. of Library Science, 1973.

McClure, C. R. "Planning Process: Strategies for Action." *College and Research Libraries* 39 (1978): 456–466.

McConkie, M. L. "A Clarification of the Goal Setting and Appraisal Processes in MBO." *Academy of Management Review* 4 (1979): 29–40.

McNichols, T. J. *Policy-Making and Executive Action.* 5th ed. New York: McGraw-Hill, 1977.

Mann, C. W. "The Use of A Model In Long-Term Planning—A Case History." *Long Range Planning* 11 (1978): 55–62.

Martin, L. A. "User Studies and Library Planning." *Library Trends* 24 (1976): 438–496.

Meeth, L. R. "Functional Long-range Planning." *Liberal Education* 53 (1967): 375–384.

Merrill, I. R., and Drob, H. A. *Criteria for Planning the College and University Learning Resources Center.* Washington, D. C.: Association for Educational Communications and Technology, 1977.

Mockler, R. J. "Theory and Practice of Planning." *Harvard Business Review* 48 (1970): 148–159.

Morford, T. G. "Long Range Planning—An Evaluative Approach." *Managerial Planning* 27 (1979): 13–15.

Murdick, R. G. "The Long-range Planning Matrix." *California Management Review* 7 (1964): 35–42.

Murphy, M., and Johns, C. J. *Handbook of Library Regulations.* New York: Dekker, 1977.

Myers, D. W., and Archer, E. R. "When the Suggestion Box Fails." *Personnel* 55 (1978): 37–42.

Nachimas, D. *The Practice of Policy Evaluation.* New York: St. Martin's, 1980.

Nakamura, R. T., and Smallwood, F.*The Politics of Policy Implementation.* New York: St. Martin's, 1980.

Nash, W. V. "Policy-making in Libraries." *Illinois Libraries* 44 (1962): 348–354.

Newell, W. T. "Long-Range Planning for Library Managers." *PNLA Quarterly* 31 (1966): 21–35.

Osgood, W. R. *Basics of Successful Business Planning.* New York: AMACOM, 1980.

Paine, F. T., and Naumes, W. *Organizational Strategy and Policy.* 2nd. ed. Philadelphia: Saunders, 1978.

Palmour, V. E. *A Planning Process for Public Libraries.* Chicago: ALA, 1980.

Palmour, V. E. "Planning in Public Libraries: Role of Citizens and Library Staff." *Drexel Library Quarterly* 13 (1977): 33–43.

Penna, C. V. "Planning Library Services. *UNESCO Bulletin for Libraries* 21 (1967): 60–92.

Quick, J. C. "Dyadic Goal Setting Within Organizations: Role-Making and Motivation Considerations." *Academy of Management Review* 4 (1979): 369–380.

Roalman, A. R. "A Peculiar, Costly Problem." *Management Review* 65 (1976): 11–15.

Robbins, J. *Citizen Participation and Public Library Policy.* Metuchen, N.J.: Scarecrow, 1975.

St. Angelo, D. *State Library Policy: Its Legislative and Environmental Contexts.* Chicago: ALA, 1971.

Sanderson, M. "Coping With Turbulence: More Flexible and Powerful Problem Solving and Policy Setting Methodology." *Journal of Academic Librarianship* 4 (1978): 192–195.

Sewell, P. H. "Development of Library Services: The Basis of Their Planning and Assessment." *Journal of Librarianship* 2 (1970): 32–42.

Sharkansky, I. *Public Administration; Policy-Making In Government Agencies.* 4th ed. Chicago: Rand McNally, 1978.

Sokolik, S. L. "A Strategy for Planning." *MSU Business Topics* 26 (1978): 57–64.

Steiner, G. A. *Strategic Planning; What Every Manager Must Know.* New York: Free Press, 1979.

Stokey, E., and Zeckhauser, R. *A Primer for Policy Analysis.* New York: W. W. Norton, 1978.

Tansik, D. A. "Management by Objectives in the Library." *Catholic Library World* 50 (1979): 418–421.

Warby, W. R. "Building a Better Procedures Manual." *Management World* 9 (1980): 22–23.

Wasserman, P. "Policy Formulation in Libraries." *Illinois Libraries* 43 (1961): 772–779.

Webster, D. E. *Library Policies: Analysis, Formulation and Use in Academic Institutions.* Washington, D.C.: Office of University Library Management Studies. Association of Research Libraries, 1972.

Young, A. P. "Generating Library Goals and Objectives." *Illinois Libraries* 56 (1974): 862–866.

9. Communication

Effective library managers and supervisors know that, ultimately, their success depends on their communication skills. Since management accomplishes things through people, it is essential that meaningful, understandable, clear communication (both oral and written) takes place at all levels of the library. The library manager, like the manager in any other service organization, must be concerned with communicating effectively with patrons as well as with staff.

Poor, ineffective, or nonexistent communication can be and often is the main complaint of library staff members. As noted in the first chapter, facing real problems is often avoided by blaming a situation on poor communication. Nevertheless, communication problems can almost always be identified and most persons can improve their communication skills. We often forget that communication is both a complex pattern of personal behavior (influenced by each person's entire life) and a two-way process (wherein the receiver has as much responsibility as the sender). True communication takes place when a person receives the identical meaning and emotion meant and felt by the communicator. Therefore, both sender and receiver should verify what was said and understood, because verification is essential to complete communication. The extra time spent verifying messages results in better performance and better relations, and, in the long run, it saves the library time and money.

More than 70% of the average person's time goes into listening, speaking, reading, and writing.[1] In addition, messages are often sent and received solely by nonverbal means. If a person's nonverbal (observation) time is included, the total time is even greater. Communication, then, is a pervasive phenomenon.

Yet, despite all the energy and time devoted to the communication process, it is more often marked by failure than by success—especially if success is defined as complete agreement on the content of a message. The general sense of a message is usually communicated, but the precise meaning is often misinterpreted. Given all the problems of communicating, it is surprising that people are able to communicate at all.

Some years ago, Ralph Waldo Emerson is supposed to have said, "Communication is like a piece of driftwood in a sea of conflicting currents. Sometimes the shore will be littered with debris, sometimes it will be bare. The amount and direction of movement is not aimless nor nondirectional at all, but is a response to all the forces, winds and tides or current which come into play." In libraries, where the staff must be concerned with both internal and external communication, all too often the currents and tides become obstacles to effective communication.

OBSTACLES TO UNDERSTANDING

In order to understand library communication, it helps to have some knowledge of general semantics. General semantics is the study of the origins and effects of communication habits. If individuals understand the effects of their communication habits, then they may be able to control them. Certainly, every librarian, whether interested in management or not, should be well versed in semantics. Reference librarians especially are constantly involved in communicating, and, if they do not really understand the process, they cannot hope to be successful, or as helpful as they ought to be.

As A. Korzybski pointed out in *Science and Sanity* (1948),[2] all semantic work is based on three premises. First, words are not the things they represent. If they were, there would be a universal language and there would be no language-barrier problems. Second, words can never say everything about anything. Some factors must be left out; otherwise, one could never complete a sentence. Consider the sentence "The card is on the table," for instance. *Card* seems to be specific, but is it a playing card, a greeting card, a catalog card? What color? What size? What about the table—its physical description, its history? And just how did the card get there? Is that relevant? So, because these factors have been ignored, total communication does not take place. Third, it is possible to use words about words about words to an infinite level of abstraction. This abstract and symbolic nature of words causes the most difficulty in the communication process.

People are able to learn new labels for physical objects because there is a common reference point—for example, *boghandel, libreria, könyvker-eskedés, librairie, bookstore.* And usually, even when many of the characteristics of a physical object are left out of a message, one can still have a general understanding of what is meant. When any critical aspects are left out, however, one usually can identify them easily and add them to the message. Try this sentence: "The new 3×5 buff unit card that you could not find is stuck in the crack in the old wooden table in the corner of the staff lounge." The message is much clearer, because important elements that were not in the first sentence have been identified. These are physical characteristics—observable and identifiable.

Problems develop, however, when there are no physical reference points—when abstract feelings and concepts are to be conveyed. "You're a good friend," "You're not doing as well as I expected," "You did a good job," and especially "I love you" are all statements that are open to a wide range of interpretation (and misinterpretation). You know what a card catalog is, but do your nonlibrary friends share your definition of what term? How many new library patrons know what to do when they are told to "Look it up in the card catalog"?

A psychological factor also can lead to communication problems. It has been observed that, when first meeting, animals tend to size one another up in order to establish dominant–submissive hierarchies. Abraham Maslow has shown that people attempt to establish a similar relationship, usually after a brief initial exchange of seemingly neutral information.[3] Again, this involves nonverbal as well as verbal behavior. When person A goes into person B's office to discuss a problem but person B continues working as if no one is present, A is placed in a subordinate position. When this happens, A is unlikely to be receptive to ideas and suggestions. This factor can be critical in library staff–patron interactions, because a reference interview can very often take on the superior-–subordinate character very quickly, which makes good communication very difficult.

A person can have a truly "open mind" only during the first few hours of life; after that, experiences begin to shape both ideas and as set of unique values. These underlying values and assumptions become important in the communication process, and, if they are thrown into a dominant–submissive relationship, almost no communication will occur. F. C. Bartlett[4] suggested that the mind constantly tries to link new materials into the existing mental patterns in order to make the new material meaningful. The relating of new information to old, unstated preconceptions, and domination are the three major psychological stumbling blocks to communication.

Each person constantly confronts the problem of determining to what degree the "real" world agrees with the symbolic world and to what degree his or her conception of both agrees with anyone else's. The greater the similarity, the greater the possibility that meaningful communication can take place.

Another major problem in the communication process involves meaning—words have more than one meaning, and meanings often change in relation to the environment in which they are used. Certainly there are a great many more meanings than there are words. The *Random House Dictionary* (unabridged) lists 31 meanings for the word *fair* alone; some of the meanings are archaic or obsolete, illustrating the changing nature of word usage. In library work, the word *classification* covers a variety of systems of arranging library materials. To say, "I classified 50 books yesterday" tells the listener nothing about the system used—it could have been UDC, LC, DDC, faceted, or any of the other existing systems. If the listener is from a library that uses a system that differs from the one used in the speaker's library, then confusion would probably reign until it became apparent through further conversation (verification and clarification) that two different reference points were involved. Given the differences in the classification systems and their ease of use, the statement may or may not be impressive. The listener cannot judge until the statement is clarified.

Language structure also may create difficulties in communication. Most Indo-European languages are based on a two-value orientation: good/bad, black/white. Yet other language families have different bases, such as the multivalue system of Chinese. A person who is only partially conversant in another language rather than truly bilingual (especially if the second language has a different value base) will probably miss a great deal of what is meant when someone speaks or writes in that second language. If the library staff is multicultural, as is common in large libraries, the manager should take extra precautions in preparing memos and instructions.

Syntax and morphology also contribute to problems in communication. It is naive to think that, if only one is very careful, then the "right" word will be found—the word that will solve all problems. (The right word would be one having identical meaning to sender and receiver, but this can happen only when they have the same background, knowledge, and experience.) A general transfer of meaning might take place, but not the "perfect understanding" so often sought. When staff members complain about lack of communication, the situation usually has resulted from people assuming that everything they have said has been understood.

If everyone in the library is careful to use job-related terms in a consistent manner, then true communication can take place. Without this consistency, people tend to develop individualized meanings for words, and things become hazy. For example, we have discussed the differences between *policy* and *rule*; these terms should be explained to new employees, with the differences made clear. This can be particularly important in matters of personnel action, salaries, and sick leave, where the difference between rule and policy can be critical. An individual may feel that policy is something that *must* occur rather than something that *can* occur.

The environment in which something is spoken influences listeners' interpretations of what was meant. Physical factors, such as crowds or confined space, can significantly alter the meanings that people place on words—witness the difference between hearing the word *fire* in a restau-

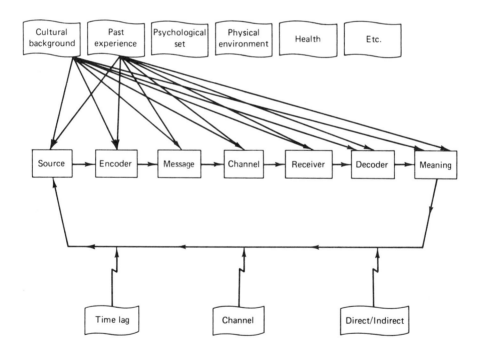

Figure 9.1 Communication model.

rant with a large fireplace in the lounge and hearing it in an overcrowded lobby at a rock concert. In the first instance, the word might connote coziness, while, in the second, it could create panic. The emotional environment is included here as well; Oftentimes, workers who are anxious or worried about something will be extra-sensitive to what they perceive as hidden meanings in chance statements made by supervisors. Consider expectations and anxieties (especially if they are at a high level) when preparing any message that will be delivered in the working situation.

The way in which something is said—the emphasis, lack of emphasis, omissions, order of presentation—also influences meaning. Only when one has had long work experience with the same people will the meanings of their word order, tone of voice, facial expressions, and other nonverbals characteristics be clear. Such familiarity is not always possible; hence, it is best to remain constantly alert to such matters, no matter how well you know the other parties.

Figure 9.1 represents an overview of the communication process, but it includes only a few of the noise factors that can alter a message. These factors are not physical sounds but psychological deterrents to understanding. In this sense, the factors that have been discussed here are *noise*, and they all affect the chain of communication. Given all the barriers, it is amazing that the sender's message and the received meaning are in agreement even 50% of the time.

ORGANIZATIONAL BARRIERS TO COMMUNICATION

Up to this point, we have been concerned with individuals' problems in communicating, but the list of potential problems does not end there, unfortunately. The library's organization itself can influence the way in which messages are interpreted. A library is a series of overlapping and interdependent groups, each with its own immediate and long-range objectives. Thus, each group tends to interpret messages in light of these objectives, and this results in problems down the line if carried too far.

Work relationships, authority structure, and status also affect the communication process by influencing people's expectations regarding who should communicate with whom, about what, and in what way. It should be pointed out that varying interpretations of relationships within an organization cause many communication difficulties. These are then magnified by the continuous flux of personal as well as professional relationships within the library. Therefore, one cannot even count on consistent *mis*interpretation.

Regular meetings of all staff from all units can help to alleviate some of these barriers to communication. In that way, the goals and activities of each unit, as well as those of the library overall, can be reviewed and discussed. Such direct feedback can help to resolve differences of opinion and priorities quickly and early on in any process.

COMMUNICATION NEEDS

Two elements necessary for effective communication on the job are time and feedback. Time is needed for any group of persons to get to know one another and to start building a base of shared experiences and meanings. Two forms of feedback are needed. First, there must be direct and immediate feedback regarding what was understood by an attempted communication. If you do not understand a communication directed to you, or if you feel that it requires you to assume certain things in order to completely carry out management's wishes, then it is your responsibility to clarify the message. In the absence of contrary feedback (questions or restatements of the message), the person sending the message will assume that it was received and *understood in the sense intended.* Perhaps even more important is the second form of feedback, which consists of letting people who will be communicating with you know exactly what you want to know and need to know. A communication system can just as easily overload as it can wither for lack of information. Either process will prove unsatisfactory. By knowing what everyone wants and needs to know, you can save time and avoid frustration.

Occasionally, a library school student will question the need to discuss communication in a course in library management. Perhaps we all know about the process, but our execution of it usually leaves much to be desired. One way to see how complex library communication is, and how many flaws may exist in a system, is to review a list of "communication needs" that were identified by a committee of staff members in a large library system a few years ago. My own experience as a library management consultant leads me to believe that a list similar in length and content could be drawn up by such a committee in almost any large library. (This list, and other samples of library communication in the book, have been drawn from real situations.)

The list is long, ranging from some very general items to some very specific problems and needs. Certainly, such a list indicates problems in library communications. Perhaps more time should be spent teaching both personal and organizational communication in library school.

Needs Relating to the Effective Use of Basic Communication Techniques

Get information out before the fact rather than during or after the fact.

Identify and communicate problem areas in order to provide guidance and assistance in resolving problems before they reach the crisis stage.

Define what is confidential.

Overcome "personality" blocks in communication.

Educate staff members in interpersonal communication.

Distribute information without creating paper overload.

Develop communication skills and techniques in all staff.

Basic Organizational Communication Needs

Encourage all levels of staff to speak out without fear of reprisal.

Provide a clear picture of each staff member's place in the organizational structure and clarify the chain of command.

Establish links with communication systems outside the organizational hierarchy.

Ensure that administrators are visible.

Maintain personal contact between administrators and staff.

Provide effective leadership and communication.

Supply administrative feedback to upward communication.

Keep open input and response channels in all directions, primarily upward.

Ensure that the system is interested in communicating with the individual.

Reduce communication barriers between library groups (for example, between librarians and nonlibrarians).

Overcome communication problems caused by geographic locations of units.

Define who needs to know what and when.

Establish a system-wide rapid communication mechanism for pressing matters.

Know the people with whom you interface in other units.

Maintain lateral communication between/among units/sections/staff performing similar functions.

Maintain lateral communication between/among units/sections/staff performing dissimilar functions.

Create a mechanism that will provide opportunity for ongoing consultation and understanding between units.

Specific Communication Needs

Staff

Publicize staff development opportunities.

Provide a clear description of criteria for evaluation and promotion of both librarians and nonlibrarians.

Publicize salary schedules.

Provide grievance policy and procedure information.

Tell the staff where they can obtain information.

Clarify the library's goals.

Generate and encourage an interest in system goals at the beginning.

Provide consistent orientation.

Ensure that supervisors, including unit heads, obtain training and orientation from those to whom they are responsible.

Public

Identify the composition of the public you serve.

Identify and establish priorities for service to the public.

Provide communication channels to all the public.

Policy Dissemination

Provide information regarding planning, goals, policy, and budget at unit, library, and jurisdiction levels.

Publicize availability and disbursement of travel funds.

Ensure that policies are printed and made available.

Decision Making

Provide staff members with the opportunity to participate in decision-making processes that affect their work.

Keep the staff up-to-date during a decision-making process.

Schedule adequate response time in a decision-making process.

Explain the rationale for determining who needs to be notified of individual decisions.

Inform staff members of budget decisons.

Individual Interest

Provide an opportunity for interested staff members to explore and develop library-related interests.

Obtain feedback from staff members who attend conferences and meetings.

Gather news from other libraries.

Keep staff current on local applications of changes in library technology and information science.

System-wide Consistency and Accountability

Provide consistent orientation.

Monitor morale in all units.

Establish methods of monitoring communications management.

Make people accountable for their communications effectiveness, and make them aware of their deficiencies.

Maintain a consistent approach to the distribution of information in all units.

Equalize information delivery time to all units.

Ensure consistent and timely distribution of job postings.

Provide equal treatment and opportunity for all staff in receiving and providing information.

Observe and enforce deadlines throughout the system.

Standardize annual report procedures.

Standardize reporting procedures in general.

Ensure that policies are consistent, printed, and available.

The list shows very clearly how almost any management problem (budget, staffing, decision making, organization policy and procedures, patrons, services, and so on) can be tied to a communication problem. It also illustrates the importance of communication to good management. This list was made up by working librarians, not academic researchers— they were people reporting their real frustrations and needs regarding on-the-job communication. The following sections explore some steps that can be taken to meet needs of the types identified by librarians.

COMMUNICATION ROLE OF SUPERVISORS

As elsewhere, the supervisor in the library is the key communicator. Because the library is departmentalized, with supervisors for each unit, supervisors communicate both up and down the hierarchy as well as with the public. If you are the supervisor who is responsible for orienting a new employee to the library, you will be interviewing, introducing, instructing, discussing, suggesting, giving orders, reporting, and disciplining.These things will be taking place as the new worker meets coworkers, learns about the library's structure, learns about the job at hand, and tries to absorb a seemingly endless flow of information. If that person makes a mistake, much of the work will have to be done over— reinstructing, sustaining confidence, motivating—until performance becomes satisfactory. But the entire communicating process provides the opportunity for shared experiences and meaning and for learning how each person reacts and thinks and what each person needs to know in order to work with the others.

Graham and Valentine point out one of the important facts a supervisor must remember about the communication process:

> The communication problem is even more complex when the "established" or "official" channels are involved. These are in themselves seen as manipulative and, therefore, received if at all, with considerable cynicism.
>
> But the fundamental problem is even more serious: the act of communicating at all is inherently manipulative. Attempts at communication are often evaluated in terms of observed change in behavior on the part of the receivers of the message.[5]

Since the audience does perceive this manipulative intent, the manager should always remain aware that a degree of hostility is present. The manager does have means, though, to combat this hostility. First, a manager should try to establish *authenticity* by achieving human rapport with the staff—engendering an atmosphere wherein they feel free to discuss problems without fear of reprisal. Also, the supervisor can shorten the period of time between work activities and their evaluation. Job evaluation is less threatening when it involves the immediate situation rather than a review of a person's entire career. The third thing that the supervisor can do is involve the worker in the entire process of the unit, giving each person an opportunity to see each job's importance to the unit's success. This can bring not only increased concern and commitment but also suggestions for improving production and performance.

WRITTEN AND ORAL COMMUNICATION

Deciding when to write and when to talk is a matter of the finest judgment. Communication within the library is both informal and formal, and there are certain situations in which either one or the other seems more appropriate.

Written Communication

At times, it is best to provide written statements and then clarify them orally through question-and-answer exchanges. Policies should always be written up, as noted earlier, and it helps a great deal if instructions and procedures are written as well. It is essential, however, that the written document be accompanied by an oral presentation that will clarify matters.

Every letter and memo should be a "sales" letter of some kind, even if it attempts to sell a point of view on a minor matter. Persuasion will result from fine directional hinting, not from overtly blunt or offensive statements. It is vital that written communications be composed with utmost care, yet people usually spend as little time on them as they do on oral presentations. The fact that something is written down does not necessarily mean that it is clear.

In the following memo, the blunt approach has been used. It should be noted that the supervisor who composed this memo received feedback both from superiors and subordinates. While the "sales" point was made, even long-time staffers misread the attempted "humor." Part of the problem arose from too much haste in writing as well as from the external employment situation for librarians at the time (few jobs, many applicants):

DATE: 1 May 1979
TO: Reference Librarians
FROM: JKL
SUBJECT: Night Work

REMARKS: At present Circulation is minus aides so is Serials. Therefore it will be necessary for the Reference Librarians to be more active in the closing routine. If there is not an aide available and even if there is, please be helpful and place the current issues of the magazines on the slant shelves. Do not pile them up in the microfilm area. Do not put information file material in the microfilm area. Be responsible and do your part. You are lucky to be employed the way things are. Read and initial.

Shared vocabulary is essential for any on-the-job communications, whether with workers or with superiors. The important thing to consider is the degree of abstraction of the material under consideration—use simple sentences to communicate material. Restrict inspirational flights of prose to situations that are general in nature and concrete in subject matter. Jargon or shoptalk is all right *if* the reader understands it and *if* it does not actively interfere with (complicate) a message.

Another staff memo may help to clarify the importance of thinking through a piece of written communication before sending it out in final form and the importance of being clear about what is wanted.

BULLETIN 79-63   6 July 1980

SUBJECT: Summer comfort

REMARKS:

1. Due to the necessity for energy conservation measures, temperatures must be maintained at somewhat higher levels during the summer months than has been the practice in the past. Accordingly, in the interest of good health and on-the-job effectiveness, employees should dress comfortably within the limits of good taste.

2. For male employees, neat-looking, open-neck short-sleeve dress shirts are appropriate. Of course, there will still be occasions or situations when coats and neckties would be more suitable and should be worn. Similarly, female employees should feel free to wear neat, comfortable clothes.

3. This attention to added comfort does not diminish the responsibility of every employee to dress in a manner that is considerate of fellow employees and suitable for a government facility, nor does it modify existing requirements with respect to the wearing of uniforms.

4. Those employees who have questions concerning the appropriateness of clothing should discuss them with their immediate supervisors. Supervisors are responsible for assuring that employees dress appropriately and should not allow inappropriate attire in areas they supervise.

5. You are reminded that we can minimize the impact of higher summer temperatures by observing and controlling our work environment through measures [such] as:
   a. Closing blinds.
   b. Keeping corridor doors closed.
   c. Turning off lights in rooms with adequate natural light.
   d. Turning off lights in unoccupied areas.
   e. Turning off electrical equipment when it is not being used.

6. Authority: Director's letter IL 10-78-34

In this memo, what is meant by good taste? Does that include sandals? For both men and women? What are the situations that require coat and tie? Where is the decision regarding this made? Will all supervisors define *appropriate* in the same way? Time and energy could have been easily saved if the director had written a specific memo about what was wanted. As it turned out, it took most of the summer to decide exactly what was desired of employees with regard to apparel.

The most important aspect in business communication is readability. Such communication should include: a frame of reference (established at the beginning), a clear, well-thought-out statement of what is meant or desired, and an explanation of how, when, and where expectations may be met.

Oral Communication

The supervisor needs to keep the following points in mind regarding oral communication.

Do not take your position (supervisory) *too* seriously.

Do let other people talk.

Do not become overcommitted to an idea.

Do try to keep the discussion from wandering aimlessly.

Do keep it simple and straight.

Do try to get to know the level of understanding of the person you are talking with.

Do not argue.

A speaker's position will naturally affect the way in which people respond and listen to that person. If someone who holds a superior position acts in a superior manner, that person will have problems talking with subordinates. One danger for the new manager (as well as for the experienced manager) is that of becoming an instant expert on something, once given a supervisory post. An instant expert never hears anything that others say, unless it provides him or her with a springboard. Subordinates of such a person just stop listening.

Total commitment to one idea—to the exclusion of entertaining a discussion of the idea's possible defects—is another way to lose an audience. When the manager is convinced that one way is right, and the workers know from experience that it is not working, then the workers usually just remain quiet until the system collapses.

Staying with the point of the conversation is essential in the library from two points of view—internal and patron. Provide only the details that are necessary for people to adequately get the job done. And remember that patrons may not warm to someone who consistently gives more information than can be used (or information that has only slight relevance). Keep messages short and simple. This allows for greater clarity, and it saves time.

Know your audience, and address yourself appropriately Choose your words and the manner in which you will deliver them. Overcomplication can cloud issues; simplistic approaches an insult an audience and reduce matters of complexity to clichés. A little time spent determining the level of an audience's understanding will result in improved communication.

Arguments seldom solve problems, and they do not lead to understanding, but the line between discussion and argument is often quite fine. To say "I disagree with that!" or "You are dead wrong!" is a very good way to turn a discussion into an argument; and that is a very good way to lose any points that might have been made. Such statements should never be made by a supervisor. Supervisors who cut subordinates off (and down) in this way almost guarantee themselves serious personnel problems.

Although there are times when the direct approach is best, the indirect tack is usually the one to take when attempting to discuss personal feelings and behavior. This approach often uses third-party or hypothetical situations (based on actual knowledge of circumstances). However, if the indirect approach is not followed up by a more direct discussion, the entire point may well be lost or misunderstandings of a serious nature may occur.

CHANNELS, DIRECTION, LEGITIMACY OF COMMUNICATION

Channels of communication run up, down, and across an organization. In cases of upward communication, tact can be very important. Also, sensitive topics, such as disagreements with a supervisor's actions, probably should be discussed orally (with considerable supporting detail). Distinguish clearly between fact and opinion, being neither subservient nor truculent. In these ways, you may influence the decison maker.

In downward communication, diplomacy is in order. Avoid carelessness, as it indicates a lack of respect for the person receiving the message. In union contract talks, careless speech has been known to lead to strikes. In libraries, it can seriously threaten morale. A manager must give explanations for actions rather than allow the workers' imaginations to fill the gap.

Superiors should always encourage subordinates to ask questions and to contribute ideas. Only in such ways can the manager know whether communication is effective, and to what degree. If management encourages such behavior on all levels, the result is likely to be greater appreciation and loyalty—throughout the library.

Although the classical function of the manager is to make decisions and to give orders, this does, in fact, occupy only a little of the time spent in communicating. In a library, a vast amount of communicating goes on among peers in order to get things done. This type of communication in a collective enterprise involves not only the formal structure but also the informal structures of the library (status structure, friendship structure, prestige structure, etc). All these are in constant flux, belying the notion that all communication in an organization is downward and horizontal.

People communicate in order to achieve a goal, to satisfy a personal need, or to improve their immediate situation with respect to their personal desires. People need to communicate with persons of higher status than themselves, which means that supervisors need to spend time with their subordinates. The effectivness of this will depend on the individual relationships between supervisors and subordinates and the degree to which each subordinate's needs are satisfied by upward communication.

Be honest and friendly. This is as essential as allowing a person to speak in the first place. When interviewing, do not worry about nervousness. Everyone is nervous. Remain dignified yet informal, and respect the individual's right to courtesy, dignity, and the facts. Remember that you represent the library; a person's impressions of an institution stem from contact with its staff as often as they stem from inspection of its facilities. If you are relaxed and responsive while representing the library, you will convey the impression that the library itself is a relaxed place that is responsive to the vagaries of individual situations.

Effective communication depends on the active cooperation and effort of all parties. As long as one is passive, little communication or understanding can ever really take place. In the library, improved understanding can lead to better working conditions, higher morale, and greater staff commitment; it is the responsibility of the supervisor to provide these benefits by ensuring that communications are as honest, clear, and open to discussion as possible.

BIBLIOGRAPHY

1. D. K. Berlo, *The Process of Communication* (New York: Holt, 1960).
2. A. Korzybski, *Science and Society* (Lakeville, Conn.: International Non-Aristotelian Library Publis. Co., 1948).

3. A. H. Maslow, "Dominance-feeling, Behavior and Status," *Psychological Review* 44 (Sept. 1937): 404–429.
4. F. C. Bartlett, *The Mind at Work and Play* (London: Allen & Unwin, 1951).
5. R. Graham, and M. Valentine, "Management, Communication and the Destandardized Man," *Personnel Journal* 52 (Nov. 1973): 962–979.

FURTHER READING

Allen, R. K. *Organizational Management Through Communication.* New York: Harper, 1977.

Anderson, M. "Communication Barriers and How to Scale Them." *Supervision* 41 (1979): 14–16.

Ball, D. L. "Communication in an Industrial Library." *North Carolina Libraries* 36 (1978): 11–16.

Baron, A. "The Key to Open Communication." *Personnel Administrator* 21 (1976): 49–52.

Bates, V. D. *Writing With Precision; How to Write So That You Cannot Possibly Be Understood.* 2d. ed. Washington, D.C.: Acropolis Books, 1978.

Berlo, D. K. *The Process of Communication.* New York: Holt, 1960.

Blagden, J. F. "Communication: A Key Library Management Problem." *ASLIB Proceedings* 27 (1975): 319–326.

Boyd, B. B. "An Analysis of Communication Between Departments—Roadblocks and Bypasses." *Personnel Administration* 28 (1965): 33–38.

Burger, R. H. "Kanawha County Textbook Controversy: A Study of Communication and Power." *Library Quarterly* 48 (1978): 143–162.

Busignies, H. "Communication and Information: Technical, Administrative, Social Challenges. *ASIS Bulletin* 2 (1975): 3–4.

Clausen, A. W. "Listening and Responding to Employees' Concerns." *Harvard Business Review* 80, 1 (1980): 101–114.

Communication in Organizations St. Paul: West Pub, 1976.

Cooper, K. *Nonverbal Communication for Business Success.* New York: AMACOM, 1979.

Deutsch, A. *The Human Resources Revolution: Communicate or Litigate.* New York: McGraw-Hill, 1979.

DiSalvo, V. *Business and Professional Communication: Basic Skills and Principles.* Columbus: Merrill, 1977.

Eichman, T. L. "Complex Nature of Opening Reference Questions." *RQ* 17 (1978): 212–222.

Emery, R. *Staff Communication in Libraries.* London: Clive Bingley, 1975.

Fair, E. W. "Put Those Instructions Across." *Supervision* 5 (1978): 9–10.

Feller, J. M. "Communicating With People: Some Thoughts Related to the Conference Theme." *Pennsylvania Library Association Bulletin* 32 (1977): 82.

Goldberg, M. "Communication, Perception, and Motivation." *Special Libraries* 51 (1960): 193–199.

Gordon, W. I. *Communication, Personal and Public.* Sherman Oaks, Calif.: Alfred Publishing, 1977.

Graham, R., and Valentine, M. "Management, Communication, and the Destandardized Man." *Personnel Journal* 52 (1973): 962–969.

Griffen, A. M. "On Communicating with Supervisors." *Unabashed Librarian* 22 (1977): 28–29.

Guillet, D. R. "Dictation Systems—Management Says They're Working." *Administrative Management* 40 (1979): 51–52+.

Halloran, J. D. "Information and Communication." *ASLIB Proceedings* 31 (1979): 21–27.

Haney, W. V. "Serial Communication of Information in Organizations." *ETC.* 21 (1964): 13–29.

Hepworth, J. B. "Communications and Library Management." *Library World* 67 (1966): 324–329.

Hoover, J. D. "Increasing Human Potential Through Communicative Effectiveness." *Supervisory Management* 22 (1977): 8–15.

Hurston, C. J. "Ten Tips for a Better Letter." *Management World* 8 (1979): 13–15.

Huseman, R. C. *Interpersonal Communication in Organizations: A Perceptual Approach.* Boston: Holbrook Press, 1976.

Jacobi, E. *Writing at Work: Dos, Don'ts and How Tos.* Rochelle Park, N.J.: Hayden Book, 1976.

King, C. P. "Keep Your Communication Climate Healthy." *Personnel Journal* 57 (1978): 204–206.

Kirby, J. "Staff Communication." *New Library World* 79 (1978): 105–106.

Korzbyski, A. *Science and Sanity.* Lakeville, Conn.: International Non-Aristotelian Library Publis. Co., 1948.

"Library Public Relations and Library Staff Communications." *Catholic Library World* 50 (1979): entire issue.

Littlejohn, S. W. *Theories of Human Communication.* Columbus: Merrill, 1978.

Lopez-Muñoz, J. "The Significance of Nonverbal Communication in the Reference Interview." *RQ* 16 (1977): 220–224.

Lumsdon, C. A. "Communication Within the Organization: Organizational Development Team Making and Informal Meetings." *ASLIB Proceedings* 27 (1975): 327–338.

McAuley, J. G. *People to People; Essentials of Personal and Public Communication.* Belmont, Calif.: Wadsworth, 1979.

McCaskey, M. B. "The Hidden Messages Managers Send." *Harvard Business Review* 57 (1979): 135–148.

McMahon, J. "Make Your Meetings Pay Off." *Supervision* 41 (1979): 3–5.

Maslow, A. H. "Dominance-feeling, Behavior and Status." *Psychological Review* 44 (1937): 404–429.

Miller, G. R., and Steinberg, M. *Between People: A New Analysis of Interpersonal Communication.* Chicago: Science Research Assoc., 1975.

Murphy, H. A., and Peck, C. E. *Effective Business Communications.* 2d. ed. New York: McGraw-Hill, 1976.

Poole, M. S. "An Information–task Approach to Organizational Communication." *The Academy of Management Review* 3 (1978): 493–504.

Pratt, A. A. "Information of the Image: A Model of the Communications Process." *Libri* 27 (1977): 204–220.

Preston, P. *Communication for Managers.* Englewood Cliffs, N.J.: Prentice-Hall, 1979.

Rice, B. *Public Relations for Public Libraries.* New York: H. W. Wilson, 1972.

Rogers, E. M., and Agawala-Rogers, R. *Communication in Organizations.* New York: The Free Press, 1976.

Roloff, M. E. "Communication at the User–System Interface: A Review of Research." *Library Research* 1 (1979): 1–18.

Schneider, A. E. "Communication Climate Within an Organization." *Management Controls* 23 (1976): 159–162.

Shapiro, L. "Lost Cord Between Communication and Understanding." *Arkansas Libraries* 35 (1978): 18–24.

Stevenson, G. "Public Library in a Communications Setting." *Library Quarterly* 48 (1978): 393–415.

Thompson, W. N. *Responsible and Effective Communication.* Boston: Houghton, 1978.

Timko, L. C. "Teaching Communication With Problem Patrons in Emergency Situations." *Journal of Educational Librarianship* 18 (1978): 244–246.

Timm, P. L. *Managerial Communication; A Finger on the Pulse.* Englewood Cliffs, N.J.: Prentice-Hall, 1980.

Toyne, M. C. "Prometheus vs Pandora: Effective Communications in the Library." *Georgia Librarian* 14 (1977): 27–28+.

"Upward/Downward Communication Channels." *Small Business Reports* 4 (1979): 12–15.

Weiss, W. H. "Communication: 'Tool of Good Management'." *Supervision* 41 (1979): 10–12.

Wilkenson, J. P. "Psycho-organizational Approach to Staff Communication in Libraries." *Journal of Academic Librarianship* 4 (1978): 21–26.

Yorks, L. "Managing Professional Relationships. P+2 Influencing Skills." *Journal of Systems Management* 28 (1977): 6–11.

Young, A. E. "Mean Business in Your Writing." *Administrative Management* 40 (1979): 62–64.

Zacharis, J. C., and Bender, C. C. *Speech Communication: A Rational Approach.* New York: Wiley, 1976.

10. Motivation

As we saw in the first chapter, libraries are highly structured organizations that fit Weber's model of a bureaucratic institution. One characteristic of a bureaucracy is a dependence on hierarchy organizational structure and on procedures and rules that maintain its operational fitness. Such a work environment usually means little room for innovation, flexibility, or independent action. Staff members often feel that they are at the bottom of the ladder and that no one above them cares what they think as long as the job is done. When this happens, morale usually drops until management takes action. Quality of work suffers, and patrons notice this in the quality of service they receive.

For all too many person, this lack of enthusiasm for (or downright dislike of) their jobs is a lifelong experience. To me, nothing can be sadder; it represents a tremendous waste of human energy and ability. Over the past 30 years, management specialists have explored the factors that motivate people in the work environment. But there is still no single answer to the following question: How do you most effectively motivate employees, achieve high volume and quality of work, and not create human-relations problems? You may recall from Chapter 2 that the consensus was that a combination of economic factors (as Taylor noted) and peer pressure and acceptance (investigated by Mayo) were dominant concerns of employees, along with personal feelings of success, accomplishment, and self-satisfaction.

Recently, librarians have been reading and talking about *participative management*. In order to understand the basic elements of participative management, a person needs to know something about the various theories of work motivation. These basic theories are discussed here.

MOTIVATION AND BEHAVIOR

Motivation has its roots in the drives within a person that induce a particular behavior pattern. Motives evolve partly through physiologically based needs (such as hunger, thirst, and sex); they cause a person to seek to satisfy those needs by mean of food, drink, a sex partner, etc. In 1943[1] Abraham Maslow used this approach in developing his theory of a hierarchy of needs. He also took psychological and social factors into consideration, because many motives are acquired through conditioning.

The culture-based conditioning that all people receive may result in motivations diametrically opposed to work. It would be rare if the motives held by a Swede were also those held by a South African bushman. And even within a society, motives will differ. Studies have indicated that the motives of big-city slum dwellers differ from those of middle-class residents of the same city. It has also been found that the motives of executives from lower-income backgrounds differ significantly from those of executives from upper-income families.[2] A manager should not expect, then, to find that all individuals in the organization have the same motives for doing their work.

The basic unit of behavior is activity—talking, eating, running, and reading, for example. At any moment, a person can choose to combine activities (eat while reading, for example) or to change from one activity to another. But why do individuals choose one activity over another? And why do they change activities? Although the supervisor rarely has total control of employees' behavior, the ability to anticipate changes in behavior may provide a chance to direct them, and this can help to improve effectiveness in a given work unit.

Behavior is basically goal oriented—even if the specific goal is not recognized as such by the individual. Certainly a majority of the drives motivating distinctive individual behavior patterns are subconscious and not easily examined. Sigmund Freud gained much of his fame as a result of his work in subconscious motivation. He pointed out that people do not always know what they want. He drew an analogy between human consciousness and an iceberg—the greatest portion lies below the surface. Sometimes, if an individual does no introspection, someone else who studies that person may have more knowledge of his or her motivation than the person does.

Motives and needs are internal; goals are external. Goals (incentives) are anticipated rewards toward which individuals gear their activities. Many managers are successful in providing the incentives that motivate their subordinates, but the trick is always to do so without making the incentive the focus of conflict. Incentives can be tangible (for example, pay increases, better working conditions, better fringe benefits, or new lounge facilities) or they can be intangible (for example, praise, approval, sympathy, understanding, or recognition of achievement in front of peers). Each employee will have a combination of incentives, and the intangible are probably more important—and also harder to identify.

In any particular situation, needs and motives may fluctuate in importance. An individual engages in a particular activity to satisfy some need. If it is impossible to satisfy a nonphysiological need in a given situation, people often suppress the need until it can be satisfied in one way or another. We can exercise control of varying degrees over our physiological needs.

Behavior can generally be classified as either *goal directed* or *goal activity*. Goal-directed behavior is directed at reaching a certain goal. (If a person is hungry, the ways of looking for food would be a goal-directed activity.) Goal activity is engaging in the goal that had been sought. In the example given here, eating is the goal activity. The *strength of need* increases during a period of goal-directed activity, and it decreases once the goal has been achieved.

The factors affecting the strength of a need are *expectancy* and *availability*. Expectancy affects motives and needs; availability affects the perception of goals and incentives. The former is based on experience and perceived probability of satisfying the need; the latter is an assessment of how accessible certain goals and incentives actually are.

People act on their needs in accordance with their perception of the real world. Supervisors should always remain aware that their personal real world will differ quite a bit from that of their peers and subordinates. However, there are some factors that can help to determine what an employee's goals are and what types of activities and behaviors that person is likely to engage in.

Cultural norms and values.

Inherited biological capabilities, that is, physical or mental limitations.

Any experience in similar situations. (If it was positive, the person will be likely to repeat the type of behavior that created the reward. If it was unpleasant, a new solution may be sought.)

The individual's mobility, either physical or social. If a person cannot get away from an uncomfortable situation physically, he or she will respond accordingly. (This could include finding new employment in the area. The availability of other jobs can affect employee behavior in your library.)

The preceding points imply that similar actions do not necessarily reflect similar desires or wants. For example, a librarian may agree to take responsibility for photoduplication as an added duty. That person may be motivated by empire building; or the individual may have genuine interest in duplication processes and photography.

An obvious corollary to this is that different actions may refelct similar desires. In the preceding example, a person who is interested in empire building might accept the new responsibility; but that same desire for advancement and recognition could lead a person to turn down such a task in order to devote more attention to current responsibilities. (This would imply a belief that "shining" in one area will lead to advancement just as well as acquiring a dull gloss in several areas.)

Consequently, when you see someone do something, do not assume that you know exactly why they are doing it. Only by carefully observing actions, and later drawing conclusions based on those actions and any additional relevant information, can the supervisor determine an individual's underlying motivations. The biggest mistake a supervisor can make is to project his or her needs on subordinates.

MASLOW'S THEORY OF MOTIVATION

Abraham Maslow's article, "Theory of Human Motivation,"[3] has become a basic source in almost all work in the field of employee motivation. His theory is based on three basic propositions about human behavior. First, humans are wanting beings—they always want, and those wants are unending. When a strong need is satisfied, its strength may diminish, but another need immediately replaces it. The human condition, then, is one of always demanding that a need be satisfied. Second, a need that has been satisfied is not a motivator of behavior. Unsatisfied needs are the only motivators. Third, human needs present themselves in a series of levels. As basic need are met, needs at the next highest level will demand attention and satifaction.

Maslow posits a need hierarchy of five levels; until the physiological needs are fulfilled, however, none of the higher needs will be strong enough to motivate behavior. The levels, and an illustration of their hierarchical order, are indicated in Figure 10.1.

1. Physiological
2. Security
3. Social
4. Esteem
5. Self-actualization

Hierarchy of needs

Figure 10.1 Maslow's hierarchy of needs.

Physiological needs, the most basic, tend to be relatively independent of one another. Usually they are identified with a bodily function, and they are often quite localized. In an affluent society, physiological needs are not usually effective motivators of work behavior, because they are easily satisfied. However, because levels of expectation rise in an affluent society, the definition of satisfactory fulfillment can vary. And there are always people who must be concerned about fulfilling these needs, no matter how affluent the society in which they live. (Naturally, needs for eating and sleeping must be satisfied frequently.)

The next level consists of the need for *security or safety*, which serves the need for self-preservation. It also goes beyond that in an economic sense, because money does enter into the process of obtaining reasonable shelter and protection. A concern for safety often manifests itself in the preference for the familiar over the unfamiliar. Therefore, a supervisor needs to realize that the frequency with which changes are made has an influence on staff morale. People need an orderly, predictable environment. A stable physical environment is an important as knowing one's place in the library hierarchy. Knowledge of the limits of acceptable behavior falls into the area of safety needs. When unacceptable behavior has been defined and penalties set forth, this represents security. If the limits are not set, then people will test until they find them. Almost anything relating to job security, promotions, and salary matters falls under safety needs.

Social needs include the desire for acceptance by co-workers, a friendly relationship with at least a few individuals, and the opportunity to associate with and discuss problems with co-workers. The informal organization accompanying every formal one arises from this set of desires.

Satisfying *esteem needs* includes gaining both self-esteem and the esteem of others. Such things as self-confidence, achievement, self-respect, and independence are factors to be taken into account. When some people find their work unchallenging, they may seek employment elsewhere because of lack of satisfaction. Another person may find the same job challenging and stay with it over several years, despite low pay, if the self-esteem received is significant. The competitive desire enters into satisfying needs for esteem. This can include the desire to compete with people within the organization as well as with people outside of it. This desire may not hold for everyone, but it is certainly strong in Western European cultures.

Self-esteem needs are rarely, if ever, completely satisfied. Physiological, security, and social needs are more likely to be completely satisfied. To some extent, this arises because new goals for self-esteem crop up all the time. Certainly, esteem needs can be a useful incentive when attempting to motivate work behavior, and, if they are tied to intangible incentives, then work performance can be much higher than it might otherwise be.

Self-actualization—the need to realize one's own potential—is the final level of need. This assumes a clear perception of one's potential and of one's limitations. Largely because most people do not have such a clear perception, this need is never satisfied. Even those who have attained the highest positions rarely feel that they have achieved their potential, but perhaps they are simply unable to see that they have achieved their own level of incompetence (remember the Peter Principle![4]).

While the conceptualization of needs as a series of steps in a hierarchy is probably accurate to a large degree, they might be better thought of as a series of waves in which a need peaks, is satisfied, tapers off, and is followed by a new need that arises in its place. Figure 10.2 illustrates this approach, which resembles a biorhythm chart. Maslow believed that extended existence at any of the lower levels tends to deaden and eliminate any higher aspirations. People who are forced to live at the physiological and security levels have very little need, if any, for self-esteem and self-actualization—they simply do not have the time and energy left after securing food and shelter.

The belief that need stimulus automatically elicits a certain behavior is not always accurate. Maslow has suggested that an individual who is deprived of two needs will tend to seek to fulfill the most basic one. However, when this choice is culturally or experimentally influenced, the person may not select the option that fills the most basic need. Finally, most action and behavior results from a complex of needs in which one need may happen to dominate rather than from a single deep need.

Maslow's theory has been widely discussed and, to some extent, accepted without the support of research evidence. In many respects, the theory is not formulated in a manner that allows for testing. For example, it is difficult to determine, on a conceptual level, where safety needs separate from physiological needs at the lower level, and from love needs at the higher level. Because of such problems, researchers have not been

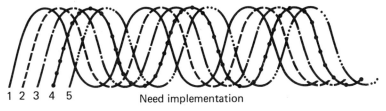

1 2 3 4 5   Need implementation

Figure 10.2   "Wave theory" of needs occurence.

able to adequately support or refute Maslow's theory. However, many researchers, in particular Clayton Alderfer, have questioned the value of the theory. Alderfer,[5] on the basis of one experiment in one organization, suggests that a modified form of the Maslow theory is a more promising approach to the basic issues of human motivation. He retained the concepts of a need hierarchy without the requirement that "it be strictly ordered."[6] Despite criticism, no other theory has been put forward that has gained as much acceptance as Maslow's.

McGREGOR: THEORY X AND THEORY Y

Douglas McGregor formulated the now classic Theory X and Theory Y in the late 1950s.[7] According to McGregor, the traditional organization (centralized decision making, superior–subordinate pyramid, and external control of work) is based on a set of assumptions about human nature and motivation. He proposed a continuum of assumptions with the end points, X and Y, representing opposite views of what motivates a worker.

Theory X assumes the following: (1) work is inherently distasteful to most people; (2) most people are not ambitious, they have little desire for responsibility, and they prefer to be directed; (3) most people have little capacity for creativity and for solving organizational problems; (4) motivation occurs only at the physiological and security levels; and (5) most people must be closely controlled and often coerced to achieve organizational objectives.

On the other hand, Theory Y assumes the following:

(1) the expenditure of physical and mental effort in work is as natural as play or rest. The average human being does not inherently dislike work; depending upon controllable conditions, work may be a source of satisfaction (and will be voluntarily performed) or a source of punishment (and will be avoided, if possible). (2) External control and the threat of punishment are not the only means for bringing about effort toward organizational objectives. Man will exercise self-direction and self-control in the service of those objectives to which he is committed. (3) Commitment to objectives is a function of rewards associated with their achievement. The most significant of such rewards, e.g., the satisfaction of ego and self-actualization needs can be direct products of effort directed toward organizational objectives. (4) The average human being learns, under proper conditions, not only to accept but to seek responsibility. Avoidance of responsibility, a lack of ambition, an emphasis on security are generally consequences of experience, not an inherent human characteristic. (5) The capacity to exercise a relatively high degree of creativity in the solution of organizational problems is widely, not narrowly distributed in a population. (6) Under the conditions of modern industrial life, the intellectual potentialities of the average human being are only partially utilized.[8] [From *The Human Side of Enterprise* by D. McGregor. Copyright © 1960, McGraw-Hill. Used by permission of the publisher.]

Theory X assumes that employees' personal goals are totally incompatible with organizational objectives. Authority is used as the instrument of command and control. Theory Y asserts that people have much to offer an organization if only they can be persuaded to accept its objectives. The use of authority is thought to impede the development of this capability, although authority may be necessary if people will not cooperate. The basic difference between the two theories is that Theory X precludes the use of motivational techniques (because of its assumptions regarding human nature), while Theory Y opens the door to their use. Managers who accept Theory X set up closely supervised rigid structures, because they clearly feel that this is the appropriate response to unreliable, irresponsible, and immature people.

On the basis of experiments and studies in the behavioral sciences, Mc McGregor questioned whether the Theory X view of human beings was correct. He concluded that it was generally inadequate and that management approaches developed from Theory X assumptions often fail to motivate people whose basic needs are satisfied and who seek to fulfill their social, esteem, and self-actualization needs.

Managers operating under Theory Y do not usually try to structure the work environment too closely or supervise constantly. Instead, they try to help employees develop by exposing them to progressively less external control, thereby allowing them to assume more and more self-control. Employees can receive the satisfaction of affiliation, esteem, and self-actualization in this kind of environment.

In a job fails to provide satisfaction at every level, high turnover and absenteeism will result. McGregor states that, if Theory X were employed, this would have to be the case. But two factors need to be examined in such cases. First, look at the supervisory philosophy and the methods of the manager of the unit having problems; a discussion of techniques may be in order. Second, look at the supervisor as an individual person, and consider whether that person is basically adequate as a supervisor. In other words, Theory X may be a factor, but it may be only part of the total problem.

Management is concerned with work, and McGregor believes that work is as natural and often as satisfying for people as is play. Since both are mental/physical activities, there appears to be no difference. But, according to Theory X, a distinction is drawn on the basis of need satisfaction— play is controlled by the individual, but work is externally controlled by others. Yet this assumption actually leads people to think of work as a necessary evil, not as a source of personal challenge and satisfaction. Persons who are stifled at work usually look for excuses to spend more and more time away from work. This is most unfortunate, especially in organizations where cohesive work groups could be formed whose goals would parallel those of the organization as a whole. In such situations, productivity is high and people are happy in their work, and there is little, if any, of the externally imposed control that causes a worker to feel dissatisfied with the job.

Occasionally, motivation concepts are either misunderstood or misused. The following example illustrates what can happen in such instances when a person misused the X–Y concept in the footnote of a memo. Using concepts in this manner often generates strong negative feelings; these feelings can be directed toward the person writing the memo as well as toward the concepts themselves and the ideal of learning about and using work motivation techniques.

INTERDEPARTMENTAL COMMUNICATION

DATE: 17 January 1980

TO: Division heads; branch librarians

FROM: Library Director

SUBJECT: Vacation

The budget situation for the remainder of the fiscal year is touch-and-go. We want to be sure we have a positive balance as of the end of June.

To this end, we want to reduce all possible expenditures without adversely affecting public service. One way we can save some money is by asking everyone to postpone vacations until July or later if this will not cause a hardship. This will not only save vacation pay, but will eliminate the need for additional part-time hours to cover vacation absences.

We are facing a year-end deficit. We cannot have a year-end deficit. This is one way a year-end deficit can be avoided.

Please explain this to the people in your division. If they have not made long-range plans, and if they can just as well take vacation after July 1, please urge them to do so. Review any vacation requests submitted to you, with postponement in mind.

GEE:ROL:dl

Footnote:

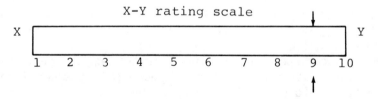

This is a Theory Y memo. It is based on the assumption that the staff will cooperate.

ARGYRIS' IMMATURITY/MATURITY THEORY

In the late 1950s and early 1960s, a number of people worked in the area of motivation research, building on the work of Maslow, McGregor, and others. The next three sections will discuss the work of C. Argyris, F. Herzberg, and R. Likert, and their findings will be related to the general library scene.

Argyris examined industrial organizations to see what effect management practices had on individual behavior and personal growth within the work environment. According to him,[9] seven changes take place in the personality of an individual as he or she develops into a mature person:

An individual moves from a passive state as an infant to a state of increasing activity as an adult.

An individual develops from a state of dependency to a state of relative independence as an adult.

An individual behaves in only a few ways as an infant but is capable of behaving in many ways as an adult.

As an infant, the individual has erratic, casual, and shallow interests but develops deeper, stronger interests as an adult.

The child's time perspective is very short, involving only the present, but with maturity, the time perspective involves both past and future.

An infant is subordinate to everyone, but moves to an equal or a superior position as an adult.

The child lacks selfawareness, but an adult is not only aware of the self but is also able to control this awareness.

Argyris postulates that these changes exist as a continuum and that the healthy personality develops along the continuum from immaturity to maturity (see Table 10.1).

Argyris was also concerned with the effects of the work place on an employee's maturation, specifically addressing the question of individual laziness. He concluded that an individual worker is often kept from maturing by the very management practices that are supposed to bring everyone to peak efficiency. Individuals may express immaturity in a number of ways, for example, absenteeism or not wanting to go to work, and in many organizations, this is what is expected. Oftentimes, managers are uncomfortable with a group of people who are able to think and act on their own.

According to Argyris, the formal organization has a built-in need to keep people in an immature state. He argued that the formal organization often reflects its founder's conception of how the institution's objectives are to be achieved. In such structures, the design comes first—based as it is on scientific management concepts of task specialization, chain of command, unity of direction, and span of control. In such situations, management

TABLE 10.1 THE ARGYRIS CONTINUUM

Immaturity	Maturity
Passive	Increased activity
Dependence	Independence
Limited behavior patterns	Multiple behavior patterns
Erratic shallow interests	Deeper and stronger interests
Short time-perspective	Long time-perspective
Subordinate position	Equal or superordinate position
Lack of awareness of self	Awareness and control over self

conceives of workers as interchangeable elements in the organizational machine; that would seem to allow for greater efficiency.

To illustrate that work is often designed for an extremely low level, Argyris cited the use of mentally retarded people in unskilled jobs. The managers were not immediately informed that the employees were mentally retarded. The following is their assessment of the workers after the fact was known.

> The girls proved to be exceptionally well-behaved, particularly obedient, strictly honest, trustworthy. They carried out work required of them with such a degree of efficiency that *we were surprised they were classified as sub-normals for their age.* Their attendance was good, their behavior was, if anything, certainly better than any other employee of the same age [emphasis added].[10]

The assumptions inherent in this statement are indicative, as Argyris saw it, of the opinions of managers and management in general.

One of Argyris' consulting jobs involved a plant wherein workers were told to assemble the product in whatever way they thought best. They had to inspect the product, sign it, and handle complaints about it. At first, production dropped 70% and morale was bad. After 2 months, production went up a bit, and after 4 months, production was at an all-time high—all without supervisors thrusting their opinions into the process. And most impressive was a decrease of 94% in waste and error and a 96% drop in complaints. Obviously, quality had vastly improved. This rather unusual experiment was repeated in several other firms with consistent results. The main stumbling block, it seems, is that management rarely can accept the fact that great numbers of employees experience an increase in motivation when they are given proper incentives and responsibility.

Libraries could possibly make use of this, although some experiments along this line have been conducted without much success. In the main, those were experiments in which people did the selecting, cataloging, and reference work for a particular subject area. However, perhaps by starting with smaller units within technical services, libraries might be able to put together work packages involving a complete activity—something in which a worker can take pride. Such an approach allows the individual to see her or his place in the organization.

Finally, Argyris' work, which was done in the 1950s and early 1960s, may no longer hold true for most organizations. Management today views its position and function differently than it did then. This shift was due in part to Argyris and his work.

THE HERZBERG STUDIES

Dr. Frederick Herzberg and his colleagues conducted a number of experiments in 1959. They concluded that the job itself was the most important motivator in the work environment.[11] Engineers and accountants (who like librarians are semiprofessionals) were interviewed as to what produced positive and negative feelings toward their jobs. Positive feelings were found to be highest when something showed them that they were doing a good job or were considered expert in their job or field. Fringe benefits did not produce positive feelings, but they did enter the picture to produce negative feelings when they were seen as inadequate. The same was true of salary. Negative feelings, then, resulted from physiological and security aspects of the job; positive feelings resulted from self-actualization, self-esteem, and social needs.

Job attitudes directly affected the quality of work. When people felt good about their jobs, they used more creativity, were more careful, and tried harder to achieve excellence. When they were unhappy, they were likely to put in a minimum performance.

Herzberg proposed two sets of stimuli that produce job satisfaction or dissatisfaction: *motivators* and *hygienic factors*. Motivators produced improvement in performance and attitudes. Hygienic factors merely maintained morale and efficiency. For the interviewees, motivators were chances to become more expert and to handle more demanding assignments.

These conclusions are quite compatible with Maslow's hierarchy, in that the hygienic (environmental) factors and the motivators (the job itself) concern the various levels in the hierarchy. (Esteem needs are divided, because recognition is an earned personal quality, whereas status usually is a function of the job itself; consequently, status is a physiological need, whereas recognition is a motivator.)

Prior to Herzberg's work, emphasis was placed on what was called *job enlargement,* that is, an increase in the number of operations performed by an individual. Herzberg replied that doing a little of this and a little of that was no way to motivate people—its is similar to being allowed to wash silverware, then pots, and then pans, in addition to being regularly assigned to washing dishes. Variety of this sort can go only a short way toward alleviating boredom. So Herzberg proposed *job enrichment*—a deliberate upgrading of the scope, challenge, and responsibility of a person's work. An investigation of this area could prove to be profitable for libraries, as Herzberg seems to have identified (his critics notwithstanding) the key motivator—*the job itself.* And this may well explain why the emphasis on fringe benefits over the past 20 years, as well as the hubbub over new supervisory techniques, has not really motivated employees.

Two points should be borne in mind concerning the Herzberg findings. First, even a job with tremendous motivators cannot overcome a negative hygienic situation, at least not over a long period of time. And the converse is true: if a job is seen as a dead end, then no amount of manipulation of the environment can be substituted for that fact. If an employee is in such a situation but stays on because of conditions (fringe benefits, and so on), that employee will be especially devastated by changes in those conditions if those are seen as negative changes.

The other thing to remember is that those interviewed in the first study were semiprofessionals. Later experiments by Robert Ford with blue-collar workers and lower-level white-collar workers at American Telephone and Telegraph Company bore out Herzberg's findings in these situations as well.[12] Thus, it can be said that, along with supervisory ability, planning, decision making, and other techniques in the management arsenal, the job itself (one of the greatest motivators) is something managers should pay close attention to. The work of K. Plate[13] was an early effort to apply the Herzberg ideas to a library setting.

Despite the results some researchers have presented supporting Herzberg's concepts, other researchers have raised a number of questions. V. M. Bockman's article[14] summarizes the views of a number of Herzberg critics. In essence, they feel that Herzberg erred in equating satisfaction with motivation and in relating extrinsic factors to lower order needs and intrinsic factors to higher order needs. Again, as with Maslow, not all the evidence is in, and Herzberg's concepts are still widely held and are at least partially supported by research findings.

MANAGEMENT SYSTEMS: LIKERT

A study by Rensis Likert in 1958 concluded that there were two categories of supervisors—production centered and employee centered.[15] The production-centered supervisors advocate strict control of the work environment and think of employees as instruments for getting the job done. They actively interfere in the work at all stages, and they are very hard driving. The employee-centered supervisors consider supervision rather than production to be their main task. Therefore, they provide general outlines of what needs to be done, and then they leave employees to do their work and to ask questions if problems arise. The researchers concluded that high-production groups had employee-centered supervisors, while low-production groups had production-centered supervisors.

Likert then described a number of management styles in organizations. These styles could be placed on a continuum, as in Table 10.2.

System 1 prevails when management has no confidence in subordinates and so does not involve them in decision making at any levels. Fear, threats of punishment, and very occasional rewards characterize the motivation system at work here. Control is concentrated at top management, and the informal organization generally develops opposing the formal organization's goals.

System 2 can be seen as a master–servant relationship. Although there is more trust involved than in System 1, condescension usually characterizes top management. Major decisions and goal setting occur at the

TABLE 10.2 LIKERT SCALE

Organizational variable	Leadership process used			
	System 1	System 2	System 3	System 4
Supervisors' confidence in subordinates	No confidence in subordinates	Condescending confidence such as master/servant	Substantial, but not complete confidence, controls decisions	Complete confidence
Motivational forces Manner in which motives are used	Fears and threats	Some rewards but actual punishment	Rewards and occasional punishment, some involvement	Participation, many rewards
Interaction Amount and character of interaction	Little, and always with fear and distrust	Little, with condescension	Moderate	Extensive

top, but many decisions are made on lower levels. Punishment and reward make up the motivation system. Subordinates are guarded and sometimes fearful. The informal organization resists formal organizational goals but does not oppose them outright.

System 3 is marked by substantial but not complete confidence in subordinates. Broad policy and general decisions are made at the top, but more decisions are delegated downward. Communication flows up and down, and rewards are common. Superiors and subordinates interact, often with a fair degree of confidence. If an informal organization develops, it may either support or partially resist the formal organization's goals.

System 4 exists when management has complete confidence in subordinates. Decision making is dispersed and thoroughly integrated throughout the organization. Communication flows upward, downward, and laterally. Motivation is handled through participation in developing economic rewards, setting goals, improving methods, and appraising progress toward goals. Superiors and subordinates interact in a friendly, confident manner. The informal and formal organizations are often one and the same, because the social forces support the organization's goals.

Libraries tend to be either System 2 or System 3, although a very few are System 1 and some do employ System 4. A trend toward System 4 has been evident, both in libraries as a whole and by individual supervisors in libraries with no such policy. But, as we shall see in the discussion of participative management, this system also has problems.

Some subsequent studies, particularly those conducted by Vroom and Mann (1960)[16] and by Fiedler (1967),[17] contradicted Likert's conclusion that employee-centered supervisors are responsible for high production. One study found a higher production figure for a production-centered supervisor's group than for a group with an employee-centered supervisor. Another study concluded that the nature of the job determined the type of supervision that would work best. For instance, in situations that demand a high degree of worker confidence (when workers know what is expected), a firm, no-nonsense attitude on the part of the supervisor is most effective.

Although the personality of the manager has an effect on the work situation, the personality of the worker is equally important. A worker who is unawed by superiors will want to have more say in decisions affecting work; this type of person would probably do best under an employee-centered supervisor. Yet there are many people who prefer carrying out the orders of a strong supervisor instead of deciding matters for themselves. Managers, then, are given a choice of styles; they must choose the most effective style, taking into account the organization's goals, the work environment, and the individuals who work within the unit(s).

MANAGING BY RESULTS

Many supervisors attempt to follow a middle-of-the-road approach to motivation that has been labeled *managing by results*. When an individual behaves compatibly with organizational goals, the behavior is reinforced by means of a reward. If the behavior is antiorganizational, the supervisor chooses from among three alternatives: (1) use negative reinforcement (punishment) to achieve goals (although other alternatives avoid some negative aspects of punishment); (2) reevaluate both the stimulus and the person, as a different approach might well do the job; or (3) fire the person, which is a last resort and an indication of failure on both sides.

The supervisor establishes job content and performance standards for the subordinate, but the individual can vary the pattern so long as the required result is achieved.* This approach requires initiative on the part of the employee, but that can only come about as part of a gradual process; to expect overnight maturity is unrealistic as well as unfair.

This approach also demands that the individual know that performance evaluation will be in terms of production and what the method of evaluation will be. The ground rules for any value judgment must be made clear prior to the point at which the judgment will be made.

Finally, allowance must be made for the time and effort required to train future managers and supervisory personnel. It will be well worth the investment to have qualified individuals in management positions.

Careful definition of the boundaries of acceptable employee behavior is always a good idea, and it becomes vital here. The levels in at which decisions may and may not be made must be quite clear. Yet, freedom to act within those boundaries must also be present, because the result is what matters, not the performance of activities leading to the result. The great temptation is to judge the activities, but this can do more harm than good in the working environment.

Supervisor and employee alike must realize that this system requires a great deal of interdependence. Moving in this direction is a risk for the supervisor, because that one person is ultimately responsible for the results. The supervisor must trust subordinates, and the workers must

---

*This differs from MBO in that the content and standard are set by the supervisors alone, not in cooperation with the employees.

realize that both they and the supervisor are vulnerable. Thus, the organizational goal must be kept foremost in the minds of all concerned as they cooperate to achieve it.

THE MANAGERIAL GRID

In 1964, Robert Blake and Jan Mouton proposed a method of plotting different theories of management leadership styles (see Figure 10.3). It involves a grid with two variables: concern for people and concern for production. This method summarizes all of the preceding approaches.

In the grid, styles are located in a matrix, with concern for production on the horizontal axis (scale 1–9) and concern for people on the vertical axis (scale 1–9). As either factor increases, its number becomes higher. Blake and Mouton describe five leadership styles.

1. *Impoverished* The least possible amount of energy is used to accomplish required work, and only enough effort to sustain organizational membership is exerted.

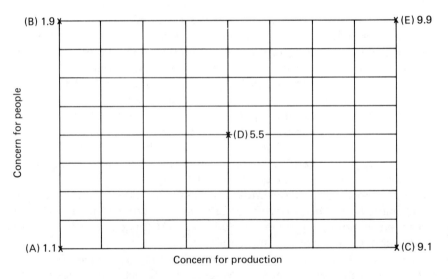

A. Impoverished
B. Country club
C. Task
D. Middle of the road
E. Team

Figure 10.3 Managerial grid. (Based on R. Blake and J. Mouton, *The Managerial Grid*, Houston: Gulf Publishing, 1964.)

2. *Country club* Thoughtful attention is given to people's needs for interpersonal relationships, but the atmosphere is so friendly that production is poor.
3. *Task* Operational efficiency results from arranging work so that human elements produce the least amount of interference.
4. *Middle of the road* Adequate performance is achieved by balancing the necessity for production with the maintenance of morale.
5. *Team* Motivated persons producing for a common goal maintain both high production and high morale.

Style 1.1 on the grid (lower left) represents a laissez-faire style of supervision—minimal concern for both production and people. Style 1.9 (top left) represents maximum concern for people and minimum concern for production—the human-relations school. The 9.1 style (lower right) shows maximum concern for production and minimal concern for people—authoritarian supervision. And the 9.9 style (top right) demonstrates maximum concern for both production and people—the ideal form of leadership insofar as Blake and Mouton are concerned.

The 5.5 style (middle of the grid) is that of the middle-of-the-road supervisor who would rather suppress or compromise than bring conflict into the open and resolve it. The ideal 9.9, on the other hand, develops committed employees who share common goals. Conflicts are faced squarely and resolved in an atmosphere of openness and trust.

Naturally, every one of these styles has its drawbacks, including the 9.9—it is hard to develop committed people, and a willingness to bring conflict into the open often backfires. Even if a group is used to this type of approach, it is never certain how open conflict and competition will be resolved.

PARTICIPATIVE MANAGEMENT

As noted earlier, participative management has been a catch phrase among librarians for the past 10 years.[18] In fact, reading and listening to discussions might convince a person that this was the solution for all library problems. Yet, the application of participative management in libraries has not resulted in the solution of very many management problems; in fact, it has created new ones.

The concept is based on Lidert's System 4, with other facets taken from various researchers in the field of motivation. Figure 10.4 is an attempt to depict the way in which all the motivation concepts in this chapter relate with one another and where participative management fits in the picture.

As the term *participative management* implies, the entire staff should

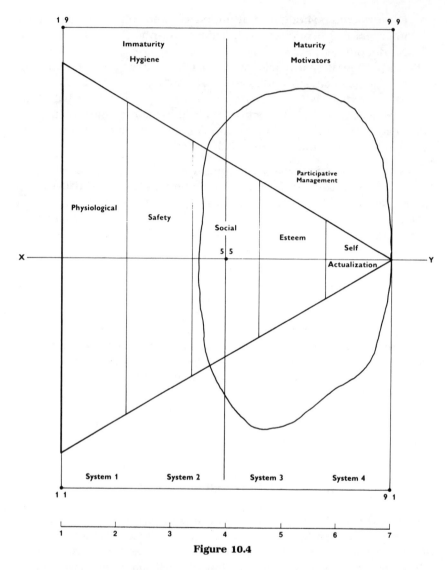

Figure 10.4

participate in the management of the library—professionals, paraprofessionals, and clerical, full-time and part-time employees. Also implied but seldom practiced is full participation by patrons. Ultimately, this whole process relies on group decision making; in order to achieve this, there must be group discussions. M. Marchant, author of several articles on this subject, states the following in his book *Participative Management in Academic Libraries.*

Participative management requires group discussion, and each group should be small enough that all may take part. The group is concerned with issues of mutual concern. Thus, the director would not discuss cataloging changes without involving public services personnel. Nor would he allow the discussion to center on personalities but would hold it to resolution of the mutual problem.[19]

Two factors stand out in this statement. One of them is that everyone must meet in small groups—and this quickly translates into costs of staff time. (Anyone who has been involved in committee meetings knows how long it takes to reach a majority opinion or a consensus on an important issue.) When there is a public to be served, time is a precious commodity, and hours of discussion do not serve the public. One library estimated that committee decisions on major issues cost approximately $5000 per decision in staff salaries alone; several of the sample decision cost figures are twice as high. Extensive use of committees also can generate hostility over a period of time.

Over the past 5 years, I have occasionally used a case study about participative management in my management courses. The case is based on a letter that appeared in a newspaper; the letter is reprinted here in its entirety. However, because the letter could cause some embarrassment, no citation is provided.

TO: The City Librarian

Most of the time when I try to reach someone in a supervisory capacity in the library, I am told that they are in a meeting. When I ask for them to call back, the return call often takes hours, or sometimes, the call isn't returned until the next day. The frequency of meetings, combined with the time lag to return a call, has led me to the subjective judgment that librarians are in more and longer meetings than city council members and that librarians' meetings' length factor approaches that of the run-of-the-mill city manager.

It is obvious that the efficiency of the library system would be vastly improved if the number of meetings, their length, and the number of people in each meeting could be decreased. Since librarians are hired on their qualifications as bibliognosts and not as conclavists (sic), I present the solution to the meetings problem: hire a Professional Meeter.

The Professional Meeter would be highly trained in attending and chairing meetings, making wise-sounding noises, raising spurious and substantive points, and suggesting that the decision can be made at a subsequent meeting. Whenever someone wants to call a meeting, he must call only the Professional Meeter, thus saving everyone else the trouble of attending. The Professional Meeter would also be trained to recognize the terminal syndrome of Library Meetingitis. In such cases, whenever some library administrator has the unnatural urges to call too many meetings, too lengthy ones, and/or too large ones, the Professional Meeter calls the Rape Crisis Line, the Hot Line, Escort Service, or similar instant source of help. Even the City Librarian might be contacted.

Think of all the time that would be saved. By hiring a single Professional Meeter, thousands of hours of time would be saved on the part of everyone else in the library system. With all the money thus saved, part could be used by the library and part

would go to promote the Professional Meeter through the ranks to Senior Professional
Meeter, Principal Professional Meeter, and (heaven help us) Supervising Professional
Meeter. And everyone else in the library could get back to work.

Arthur D. Honeywell
Library Consumer

Although the letter is overstated, it does reflect a valid concern of
patrons and staff. How can people be active in committee work (a major
element in participative management) and still provide adequate service?

One major difficulty with the concept of participative management
concerns accountability. A committee simply is not accountable, as was
pointed out in Chapter 5. Accountability, and how to handle it in a
participative management environment, is a problem that is rarely, if
ever, identified in books or articles on the subject. Yet, decisions requiring accountability are made in precisely those areas in which the staff
wants the most input. Given the authority relationships for agencies that
receive government funds, accountability must be present. So, how do
you have both accountability and staff input on the levels desired?

If you first determine staff views and then reserve the actual decision
making for yourself (as director) and a small group of staff members, this
is not participative management. It might be called consultative management. Misuse of the label *participative management* by directors of libraries, when they really mean *consultative management*, has probably
caused more anger and frustration than people realize.

People may assume at first that they are involved in a "textbook case"
(a library that is well run, with good staff relations and excellent patron
good will), making participative management easy, but the need for
accountability quickly becomes clear, especially if the library board calls
the director on the carpet for a "bad" decision. Then, management begins to view committee deliberations as advisory rather than as binding
decisions, and staff begins to feel "used" once this change is made clear
to them. So, "why trust management?" becomes the question.

Certainly, all this presents a bleak picture of participative management.
Currently, although a person may philosophically support the concept, it
is difficult to see how it can be applied practically in libraries. Until such
items as serving the public effectively while still attending the necessary
meetings and maintaining accountability can be solved, the idea should
be implemented with caution and selectivity.

It is best, then, not to suggest that you are going to use participative
management. Simply ask for advice and input from staff on decisions
regarding them and the library in general. This is consultative management. Make it clear that their voice needs to be heard but that the decision will be made by the appropriate party—the one with responsibility,

authority, and accountability for the area affected. If you fully explain the issues while using this approach, you can gain many of the benefits and few of the problems of participative management.

Naturally, this will not satisfy everyone. But I know of no organizations (except fully professional ones in Etzioni's sense) that have been able to implement participative management and operate successfully for more than a few years. Selective use of the elements of the concept in concert with other ideas regarding work motivation can achieve positive results and avoid many of the pitfalls that result from jumping on the bandwagon of a popular idea that was not developed with the special aspects of library organization in mind.

Motivation is inseparable from an individual's goals, values, psychic needs, and life experiences. What motivates one person may completely fail to strike a responsive chord in another.

Most people modify their personal goals as they go through life. Some will set continuously higher goals and challenges for themselves, whereas others restrict their ambitions and goals. A person who has lost motivation and self-confidence through a series of misfortunes may regain them if the opportunity to try again is met with success. Such a person would be fortunate to work for a supervisor who is sensitive and alert to the potential beneath the protective coat of caution and pessimism—one who will give the support and encouragement necessary for success.

In concert with job performance or accomplishment, salary can be a powerful motivator—witness the salesperson on commission as compared with one on a straight salary. Libraries can work toward a similar end, though not quite in the same manner. A good motivator in this setting might be more time off with pay.

Supervisors should see that employees in their area are treated equitably and that they are given recognition and rewards for superior achievement. Keeping communication channels open can usually help toward nipping problems in the bud.

If you have a sound understanding of the basics of library organization and operation, and of human psychology—and if you read and think about new ideas regarding work motivation, and then choose those that seem most appropriate for your unit—then you should be a good supervisor. *Flexibility* is the key word in a good motivation system. No two people are alike, and human behavior is too complex for anyone to achieve long-term success as a manager if that person depends on rules, formulas, or one single system for handling every person and problem. In essence, good supervision requires situational thinking; that is, each case should be approached as though it were unique. In fact, most cases are unique to some degree. It comes down to a frequently repeated formula:

If you treat staff members as you wish to be treated, you will have very few motivation or morale problems in your unit.

BIBLIOGRAPHY

1. A. H. Maslow, *Motivation and Personality* (New York: Harper, 1954).
2. A. Davis, "The Motivation of the Underprivileged Worker," in *Industry and Society,* ed. by W. F. Whyte (New York: McGraw-Hill, 1946).
3. A. H. Maslow, "A Preface to Motivational Theory," *Psychosomatic Medicine* 23 (1943): 85–99.
4. L. Peter, *The Peter Principle* (New York: Morrow, 1969).
5. C. P. Alderfer, "An Empirical Test of A New Theory of Human Needs," *Organizational Behavior and Human Performance* 4 (1969): 142–175.
6. Alderfer, p. 154.
7. D. McGregor, *The Human Side of Enterprise* (New York: McGraw-Hill, 1960).
8. McGregor, p. 46–48.
9. C. Argyris, *Integrating the Individual and the Organization* (New York: Wiley, 1965). "Personality and Organization Theory Revisited," *Administrative Science Quarterly* 18 (1973): 747–767.
10. C. Argyris, (1965), p. 32.
11. F. Herzberg, *Motivation to Work* 2d. ed. (New York: Wiley, 1959).
12. R. N. Ford, *Why Jobs Die and What to Do About It* (New York: AMACOM, 1979).
13. K. P. Plate, and E. W. Stone, "Factors Affecting Librarians' Job Satisfaction: A Report of Two Studies," *Library Quarterly* 44 (1974): 97–110.
14. V. M. Bockman, "The Herzberg Controversy," *Personnel Psychology* 24 (1971): 155–189.
15. R. Likert, "Measuring Organizational Performance," *Harvard Business Review* 36 (1958): 41–50. *The Human Organization* (New York: McGraw-Hill, 1967).
16. V. H. Vroom, and F. C. Mann, "Leader Authoritarianism and Employee Attitudes," *Personnel Psychology* 13 (1960): 125–140.
17. F. E. Fielder, *A Theory of Leadership Effectiveness* (New York: McGraw-Hill, 1967).
18. *Participative Management, Quality of Worklife and Job Enrichment* (Parkridge, N.J.: Noyes Data Corporation, 1977).
19. M. P. Marchart, Participative Management in Academic Libraries (Westport, Conn.: Greenwood, 1976).

FURTHER READING

Alber, A. F. "How (and How Not) to Approach Job Enrichment." *Personnel Journal* 58 (1979): 337–341.
Archer, E. R. "The Myth of Motivation." *Personnel Administrator* 23 (1978): 57–65.
Argyris, C. "Personality and Organization Theory Revisited." *Administrative Science Quarterly* 18 (1973): 747–767.
Argyris, C. *Integrating the Individual and the Organization.* New York: Wiley, 1965.
Berry, L. "Motivation Management." *Journal of Systems Management* 30 (1979): 30–32.
Bittel, L. R. *What Every Supervisor Should Know.* 3rd ed. New York: McGraw-Hill, 1974.
Blake, R. F., and Mouton, J. S. *Making Experience Work; The Approach to Critique.* New York: McGraw-Hill, 1978.

Blake, R. F., and Mouton, J. S. *The New Managerial Grid.* Houston: Gulf Publishing, 1978.

Bolles, R. C. *Theory of Motivation* 2d. ed. New York: Harper, 1975.

Brooker, M. "Does Traditional Organization Theory Conflict with Theory Y?" *Personnel* 41 (1964): 65–68.

Brown, M. A. "Values—A Necessary But Neglected Ingredient of Motivation on the Job." *Academy of Management Review* 1 (1976): 15–23.

Clark, J. V. "Motivation in Work Groups." *Human Organization* 19 (1960): 199–208.

Cook, S. H. "From X to Y—A Fresh Look at the Basics." *Management World* 6 (1977): 10–14.

Davis, A. "The Motivation of the Underprivileged Worker." In *Industry and Society,* edited by W. F. Whyte. New York: McGraw-Hill, 1946.

Dowling, W. F., and Sayles, L. R. *How Managers Motivate: The Imperative of Supervision.* 2d ed. New York: McGraw-Hill, 1978.

Dubois, P. "La Motivation au Travail: Quelques Considérations Théoriques et Pratiques." *Documentation et Bibliothèques* 21 (1975): 123–128.

Fielder, F. E. *A Theory of Leadership Effectiveness.* New York: McGraw-Hill, 1967.

Fleishman, E. A. "Patterns of Leadership Behavior Related to Employee Grievances and Turnover." *Personnel Psychology* 15 (1962): 43–56.

Ford, R. N. *Why Jobs Die and What to Do About It; Job Redesign and Future Productivity.* New York: AMACOM, 1979.

Friedlander, F. "Performance and Interactional Dimensions of Organizational Work Groups." *Journal of Applied Psychology* 50 (1966): 257–265.

Gayle, J. B., and Searle, F. R. "Maslow, Motivation and the Manager." *Management World* 9 (1980): 19–20.

Goodman, C. H. "Employee Motivation." *Library Trends* 20 (1971): 39–47.

Grant, P. C. "Do You Know What Your Employees Really Want?" *Management World* 7 (1978): 13–15.

Hanson, C. A., and Donna K. "Motivation: Are the Old Theories Still True?" *Supervisory Management* 23 (1978): 9–15.

Herzberg, F. *The Motivation to Work.* 2d ed. New York: Wiley, 1959.

Herzberg, F. *The Managerial Choice: To Be Effecient and to Be Human.* Homwood, Ill.: Dow Jones-Irwin, 1976.

Huberman, J. "Discipline Without Punishment." *Harvard Business Review* 42 (1964): 62–68.

Katz, D. "The Motivational Basis of Organization Behavior." *Behavioral Science* 9 (1964): 131–146.

Katz, R. "Job Longevity as a Situational Factor in Job Satisfaction." *Administrative Science Quarterly* 23 (1978): 204–223.

Krenta, N. "Middle Management, Motivation and Communication." *Canadian Library Association Feliciter* 10 (1964): 3–5.

Lewis, M. "Management by Objectives: Review, Application, and Relationships with Job Satisfaction and Performance." *Journal of Academic Librarianship* 5 (1980): 329–334.

Likert, R. *The Human Organization.* New York: McGraw-Hill, 1967.

Likert, R. "Measuring Organizational Performance." *Harvard Business Review* 36 (1958): 41–50.

McGregor, D. *The Human Side of Enterprise.* New York: McGraw-Hill, 1960.

McMurry, R. N. "Conflicts in Human Values." *Harvard Business Review* 50 (1943): 370–396.

May, B. R. "Give Employee Morale a Boost." *Supervision* 41 (1979): 3–4.

May, B. R. "Motivation: The Key to Productivity." *Supervision* 41 (1979): 13–15.

Meyer, M. C. "Demotivation—Its Cause and Cure." *Personnel Journal* 57 (1978): 260–266.

Morton, D. J. "Applying Theory Y to Library Management." *College and Research Libraries* 36 (1975): 302–307.

Norton, S. D. "Is Job Enrichment a Success or a Failure?" *Human Resource Management* 18 (Winter 1979): 28–36.

Participative Management, Quality of Worklife and Job Enrichment. Parkridge: N.J.: Noyes Data Corporation, 1977.

Plate, K. H., and Stone, E. W. "Factors Affecting Librarians' Job Satisfaction: A Report of Two Studies." *Library Quarterly* 44 (1974): 97–110.

Sandell, R. M. "Promoting Employee Suggestions." *Supervision* 41 (1979): 11–13.

Schneier, C. E. "Improving Performance in the Public Sector Through Behavior Modification and Positive Reinforcement." *Public Personnel Management* 8 (1979): 101–111.

Strauss, P. S. "Is Job Enrichment Really the Answer?" In *Personnel Development in Libraries,* edited by K. Maloney. New Brunswick, N.J.: Rutgers University Graduate School of Library Science, 1976.

"Understanding the Attitudes of Today's Employees: An Interview with Dr. John Mee." *Nations Business* 64 (1976): 22–24.

Unstot, D. D. "Effects of Job Enrichment and Task Goals on Satisfaction and Productivity: Implications for Job Design." *Journal of Applied Psychology* 61 (1976): 379–394.

Von der Embse, T. J., and Brown, H. E. "Authentic Motivation: How Psychological Touching Works." *Supervisory Management* 24 (1979): 19–23.

Vroom, V. H., and Mann, F. C. "Leader Authoritarianism and Employee Attitudes." *Personnel Psychology* 13 (1960): 125–140.

Roy W. Walters & Associates. *Job Enrichment for Results: Strategies for Successful Implementation.* Reading, Mass.: Addison-Wesley, 1975.

Weaver, C. N. "Sex Differences in the Determinants of Job Satisfaction." *Academy of Management Journal* 21 (1978): 265–274.

11. Leadership in Management

What is leadership? What makes a good leader? Can a person become a leader? Questions such as these have been of interest to people for almost as long as people have lived in groups. Until the 1960s, the common assumption (despite ample evidence to the contrary) was "once a leader, always a leader" (and, obviously, "once a person has failed as a leader, that person can never lead again"). What have been the results of recent interest, study, and research in the area of leadership? "Styles of leadership have been studied and restudied; prescriptions for leadership have been written and revised; and exercise of leadership has been carefully analyzed and often sharply criticized. Yet, despite all this attention, the question of 'what it takes to be an effective leader' is still far from settled."[1]

Definitions of leadership are as varied as the number of writers and speakers on the subject. A person is assumed to have taken on a leadership role when that person exercises influence over a group, including directing group activities toward a goal. The group voluntarily accepts this influence and direction for a number of reasons: outstanding skill in a particular area, extensive experience in the area of concern, or specific personality traits. As long as the group is successful, the person retains leadership; a series of failures usually results in a change.

Libraries and other organizations through which people earn a living and contribute to society are not volunary groups. Individuals are hired, retained, or dismissed on the basis of their individual skills, knowledge, and ability to do the required work. Yet, since library directors and supervisors are seldom voted into office by the library staff, can one really talk about leadership in the organization setting? The answer is a qualified "yes." The major difference in leadership in an organization is that there is no voluntary group acceptance; instead, acceptance must be earned from the staff. Because the library environment is highly structured, a person must prove leadership abilities in a limited framework—a difficult task at best.

APPROACHES TO LEADERSHIP

Until the 1950s, the study of leadership had focused on the personality traits of the individual leader. Thus, it was generally assumed that a person was born either a leader or a follower. However, as is the case with so many other personality studies (of the creative person, the successful writer, the famous singer, the great dancer, and so on), the list of general personality traits became very long and contradictory. Eventually, it became clear to researchers that no degree of study would produce a definitive list of a leader's personality traits.

Consequently, focus shifted to the environment in which leadership exists—the "situational approach." Studies were (and are being) conducted on such factors as the interactions between the manager (leader) and the staff (followers), the organization's needs at any given time, the type of work that the organization performs, and/or the group's values, ethics, experiences, etc. Both experience and studies have indicated that the environment is indeed important in the success or failure of a leader.

For instance, several times in the past, libraries have hired persons for directorships who had been successful managers in business or other activities. Sometimes these individuals succeeded, but they often failed. Knowledge in one area, success in one field, the ability to work with people in a particular field—none of these are guaranteed to transfer from one field to another. Even within a single field, leaders are affected by changes in environmental needs, expectations, and roles of followers. During the late 1960s, American academic leadership went through a series of rapid changes (or saw earlier changes culminate), the end result being an extensive change in leadership (directorships).[2] Most of the directors who resigned, or were fired, were some years away from retirement age. They would have been rated as successful leaders 5 or 10 years earlier, even by the same staffs who would come to support their vacating the directorships. The key was that, in most cases, the directors had not changed in personality or style of management, even though the environment around those people had changed. Successful leadership in 1958, 1960, or 1962 was inadequate, or barely acceptable, in the 1968, 1970, or 1972 library situation.

One of the more successful approaches to leadership was developed by F. E. Fiedler and the staff at the University of Illinois Group Effective-ness Research Laboratory.[3] They identified three major factors that affect a person's leader-ship effectiveness: (1) the leader's power or authority, as defined by the official position held; (2) the nature of the work being performed by the group; and (3) the personal relationship between the leader and the group. Their basic conclusion was not too surprising: "The leader who is liked by his group and has a clear-cut task and high position power . . . has everything in his favor. The leader who has poor relationships with his group members, an unstructured task and weak position power likely will be unable to exert much influence over the group."[4]

From the librarians' point of view, the director's power position vis-à-vis outside agencies (because the library is part of a whole) is generally low. Thus, when the library needs strong leadership in its relationship with either agencies and organizations, there is a problem. Frequently, though, the library staff fails to remember this constraint on the director when assessing that person's success with outside groups. Within the library, an individual will usually have a clearly defined position of power, due to the hierarchical structure that most libraries favor. Again, the more structured the work environment, the less room there is for maneuvering in order to obtain a desired result for the group.

As far as the nature of the work is concerned, most of the library's internal work is reasonably well defined, so the manager should have little problem in this regard. Problems may arise regarding the expecta-tions held by outside groups as to what the library should be doing. This is, indeed, highly probable if the library's objectives have not been stated clearly and precisely. (Vague statements lead to variety in interpreta-tions.) It is also wise to avoid being caught between staff expectations and knowledge and public expectations. The director can do this by making certain that library objectives meet the criteria for good objectives.

Of the three factors identified by Fiedler's group, the one over which the leader has the most control is personal relations. By working on this aspect of leadership, an individual can achieve a certain degree of suc-cess, even if the other two factors are not as favorable as they might be. The remainder of this chapter, then, focuses on the personal aspect of leadership. In essence, this chapter is directly related to Chapters 3 through 10, because one must know and implement the concepts dis-cussed in those chapters in order to develop good staff relations.

ASSUMPTIONS REGARDING LEADERSHIP

Several assumptions regarding leadership underlie this chapter. One major assumption is that a leader attains or assumes a position of leadership in a library through an appointment process in which the staff does *not* have the final say. Systems may vary from no input, to a staff vote on several candidates; but the actual hiring decision rests with an outside body. Therefore, in the minds of staff, the director or leader is, to some degree, appointed by decree of a higher authority. Also, the new employee's power position is understood, and all that can be varied is the degree of informal influence that can be exerted on higher positions or outside bodies.

The second assumption is that a person starts off in every position with only the rank and authority that is derived from the office. Initially, there is no leadership. People in the unit do the work because the supervisor is "boss," and because that work is their job. A "good" manager will quickly move beyond this "do-it-because-I-told-you-to" approach and use leadership rather than authority to accomplish things through people. Failure to move from strict reliance on authority almost always generates a tension-filled environment laced with distrust, suspicion, and hostility.

In professional or semiprofessional organizations, it is almost a given that the professional staff shares to some degree the organizational goals and objectives.[5] Nonprofessional staff are less likely to share the goals completely, but in a library, one may assume that most full-time staff members who have been there for more than five years share the organizational objectives. In particular, Robert Presthus found that there is a close correlation between the values of professional and nonprofessional staff.[6] This means that the quality of work performed will be strongly influenced by the supervisor's mode of operation.

The third assumption is two-edged: no one is a born leader; leadership is a skill that can be learned (at least insofar as human relations are concerned). To some degree, everyone has leadership potential in some situations, which means that you should be careful about saying that someone has no leadership potential. You need to clarify the exact situations that you have in mind whenever you cast doubt on someone else's leadership ability. It may now be more clear precisely why it has been pointed out that leadership is a complex process that depends on a combination of people and environmental factors.

FUNCTIONS OF LEADERSHIP

Up to this point, no functions or roles have been identified for the organizational leader. Several years ago, in a book on social psychology, Kreck, Crutchfield, and Ballachey produced a reasonably comprehensive list of the functions of a leader. The following list is derived from that work; in many ways, it is similar to Mintzberg's list (see p. 31), although Mintzberg indicates that he is describing the manager's role.

Executive or top coordinator of group activities. To coordinate activities, the leader needs to devote considerable time and energy to reconciling personal (own and staff's) and organizational goals.

Planner for the group. As the person in charge, and presumably the one who has more time and information, the leader must develop new ideas, anticipate changes, and propose adjustments in the group's activities. A leader who has no plans is not a leader.

Policy maker within limits. A manager who operates only on authority receives policy guidelines from above and may delegate some policy making to subordinates. A true leader derives policy-making power from a third source—the subordinates. That is to say, because of subordinates' trust and desire, the leader formulates policy for them.

Expert in the field. The difference between a manager and a leader lies in attitude. The leader share knowledge and skills willingly and in a manner suggesting an equal relationship, not a superior–subordinate relationship.

Example setter. Both in attitude and performance, the leader sets the tone and pace for the group. It is not surprising to find the staff of a leader emulating that person's methods of working, attitudes, and occasionally, even style of dress.

Controller of internal relations. In a unit supervised by a leader, the formal and informal structures usually are very similar (a situation that is rare for the nonleader). More often than not, the leader is the hub around which all activities revolve.

Arbitrator and mediator. Although the leader and manger have this role thrust upon them, the leader actually takes more of it on voluntarily. Because of the staff's respect for and trust in the leader, they bring most of their problems to that person for resolution. Many of these are the types of problems that the nonleading manager would never even hear about.

Purveyor of rewards and punishment. Again, this role is held both by the leader and by the plain manager. Although neither one may personally administer rewards and punishment, both approve or recommend such actions. The difference is that the manager will find that even rewards are questioned (as well as punishments); this is something that never occurs in the case of a leader.

Substitute for individual responsibility. A leader will often tell a subordinate, "Go ahead and do X, and if there's any flak about it, I'll take the blame." The subordinate knows that this will be the case with a leader. Nonleaders either force the subordinate to take the blame or, after saying that they will accept the responsibility, they avoid it.

Symbol of the group. Because they set its tone, leaders tend to be regarded both by members of the group and by people outside it as the symbol of the group. In the work group, this is tied to the manager's accountability, but it goes far beyond that for a leader.

Representative to nongroup persons. A group expects that its leader will be its spokesperson to outsiders. Other persons may be capable of assuming this role, but the majority of people are secure in the belief that the leader is best qualified to present the group's position and protect its interests. Nonleaders also represent the group to outsiders, but the group's feelings are very different toward them in this role.

Scapegoat. True leaders know that they will at times receive the blame for things they have no way of controlling. They accept this as readily as they accept the accountability that accompanies their position. Nonleader managers often have difficulty accepting the accountability of their position, let alone other responsibilities.

Given this rather broad range of roles—many of which are similar for leaders and managers alike—what should a person do to become a leader? First of all, realize that there is a variety of leadership styles, just as their is a variety of managerial styles. However, leadership styles vary more often as situations change. Fiedler and his associates suggest that, when tasks are clear-cut (as in the library), when relationships between staff and manager are positive, and when the position is strong (seldom the case outside the library), then the leader should be strongly directive rather than democratic nondirective. As the situation shifts toward the other extreme, the leader is advised to become less and less directive and increasingly participative in approach. Therefore, within the mythical average library, it would seem advisable to use a moderate-to-strong directive approach based on moderate-to-strong staff input. For relations with other agencies, it would seem advisable to use the strongly democratic–nondirective approach.

Table 11.1 is based on Keith Davis' classification system for leader-ship styles.[7] This, along with Tannanbaum and Schmidt's seven-point scale of leadership behavior, gives an idea of the variety of available styles.[8] Referring back to Figure 10.4, the seven digits below the X–Y line represent the seven points of the Tannanbaum–Schmidt scale. This illustrates the degree to which leadership and moderation are interrelated. The seven

TABLE 11.1 LEADERSHIP STYLES[a]

	Autocratic	Custodial	Supportive	Collegial
	Power	Economic resources	Leadership	Mutual contribution
Managerial orientation	Authority	Material reward	Support	Teamwork
Employee orientation	Obedience	Security	Performance	Responsibility
Employee psychological result	Personal dependency	Organization dependency	Participation	Self-discipline
Employee needs met	Subsistence	Maintenance	Higher order	Self-realization
Performance result	Minimum	Passive cooperation	Achieved drives	Some enthusiasm

[a]Based upon K. Davis' work in *Human Behavior at Work: Human Relations and Organizational Behavior.* New York: McGraw-Hill, copyright © 1972, p. 498. Used with the permission of McGraw-Hill Book Company.

points (moving from *X* to *Y*) are: (1) the manager is able to make a decision that nonmanagers accept; (2) the manager must "sell" the decision before gaining acceptance; (3) the manager presents the decision but must respond to questions from nonmanagers; (4) the manager presents a tentative decision, subject to change after nonmanagerial input; (5) the manager presents a problem, gets input from nonmanagers, then decides; (6) the manager determines the limits within which nonmanagers may make decision; and (7) managers and nonmanagers make decisions jointly within limits defined by organizational constraints.

GIVING ORDERS

Ultimately, if the manager is to accomplish things through people with only an official grant of authority, he or she must give orders (directions). Without question, giving orders or directions has more to do with being a leader than any other activity. The position already has its inherent authority; you need to develop the authority of respect if you hope to become a leader. Authority of respect is *earned,* and it is earled *slowly.* It can be earned through shared experiences in which subordinates feel they have received fair treatment, proper recognition for work well done, sound advice and firm direction, recognition and fair treatment of poor performance, and a fair hearing for their interests and concerns. If all this comes about, the staff will give more than is expected, and they will do so voluntarily. A climate of cooperation will exist, and the them-versus-us syndrome will cease to exist—at least insofar as the immediate supervisor is concerned.

From the leader's point of view, there are three broad categories of work climate: cooperation, compliance, and hostile compliance. (In merit systems, and very rarely in other systems, a fourth type exists: noncompliance. It is normally short-lived, because someone will leave unless things change; it is usually found in places in which there is a high degree of job security.) Naturally, the climate of cooperation is the one to be preferred, but this can only come about over a long period of time, because it requires mutual trust.

Most typical is the climate of compliance. People do what they are told to do (what is expected), but they do no more and no less. Enthusiasm is lacking, no initiative is shown, mistakes are common, and mistakes often result from following the letter of an order even though it does not conform to previous practice. ("Look, I did just what you told me to do. If there's a problem in the procedure, *you* correct it. That's what they pay you for!") This is a typical reaction when a procedure goes wrong in a compliance climate. Yet, if the supervisor knows that the problem could have been avoided, hostility and resentment come into the picture. If the feelings are allowed to carry over to the next activity, more distrust will be generated. The situation can slide rather quickly from compliance to hostile compliance.

Hostile compliance can exist over a long period of time. Sides are taken, and each side does its best to catch the other side off guard. Civilities usually are observed, and work is done—but at the absolute minimum level. The supervisor gathers evidence to justify disciplinary action. The staff usually is well aware of this, but it hopes to cause the supervisor difficulties by keeping production to the absolute minimum in quality and quantity (so that higher-ups will notice). They also wait for the order that, if carried out to the letter, will cause disaster for the supervisor. If mutual respect and trust are present from the beginning, though, one poorly given order will not create a hostile-compliance environment.

What can you do to develop the climate of cooperation, which is an essential element in leadership? You can begin with delegation. Even within the smallest unit, some tasks can usually be delegated. Give authority along with the delegation, so that the staff learns that you trust them. (This can be a problem in strict merit systems, wherein delegation beyond the job description can affect classification and salary. Walk softly in these cases.) Such delegation will also give the staff an opportunity to develop new skills. Because staff members usually welcome growth opportunities, you can enhance their positive feelings and encourage co-operation through delegation. Delegation also provides you with more time for planning and working on problems; this will help to establish your reputation as a planner and an expert, both of which are needed for strong leadership.

Mistakes will occur whenever individuals take on new duties and try to perform activities that they have never attempted. By treating these mistakes as learning and teaching experiences, you can enhance your reputation as an expert. By approaching the work in a positive manner, you will begin to fill the role of example setter—enthusiasm is contagious! If mistakes are expected, and if teaching and correction is undertaken in a peer relationship (not a superior–subordinate atmosphere), the experience can be positive for everyone.

You must check on the progress of all delegated work. After all, you are responsible for the overall completion of the tasks assigned to the unit. More important, though, is to check properly and not too often—in this way, you let the staff know that you are interested in their progress and ready and willing to help when needed. At the beginning, a weekly or biweekly progress report is a good means of learning about progress and problems. Such reports also dispel the image of someone hovering over employees' shoulders and worrying about what is happening. If you use these reports in your own reports to superiors, then the staff will see you in the role of group representative.

When it comes to actually issuing an order or directive, you have two modes of presentation: a demand or a request. The factors discussed in Chapter 9 will influence the way in which your directive is perceived— both its content and the intent behind it. Oral communication always contains nonverbal elements, and situational factors also enter into the process of interpreting a message.

People respond to requests more quickly than they respond to demands in the cooperative and compliance environments. The mutual dependence between supervisor and staff is made clear, and the recipient of the order feels a recognition of individual humanity. Requests are easier to modify than are demands, should that prove necessary.

Certain persons do, however, require that demands be issued to them. Usually, this attitude is a result of past experience, that it resists change. Sometimes it cannot be changed. Of course, some people are lazy and need threats to keep them functioning above the minimum level. Others may simply be careless or indifferent, and they may need the threat of a demand to put out a more effective work effort.

An order must be clear; and normally, an explanation of the reason for it can gain goodwill. Unclear orders will produce poor staff effort and quickly undermine confidence in the supervisor. No order should leave doubt in the staff's mind as to what is to be done and how soon. When you do not convey this information, you are asking for trouble. On the other hand, when you convey too much detail, the staff will wonder whether you respect their ability. In other words, be clear and strike a balance, telling everything that they need to know but not so much as to confuse matters.

Nothing will destroy your credibility as a supervisor more quickly than issuing unreasonable orders. Orders can be unreasonable in terms of time, volume of work, or the resources available to do the work. When pressured from above, it is easy to promise something that cannot be done in the time available. You should remember this and not give in, unless it is an emergency—and even then, be careful not to promise more than your best effort. Emergency or high-pressure situations will occur, but not too often in a well-managed organization. And, if staff and supervisor work well together, these situations will be handled effectively. The occurrence of too many high-pressure situations indicates a lack of planning and control by the manager; this will cause staff distrust, as well it should. Reasonable orders provide realistic goals and adequate time for accomplishment.

Starting off in a new supervisory position with these guidelines in mind, it is possible to move smoothly and in a reasonable period of time from having only authority of position to having the authority of respect and trust. Individuals who move into a leadership mode of management will find their work easier than before, despite the many jobs that the leader do, because there will be much greater staff support. In essence, one person fills the formal leadership role, while others in the group take on supporting leadership roles. Thus, the unit moves to a collegial system without being aware of what is happening. Collegial management is about as close as one is likely to come to group leadership (as opposed to individual leadership) in a complex, highly structured organization such as a library.

BIBLIOGRAPHY

1. J. Gordon, *Public Administration in America* (New York: St. Martin's, 1978), p. 212.
2. E. Holly, "Who Runs Libraries?" *Wilson Library Bulletin* 47 (1973): 42–50.
    A. M. McAnally, and R. B. Downs, "The Changing Role of Directors of University Libraries," *College and Research Libraries* 34 (1973): 103–125.
3. F. E. Fiedler, "Style or Circumstances: The Leadership Enigma," *Psychology Today* 2 (March 1969): 39–43.
4. Fiedler, p. 42.

5. D. Krech, R. S. Crutchfield, and E. L. Ballachey, *Individual in Society* (New York: McGraw-Hill, 1962).

6. R. Presthus, *Technological Change and Occupational Response: A Study of Librarians* Final Report Project 07–1084, Contract OEC 1–7–07084–5017 (Washington, D.C.: Office of Education, 1970).

7. K. Davis, Human Behavior at Work (New York: McGraw-Hill, 1972), p. 498.

8. R. Tannanbaum, and W. H. Schmidt, "How to Choose a Leadership Pattern," *Harvard Business Review* 51 (1973): 162–175.

FURTHER READING

Abboud, M. J., and Richardson, H. L. "What Do Supervisors Want From Their Jobs?" *Personnel Journal* 57 (1978): 308–312.

Braun, A. "Assessing Supervisory Training Needs and Evaluating Effectiveness." *Training and Development* 33 (1979): 3–5.

Burns, J. M. *Leadership*. New York: Harper, 1979.

Carroll, A. B. "Paving the Rocky Road to Managerial Success." *Supervisory Management* 24 (1979): 9–13.

Culbertson, K., and Thompson, M. "An Analysis of Supervisory Training Needs." *Training and Development Journal* 34 (1980): 58–60+.

Ellison, J. W., and Molenda, C. "Making Yourself Approachable." *New Library World* 77 (1976): 214–215.

Fiedler, F. E., and Chemers, M. M. *Leadership and Effective Management*. Glenview, Ill.: Scott, Foresman, 1974.

Goldberg, T. "Changing Role of Supportive Staff." *Ohio Library Association Bulletin* 47 (1977): 23–25.

Haimann, T., and Hilgert, R. L. *Supervision: Concepts and Practices of Management*. Palo Alto, Calif.: South Western Publishing, 1977.

Hannah, C. "Supervising Temporary Employees." *Supervisory Management* 25 (1980): 22–28.

Henselman, F. "Supervisory Responsibilities and Qualities." *Library Journal* 85: (1960): 1329–1333.

Hollander, E. P. *Leadership Dynamics; A Practical Guide to Effective Relationships*. New York: Free Press, 1978.

Imudo, L. V. *Effective Supervisor's Handbook*. New York: AMACOM, 1980.

Kets de Vries, M. F. R. "Managers Can Drive Their Subordinates Mad." *Harvard Business Review* 57 (1979): 125–134.

Lawson, J. D. *Leadership is Everybody's Business*. San Luis Obispo, Calif.: Impact Pub., 1976.

Loban, N. "Supervision—More Than A Hat Trick." *Supervision* 41 (1979): 15–17.

Melcher, A. J. "Participation: A Critical Review of Research Findings." *Human Resources Management* 15 (1976): 12–21.

Murdock, W. J. "Leadership and the Librarian." *LACUNY Journal* 1 (1977): 16–20.

Peters, T. J. "Leadership: Sad Facts and Silver Linings." *Harvard Business Review* 57 (1979): 164–172.

Pryor, M. G., and Mondy, R. W. "Mutual Respect: Key to Increased Productivity." *Supervisory Management* 23 (1978): 10–17.

Sager, D. J. "Leadership and Employee Motivation." In *Supervison of Employees in Libraries*, edited by R. E. Stevens. Urbana, Ill.: University of Illinois Graduate School of Library Science, 1979.

Sandell, R. M. "What It Takes to Lead Your Work Force." *Supervision* 42 (1980): 15–16.

Sasser, W. E., and Leonard, F. S. "Let First-level Supervisors Do Their Job." *Harvard Business Review* 80, 2 (1980): 113–121.

Sayles, L. R. *Leadership; What Effective Managers Really Do . . . and How They Do It.* New York: McGraw-Hill, 1979.

Schoemberg, R. J. *The Art of Being a Boss.* New York: Lippincott, 1979.

Schriesheim, C. A. "Leadership Theory: Some Implications for Managers." *MSU Business Topics* 26 (1978): 34–40.

Stevens, R. E., ed. *Supervision of Employees in Libraries.* Ubrana, Ill.: University of Illinois Graduate School of Library Science, 1979.

Thompson, K., and Pitts, R. E. "The Supervisor's Survival Guide: The Great Balancing Act." *Supervisory Management* 24 (1979): 22–30.

Thompson, K., and Pitts, R. E. "The Supervisor's Survival Guide: Being Group Leaders." *Supervisory Management* 24 (1979): 24–31.

Wasmuth, W. J., and Greenhalgh, L. *Effective Supervision; Developing Your Skills Through Critical Incidents.* Englewood Cliffs, N.J.: Prentice-Hall, 1979.

Weinrich, H. "How to Change a Leadership Pattern." *Management Review* 68 (1979): 26–28+.

Weiss, A. J. "Surviving and Succeeding in the 'Political' Organization: Becoming A Leader." *Supervisory Management* 23 (1978): 27–35.

12. Personnel: The Human Side

Library personnel work, while never simple, has become more and more complex over the past 15 years. Increasing government regulations regarding employment practices (from recruitment to dismissal, resignation, and retirement), decreasing or "stable" budgets that require adjustments in staffing patterns, and increasing staff concern with work conditions and benefits have combined to make personnel work time-consuming, complicated, and, often, frustrating. It is difficult to know precisely what government regulations are, as they seem to change almost everyday. Indeed, full courses on the subject are now being given in many library schools; textbooks will undoubtedly follow. Within the scope of this book, however, I shall only highlight the topic in one of two chapters on personnel. This chapter deals with the people aspect of personnel work; the following chapter deals with the systems side of the field—merit and civil service, collective bargaining, and unionization.

As discussed previously, money and things are relatively easy to control and predict—people (the patrons, the managers, and the staff) are not. The vast majority of a library's problems relate to people in one way or another. Probably 90% of a supervisor's attention will be given to people problems rather than to technical problems. The bulk of the preceding chapters has dealt with people in terms of specific management activities. In this chapter, we are concerned with how employees are brought into the library and how they are treated as employees.

KNOWING WHAT YOU NEED

Many libraries today, especially those in the United States, do not know what they need from a personnel standpoint. In the past, a few relatively simple steps could be taken to estimate how many new staff members might be needed during an upcoming fiscal year. These steps still need to be taken, but a manager needs to know more than this. You may need to know the percentages of male and female employees at each employment level, their ethnic backgrounds, ages, and many other characteristics. Some government jurisdictions require a balance (ethnic and sexual) that reflects the composition of the local labor pool—a 25% Hispanic local population would then necessitate hiring 25% of the library's staff from the Hispanic population. Of course, populations change so rapidly that the "acceptable" staff of one year might not reflect the library's community in another year or two. A final complicating factor is that merit systems to which many libraries are subject make it illegal to give preferential treatment. Thus, many American libraries have been trying to deal with a real need to ensure equal employment opportunities and fair treatment, the real difficulty of meeting the library's true staffing needs by drawing from the local population, and equally real (and often unrealistic) government formulas and guidelines.

A first-hand example will illustrate the strange situations that have developed as a result of affirmative-action programs. One library's professional staffing pattern was reviewed by the local government and received a complimentary letter indicating that the library had done a fine job of meeting the required percentages—with one exception. The exception was that the library was "underutilizing male Chicanos in the AA [Administrative Assistant] positions," and steps needed to be taken to rectify this imbalance. The real predicament for the library was that it had only one AA position, and it was held by a Black female. The issue was slowly resolved over the next several months, but only after several working days had been wasted (for staff meetings) and large quantities of paper had been consumed. The library agreed that, while the incumbent would be allowed to remain, upon her resignation, the library would try very hard to find a qualified male Chicano who would accept the position.

Most merit systems have examined, or are constantly examining, all the jobs being performed in the system in an attempt to create what is called a position classification. Each job is assigned to a category in the classification scheme. Normally, each category carries with it a salary range and a list of basic qualifications for holding a job in that category. The ultimate objective is to create a situation in which all persons in the jurisdiction who are covered by the merit system will receive equal pay for equal work (see Table 12.1). Under the system illustrated, a Secretary II would receive the same pay (within the range) regardless of which department he or she worked for. It also is true that a person might be classified as a Bibliographer I or Library Assistant I and *not* work in the library. The category label (Bibliographer, Library Bookmender, or Library Assistant, for example) is applied to the job no matter where it is performed, if the actual duties fit the category. Individuals who work in the personnel office take the information supplied by the supervisor about the job to be performed (a job description) and place it in a category, thereby determining the salary range and, to some extent, the skills or knowledge required to fill the job. A job may be "reclassified" after someone starts doing the work, if the duties of the job turn out to be different from what was initially anticipated. This means an employee may be moved to a category where the pay range is higher or lower than the one first assigned.

All this means that the supervisor must spend some time carefully preparing job descriptions. By doing so, he or she can avoid problems with workers and with budgets. (If the salary range is increased by $100 per month, there may not be enough money in the library budget to pay the required salary.) If job descriptions cover the following points and come close to the examples given in this chapter, most problems should be avoided.

An advantage in defining precisely what you need is that you will keep the library well informed about the community and any changes in it. However, this advantage is far outweighed by the additional time that must go into all phases of personnel work—but without additional staffing to handle the increased load. Regardless of the pros and cons of such precise requirements, though, they exist, and steps can be taken to ensure that information is available when someone asks for it.

Job descriptions, then, should provide the following:

Provide a clear delineation of duties and responsibilities. ("And so forth" or "etc." should never appear in a job description.) New duties are added only by mutual agreement, and they are incorporated immediately into the written statement.

Identify the relationship of the position to the whole organization. Who does the employee report to? Are there subordinates? What is the relationship between this postion and other positions at an equal level? These questions must be answered by the job description.

Give an explanation of the need for the particular services. The personnel office usually provides this in order to justify a position. Is a new person needed to fill an old position, or is a new position being created?

Make an explicit statement of the qualifications required to fill the position. These should be clear, and they should apply to every applicant. Also, there should be *no* "unwritten" qualifications of any sort.

A statement of the desired salary range.*

Remember, unless you have a clear idea of what attributes and skills you are looking for in a person, you may have trouble knowing when you meet the person you want and need. Each of the following job descriptions (reproduced by permission of the Inglewood [California] Public Library) provides a fairly good description of a position. (The question of need for the position is addressed in the city's internal documents, and overall qualification and compensation are included in Inglewood's city personnel code; thus, they are available but are not included here.)

Job Title	HEAD—YOUNG ADULT DIVISION
Class title	Librarian
Reports to	Library Director
Supervises	Clerks and aides as assigned
Location	Main Library

Summary.   The Head—Young Adult Division directs young adult services and programs and selects young adult materials.

Qualifications.   In addition to standard academic qualifications, the young adult librarian should have an interest in and be compatible with young adults. Specialized courses in work with young adults would be desirable.

Duties	Percent
1) Plans and develops programs for young adults. *May consult* library division heads, city recreation department.	40%
2) Selects and orders library materials suitable for young adults; administers book account; analyzes the collections; withdraws materials regarded as no longer suitable. *Must consult* order–receiving clerks; technical processes personnel in withdrawing materials.	35%
3) Coordinates the young adult service with other library divisions. *Must consult* library division heads.	5%

*After the position has been established and classified, most of these items will be used in the published job announcements—sometimes also called the job description.

4) Prepares reports and statistics. 5%

5) Establishes liaison with other related agencies or groups; is
aware of the community's young adult requirements. 4%
May consult city recreation department.

6) Attends conferences and meetings; reads professional literature; is aware of new trends and practices. 4%

7) Supervises non-professional assistants. 2%

8) Prepares division budget; reviews and reports on budget
periodically. 2%
Must consult Administrative Assistant in budget preparation.

9) Assists and recommends to the Library Director policies and
procedures relating to young adult service. 1%

10) Reports on problem areas and recommends procedural
changes. %

11) Reviews personnel record, makes efficiency reports, and
interviews applicants for new positions. 1%
Must notify business office.

12) Serves as Reference Librarian when required. —

Job Title	CIRCULATION SUPERVISOR (Branch Library)
Class title	Library Assistant
Reports to	Branch Librarian
Supervises	Branch Library clerks and aides when assigned to circulation duties
Location	Branch Library

Summary. The Circulation Supervisor (Branch Library) directs the branch library circulation function, stack maintenance, and supervises clerks and
aides assigned to circulation duties.

The position differs from that of Circulation Supervisor (Main Library) in that
the Circulation Supervisor (Branch Library) supervises clerical functions in
the branch library and is "in charge" in the absence of a librarian.

Duties	Percent
1) Performs loan desk routines, as the job is considered a "working" position.	50%
2) Supervises receiving and routing of library materials.	10%
3) Supervises clerks and aides.	10%
4) Coordinates branch circulation activities with Circulation Control and other relaed divisions. *Must consult* circulation control personnel and personnel affected.	5%

5) Coordinates the work of clerical personnel relating to branch librarian's assignments (card filing, transferring books, exhibits, special programs, etc.).   5%

6) Supervises branch library registration and reserve book procedures.   5%
   Must consult Registration Clerk and Reserve Control Clerk.

7) Interprets and explains library circulation policies and interprets fine and damage policies to the public.   4%

8) Inventories and requests branch library supplies.   2%
   Must notify library business office.

9) Makes schedules; supervises time sheets; assigns clerical duties.   2%
   Must notify Circulation Supervisor (Main Library) for additional personnel requirements; library business office concerning time sheets.

10) Receives records and transfers money to the library business office or the Circulation Supervisor (Main Library).   2%
    Must notify library business office.

11) Maintains circulation records and statistics.   1%
    Must notify library business office.

12) Confers with circulation supervisors. Reports on problem areas and recommends procedural changes.   1%

13) Directs activities of volunteer workers.   1%

14) Surveys the library in order to determine maintenance requirements.   1%
    Must notify library business office.

15) Inspects and reports condition of furniture and equipment.   1%
    Must notify library business office.

Job Title	INFORMATION ASSISTANT
Class title	Senior Library Clerk
Reports to	Head—Reference and Information Division
Supervises	—
Location	Main Library

Summary.   The Information Assistant, stationed at the information desk (near the entrance of the library and adjacent to the public catalog), provides general information on the use of the library, assists the public in the use of the author–title catalog and in locating materials, and answers and routes telephone calls.*

Qualifications.   The person holding this position should be conversant with the library's resources, services, classification system, and policies. The person should have a college background, be interested in books and reading, and be aware of community activities. Ability to work with and be responsive to the public is a basic requirement.

Duties	Percent
1) Assists the public in the use of the author–title catalog and in the location of library materials.	30%
2) Explains library resources and services and gives directional information.	20%
3) Answers the telephone and routes calls (main library public service areas).	15%
4) Identifies library materials from telephone requests.	10%
5) Receives book requests; edits and completes forms with additional bibliographic information.	5%
6) Interprets trade bibliographic information to the public from sources at the information desk.	5%
7) Provides basic ready reference information from such sources located at the information desk (dictionaries, almanacs, city directories, gazetteers, telephone directories, etc.).	5%
8) Screens information requests and refers questions to reference librarians.	5%
9) Maintains local organization files and provides general information on the area, including community events.	5%

*[Because of the physical demands of working with the public, the job, as with that of Reference Librarian, is scheduled in shifts, and the person holding this position is assigned other job-related duties when off the desk. The amount of time spent is not included in the percentage account of the position. During non-busy periods, the information assistant will work on assignments related to other duties that can be accomplished at the information desk.]

Job Title	MECHANICAL PROCESSES AIDE
Class title	Library Aide
Reports to	Catalog Supervisor
Supervises	—
Location	Main Library

<u>Summary.</u>   The Mechanical Processes Aide files and arranges catalog cards and performs mechanical processing functions and materials handling.

Duties	Percent
1) Edits books after processing, including labels and catalog; maintains statistics.	35%

2) Assists technical processes personnel in special projects and specific assignments.   15%

3) Sorts and files catalog cards.   10%

4) Transfers books within the library, including record changes, processings, and statistics.   10%

5) Pastes book pockets and maintains electric pasting machine.   10%

6) Boxes and moves library materials and equipment; prepares shipments to main and branch libraries.   10%

7) Unpacks shipments and arranges materials.   5%

8) Multiliths catalog cards.   3%

9) Assists in the mending of books on a project basis.   2%

To provide some insight into pay schedules in large libraries, Table 12.1 presents the pay classification for a large municipality that includes a library. In most large systems, such a chart can run to many pages and is usually subdivided so that librarians are in one group, paraprofessionals in another, and clerical in still another. If you have a specific task in mind, locating the proper level of personnel to perform that task may be very time consuming, as what you want done will probably not fit precisely into any existing job description. So, you must first describe the work, and then look for a matching classification (with salary predetermined). In Figure 12.1, then, a job matching the description for Library Assistant III would pay between $949 and $1137; the exact salary would depend on qualifications, experience, and, to some extent, the degree of difficulty in filling the position.

The second step in knowing your needs is to anticipate as much as possible the number of vacancies that the library is likely to have in the next fiscal year. The following things should be considered in this review-planning process.

How many of the present staff appear to be capable of promotion?

How many of the staff do not appear to be capable or promotion but are capable of continuing at their present level indefinitely?

How many (and all too often, *if any*) staff members ought to be released and replaced? (Merit systems have a reputation for retaining incompetent employees.)

How many people are near retirement?

How many new positions are desired, and how many new positions are likely to be funded? (The first number is almost invariably higher than the second.)

How many resignations are likely? (These can be expected from per-

TABLE 12.1 PAY SCHEDULE

LOS ANGELES   TITLE AND PAY PLAN - OCCUPATIONAL SUBGROUP SEQUENCE 07/26/77

Title Code	Use	Name	Range	Step	S D	O E S	F O C
5007	T	Secretary II	831.00 - 991.00	5	Yes	N	D
5008	T	Secretary I	727.00 - 868.00	5	Yes	N	D
5009	T	Secretary I Shorthand	760.00 - 908.00	5	Yes	N	D
6456	T	Program Assistant II	949.00 - 1137.00	5	Yes	N	D
6457	T	Program Assistant I	831.00 - 991.00	5	Yes	N	D
6650	T	Language Assistant	1087.00 - 1305.00	5	Yes	N	C
6652	T	Senior Linguistic Informant	868.00 - 1040.00	5	Yes	N	C
6653	T	Linguistic Informant	794.00 - 949.00	5	Yes	N	C
6677	L	Reader For The Blind	- 638.00	1	Yes	N	C
6693	T	Translator-Nontechnical	794.00 - 949.00	5	Yes	N	C
6694	T	Translator-Technical	868.00 - 1040.00	5	Yes	N	C
6732	T	Bibliographer II	831.00 - 991.00	5	Yes	N	D
6733	T	Bibliographer I	727.00 - 868.00	5	Yes	N	D
6759	T	Library Assistant IV	1087.00 - 1305.00	5	Yes	N	D
6760	T	Library Assistant III	949.00 - 1137.00	5	Yes	N	D
6761	T	Library Assistant II	831.00 - 991.00	5	Yes	N	D
6762	T	Library Assistant I	727.00 - 868.00	5	Yes	N	D
6772	T	Senior Library Bookmender	949.00 - 1137.00	5	Yes	N	E
6773	T	Library Bookmender	727.00 - 868.00	5	Yes	N	E
6774	T	Library Bookmender Trainee	638.00 - 760.00	5	Yes	N	F
7231	T	Survey Supervisor	969.00 - 1161.00	5	No	E	A
7232	L	Senior Survey Worker	831.00 - 991.00	5	Yes	N	D
7233	T	Survey Worker	727.00 - 868.00	5	Yes	N	D
9030	T	Admitting Worker Supervisor	1087.00 - 1305.00	5	Yes	N	D
9031	T	Principal Admitting Worker	949.00 - 1137.00	5	Yes	N	D
9032	T	Senior Admitting Worker	831.00 - 991.00	5	Yes	N	D
9033	T	Admitting Worker	727.00 - 868.00	5	Yes	N	D
B.20 Key Entry Operations							
4770	T	Key Entry Supervisor II	991.00 - 1191.00	5	Yes	N	D
4771	T	Key Entry Supervisor I	868.00 - 1040.00	5	Yes	N	D
4772	T	Lead Key Entry Operator	831.00 - 991.00	5	Yes	N	D
4773	T	Key Entry Operator	760.00 - 908.00	5	Yes	N	D
4774	T	Assistant Key Entry Operator	695.00 - 794.00	4	Yes	N	D
B.30 Storekeeping							
5060	T	Senior Stores Supervisor	1336.00 - 1607.00	5	No	E	D
5061	T	Stores Supervisor	1217.00 - 1464.00	5	No	E	D
5062	T	Senior Storekeeper	969.00 - 1161.00	5	Yes	N	D
5063	T	Stores Worker	888.00 - 1063.00	5	Yes	N	F
5064	T	Storekeeper	848.00 - 1015.00	5	Yes	N	D
5065	T	Assistant Storekeeper	743.00 - 888.00	5	Yes	N	D
5066	T	Delivery Worker	727.00 - 868.00	5	Yes	N	F
C FOOD AND LINEN SERVICES							
C.10 DIETITIANS							
5410	L	Chief Dietitian	1805.00 - 2179.00	5	No	E	A
5411	L	Principal Dietitian	1569.00 - 1893.00	5	No	E	A
5412	L	Senior Dietitian	1365.00 - 1644.00	5	No	E	B
5413	L	Dietitian	1191.00 - 1429.00	5	No	E	B

sons who appear to be promotable, because they will probably be attractive candidates for higher positions in systems other than your own.)

JOB REQUIREMENTS

You can avoid many performance problems by selecting new employees very carefully, by giving them proper training, and by observing their progress during the first few months of their employment. Selection and training go hand in hand; if one is deficient, the other cannot possibly succeed. No amount of training can make a good worker out of someone who lacks the basic qualifications and aptitude for the task at hand. Likewise, the best selection practices will be nullified by a poor training program (or none at all).

Yet training and experience requirements for a job should not be so narrow that they rule out promising applicants who might not quite meet them. Many jobs can be performed by people with a fairly wide range of backgrounds. A secretary, for example, can be someone with good typing speed, shorthand, command of the basics of the language(s) used in the office, knowledge of office procedures, a good personality, and the ability to follow through on a number of details without close supervision. It need *not* necessarily be a person who has had specific training to be a secretary.

Unfortunately, libraries tend to set unrealistic educational requirements for positions. Certainly, placing an accountant in a minor clerical position is wasteful of skills, as would be placing a college graduate in a dead-end clerical position. Yet, almost every job announcement indicates that a high school education is required, and frequently, a college degree is required to fill clerical positions. By now, though, most formal educational requirements have been challenged in court. As a result of the challenges, most statements of desired qualifications conclude with the phrase, "or equivalent." Some people have questioned, on occasion, the need for formal library school training for appointment to professional positions.

Factors other than essential skills, knowledge, training, and aptitude come into play when considering job requirements. Any employer prefers to hire persons who are likely to remain with the organization for some time, who will work and be interested in the work, who can get along with co-workers and the supervisor, and who will be prompt and regular in attendance. Personal appearance and manner of speaking also are important in public service positions. Handicapped persons are perfectly capable of handling many public service activities. And from a qualification standpoint, you should not (and in many jurisdictions, you *cannot*) cite a physical handicap as a reason for disqualification. On the other hand, some nonhandicapped persons avoid contact with the handicapped. Can you hope to change attitudes by confronting people with their prejudices? In time, confrontation might cause a change in attitude, or there may be complaints and loss of patrons. But remember that social ability, initiative, and drive are essential in any job dealing with the public, such as in the reference department, where the library employee must be able to approach clients and make them comfortable. In any event, you must be very careful about including personality or appearance requirements in a job description.

RECRUITMENT

Once you have determined your needs, you begin to search for applicants. Most large libraries conduct national searches for qualified persons for their professional positions and draw the majority of their nonprofessionals from the local area. Advertisements for openings must provide the same basic information contained in the job description and indicate where and when a person should apply. Applicants should be given ample time to apply—a minimum of 1 month, unless it is an emergency situation. A brief application period usually results in a small pool of applicants (not very many of whom are fully qualified).

SELECTION

Once applications have been received, the review process begins. The process involves several steps: the application forms, the preemployment tests (if required), a personal interview, and verification of qualifications and past work experience. Normally, only a few persons will be interviewed on the basis of their application forms and supporting documents. Also, you do not normally verify qualifications and past work experience until you have reduced the list of applicants to the most promising group.

APPLICATION FORMS

The application blank provides a great deal of information about the person filling it out, not only from the raw data but by the manner in which information is given. It can reveal a good deal about the individual's motivation, drive, maturity, and language skills. Such forms should cover the following areas of concern:

Has the applicant shown steady career growth and progress, or has the person simply moved from position to position for no apparent reason (and within a short period of time)? If the answer is not clear, this should be brought up in the interview to determine whether a personal problem might be the cause.

Does the application reveal definite educational goals and objectives? Does the candidate appear to have a certain direction and drive that could be useful in the position being filled?

Are there unexplained gaps in the work history? If so, the applicant should be asked to explain the situation.

Remember, though, that certain questions may not be asked, either on the application blank or during the interview, if the library is to comply with equal employment programs. Obvious questions about race and religion are out. Age and sex are in the questionable area; most forms still ask for this information, but if someone challenges your right to ask, it is best to drop the matter. Formerly, you could ask any question you wanted to on an application form, and you still can—*if* you can prove the question's direct relevance to the open position. If you cannot answer "yes" to the question, "Does the answer to question x really matter in the performance of the job?" then you ought to omit it.

If, in your job description, you used the phrase "or equivalent," then you must be ready to clearly state what is and is not equivalent. Naturally, because the application form provides the basis for initial selection of candidates for interviews, that form should provide space to list information regarding equivalent training and experience. Individuals who were not chosen for interviews and lack formal requirements have often claimed that they were discriminated against, even though they have equivalent background. If a formal complaint is filed, be ready to explain your definition of *equivalent*.

Review the applications a day or two after the deadline for applying. Individuals who clearly lack either formal or equivalent requirements (and there always seem to be some) may be eliminated from further consideration. (Naturally, these people should be notified immediately that they are not in the running.) Then begins the hard work of choosing who to invite and who not to invite for further consideration. Some positions (beginning clerk to begging professional) may require that everyone who wishes to be considered take a test on a certain day (usually only in municipal library systems, though). If the position is to be filled from the local area, then of course, all qualified applicants ought to be invited.

National searches present a different problem. Given the expense of travel and lodging, few libraries can pay for all candidates' expenses, and it is unreasonable to expect candidates to pay their own way, unless they have a very good chance of getting the job. Library association conventions and meetings are means of solving the problem, as many national associations operate "placement" centers at their annual meetings, which allow prospective employees and employers to easily contact a large number of persons. Placement centers, though, are only partial solutions, and almost always, some persons are rejected or invited on the basis of the application form and letters of reference.

Evaluating applications always seems to take much longer than expected. Even with experience, you are never absolutely certain that you have not made a mistake; however, once you have made your decisions, issue the invitations and start to schedule the interviews.

TESTS

If the job to be filled calls for certain "testable" skills, it is very useful to employ appropriate preinterview tests. Of course, testing has been attacked on several grounds—invalidity, invasion of privacy, or discrimination against certain classes of applicants. The only preemployment tests that are useful in library settings are those that measure a manual skill—typing, filing, numerical computation, and other measurable traits. A number of such tests are available, and they are valid. Why hire someone as a typist if that person cannot type at the speed required for the job?

Failure to use skill tests can be quite costly—not only in terms of production. The person who was hired and then dismissed loses confidence and becomes frustrated. Also, it cost money and time to train (or attempt to train) that person, and this effort must be repeated with the next person hired. Indeed, the entire selection process must be repeated. By using a simple test that illustrates the work to be done, or that actually involves a facet of the job, the library can give the applicants a clear picture of the job they have applied for and assure itself of potential employees' skills and aptitudes.

Skill tests can be used to further advantage during the interview, as they permit the interviewer to discuss test results with the applicant. Someone who lacks the necessary skill for a particular job will usually recognize this fact while reviewing the test results. Such recognition may provide motivation to improve in certain skill areas in order to pass similar tests in the future. (Even in programming, where actual hands-on testing cannot be used, some pencil-and-paper programming will supply an indication of capacities.)

INTERVIEWS

The preemployment interview supplements the application form and tests, as it gives the interviewer a chance to measure an applicant's technical and professional knowledge as well as depth of experience. The supervisor can also evaluate the applicant's personal and emotional characteristics—something not easily done on the basis of the application form. The applicant can use the interview, too, in order to find out about the job (in depth) and the staff of the library. It is also an excellent time to clarify any gray areas for both supervisor and applicant.

The interview should have a definite purpose and plan; this requires careful preparation prior to the meeting. If the application has been received beforehand, it should be evaluated prior to the interview; if it is completed only when the applicant arrives, it still should be reviewed by the supervisor in private. That way, notes can be taken regarding areas to discuss and items to verify. Above all, do not waste time—yours or the applicant's.

Some interviewers do entirely too much talking, when what is needed is to get the applicant to discuss the pertinent facts, with the interviewer as a guide. If the interviewer spends the entire time discussing the organization, nothing significant about the applicant can emerge. A balance should be maintained between providing the applicant with necessary information and getting the applicant to "flesh out" the application form.

The interview should *not* take on the air of an interrogation; if it does, it is a poor interview. The applicant should always be given a few minutes in which to relax and become more nearly "normal." If this is done, the person's answers will be more reflective of the individual's true abilities. A good place to start is with a general description of the job and its place in the organization. (Not to many details here, as the applicant may not get the job; overexplanation may raise false hopes.) The main point is to provide time for the applicant to relax while you move from the job to the applicant as the primary focus of attention. It is easy to begin with education and work history, then to proceed slowly into more personal areas if necessary (but these should be strictly related to the decision to hire a particular person to fill a particular position).

The key is to listen. Open-ended questions are fine for bringing out information, but, unless the interviewer actually hears the total responses, little is accomplished. Novice interviewers should be careful not to get so involved in determining the next question that they miss the answer to the one they just asked.

The interviewed should be a mixture of open-ended and specific questions. The former type requires the applicant to organize thoughts before answering ("What specifically qualifies you for this job—education, experience, etc.?"). The disadvantage is that open-ended questions do not allow comparison among candidates. Specific questions requiring specific answers do allow for some such comparisons. Such questions are usually technical and job related. They might involve asking about unit cards or hanging indentions (if the job involves cataloging), or about multiple copy order forms or on line verification techniques (if the job is in acquisitions). Avoid leading questions that imply the correct answer. "Are you good at detail?" would hardly be answered "no" by someone applying for a job involving details.

Interviews should be of equal length—20 minutes should be sufficient time for an interview for a beginning or nonmanagerial position. If the applicant is so reluctant or withdrawn that the interviewer cannot get any information beyond monosyllables, the interview should be terminated after a reasonable effort has been made. If a person is clearly unqualified, this should be said plainly to the applicant.

If several candidates are applying for a position, each interviewee should be told this. Each person also should be given an idea of when he or she can expect to hear results. The results should be given as promised, and they should be given soon after the interview.

To review briefly, it might help to list things *not* to do. Do not ask questions that might be considered discriminatory. ("How many children do you have, Mrs. Gascoyne, and how old are they? And does your husband's job entail transfer?" or "Do you make religion a part of your daily life?") Do not allow interviews to be interrupted. This is both rude and inefficient. Only extreme emergencies cannot be delayed for a few minutes. Do not let the interview drift aimlessly. If you are doing your job as an interviewer, you have a list of questions ready for each session. Do not allow the staff to evaluate candidates as to their social acceptability. Your concern is the organization, not a bridge coterie or a movie club. Do not use subtle "psychological" tests to determine what a person "is really like." First, only professionals in the field of psychology should use these instruments; second, there is no single set of ideal characteristics for a library employee.

VERIFICATION AND EVALUATION

One of the more difficult and sensitive areas in any hiring procedure is verification of an applicant's education and work history. Letters of recommendation from former teachers and employers are often required, as are school attendance records and employment dates. These provide a picture of the person that will usually be crucial in any decision to hire. However, letters of recommendation are being used less frequently, as many interviewers prefer to speak directly with the persons listed as references.

The problem of confidentiality occurs with references—is the interviewee to be informed of the contents of a letter? From the applicant's standpoint, it is unfortunate to keep using a person as a reference if that person is providing highly negative comments. On the other hand, it is quite hard to get an honest opinion in writing if the writer knows that the subject of a letter will see its contents. Some states (California and Colorado, for example) have open records laws that allow such examination, so use of letters may become even more of a rarity.

A genuine problem is posed by the applicant who fakes a work history. People who claim to have worked in several cities but who are vague as to the addresses of previous employers or names of immediate past supervisors may well have submitted a false application. By checking with the organizations listed, you can determine whether or not the person was actually employed there in the capacity claimed. A way to possibly circumvent this time-consuming procedure, though, might be simply to ask, "Whom can we contact at the Dingy Company regarding your employment there" (Be wary of applicants who claim that their former employers cannot be contacted; an employee's former associates may well have died or moved to Tierra del Fuego, but the chances of this happening are remote.) If you cannot verify most of a history, it becomes very suspect.

Confirm educational background directly from the school(s) listed. Obtain official transcripts. If licensing is involved, check with the appropriate licensing agencies. Libraries often hire full-time repair technicians for large-scale media programs; such people may well have to be licensed. If professional certification, which is a factor in some libraries, is needed, it may have to be verified.

FINAL DECISION

All of the preceding processes lead to a decision by the supervisor. The application form, the tests, and the interview are synthesized and summarized, and an individual is offered the job. Making such evaluations often involves overcoming a narrow personal view of what it takes to fill a certain position successfully. Any time a supervisor discovers himself or herself accepting a stereotyped view of a job, it may be wise to have someone else sit in on the interview, or at least sit in on the evaluation.

Another mistake is to hire someone out of sympathy while disregarding obvious things that would disqualify anyone else. This kindness usually is misplaced. It can create trouble for the supervisor and the employee, not to mention the entire staff. Although an applicant may need help, giving a job to a person who cannot do it is hardly helping that person. Moreover, this practice can do genuine harm to the organization and to the morale of other employees.

THE NEW EMPLOYEE

The first step in the training process—orientation—is very important. It begins the moment the person accepts the job, and involves overcoming the natural reaction of *any* new employee of feeling a little lost and a little strange in a new organization. People must be met—and remembered both as people and as employees. A new physical layout must be learned. Policies must be gone over, rules and practices must be explained, and the dress code (if any) must be defined. Because so much goes on in addition to simply getting the person started in the physical job, the first few weeks are critical in shaping a person's attitudes toward an organization.

The first day should cover organizational procedures. Co-workers should be introduced, but limit this (at first) to those people with whom the new person will be working, if there are very many to meet. (Meeting people right and left and briefly creates confusion, not security). A tour of the physical facility should be made, and the overall structure of the organization, including key people, should be explained.

Naturally, the job duties will be discussed in detail, along with the training—type, length, and instructor or supervisor. For a librarian in technical services, training may last from 2 days to 3 months, depending on the complexity of the work. If a senior employee is involved directly in the training (because the supervisor cannot be), the senior employee should be interested in and understand the work at hand.

New employees often find the first several days confusing and unsettling, but two things can help to alleviate this somewhat. First, allow them to actually do some work undisturbed for a few hours on the first day. Second, you should spread orientation out over several days rather than try to fit it all into 2 or 3 days. Even if new employees have actually read 5 policy or procedure manuals, this does not mean that they have a context for the information contained in those manuals. The training also should be flexible, in order to adapt to various learning speeds.

A new employee's past work experience usually influences the way in which that person will be trained. Experienced professional or supervisory personnel may not need detailed instructions—they may require only an explanation of objectives, policies, practices, and potential problems. And, because beginning librarians should know the fundamentals of any job they might get, only local variations need to be explained.

Most clerical jobs demand careful, specific instruction, as do manual and unskilled jobs. Routines will vary, and a considerable amount of detail is usually involved, whether it involves technical services, shelf reading, or filing cards. Group training programs are very efficient for such positions, but turnover and the creation of new positions seldom allow a large number of new employees to begin work at the same time. Libraries that hire a large number of part-time workers, though, might consider doing this: Plan to hire a group, and plan to have them trained as a group.

Yet another plan is involved here—the plan behind the training. Trainees must be taken through a clear-cut sequence, and there should be active involvement ("hands-on learning") as soon as possible. Explain why tasks are done as they are, why they are done at all, and what they mean to the organization. If the trainee does not understand these things, he or she may have no inclination to learn the task at all.

If classroom techniques can be used, be sure that they include instruction, demonstration, and practice work, followed by evaluation. Active participation seems to be one of the best ways of learning, and, coupled with strong feedback, it can prove invaluable to new employees.

TRAINING PROFESSIONAL STAFF

A number of training programs are designed especially for professionals and managerial employees. The concept of staff development has increasingly become the subject of many articles and books.[1] The basic issue is the same: to enhance the library employee's ability to do the work for which that person was hired, and thereby enhance the efficiency of the library. Staff-development programs can occur both in the library and outside it, but they retain a common goal; and they share a common problem. The problem is the varying motivations of individuals who might be affected—if programs are mandatory, many people will participate at a minimal level, and if they are voluntary, many people will not elect to give up individual time to enhance their work performance.

Several techniques might be used within the library to train professional staff. *Planned progression* sets out an interlocking pattern of on-the-job training and advancement that can help to ensure the possibility of promotion. Everyone knows what the sequence is, and the technique familarizes everyone with the system as a whole (including rotation to branch libraries, if they are part of the system). *Job rotation* is another approach to learning the entire system; however, with professionals, it usually is confined to observation. Observation has been seen to be too passive a learning tool, though, and trying to learn by observing an almost invisible activity seems extremely inefficient. Job rotation involving actual performance of management functions by a trainee appears to work better than observation does, and trainee positions are commonly created for just that purpose. A problem of how to treat a temporary employee then arises, for both management and co-workers. In attempts to solve that problem, assistant positions have been created; however, their permanence does not allow for the rotation that provides breadth of experience.

The *temporary promotion* has been used, especially in small or medium-sized libraries, to acquaint employees with new facets of the organization. Yet, people will hesitate to make decisions in such situations (rightly so), and they tend to think on a day-to-day basis while waiting for replacement. *Junior boards* (committees of trainees assigned to tackle specific problems) are used to great advantage—both in problem solving and in training; the disadvantages involve great use of time and an air of paternalistic experimentation.

Devices and opportunities for training can, as noted, be found outside the library; here, the problem of individual motivation is strongest. Conference programs at meetings of professional associations often cover management-related topics, but they are not *training* devices per se. Usually, they present information that might lead one to want actual training, but they rarely provide anything beyond the most fundamental type of training. Their value lies in other areas.

Most valuable are those programs offered by schools of business and management, or political science/public administration programs and management workshops presented by various professional groups. The advantage of this method of training over conference programs is that, although fewer topics may be covered, the level of presentation will probably be significantly higher and the topics will be covered in greater depth. The focus will be on a particular area (budgeting, personnel management, etc.) rather than on a professional groups, such as librarians.

Probably the best such program in the United States is that offered by the American Management Association, which offers workshops all across the country.

Naturally, individual libraries will offer their own training, oftentimes using a combination of approaches. The training techniques described here, however, represent the basic types that you might expect to encounter. Their particular advantages and disadvantages will depend on how they are administered with the individual employee, who must always remain the focus.

PERFORMANCE EVALUATION

Conventional management theory in the United States holds that performance evaluation is essential to the successful operation of any organization, including the library. In theory, it will help the worker to improve performance. Yet, after teaching management in both American and Scandinavian library schools fo 6 years, I have found that the concept of formally evaluating someone for the purpose of granting raises, promotion, or for firing that person is almost incomprehensible to most Scandinavian librarians, practitioners, and students. On the other hand, Americans find the failure to formally evaluate equally incomprehensible. (Typically, the British seem to strike a balance between the two extremes.) All these countries have good library systems—although the Scandinavian seem the most progressive, and British academic librarianship is a bit more innovative than the others—therefore, it does not appear true that failure to conduct formal personal performance evaluations will lead to failure on the part of the library.

Based on personal research, I maintain that Southern Californian and Scandinavian[2] librarians dislike conducting performance evaluations because of the anxiety, tension, and hostility that the process often generates. It seems that, no matter how the process is presented, people feel their security threatened. A negative evaluation can affect salary and even job security. People naturally worry about a process over which they feel they have little control. Perhaps if the process was treated as a teaching and training device, some of this hostility might be abated. However, for many years the process has been tied to job security. It would be very difficult to change feelings that have been built up over a long period of time.

In actuality, performance evaluations provide employees with formal feedback; however, the supervisor should provide informal daily comments and periodic written comments as well. This is the supervisor's job. In addition to the feedback, evaluations provide a chance to discuss long-term problems and goals. If they are not approached in a positive way, formal evaluations can do more harm than good.

One step to take to avoid problems is to make evaluation a continuous process so that the people coming up for evaluation every 6 months or once a year do not have a long period of time of uncertainty regarding what will be said. Constant informal evaluation and occasional written comments during the year can significantly reduce staff stress.

Naturally, supervisors should discuss performance problems as they occur. The tendency is to avoid any unpleasantness and to let the problem slide. If this is done, the employee may well not see that anything wrong has taken place. Also, despite the contentions of the human-relations school, supervisors should be willing to show displeasure when an individual performs in a grossly unacceptable manner—especially when it is a matter of willfulness or neglect. The idea that the superior--subordinate relationship is a delicate, fragile thing that is too easily destroyed by a hasty word or an ill-timed move on the part of the supervisor is overemphasized by the human-relations school.

A healthy system provides for a two-way exchange between supervisor and subordinate. Each should be free to voice satisfaction or dissatisfaction. Attempts to avoid strain or problems will bring great pressure on everyone involved and will solve nothing.

Whatever the error, no supervisor has the right to humiliate an employee by giving a public reprimand. The conversation should take place as soon as possible, but it should be private. Criticism should be in terms of the error, never in terms of the individual's personality or worth as a human being. Abusive or profane language is inexcusable—the use of such language in an evaluation marks a person who simply does not deserve to be a supervision.

The supervisor needs to be consistent in evaluation. Standards should not shift from one week to the next or alter from one employee to another. Remember, it is the end result that is being evaluated, not the approach (so long as the approach does not cause trouble or problems).

Flexibility needs to go in concert with consistent evaluation, but flexibility comes in the discipline. A new employee should not be held as closely accountable for an error as an older, experienced worker, even though the difficulty does need to be resolved. (A problem with a new employee could have its roots in the training, so that should be checked.) Naturally, a person who simply lacks the skill to do a task should not be overly criticized; rather, training should be provided. If the training does not work, then other adjustments should be made. A simple reprimand will hardly solve the problem.

When a supervisor has determined that an employee's poor performance is due to laziness, lack of application, or indifference, then the supervisor must make it clear that the individual is expected to improve or face the consequences. This is appropriate, regardless of the personality type of the employee.

A real problem in appraisal is that many supervisors have only vague impressions of the ability and worth of their subordinates. They will very often praise them in general terms—"One of the best," "Real potential," "A great asset!"—yet they seldom have specific incidents to back these statements. This can occur as a result of the "halo effect"—a single incident, good or bad, can actually form a person's entire opinion of someone else, and all this can take place quite unconsciously. This is hardly desirable, but many evaluation forms (see Figure 12.1) call for appraisal of very nebulous traits.

Many managers tend to rate all employees in the middle of whatever scale they are using. This accomplishes nothing. No one learns from it, and the supervisor avoids making decisions. This also helps to avoid conflicts—except with people who feel they should have been rated higher. Obviously, there is an average performance level in a library, but some employees perform below that level and some perform above it—otherwise, it sould not be an average.

Attempts have been made to design rating forms that are more accurate. The "forced choice" form has been examined in particular. Equally attractive statements are presented, but the supervisor can choose only one. Thus, performance is supposedly examined without the halo effect. (Hasty checking simply to get through the form will defeat its purpose.)

The supervisor should be aware of a subtle pressure in the evaluation process: the supervisor's own ego needs and the extent to which individual subordinates fulfill or fail to fulfill these needs. A person who is unable to delegate authority tends to choose subordinates who are deferential and lacking in initiative. When these people are evaluated, they will probably do well, precisely because they were chosen and evaluated on the basis of personality traits. A technically incompetent supervisor tends to select and retain persons who are even less competent, and then give these people high ratings because they are not a threat. Only through careful observation over a long period of time can the manager prevent personality factors from interfering unduly in the evaluation process.

The frequency of formal ratings varies a good deal. During the first 6 months especially, they should be made frequently. Even if formal ratings are not required by the library, the supervisor should undertake them independently. During the first year, then, evaluate every 2 months during the first 6 months, evaluate again 3 months later, and finally, evaluate

PERFORMANCE RATING FOR CASUAL EMPLOYEES

Name_____Date hired_____Unit_____

Position held (include brief statement of duties)_____

_____

Date terminated_____Reason_____Would you rehire?_____

E x c e p t i o n a l	V e r y G o o d	S a t i s f a c t o r y	F a i r	U n s a t i s f a c t o r y	
					The rating should be made with great care and fairness for the interest of the employee and the Library. Base your judgment on the entire period covered and not on isolated incidents alone. (Comments on critical incidents and unusual or out-standing task performance may be cited in the space provided below.) Do not rate any item if you do not have adequate basis for making a judgment. This report is to be sent to the Administrative Office at the time a part-time employee is re-commended for a pay increase or is terminated.
					QUANTITY: The amount of satisfactory work regularly produced.
					QUALITY: The degree to which work produced meets established standards of quality.
					DEPENDABILITY: Employee's attendance and tardiness record, degree to which employee meets scheduled work hours, the care employee gives library property, and ex-tend to which employee carries out instructions.
					JOB ATTITUDE: Employee's enthusiasm and interest for work; cooperation with other employees.
					JOB KNOWLEDGE: Employee's understanding of the type of work to be performed and possession of information needed to perform adequately.
					JUDGMENT: Employee's ability to decide correct course of action when decisions are required.
					RELATIONS WITH PUBLIC: Employee's attitude in dealing with public and manner in which he or she behaves in contacts with public on job.
					DRESS AND PERSONAL APPEARANCE: Manner and neatness of employee's usual dress and personal appearance during working hours.

General
Rating: Exceptional [ ] Very Good [ ] Satisfactory [ ] Fair [ ] Unsatisfactory [ ]

What are employee's strong points?
What are employee's weak points?
Comments on above factors and summary statement:

Dept Head:_____Supervisor:_____Date_____

How long have you supervised   Has this rating sheet been discussed with employee?
this employee?_____   Yes_____No_____

Figure 12.1 Sample evaluation form.

at the end of the year. The employee then knows exactly how the supervisor interprets the evaluation criteria. After the first year, a formal review twice a year should be sufficient—once for personnel requirements, and once for the supervisor's benefit. The latter would be especially helpful if performance started to slip, because waiting a year without taking action would be unfair and unproductive.

As was pointed out previously, the ideal evaluation is ongoing and is both informal (verbal) and formal (written). The informal evaluation allows for flexibility and helps to provide a basis for the formal evaluation, which allows structure, continuity, and consistency throughout the organization.

THE UNSATISFACTORY EMPLOYEE

Occasionally, the supervisor is faced with employees who are completely unsatisfactory. They consume inordinate amounts of time, are unproductive, and represent a heavy cost to the library in many ways. Sometimes, as in merit sytems, they are long-time employees. Some supervisors evade the issue by working around such persons and hiring competent people to get the work done. There are really only three methods an effective supervisor can use in dealing with an unsatisfactory employee: (1) attempt to help the employee improve his or her performance; (2) transfer the employee to a place wherein that person might be effective; or (3) discharge the employee. Each option has its value, according to the circumstances, but each also ought to be weighed heavily before any action is taken.

The primary question to consider with an unsatisfactory employee is: How long has the person's behavior been this way? Is it recent, or has it been building up over a long period of time? If it is recent, the supervisor should try to find out where the difficulties lie by discussing them with the employee. If it is a long-standing problem, there will be a record of discussions, and, when performance declines to an unacceptable level, action must be taken.

If the problem is absence or late arrival—especially in the case of a new employee—then the problem should be explored. Adjustments in the work schedule might overcome problems that might not easily be surmounted any other way. Such problems might even provide a chance to explore a concept such as "flextime" for the entire department, or a 4-day, 40-hour work week.

A problem of friction with co-workers must be resolved soon, and the result is usually either transfer or discharge. Discussion rarely works here, because such problems are almost always two-way problems.

An excellent way to avoid the problem of unsatisfactory performance is to use the probationary period* effectively. If there is still a question at the end of the period, the supervisor should either extend the probation or terminate the person. Having to discharge or fire someone is always uncomfortable, especially if that person has been with the organization for some time. But, if this is the only alternative available, then the supervisor must not be reluctant to take it on. (As the next chapter points out, merit systems have definite procedures for doing this.)

The preceding discussion assumes poor performance on the part of the employee. If a person is caught stealing or falsifying records, or is guilty of immoral conduct, it is an entirely different matter. Almost anywhere, such acts would be grounds for immediate firing, without notice and most often without terminal pay.

Experience is still the only real guide in handling unsatisfactory employees, so it is fortunate that serious problems usually are rare. Ongoing evaluation can reduce problems even further, but when they do occur, they should be dealt with promptly.

OTHER FACTORS IN PERSONNEL WORK

A supervisor has little to do with the creation of the elements in a library's personnel system. Usually the system is imposed on the library by an outside agency, although, in larger libraries, there is one person who is responsible for supervising the implementation of the system. Overseeing fringe benefits is usually the job of the personnel officer. Vacations (time earned, possible loss of accumulated time, and approval), insurance benefits, and retirement programs are all part of personnel work. Explaining differences in insurance plans, helping with claim forms, and scheduling vacations may not seem to be very important to the larger picture of personnel work, but they are quite significant to the employees (even though Herzberg sees them as only hygienic factors). Increasingly, personnel officers are responsible for employee health and safety (OSHA: Occupational Safety and Health Act)—from maintaining accident records to monitoring unsafe conditions (slippery stairs or chemical storage, for example).

Table 12.2 illustrates the variety of federal laws and a sample of state laws affecting personnel management in libraries. Because these laws and the interpretations of them change so frequently (almost daily, it

---

*A period of time (from 3 months to 2 years) in which the employer can dismiss the employee for almost any reason fairly easily. In a merit system, it is very difficult to dismiss a person who has passed probation.

TABLE 12.2 LAWS AND EMPLOYMENT PRACTICES

Type of law	Federal	CA	CO	GA	MI	PA
Discrimination–race	X	X	X	X	X	X
National origin	X	X	X	X	X	X
Religion	X	X	–	X	X	X
Sex	X	X	X	X	X	X
Age	X	X	X	X	X	X
Handicap	X	X	X	X	X	X
Veteran's readjustment	X	–	–	–	–	–
Collective bargaining	X	X	X ^{a}	X ^{a}	X	X
Reporting and disclosure	X	–	X	–	–	–
Right to strike	X	X ^{a}	X ^{a}	X ^{a}	X ^{b}	X ^{b}
Minimum wage	X	X	X	–	–	–
Equal pay	X	X	X	X	X	X
Hours	X	X	X	X	X	X
Portal to portal	X	–	X	–	–	–
Garnishment	X	X	X	–	X	X
Worker's compensation	X	X	X	X	X	X
Social security	X	–	–	–	–	–
Employment security	X	X	X	X	X	X
Occupational safety and health	X	X	–	–	X	–
Posting and records	X	X	X	X	X	X

^{a} Does not apply to public employees.

^{b} Applies only to certain public employees.

^{c} Includes the categories of wages, safety and health, worker's compensation and affirmative action.

seems), most books on personnel can provide only general guidance. If, after reading about these programs in government documents and news articles, you think you might have a problem, do not hesitate to get expert advice from your personnel department.

The library's (or its jurisdiction's) personnel office should be a source of aid to the supervisor in all phases of personnel work, from writing job descriptions to dealing with the day an employee leaves. The more you know about the system of which you are a part, the less often you will need to consult personnel offices. If 90% of your time is spent on personnel problems of one kind or another, the more time you save, the better off you will be.

In the suggestions for further reading, there are several interesting additional topics listed. There is a section on alternative methods of work scheduling—a topic for advanced course work in personnel administration. A list of materials on interviewing in all its aspects also is included. The section on legal aspects is long because laws are now central to all personnel work in the United States.

BIBLIOGRAPHY

1. B. Conroy, *Library Staff Development* (Littleton, Colo.: Libraries Unlimited, 1978).
2. G. E. Evans, "An American's View of Nordic Education Programs for Library Personnel," *Scandinavian Public Library Quarterly* 7 (1974): 2–15.

FURTHER READING

General Works

American Library Association, Personnel Administration Section. "Guidelines to the Development of Human Resources in Libraries." *Library Trends* 20 (1970): 97–117.

Beatty, R. W., and Schneier, C. E. *Personnal Administration: An Experiential/Skill Building Approach.* Reading, Mass.: Addison-Wesley, 1977.

Boyd, H. "Employment Paperwork Systems." *Personnel Journal* 56 (1977): 611–615.

Brownell, P. "Social Accounting—Go; or Not Go!" *Australian Accountant* 47 (Aug 1977): 430–433.

Bryan, W. W. "Public Library Personnel Administration: The Part of the Trustee." *Illinois Libraries* 49 (1967): 597–603.

Burack, E. H., and Miller, E. L. "The Personnel Function in Transition." *California Management Review* 18 (1976): 32–38.

Coleman, J. M. *Trustees and Personnel Policy.* In *American Library Association Yearbook, 1978.* Chicago: American Library Association, 1979.

Corbett, E. V. "Staffing of Large Municipal Libraries in England and the United States." *Journal of Librarianship* 3 (1971): 87–100.

Cronback, L. "Selection Theory for a Political World." *Public Personnel Management* 38 (1980): 37–39.

Deep, S. A. *Human Relations in Management.* Encino, Calif.: Glencoe, 1978.

Design of Jobs. 2d, ed. Santa Monica, Calif.: Goodyear Pub., 1979.

Dessler, G. *Personnel Management; Modern Concepts and Techniques.* Reston, VA: Reston Publishing, 1978.

Edwards, R. J. "Staff Organization." In *Manual of Library Economy.* London: C. Bingley, 1977.

Flener, J. G. "New Approaches to Personnel Management: Personalizing Management." *Journal of Academic Librarianship* 1 (1975): 17–20.

Franklin, R. D. "Personnel Primer: Topical Index to Library Teamwork." *Library Journal* 90 (1965): 3542–3549.

French, W. L. *The Personnel Management Process.* 4th ed. Boston: Houghton, 1978.

Glueck, W. F. *Personnel; A Diagnostic Approach.* Rev. ed. Dallas: Business Pub., 1978.

Goldstein, M. A., and Sweeney, C. M. "Aptitude Requirements for Library Assistants in Special Libraries." *Special Libraries* 70 (1979): 373–376.

Hamill, H. L. "Selection, Training and Staffing for Branch Libraries." *Library Trends* 14 (1966): 407–421.

Hasselquist, O. "The MTM Method—With Special Reference to the Physically Handicapped." *Management Services* 22 (1978): 14–19.

Kuzmits, F. E. "How Much is Absenteeism Costing Your Organization?" *Personnel Administrator* 24 (1979): 29–33.

Lee, R., and Lee, C. S. "Personnel for a Library Manpower System." *Library Trends* 20 (1970): 19–38.

Levine, E. L. "Evaluation and Use of Four Job Analysis Methods for Personnel Selection." *Public Personnel Management* 8 (1979): 146–151.

Library Administration and Management Association. Personnel Administration. *The Personnel Manual: An Outline for Libraries.* Chicago: American Library Association, 1977.

McNamara, J. R. "Why Aren't They Doing What We Trained Them to Do?" *Training* 17 (Feb 1980): 33–34.

Martin, T. N., Jr. "A Contextual Model of Employee Turnover Intentions." *Academy of Management Journal* 22 (1979): 313–324.

May, B. R. "Give Employee Morale A Boost." *Supervision* 41 (1979): 3–4.

Pardee, J. H. "Special Requirements of the Larger Unit in Personnel Administration." *Libraries Trends* 13 (1965): 353–363.

Peterson, R. B., and Tracy, L. *Systematic Management of Human Resources.* Reading, Mass.: Addison-Wesley, 1979.

Rickling, Myrl, and Booth, R. E. *Personnel Utilization in Libraries: A Systems Approach.* Prep. for the Illinois Library Task Analysis Project. Chicago: American Library Association, 1974.

Sanzotta, D. *The Manager's Guide to Interpersonal Relations.* New York: AMACOM, 1979.

Savage, A. W. *Personnel Management.* London: Library Association, 1977.

Shaughnessy, T. W. "Redesigning Library Jobs." *American Society for Information Science Journal* 29 (1978): 187–190.

Smith, H. L., and Watkins, L. E. "Management Manpower Turnover Costs." *Personnel Administrator* 23 (1978): 46–50.

Stephan, S. S. "Assignment: Administrative Volunteer." *Catholic Library World* 48 (1976): 104–108.

Swinburne, P. "Psychology and the Personnel Manager: Is A Little Knowledge A Dangerous Thing?" *Personnel Management* 11 (1979): 40–43.

Tosti, D. J. "How Not To Waste Your Training Dollars." *Administrative Management* 41 (Feb. 1980): 44–46+.

Walters, L. K., and Roach, D. "Job Satisfaction, Behavioral Intention, and Absenteeism as Predicators of Turnover." *Personnel Psychology* 32 (1979): 393–397.

Weber, D. C., and Kass, T. "Comparable Rewards: The Case for Equal Compensation for Administrative Expertise." *Library Journal* 103 (1978): 824–827.

Wilkinson, J., Plate, K., and Lee, R. "A Matrix Approach to Position Classification." *College and Research Libraries* 36 (1975): 351–363.

Williams, E. E. "Who Does What: Unprofessional Personnel Policies." *College and Research Libraries* 6 (1945): 301–310.

Yecht, E. *Work Sample Test of Reference Skills for Information Specialist Candidates.* Los Angeles: Atlantic Richfield Corporate Library, 1980.

Alternative Work Schedules

Baird, N. "Two for the Price of One [Job-Sharing]." *Kentucky Library Association Bulletin* 44 (1980): 9–11.

Barkey, P. T. "Flextime: The Workweek Revolution." *Library Journal* 103 (1978): 713–715.

Best, F. "Preferences on Work Life Scheduling and Work–Leisure Trade Offs." *Monthly Labor Review* 101 (1978): 31–37.

Finkle, A. L. "Flextime In Government." *Public Personnel Management* 8 (1979): 152–155.

Flextime Programs. Willow Grove, Penn.: Administrative Management Society, 1978.

Golembiewski, R. T., and Proehl, C. W., Jr. "Public Sector Applications of Flexible Workhours: A Review of Available Experience." *Public Administration Review* 40 (Jan.-Feb. 1980): 72–85.

Kramer, O. P. "Flexible Working Hours." *Journal of Systems Management* 29 (1978): 17–21.

Mahoney, T. P. "The Rearranged Work Week: Evaluations of Different Work Schedules." *California Management Review* 20 (1978): 31–39.

Meyer, B. J. "Longer Workday and the Shorter Workweek." *Library Resources and Technical Services* 18 (1974): 336–340.

Nollen, S. D. *New Work Patterns.* Scarsdale, New York: Work in America Institute, 1979.

Olmsted, B. "Job Sharing—A New Way to Work." *Personnel Journal* 56 (1977): 78–81.

Ronsham, S. *Flexible Working Hours Today: Practices and Experiences of Over Fifty British Organizations.* Management Survey Report No. 17. London: British Institute of Management, 1973.

Schein, V. E., Maurer, E. H., and Novak, J. F. "Supervisors' Reactions to Flexible Work Hours." *Journal of Occupational Psychology* 51 (1978): 333–337.

Snyder, C. A., and Burbach, S. J. "Flexible Scheduline: The Indiana University Experience." *Library Journal* 101 (1976): 861–864.

Sullivan, K. "Implementation of Flextime." *New Library World* 76 (1975): 18–19.

Swart, J. C. *A Flexible Approach to Working Hours.* New York: AMACOM, 1978.

Weinstein, H. G. *A Comparison of Three Alternative Work Schedules: Flexible Work Hours, Compact Work Week, and Staggered Work Hours.* Philadelphia: Univ. of Pennsylvania, The Wharton School, Industrial Research Unit, 1975.

Wells, D. P. "Coping With Schedules for Extended Hours: A Survey of Attitudes." *Journal of Academic Librarianship* 5 (1979): 24–27.

Interviewing

Creth, S. "Conducting an Effective Employment Interview." *Journal of Academic Librarianship* 4 (1978): 356–360.

Forbes, R. "Improving the Reliability of the Selection Interview." *Personnel Management* 11 (1979): 36–39.

Maag, A. F. "Design of the Library Director Interview: The Candidate's Perspective." *College and Research Libraries* 41 (1980): 112–121.

Moffat, T. L. *Selection Interviewing for Managers.* New York: Harper, 1979.

Ramsay, R. T. *Management's Guide to Effective Employment Interviewing; Fair, Valid Methods for Hiring Qualified Personnel.* Chicago: Dartnell, 1978.

Simon, B. "Personnel Selection Practices: Applications and Interviews." *American Libraries*
   9 (1978): 141–143.
Stewart, C. J., and Cash, W. B., Jr. *Interviewing; Principles and Practices.* 2d ed. Dubuque:
   W.C. Brown, 1978.

Legal Aspects

American Library Association Equal Employment Subcommittee. "Guidelines for Library
   Affirmative Action Plans." *American Libraries* 7 (1976): 451–453.
Anthony, W. P., and Bowen, M. "Affirmative Action: Problems and Promises. *Personnel
   Journal* 56 (1977): 616–621.
Brecht, A., and Mills, R. "Minorities Employed in Law Libraries." *Law Library Journal* 71
   (1978): 283–288.
Burton, G. E., and Pathak, D. W. "101 Ways to Discriminate Against Equal Employment
   Opportunity." *Personnel Administrator* 22 (1977): 42–45.
Dhanens, T. P. "Implications of the New EEOC Guidelines." *Personnel* 56 (1979): 32–39.
Dickenson, E. "Affirmative Action Plans in Review: A Report from the Equal Opportunity
   Subcommittee." *American Libraries* 10 (1979): 69–70.
English, J. W. "How to Pick the Best People Under EEO." *SAM Advanced Management
   Journal* 44 (1979): 23–30.
Fry, F. L. "The End of Affirmative Action." *Business Horizons* 23 (1980): 34–40.
Gaymon, D. "Underutilization in Affirmative Action Programs: What Is It and What Can We
   Do About It?" *Personnel Journal* 58 (1979): 457–459.
Hall, F., and Albrecht, M. H. *The Management of Affirmative Action.* Santa Monica, Calif.:
   Goodyear Pub. Co., 1979.
Hammer, T. H. "Affirmative Action Programs: Have We Forgotten the First-Line Supervisor?"
   Personnel Journal 58 (1979): 384–389.
Josey, E. J. "Can Library Affirmative Action Succeed?" *Library Journal* 100 (1975): 28–31.
Leadvinka, J. "The Statistical Definition of Fairness in the Federal Selection Guidelines and
   Its Implications for Minority Employment." *Personnel Psychology* 32 (1979): 551–562.
Loban, L. "The Handicaps—Sometimes Your Best Employee." *Supervisor* 42 (1980): 3–5.
McFeeley, N. D. "Weber Versus Affirmative Action?" *Personnel* 57 (1980): 38–51.
Miniter, J. J. "Implications of Affirmative Action in Recruitment Employment and Termina-
   tion of Personnel." *North Carolina Libraries* 36 (1978): 16–20.
Pati, G. C., and Hilton, E. F., Jr. "A Comprehensive Model For A Handicapped Affirmative
   Action Program." Personnel Journal 59 (1980): 99–108.
Pati, G. C., and Adkins, J. I. "Hire the Handicapped—Compliance Is Good Business." *Har-
   vard Business Review* 58 (1980): 14–15.
Rosen, B., and Jerdee, T. H. "Coping With Affirmative Action Backlash." *Business Horizons*
   22 (1979): 15–20.
Sahlein, S. *The Affirmative Action Handbook; Dealing With Day to Day Supervisory Problems.*
   New York: Executives Enterprises, 1978.
Treiman, D. J. *Job Evaluation: An Analytic View; Interim Report to the Equal Employment
   Opportunity Commission.* Washington, D.C.: Nat. Acad. Sci., 1979.
U.S. Civil Service Commission. Office of Federal Equal Employment Opportunity. *The Skills
   Survey; What It Is and How It works.* Personnel Management Series No. 29. Washington,
   D.C.: Government Printing Office, 1977.
U.S. Department of Labor. Bureau of Labor Statistics. *What Every Employer Needs to Know
   About OSHA Record Keeping.* Report No. 212-3. Washington, D.C.: Government Printing
   Office, 1978.

Performance Appraisal

Association of Research Libraries. Office of University Library Management Studies and McGill University Libraries. *Staff Performance Evaluation Program at the McGill University Libraries: A Program Description of a Goals-based Performance Evaluation Process with Accompanying Supervisor's Manual.* Washington, D.C.: ARL, 1976.

Bell, R. R. "Evaluating Subordinates: How Subjective Are You? *S.A.M. Advanced Management Journal* 44 (1979): 36–44.

Berkner, D. S. "Library Staff Development Through Performance Appraisal." *College and Research Libraries* 40 (1979): 335–344.

Binis, R. A. "The Performance Appraisal: The Most Needed and Neglected Supervisory Tool." *Supervisory Management* 23 (1978): 12–16.

Danzig, S. M. "What We Need To Know About Performance Appraisals." *Management Review* 69 (1980): 20–24.

Delamontagne, R. P., and Weitzul, J. B. "Performance Alignment: The Fine Art of the Perfect Fit." *Personnel Journal* 59 (1980): 115–117+.

DeProspo, E. "Personnel Evaluation as an Impetus to Growth." *Library Trends* 20 (1971): 60–70.

Dutton, B. G. "Job Assessment and Job Evaluation." *ASLIB Proceedings* 28 (1976): 144–160.

Fulmer, W. F. "Tayloring Employee Evaluation Forms to Your Organization's Needs." *Personnel* 55 (1978): 69–72.

Gardner, J. J. "Performance Evaluation in Libraries." In *Personnel Development in Libraries,* edited by K. Maloney. New Brunswick, N.J.: Rutgers University Graduate School of Library Science, 1976.

Hall, M.A. "A Funny Thing Happened On the Way to a Performance Appraisal Form." *Public Library* 17 (1978): 8–9. 13–14.

Haynes, M. G. "Developing an Appraisal Program." *Personnel Journal* 57 (1978): 14–19.

Johnson, H. "Performance Appraisal of Librarians." *College and Research Libraries* 33 (1972): 359–366.

Johnson, J. W. "Some Psychological Aspects of Employee Evaluation." *Public Management* 60 (1978): 2–4.

Johnson, S. L., and Ronan, W. W. "An Exploratory Study of Bias in Job Performance Evaluation." *Public Personnel Management* 8 (1979): 315–323.

Kaske, N. K. "Personnel and Employment Performance Appraisal." In *American Library Association Yearbook.* Chicago: ALA, 1976.

Levinson, H. "Management of What Performance?" *Harvard Business Review* 54 (1976): 30–36.

Martin, J. A. "Staff Evaluation of Supervisors." *Special Libraries* 70 (1979): 26–29.

Nicholas, P. L. "Do Public Servants Welcome or Fear Merit Evaluation of Their Performance." *Public Administration Review* 40 (1980): 214–222.

Peele, D. "Evaluating Library Employees." *Library Journal* 97 (1972): 2803–2807.

Peele, D. "Fear in the Library." *Journal of Academic Librarianship* 4 (1978): 362–369.

Sauser, W. I., Jr. "Evaluating Employee Performance: Needs, Problems and Possible Solutions." *Public Personnel Management* 9 (1980): 11–18.

Schlukier, G. "Transguessing the System: Performance Measurement and Library Development." *Canadian Library Journal* 35 (1978): 303–306.

Smith, H., and Brouwer, P. J. *Performance Appraisal and Human Development; A Practical Guide to Effective Managing.* Reading, Mass.: Addison-Wesley, 1977.

Smith, M. "Documenting Employee Performance." *Supervisory Management* 24 (1979): 30–37.

Tilton, R. C. "Performance Evaluation of Library Personnel." *Special Libraries* 69 (1978): 429–434.

242

12. Personnel: The Human Side

Yarbrough, L. N. "Performance Appraisal in Academic and Research Libraries." *ARL Management Supplement No. 3*. Washington, D.C.: ARL, 1975.

Yeh, T. Y. R. "Library Peer Evaluation; A Blessing or Nuisance." *Pacific Northwest Library Association Quarterly* 42 (1977): 10–14.

Removal and Grievances

Baer, W. E. "Discipline: When an Employee Breaks the Rule." *Supervisory Management* 11 (1966): 20–23.

Brophy, A. L. "Handling Problem Staff Members." *Illinois Libraries* 43 (1961): 750–763.

Corzine, J. E. "Structure and Utilization of a Grievance Procedure." *Personnel Journal* 46 (1967): 484–489.

Embrey, W. R. "Exit Interview: A Tool for Personnel Development." *Personnel Administrator* 24 (1979): 43–48.

Harrison, E. L. "Discipline and the Professional Employee." *Personal Administrator* 24 (1979): 35–38.

Kuzmits, F. E. "How Good Is Your Absenteeism Control System?" *SAM Advanced Management Journal* 45 (1980): 4–15.

Mosher, L. S. "What the Supervisor Should Know About Grievance Procedures." *Supervisory Management* 21 (1976): 20–26.

Potter, B. A. *Turning Around*. New York: Amaco, 1980.

Simon, B. "Developing Termination Policies and Procedures." *American Libraries* 4 (1973): 45–57.

Summers, C. W. "Protecting *All* Employees Against Unjust Dismissal." *Harvard Business Review* 80, 1 (1980): 132–139.

Weiss, W. H. "Goofing Off On the Job." *Supervision* 39 (1977): 2–4.

Special Problems

Bauman, R. "'High' Employees." *Supervision* 39 (1977): 3–4.

Filipowicz, C. A. "The Troubled Employee: Whose Responsibility?" *Personnel Administrator* 24 (1979): 17–20.

Follman, J. F., Jr. *Helping the Troubled Employee*. New York: AMACOM, 1978.

Manuso, J. S. "Executive Stress Management." *Personnel Administrator* 24 (1979): 23–26.

May, B. R. "The Problem Employee Is Your Problem." *Supervision* 40 (1978): 5–7.

Organ, D. W. "The Meaning of Stress." *Business Horizons* 22 (1979): 32–40.

Quinn, R. E., and Judge, N. A. "The Office Romance: No Bliss for the Boss." *Management Review* 67 (1978): 43–49.

Schramm, C. J. *Workers Who Drink; Their Treatment in an Industrial Setting*. Lexington, Mass.: D.C. Heath, 1978.

Student, K. R. "Personnel's Newest Challenge: Helping to Cope With Greater Stress." *Personnel Administrator* 23 (1978): 20–24.

Weiss, W. H. "You Can't Ignore the Alcoholic." *Supervision* 39 (1977): 6–8.

Staff Development

Bare, A. C. "Staffing and Training: Neglected Supervisory Functions Related to Group Performance." *Personnel Psychology* 31 (1978): 107–117.

Becker, S. "The 10 Sequential Steps of the Training Process." *Training* 17 (1980): 40–43.

Clement, R. W. "Unethical and Improper Behavior by Training and Development Professionals." *Training and Development Journal* 32 (1978): 10–12.

Conroy, B. *Library Staff Development and Continuing Education: Principles and Practices.* Littleton, Colo.: Libraries Unlimited, 1978.

Dartnell Corporation. Office Administration Service. *Why Training Programs Sometimes Fail.* New York: Dartnell, 1980.

Donaldson, L., and Scannell, E. E. *Human Resource Development; The New Trainer's Guide.* Reading, Mass.: Addison-Wesley, 1978.

Gardner, J. E. *Training the New Supervisor.* New York: AMACOM, 1980.

Hayford, S. L. "The Crisis in Public-employee Collective Bargaining." *Business Horizons* 22 (1979): 47–52.

Laird, D. *Approaches to Training and Development.* Reading, Mass.: Addison-Wesley, 1978.

Levine, M., and Hagburg, E. *Labor Relations; An Integrated Perspective.* St. Paul, Minn.: West Pub. Co., 1978.

Lewis, R. "A New Dimension in Library Administration—Negotiating a Union Contract." *ALA Bulletin* 63 (1969): 455–464.

McDongle, L. G. "The Job Description: Setting the Standard for Employee Development." *Supervisory Management* 24 (1979): 38–40.

Moss, C. E. "Bargaining's Effect on Library Management and Operation." *Library Trends* 25 (1976): 497–515.

Nelson, N. E. "Public Policy and Union Security in the Public Sector." *Journal of Collective Negotiations in the Public Sector* 7 (1978): 87–101.

Nigro, F. A. "Managers in Government and Labor Relations." *Public Administration Review* 38 (1978): 180–184.

Nigro, F. A. *The New Public Personnel Administration.* Itasca, Ill.: F. E. Peacock Pub., 1976. *Personnel Management in Government; Politics and Process.* New York: Dekker, 1978.

Pinto, P. R. "Your Trainers and the Law: Are They Breaking It In and Out of the Classroom?" *Training* 15 (1978): 17–23+.

Robb, P. P. "Changing Loyalties: Effects of Unionization on Communication Patterns in Libraries." *Canadian Library Journal* 32 (1975): 357–359.

Schlipf, F. *Collective Bargaining in Libraries.* Urbana, Ill.: Univ. of Illinois Press, 1975.

Shafritz, J. M. *The Public Personnel World: Readings on the Professional Practice.* Chicago: International Personnel Management Association, 1977.

Shaw, M. E. "On Criticism: Training and Development. *Training and Development Journal* 34 (1980): 33–35.

Suskin, H. *Job Evaluation and Pay Administration in Public Sector.* Chicago: International Personnel Management Association, 1977.

U.S. Department of Labor-Management Services Administration. *Summary of Public Sector Labor Relations Policies.* Washington, D.C.: Government Printing Office. 1979.

U.S. Office of Personnel Management. *Personnel Management in State and Local Governments.* Washington D.C.: Government Printing Office, 1979.

Weatherford, J. W. *Collective Bargaining and the Academic Librarian.* Metuchen, N.J.: Scarecrow, 1976.

Weatherford, J. W. "Collective Bargaining and the Academic Librarian." *Library Journal* 105 (1980): 481–482.

13. Personnel: The System Side

As part of a larger system (whether commercial, educational, or governmental), a library is seldom free to establish an independent personnel system. Even those libraries associated with private institutions normally have the basic rules for personnel work prescribed to them. Such issues as salary ranges, recruiting, testing methods, interviewing, and benefits are tied to comparable categories of work both within the library and in outside units. Because the majority of libraries are public institutions, this chapter emphasizes conditions in government employment, whether at the federal, state, or local level. A public librarian's salary is usually tied to salaries paid to school teachers, social workers, and other governmental professionals, as well as to the salaries paid to librarians who work for private business and industry.

CHARACTERISTICS OF THE MERIT SYSTEM

Because so many libraries are bound by either a civil service or a merit system, the basic concepts of such systems will be explored in the first part of this chapter (the term *merit system* will be used for convenience.) A merit personnel system is one created by a governmental or quasi-governmental body; in such a system, comparative merit or success on the job governs each person's selection and progress in the system. Comparisons are made by means of tests or rating schemes. Employees have a high degree of job security, and the system is designed to protect them from undue political pressure and influence.

The main goals of a merit personnel system are: (1) to secure the most competent staff possible regardless of political affiliation; (2) to ensure that salary increases and promotion are free of political or personal bias; and (3) to establish a stable work force by providing security against dismissal for political reasons. Theoretically, a merit system is based on three values or objectives: (1) competence (which affects efficiency of service), (2) neutrality in policy (which involves political neutrality), and (3) equality of opportunity (which requires an absence of favoritism). In practice, however, since every system is administered by humans, several subjective elements complicate the picture.

In a library, as in many other areas of public employment, the application of these values is difficult and may even be self-contradictory. According to American political philosophy, government consists of three branches (legislative, executive, and judicial) each with its own sphere of influence. The legislative branch, through the laws it passes, establishes basic governmental policies that in theory reflect the desires of the electorate. The executive branch is supposed to administer the policy through its various agencies. The judicial branch is expected to enforce laws as well as to provide binding interpretations of them. Theory and practice often seem to be very far apart.

The majority of merit system employees are in the executive branch. In theory, then, they should not establish policy, but rather only administer it. If employees decide only questions of fact, then a system needs only people who are qualified to deal with factual issues. Civil servants, however, often have discretionary powers involving questions of values; therefore, choosing employees involves not only evaluating their technical competence, but also determining how candidates would interpret policies that would be within their jurisdiction or responsibility. Thus, the assumption that public employees can or should be neutral on questions of value may not be valid at all. Once a person is "forced" to decide an issue in favor of one position or another, neutrality is gone. Almost all agencies decide or interpret policy, which complicates the process of choosing employees solely on the basis of ratable skills.

Precisely how to define and determine merit is another problem. What methods are available for deciding gradations of merit among candidates? We find, in fact, that as a goal, competence is a statement of good intentions rather than something that is measurable and attainable. All tests have inherent biases, whether those biases are immediately apparent or not. Another question is, do tests measure competence or perhaps only skill in test taking?

Present measures of administrative ability are so inadequate that no reasonable person would rely solely on test results as indicators of ability. The applicant's prior experience, job history, personal recommendations, and professional or other activities ought to be equally important in influencing such a decision. Of course, these too are biases, subject to interpretation. Alone, such subjective judgments can lead to a spoils system or an "old boy" network; however, *taken together with tests and other data,* personal work histories can help to shape informed recommendations. Remember, however, the goal of filling posts solely on the basis of competence is difficult at best and often not practical. (Some of the ways one can reduce the amount of bias in selection process were discussed in Chapter 12; however, the following is a brief review of the important issues.) Evaluation criteria must be based upon job duties: have written guidelines that indicate what experience is believed to provide the desired skills and knowledge; employ a selection committee or have several persons make independent judgments about candidates' qualifications; contact all references given by candidates.

The second goal in a merit system is neutrality in administering policy. Persons who favor either merit or spoils systems usually agree that having policy carried out in a neutral manner might not be the wisest course. Usually it is said that lower echelon employees need merit systems, whereas higher-ups (policy makers) ought not to be covered. But it is naive to argue that those who work with policy on a day-to-day basis and deal with the public are not capable of influencing that policy or that they do not interpret policy. Indeed, they do, and they can even come to have considerable influence on policy.

Where should the line be drawn? Should a city department head be outside a merit system because of a wide range of discretionary powers? Does (or should) the degree of controversy surrounding a job require that it be placed outside the merit system? For libraries, the common pattern has been to cover all nonprofessional categories by a merit system or its equivalent (especially in public libraries). The professional positions often are handled differently from library to library; however, the most typical pattern is for all librarians to be included in the merit system, with the exception of the director.

The third goal in the merit system is equality of opportunity. Recent federal and state legislation has made this concept a significant factor in the profit sector employment picture, not just in government. Because nearly 25% of all employed people in the United States are paid with government funds (direct or indirect), the impact of the merit system is quite clear, even though not all these persons are covered by such a system. As already noted, a true spoils system would make it difficult to anticipate a career that crosses party lines, but spoils nevertheless do enter the picture with subjective evaluations. Influence, favoritism, nepotism—all can rear their heads and destroy any semblance of equal opportunity. Also, candidates must remember that systems have preferences built into them. For example, military personnel who decide to enter civil service in the United States are given preference points. Under that system, if a veteran and nonveteran scored equally on a test, the job would go to the veteran because of preference points. Also, preference is occasionally given to people who have been in a system for some time and have seniority, although this is not always stated. The latter is especially in evidence during layoffs ("first hired, last fired").

PROBLEMS IN THE MERIT SYSTEM

The primary problem with the ideal merit system, then, is that it does not reflect reality, that is, it is not attainable. Because neutral tests are not available (and are unlikely to become so), and because people cannot always be simultaneously neutral politically and in terms of policy implementation, and because equal opportunity barriers cannot be broken totally without sound neutral tests, the best that can be done is to keep working on existing systems to try to bring them closer to the ideal. All systems, of course, have flaws and problems. Merit systems usually encounter problems in five basic areas. One problem that used to be prominent was the requirement that persons employed by a governmental agency actually live within the political jurisdiction. Thus, a person who worked in a public library would have to live within the limits of the city that supported the library. Because this concept has been challenged in courts in the United States, we may see such requirements dropped in the future. It should be noted that residency requirements actually operate against one of the concepts of the merit system, specifically, the goal of the best person for job. Instead, the search for employees is confined to the best person within the designated geographic limits (or one who is willing to move to the designated locality).

As noted previously, testing is another area in which problems can arise, especially for professional positions. Most systems use combination oral–written tests, the latter being general and both subject to change for each testing session. For clerical positions, written tests are much more important, and they usually consist of standardized tests for typing, filing, and similar mechanical skills. The problem with both kinds of tests, though, is that they cannot always predict actual behavior in the library setting. For example, a person achieving a high score on a standard typing test may not be able to effectively apply that skill to typing library order forms.

The probationary period is yet another area of concern. In theory, merit systems are designed to create career opportunities for individuals, and especially to protect them from being fired for political considerations. Once the probationary period has passed, firing a person from a merit position is extremely difficult. However, probationary periods are often too short (as little as 3 months) to give supervisors a clear idea of how well an individual will perform. Most systems allow for an extension to the probationary period, if the supervisor believes that questions exist concerning an employee's ability and motivation. Such extensions should be requested and made for both the employee's and the organization's sake, if the merit system is to be effective.

Rewarding the person who performs exceedingly well is also a problem in most merit systems. Rapid promotion is almost out of the question, as are pay differentials based upon levels of productivity. Trying to upgrade an employee by two or three steps (which usually means 5% increments in salary per step) will almost inevitably fail, as the fear of favoritism crops up and because the amount of justification paperwork is so great that most supervisors give up after a few attempts. Once beyond probation, a government employee has a greater chance of retaining a job than does someone in the private sector, even in times of great economic recessions. (The more seniority, the more security. When rare reductions in force [RIFs] do occur in government, then seniority matters.) Usually, the government simply allows natural factors (resignation, retirement, transfer, and death) to thin the ranks, thereby avoiding layoffs and related personnel problems.

Employees have security of salary as well as tenure. Most position categories (such as Librarian I, II, III, IV, V) have five or six pay steps, and in some systems, a person moves up one step each year. (Thus, a five-category librarian system with a five-step annual sequence could cover a 25-year career.) All too often, though, advancement is almost automatic, even advancement from one position category to another. In the preceding chapter's discussion of performance evaluation, it was noted that librarians worry about how evaluations affect their salary and advancement; in an automatic system, this would hardly be necessary. However, despite the almost automatic granting of one-step promotions in a government merit system, people still do worry about what their supervisor thinks about the level of performance achieved. Although one-step increases are almost automatic, supervisors have great difficulty rewarding outstanding performance. Because good performance is difficult to reward and bad performance is difficult to discipline, the usual result in a merit system is mediocre performance. In theory, poor performance can be punished; in practice it is very difficult and time consuming, because the system is designed to provide maximum protection for the employee. People will often perform at a minimum level, or slightly above, because they are safe from reprisal and have no real incentive to do better work.

The final problem for a supervisor in a merit system involves the discharge of an unsatisfactory employee—the grievance procedure is complex, it takes time (the procedure can take months), and it often does not accomplish the desired end. Tensions increase when all parties stay on the job, and time is lost by supervisors and employees in testifying. Details of procedure vary from jurisdiction to jurisdiction, but they all involve a series of reviews within the agency, and if the issue cannot be resolved in the agency, then a hearing by a "grievance" board for the system. If the employee wishes to, he or she may be represented by legal counsel. On rare occasions, the issue may have to be resolved in court. As one moves up the procedural levels, pressure increases on the supervisor to prove that the case is one of poor performance and not one of personal bias. In fact, getting an employee discharged hardly seems worth the effort to some supervisors. Such an attitude, however, will only increase the problems of poor performance.

What can the supervisor do? The supervisors must assume *all* of their responsibilities. They must train the employees properly. They must demand high levels of performance and enforce, fairly, all the work rules. They must not pass persons through probation without adequately assessing their performance. They must not tolerate violations of performance standards or rules of conduct. Failure to do these things results in an atmosphere that is lax and conducive to poor performance, which in turn results in wasteful and poor service to the clientele.

The problems outlined above have been with the merit system for years, even though politicians periodically make these problems a public issue and force some changes. Naturally since one of the aims of the merit system is to keep political influence out of the system, reforms are hard to achieve, since the party not in office is concerned that any changes may make it harder for them to gain public office. Under the Carter administration, there was an effort to change the U.S. federal system after an extensive review of the present methods of operation. For example, the study indicated that only 226 persons (out of a total federal work force of 2.1 million persons) had been dismissed for incompetence during 1977. It also indicated it took an average 2.34 years to accomplish a dismissal if the worker had passed the probationary period. The reform legislation proposed to make it possible to reward high productivity through bonuses and special stipends (Alan K. Campbell, Chairman, Civil Service Commission 1977/1978 reform study.) Despite all the efforts and public statements by politicians, the basic problems still remain as they were in 1977 or 1947, or 1907 for that matter, because no significant changes were made by Congress or the Civil Service. Only the supervisors can make a significant difference in the performance of the merit system by not tolerating poor performance before or after the probationary period.

Merit Systems and Collective Bargaining

Although it would seem that government employees have the best of employment worlds, there is a drawback, one with which labor unions are vitally concerned: governments have not traditionally allowed their employees much say regarding working conditions. For several reasons, government employees have not been allowed to join unions or to go on strike. Part of the reason for this resides in the characteristics of the services that governments offer:

They are generally more urgent than those provided by the private sector.

They are generally of a monopolistic of semimonopolistic nature.

They tend to be conducted in a precise legal context.

They are not controlled by "market" pricing (everyone receives equal services for equal prices).

Libraries do not fit these characteristics very well (nor do other government agencies such as those that deal with educational, recreational, and other social and cultural functions). However, because these activities have been deemed too essential to be relegated to the private sector, government provides such services. Because of the characteristics of government work, society has not felt that individuals working for the government should have the right to disrupt those services or unnecessarily increase their cost.

Even without union representation, government employees' associations have been rather effective in influencing legislative bodies to improving working conditions. However, working through the legislative process can be slow and frustrating. Government employees hope to gain the right to obtain improvements and the right to strike through collective bargaining. The past 20 years have seen strikes by teachers, police officers, fire fighters, librarians, doctors, nurses, and just about every other category of public employee. In essence, then, it is no longer a question of whether government employees should unionize, but rather how and when such professionals should form a union or even strike.

WHAT IS COLLECTIVE BARGAINING?

The use of the term *collective bargaining,* a term from the field of labor relations, is more appropriate for the private sector and for labor union situations than for merit systems, because it contains the idea of two equally strong groups coming together to bargain. In public employee negotiations with government, however, the parties are not at all equal, and therein lies the major difference. Even in the face of a strike, the government obviously is the stronger party (for example, as in the 1982 air traffic controllers strike in the United States). Some writers have even suggested that *collective negotiation* would be a more accurate term in such situations, but here the term *bargaining* will be used because it is more familiar. The concept, then, is that a *bargaining unit* (representatives of employees) meets with *management* (again, representatives) to discuss *bargaining issues* (perhaps changes in working conditions). Once the terms of the *agreement* are worked out, a document is prepared that incorporates all issues and their solutions; it also includes the period of time for which the agreement will be in force.

Government employees not only enter collective bargaining in a weaker position than their private sector counterparts, but they also face other limits. T. G. Stahl (1977) noted the following major differences in employees bargaining with the government as management; and from a labor point of view, they are limitations.

1. One party to the relationship (the government/employer) must and does set all the rules. It is not an ordinary employer; it is the instrument of the people.
2. Many aspects of personnel policy are and will continue to be established by law. A union is simply one of several competing interests in the political arena.
3. The subjects available for negotiation and settlement between administrative management and unions will almost invariably be more limited than in the private sector.
4. As the result of the above conditions, the negotiation and bargaining processes will differ substantially from those in private business.
5. Likewise, the settlement of disputes will follow quite different patterns from those prevailing in the private sector.

FORMING A COLLECTIVE BARGAINING UNIT

Forming a collective bargaining unit can be a long, involved process. Before there is an attempt to form a unit in a library, staff dissatisfaction with working conditions probably will have become severe. Supervisors and top administration are often fully aware of such problems and probably will have made numerous attempts to solve them, even those requiring increased funding for the library. More often than not, if the solution requires that the library receive increased funding, the funding authorities will turn down the request. All the supervisors can do is attempt to keep problems as manageable as possible and discuss with the staff those problems they can do nothing about in an effort to maintain good working relationships.

Once dissatisfaction reaches a certain level, the collective bargaining process will start. There are eight basic steps in the process (see Figure 13.1): organizing, petition, election, certification and recognition, preparation for negotiation, negotiation, and contract administration. A library is unorganized when the staff is dissatisfied but acts on an individual basis or in small semiformal protest groups. Organizing is a period of time when one or more groups actively campaign to gain staff support to form a collective bargaining unit and to vote for that group in an election. During this stage, management and individual staff members may present a case against forming a collective bargaining unit. (An example of such campaign statements from both a union group and from management is provided later in this section.) Complex rules govern what a supervisor can and cannot do during this stage of the process. Be certain to check with your personnel office director to determine what you can and cannot do if you should find yourself in a supervisory position during an organizing stage.

The petition stage is a request to hold an election under the supervision of a third party (normally a governmental agency). The election is conducted by secret ballot, and the third party counts the ballots to determine whether a majority of voters favors forming a collective bargaining unit. If one of the groups in favor of forming a unit receives 51% of the votes, the third party certifies the election results and the winning group is then recognized as the *sole* bargaining group for the staff. Both the bargaining group (agent) and management then begin to prepare for the negotiation sessions. Bargaining sessions take place and, more often than not, the sessions result in a contract without a strike being called. Once the contract is agreed upon, the supervisors in the library have two sets of concerns: What do the merit system regulations say and what does the collective bargaining agreement require? Most contracts are for 3 or 4 years, and this represents the contract administration stage.

The first step in starting the collective bargaining process is to determine whether the government jurisdiction that funds the library has made it legal for public employees to bargain collectively. Most jurisdictions today do allow some limited bargaining, but it is always wise to make sure that this is the case.

A more difficult step is determining which union or group the library staff wants to represent them. For instance, in the United States (and in other countries as well), librarians have a number of choices when deciding on bargaining agents—everything from creating an independent, unaffiliated union to affiliating with a large nationwide labor organization. At present in some countries, the national library association functions as the bargaining agent, and eventually this may come about in all countries.

The question of which group should represent the library staff is complicated and usually requires much discussion. At the University of California, Los Angeles, at least four groups have attempted to convince the library staff that only they can effectively represent them in bargaining sessions. But before any bargaining starts, one group must be designated the *sole representative*. This usually is done by means of a formal election conducted by an outside group (e.g. the U.S. National Labor Relations Board), which will ensure an honest election. Only eligible staff members may vote, and a majority vote (51%) decides the issue. In choosing from among groups, a majority must be gained (*not* a plurality); this fact often means more than one election must be held. (Once the sole bargaining agent is certified, it can be replaced only if new elections are called and it is voted out.)

Equally difficult to resolve is the question of who should be in the bargaining unit. Will the unit represent the entire library staff, the professionals, the para-professionals, or the clerical staff? Such questions can split the library staff and create problems in work relations. However, the real question is whether the needs, interests, and requirements of the entire library staff are so alike that one representative can do an adequate job *and* be assured of support from the entire staff during tough negotiations. How these questions are answered determines who will vote for or against representation. Even in the same type of library (say, academic) the question has been resolved in different ways in different states in the United States alone. Usually, the labor relations board overseeing the election decides who will or will not be allowed to vote. In some cases, the board rules that all library staff members who are not in a supervisory position are eligible. (The question of when a supervisor is not a supervisor [as far as eligibility is concerned] has proven to be equally complex.) On other occasions, boards have ruled that two or more collective bargaining units should be formed: one for librarians and one for paraprofessionals and clerical staff (sometimes these latter two are also separated). For a full discussion of board rulings in terms of libraries, see John W. Weatherford's *Collective Bargaining and the Academic Librarian* (Scarecrow Press, 1976).

As noted previously, the question of who is a supervisor/manager is complex in a library. The library director certainly is management, but what about the librarian who supervises the circulation desks but yet has no subordinate librarians? In many libraries, a strict definition of management (whether an employee supervises others) would put almost all librarians and paraprofessionals in management; thus, they could not be represented by a union. At present, no true pattern exists for employee inclusion in library unions, but middle management people usually are included. Again, this matter is resolved by the labor relations board supervising the election.

Once the election is over and a sole agent certified to represent the staff, the question arises of where the agent gets the money to carry out its work. A union or bargaining agent normally derives the money it needs to operate by levying membership dues. Naturally, the more members, the more money; but some people do not want to join a collective bargaining group. (What about the possible 49% who might have unsuccessfully opposed group representation?) From the agent's point of view, it bargains for it *all* staff members eligible for membership, not just its own members; and all eligible staff receive any benefits that are won at the bargaining table. Therefore, it is argued that those who benefit from bargaining activities should contribute to the support of those activities.

Unions and collective bargaining groups have tried three basic methods of handling this problem: closed shops, union shops, and agency shops. In a closed shop, only the union can supply candidates for employment—a practice that merit systems cannot tolerate. In a union shop, the goal is 100% union workers, but the employer does the initial selection. Then, after a certain period of time (in government a probationary term) employees must join the union. In an agency shop, one can choose whether or not to join the union formally, but union dues are deducted from everyone's wages. As long as the union really works for the well-being of all eligible staff and all eligible persons benefit, an agency or union shop can be a viable form of worker representation. But, if doubt emerges as to what percentage of the staff are union members or as to what efforts actually are being devoted to improving staff well-being, it is time to hold another election.

As this discussion has implied, securing union representation is a long, complex, and often tension-laden process. The following brief presentations are samples of actual efforts by both management (first document) and a bargaining unit (second document) to win an election (names have been deleted, but the text is as issued). The statements are not intended to be read as models to be followed. Rather, they are included to provide some of the flavor of the pre-election activity and perhaps convey some sense of the tension that can exist in a library during this time. Also, remember that during the pre-election period, supervisors must be certain that their actions and statements stay within the limits set by the labor relations board. Normally when the library goes into the pre-election stage, a representative of the merit system or the personnel office will hold some training sessions for the supervisors to help them understand what they can and cannot do.

[Management Statement]

PRE-ELECTION NOTES   AUGUST 1,19XX

PRE-ELECTION NOTES is the fourth in a series of question and answer publications to ensure that the staffs of the QED Libraries have sufficient information on the pros and cons of seeking union representation. Additional copies are available in the staff room of the main library.

QUESTIONS AND ANSWERS

Q: HOW WOULD A UNION CONTRACT AFFECT STUDENTS?

A: The National Labor Relations Board in its decision did not consider the student status of employees. Rather, the Board included anyone who worked on a regular part-time basis for purposes of voting, whether student or nonstudent. Unless special provisions are made during the negotiation period, students, like any other member of the bargaining unit, will pay dues, be subject to union actions, and be required to comply with union discipline. In any case, the future of the student's role will definitely be a part of negotiation.

Q: THE UNION HAS STATED THAT IT WILL MAKE SPECIAL PROVISIONS FOR STUDENTS IN THE CONTRACT. CAN THEY DO SO?

A: When the students return to school in the fall, they will constitute a majority of the members of the bargaining unit. Any agreement to place students in a secondary status will, of course, be subject to a majority vote of the bargaining unit. The majority are students. In addition, any contract negotiations for benefits covering staff and professionals will also require a majority vote of the unit for approval.

Q: DO THE VOTES OF PART-TIME ASSISTANTS COUNT THE SAME AS FULL-TIME STAFF IN THE ELECTION?

A: Yes. Each full- or part-time staff member on the election list votes with the same authority. A simple majority wins.

Q: IN THE EVENT A FORMAL BARGAINING UNIT IS FORMED, WILL THE PART-TIME STAFF HAVE THE SAME WEIGHT IN VOTING?

A: Yes. The part-time votes will count the same as full-time votes in approving the constitution and contractual negotiations. If this is done during the school year the part-time votes will make up a majority of the voting unit.

Q: THE Q LIBRARY STAFF ASSOCIATION DOES NOT INCLUDE STUDENT AS-

SISTANTS IN ITS MEMBERSHIP. WHY ARE THEY NOW BEING INCLUDED IN THE ELECTION?

A: Again, the National Labor Relations Board was not concerned with the student status of the employee but whether or not the employee was a regular part-time member of the staff.

Q: WHY WAS IT ASSUMED THAT A UNION SHOP (SECURITY AGREEMENT) WOULD BE THE END RESULT OF NEGOTIATIONS?

A: A review of union contracts in _____ indicates that a vast majority of contracts include the union security agreement. In fact, the percentage which does not include the union security agreement is quite small.

Q: WHEN A CONTRACT IS NEGOTIATED BETWEEN THE UNION AND AN EM-PLOYER, WILL ALL THE EMPLOYEES GET TO VOTE ON ACCEPTING IT OR ONLY THOSE WHO HAVE JOINED THE UNION?

A: With few exceptions, only employees who belong to the union vote on the contract. Therefore, an individual who chooses not to join the union but is subject to dues, does not have a vote on any future contracts until he finally becomes a member.

Q: WOULD THE Q LIBRARY BE ABLE TO GIVE SPECIAL CONSIDERATION TO STUDENT EMPLOYEES DURING EXAMS, CLOSE OF SEMESTERS, VACATION PERIODS, ETC., IF THERE IS A UNION?

A: Any kind of special provisions to any member of the bargaining unit would be a matter of negotiation.

Q: WILL THE Q EMPLOYEES BE ABLE TO CONTINUE THEIR SCHEDULES IN ORDER TO HAVE THEIR "SHORT DAY," IF THERE IS A UNION?

A: Again, this and all other benefits will be subject to negotiation at the bargaining table.

Q: IS IT CORRECT THAT UNION NEGOTIATED SALARIES GENERALLY RUN AS MUCH AS 34% HIGHER THAN THOSE IN NON-UNION COMPANIES?

A: Such a comparison is absolutely impossible to make based only upon this statement. As an example, if the comparison is between a skilled trades union with very high wages and migrant non-union farm workers, then the comparison may be statistically correct but irrelevant. If you compare union skilled trades against non-union employees in the skilled trades, the percentage difference stated is not correct.

Q: WHAT PROCESS IS FOLLOWED IN YEARS TO COME IF EMPLOYEES DECIDE TO WITHDRAW FROM UNION REPRESENTATION?

A: The employees must request the National Labor Relations Board for an election to change representation and go through essentially the same process as when first seeking representation. Management can in no way assist employees if they choose to seek other representation, nor can they provide any of the financial support necessary if the change is contested and hearings are required.

Q: IT WAS EARLIER STATED THAT UNION DUES COULD EXCEED THE $7 FIGURE ANNOUNCED BY THE UNION REPRESENTATIVE. IS THIS TRUE?

A: The union can best answer this question. Ask the union representative if the dues for all members under its representation are always $7.

Q: SOME MONTHS AGO THE PERSONNEL DIRECTOR INDICATED THAT THE COUNCIL WAS CONSIDERING A NEW GRIEVANCE PROCEDURE. IS THIS NOW IN PROCESS?

A: Yes. The new grievance procedure has been in process for approximately six months. The program calls for three basic steps for an employee who has a problem concerning any part of his or her working relationship.

First, the employee discusses it with the supervisor to try to resolve the problem at the first level of management.

Second, the individual discusses it with the business officer or Director of Personnel for Central Services to try and resolve the problem within the individual unit or central service.

If the problem cannot be resolved, then the problem is submitted to Personnel, which in turn does an investigation and analysis and submits information to an independent committee. The committee has been appointed by the Provost at the request of the Council. The committee is an impartial third party with the power to investigate and recommend to the President and/or Provost an effective solution to the problem. The committee is composed of staff members from a number of different classifications.

In one recent case, a supervisor had released two employees. The committee recommended reinstatement for one employee and reinstatement for the other with full back wages. The recommendations were accepted.

ADDITIONAL PRE-ELECTION NOTES WILL BE PUBLISHED AS QUESTIONS ARRIVE. IF YOU HAVE AN IMMEDIATE NEED FOR INFORMATION, PLEASE CONTACT THE DIRECTOR OR PERSONNEL BY TELEPHONE (EXT. XXX) OR USE THE QUESTION SHEETS AVAILABLE IN THE STAFF ROOM OF THE MAIN LIBRARY. WE ENCOURAGE YOU TO ASK QUESTIONS AS EARLY AS POSSIBLE SO THAT WE WILL HAVE THE NECESSARY TIME TO RESPOND. THANK YOU.

[Union Statement]

To Library Staff Members:

If, as Mr. Blank stated to you in his August 16 letter regarding Wednesday's NLRB election, "The College officially does not take a position," why has there been such voluminous correspondence, so many administration-led meetings on the employer's time, and such an attempt made to create uncertainty and fear concerning what is basically a very simple matter?

The promised "open forum for discussion and questions on both sides" has not been forthcoming. Reams of paper, and many working hours could have been spared, had arrangements been made for such a forum.

Instead, under the guise of neutrality, what we feel is a most unfortunate and calculated pattern has developed. Blurring the legitimate issue of collective bargaining, administration has made an attempt to manufacture fear and distrust among the staff, setting "professionals" against "non-professionals" and both groups against "students."

We are confident this attempt to cast staff as one another's enemies will fail. The staff has always worked together, respecting one another's role within the library, and also respecting one another as individuals of integrity and *judgement; collective bargaining will further strengthen this unity and cooperation.*

The organization, as an employer, is not unique in the course it has taken. Most employers whose staffs are unorganized and unrepresented would prefer to keep them that way. It is easier to say "no" to an individual, or even to an unrepresented group of employees, than to bargain in good faith with those same employees through their chosen representative.

The irony of this traditional opposition by employers is that, once the employees have won the right to collective bargaining, and the negotiations are underway, those same employers often find that dealing with their staff in an organized, orderly manner can be mutually beneficial.

In addition to administration's meetings with you, where what clearly seems to be an attempt to "divide and conquer", thereby destroying your unity of purpose, has been used, you have received (and will receive still more) purportedly objective "Pre-Election Notes", and letters from administration.

Rather than attempt here to separate truth from fiction, we are confident that it is sufficient simply to refer you to our earlier communications, and to the commitments made in meetings with Union staff.

The need for a *process* (which you are voting to try) to establish in a dignified, orderly, legal manner and through a written agreement, the terms and conditions of your employment is most apparent.

When you vote Wednesday on the question "Do you wish to be represented by Local XXX for purposes of collective bargaining?," a YES vote will be a vote in favor of a cooperative agreement, based on your proposals.

A "NO" vote would be a vote for continuance of the present policy of permitting the employer to unilaterally determine all matters affecting your working life.

No matter how beneficent a dictator he may be, an employer whose staff does not have collective bargaining has unlimited power over that staff's employment conditions. He has the unbridled authority to say "no", or to say "go", in response to any employee's request, no matter how reasonable it may be.

Collective bargaining is participatory democracy, as opposed to monarchy. We are confident you will welcome the opportunity to engage in an experiment called collective bargaining, and to realize the benefits of working together with union staff to negotiate an agreement with an employer, who, after Wednesday's election, will hopefully be *required by law to bargain in good faith with you.*

Cordially yours, ABC

P.S. Because of reports of extremely divisive tactics and rather serious distortions of fact in today's meetings with administration, we have requested of Mr. Blank that staff be afforded the opportunity to participate with *both* administration and union staff in a *true* open forum on Tuesday. Should he agree, we will see you

Tuesday morning. If not, we hope you will call us collect if issues were raised which concern you.

POSTELECTION ACTIVITY

Thus far in this chapter, some of the basic issues of collective bargaining have been covered: forming a unit, deciding on membership, choosing a sole representative, and gaining "security" (money, usually membership dues) for the unit once it is established. After this is done, the law requires that bargaining be done in "good faith," that is, genuine effort must be made to resolve differences and reach equitable agreements. And here lies another area in which public employee unions differ from those in the private sector. How will the government (and will it) impose penalties upon itself should it fail to act in good faith as an employer? More to the point, bargaining is usually done by the executive branch; however, the legislative branch controls the money and the law, and it may not agree to bargains made by the executive branch. Also, public pressure can force changes should enough citizens express disapproval of an agreement made by the government. The usual procedure in libraries is for the head of the library and a personnel officer who represents the government to negotiate issues that concern the library (hours, policies, procedures, etc.) Should the issues involve general governmental concerns (salaries, benefits, vacations, leaves, and other "economic" issues) then other persons will represent the government in the bargaining sessions.

The matter of issues that are subject to bargaining (i.e., scope of representation) is actually what the whole process is to determine. For analysis purposes, issues are usually placed in one of three groups: mandatory, consultive, and reserved. Mandatory issues must be negotiated, whether management wishes to or not. Consultive issues are brought by management to the bargaining agent by prior agreement before a change is made (but note the limitations inherent in the term *consult.*) In libraries, consultive issues might include the definition of service objectives, the opening or closing of a branch, the locations of branches or service points, or the use of on-line computer systems. Reserved issues are those not specifically identified as either mandatory or consultive; management holds the rights to these. If management wants a good working relationship with the bargaining unit, it might well consider consulting on reserved issues as well as on mandatory and consultive issues; however, the bargaining unit cannot force such consultation. That can come only freely from management.

Regarding public employees, mandatory issues need some explication. The basic issues are salary and hours, but if the first few negotiations are successful, then salary will not be the foremost item in negotiations thereafter. Other common mandatory topics include health and welfare benefits, leave and transfer policies, safety conditions, work load, employee evaluation procedures, grievance procedures, and union security (type of membership). Some bargaining units have succeeded in bringing promotion and layoff issues into the mandatory group. Some unions try to include a contract clause to the effect that seniority will be the primary consideration in granting promotions. Most government jurisdictions will not allow this, as it strikes at the comparative (best person) philosophy behind the merit system.

Impasse and difference of opinion regarding interpretation of the agreements are two other important issues. When an impasse is reached, an impartial third party, an arbitrator, is called in. Governments seldom submit to binding arbitration, however, preferring advisory arbitration, which can be interpreted as loosely or strictly as the government pleases (or ignored altogether). Naturally, the degree to which an arbitrator's advice is accepted depends largely on that person's reputation for fairness and practical solutions.

Somewhere between talking things out (negotiation) and arbitration is the process of mediation. A third party, who may actually function initially as a go-between when two parties refuse to meet, presents each party's views to the other, but without the emotionalism that may be present when the two parties face one another. Most often, the mediator will sit in on (or chair) meetings and act as fact finder when needed. Again, the theory is that an impartial third party can throw new light on subjects for both parties and can expedite an equitable agreement.

Where do strikes fit into the picture? Most agreements are reached without the use of a mediator, much less an arbitrator or even the suggestion of a strike. Threatening production or service (by means of a strike, slowdown, work stoppage, sick-in) is the bargaining unit's ultimate sanction. Both sides know this from the outset, and they also know that neither side will really benefit from a strike, especially a long-term strike.

Public employees are generally forbidden from striking, so many unions have used either work slowdowns or sick-ins to achieve the result an actual strike might achieve. "Legal" strikes may be called by the union after an agreement expires and before a new one is signed. Public employee unions tend to strike not so much over personal member grievances but to show management that they "mean business." Thus, strikes are usually brief (from a few days to a couple of weeks in duration.) Because most public employees are service-minded, they do not intend to cause the public inconvenience by striking, and this is especially true of librarians. They simply want some means of pointing out the essential nature of their services. For libraries, too, an extended strike might send people to a variety of new information sources, thereby altering their library habit. Any library union considering a strike needs to keep this in mind.

If you supervise a library unit in which a merit system is in force and there is also a bargaining unit, you need to know the details of both systems, and you need to know them inside out. What does the contract say about performance evaluation, and how does it fit into the requirements of the merit system personnel office? May you require an employee to stay overtime to finish an urgent task? What is the discipline procedure for someone who is chronically late? Will you as supervisor be allowed to decide whether the new position in your unit should be filled by a professional, a paraprofessional, or a clerical worker, or must you accept the decision reached by the personnel office and the union? Can you decide who gets the new typewriter or is this a union issue?

These represent a sample of the kinds of questions that will confront the supervisor in such a situation. You must not only know your library's system, but you must know about such systems in general, as much broader issues will affect the library than may first seem possible. Therefore, even if you have no intention of becoming a library personnel officer, you should read extensively in these areas, particularly about the situation in which you work.

BIBLIOGRAPHY

1. United States Civil Service Commission. *A Self-Inquiry with Merit Staffing.* (Washington, D.C.:G.P.O., 1976).
2. Stahl, G. O., *Public Personnel Administration* (New York: Harper, 1977), p. 337.

FURTHER READING

Aaron, S. L., "Media Supervisor and Collective Bargaining." *Drexel Library Quarterly* 14 (1978): 95–101.

Abell, M. *Collective Bargaining in Higher Education.* Chicago: American Library Association, 1977.

Bach, H. B. "The Merit Track in Local Government: Abused and Diffused." *Public Personnel Management* 6 (1977): 116–120.

Bent, A. E., and Reeves, T. Z. *Collective Bargaining in the Public Sector.* Menlo Park, Calif.: Benjamin/Cummings Pub., 1978.

Bookmark 40 (1982), no. 4. (Entire issue is in collective bargaining in libraries.)

Brandwein, L. "From Confrontation to Coexistence." *Library Journal* 104 (1979): 680–683.

Chamot, D. "Effect of Collective Bargaining on the Employee–Management Relationship." *Library Trends* 25 (1976): 489–495.

Collective Bargaining: New Dimensions in Labor Relations. Boulder, CO: Westview Press, 1979.

Decker, K. H. "Arbitrability of Public Sector Grievances After Expiration of a Contract." *Journal of Collective Negotiations* 7 (1978): 287–297.

Dwoskin, R. P. *Rights of the Public Employee.* Chicago: American Library Association, 1978.

Guyton, T. L. *Unionization: The Viewpoint of Librarians.* Chicago: American Library Association, 1975.

Henderson, J. W. "Consulting in Union Management Relations." *Library Trends* 28 (1980): 411–424.

Jaffe, M. E. "Solidarity Forever." *Library Journal* 104 (1979): 2172–2173.

Kaiser, J. B. "Civil Service and Libraries." *Library Trends* 3 (1954): 80–94.

Kovach, K. A. "State and Local Public Employee Labor Relations—Where Are They Headed?" *Journal of Collective Negotiations in the Public Sector* 8 (1979): 19–29.

14. Fiscal Management

Any major effort to provide library services will require raising funds, developing a budget, and controlling expenditures. This chapter focuses on types of budgets, uses of budgets, and methods of preparing and defending budgets. It also deals with appropriations, the most common source of library support. Supplemental sources—private donors, special grants, bond issues, etc.—will not be covered, because mastery of the basics of the appropriations process is the place to begin. All too often, libraries have failed to recognize the connection between the budget and the political process, and the logical extension to that kinship—there is a "politics" of the budgetary process.

BUDGET AS A CONTROL DEVICE

A budget is a plan. It represents choices made from alternatives for expenditures, and it is used to coordinate efforts toward a specified end. Among libraries, some develop comprehensive budgetary systems that include every phase of planning and operation. Others have only partial systems that are concerned with particular aspects of budgeting. Naturally, budgetary control—regardless of outward form—is the most widely recognized and used means of managerial control. It is the process of comparing what actually happened over a specified period of time with what had been planned to happen. A budget is formulated to be carried out at a certain cost level over a certain time span. By examining progress and comparing it with both monetary costs and time elaspsed, a manag-

263

er can adjust operations on a day-to-day, week-to-week, or month-to-month basis.

Profit-making organizations begin budgetary control by estimating sales and income; a library starts by totaling all its income from known funding sources (city, province or state, school district, private business, or national government). This will involve forecasting to a large extent. Accurate predictions can be made if one concentrates on a few key factors. Actually, all budgeting is forecasting, with the final estimate being the result of intelligent judgments based on careful analysis of the available facts.

Typically, in libraries that are government supported, the available data regarding appropriations is of a constant (rather than a variable) nature. Such libraries know fairly accurately how much money they will be allocated, and, once funds are appropriated, the budget usually becomes constant. The fact that goals tend to remain constant for libraries assists in keeping their budgets fixed. Variable income—for libraries, usually endowment monies—comes into play primarily in private institutions (both profit and nonprofit). The variable income derived from endowments may become more important for all types of libraries in the future, as governments reassess their committments to libraries; currently, however, the bulk of library funds is of a reasonably constant nature. This is not the place to explore the issue of taxpayer "revolts," other than to say that libraries that are supported by government funds suffer this form of unpredictability along with governmental units.

Budgeting is not confined to monetary units. Industry employs the physical units or labor required when budgeting. Libraries could use a similar of budgeting in technical services—cataloging, acquisition, and bindery work, for example—and, to some extent, in circulation and reference work.

Because budgets are estimates, they can be altered as circumstances change. Budgets need to be flexible in order to meet rapid shifts in needs, but alterations should be approached cautiously. Too many rapid changes can damage the integrity and stability of any budget.

Budgetary control consists of three basic steps:

1. Estimate the costs of plans for each unit in monetary terms, much as an accountant would. (Using the same terms helps.)
2. Combine all estimates into a well-balanced program. This will require investigation of each plan's financial feasibility and comparison of the program with institutional goals.
3. Compare, for a given time, the estimates derived from step 2 with the actual results, making corrections for any significant differences. (Use the budget as a standard for appraising performance.)

A library's size does not materially affect the basic budgeting process, although larger libraries naturally have more complexity at each step. As a library grows, it will probably come to employ separate budgets for departments, divisions, or work units. Because these units are somewhat independent, different performance standards are employed in different units. A very large library could have hundreds of internal budgets subsumed under the general budget heading.

Preparing a budget involves defining a set of *planning premises.* If subsidiary budgets are to be planned with consistency, planning premises are vital.

Anyone who works with the budget ought to know what assumptions have been made (or are being made) about it. Because public and technical service units are interdependent, both need to know all premises involved in preparing their separate budgets—their own premises and those of the other units. Such things as increases in unit costs and prices of materials will affect what can be processed by acquisitions and cataloging; and this naturally affects all other departments. Consequently, everyone should have estimates to use when generating their subsidiary budgets.

The second step—combining and coordinating subsidiary budgets—becomes exceedingly complicated. It certainly involves more than just totaling the small budgets. It must represent a total, feasible program that is consistent with the library's objectives. For this reason, very large libraries often have a person whose sole job it is to coordinate the budget, while smaller libraries may be able to combine this job with other functions so that it is a part-time responsibility borne by someone in a full-time position.

Finally, budget officers compare the actual performance (what has been accomplished, the volume of work, and so forth) against what was expected (budget). At the same time, supervisors and top management need to look at the existing circumstances in order to decide whether a major or a minor shift in budget allotments is necessary or desirable. By doing this every few months throughout the fiscal year, the library can help to control the unpredictability of the future. This step is most important, because budgets are often prepared 12 to 18 months before they are approved and thus may represent predictions that are 2 years old at the time of review.

As is implied here, budgeting often spurs managers on to other good management practices, ones that could be wisely used in the absence of budgetary control. Four of these practices are listed here, along with suggestions as to how budgeting might help to develop them.

Formal organization must be clear. Know who is to make each plan and who is responsible for its execution; this is the only way to measure actual performance within the budget.

Set up financial accounts for each department or unit of administration. Expenses and income that are traceable to specific managers are more easily controlled, and managers are more responsive. This will be valuable both in preparation and in evaluation.

Plan well in advance and be as specific as possible. Sloppy plans will be reflected in a floundering or stagnant department, or one that is out of touch with organizational goals. (How can money be requested if no one knows exactly what it is to be used for?)

Include long-range projections (2, 3, or even 5 years ahead) in the overall budgeting process. This can be done only after the first three steps have been taken. Libraries are prone to neglecting this aspect; consequently, they often react spasmodically to variations in money available and demands placed on them.

It is only natural that budgeting will present problems along with its many advantages. One problem is that a budget needs to be expressed in precise terms; this tends to create a potentially unhealthy emphasis on factors that are easily observed. For example, high circulation statistics may show that the library is doing a fine job. More money might then be appropriated, because the cause (increased circulation) appears to be a good one. However, this emphasis might cause the library to concentrate on buying materials for the heavy users and neglect buying to meet the needs of the entire service population.

Budgets also tend to create internal conflicts and pressures, because they highlight the efforts of every department in the same terms. The intangible results of such conflict might not be measurable, and they may not be traced to the units that produce them; however, they do exist.

A related problem arises when symptoms are treated while the actual disease is ignored. For instance, when administrative salaries appear to be quite high, efforts might be made to recruit inexperienced personnel at lower salaries. Although this may reduce salary costs, it could also worsen an already unstable situation. It could be that the solution lies in reevaluating supervisory tasks, reassigning some tasks, and possibly reducing the number of supervisors. All this could achieve the desired savings and lead to greater efficiency.

Similarly, high processing costs might indicate that a weakness is present in the processing department, not that the entire department is inefficient. Inept purchasing, rigid specifications, inadequate inspection, or old or poorly maintained equipment could cause a rise in costs. The budget shows only that a problem exists. It may hide the fact that the true cause of the problem might have arisen earlier in the system, and perhaps in a different area.

Another problem is that control of the budget can lead to dictatorial behavior on the part of top management. Terse, cold figures make it easy for managers to dictate cutbacks—say, 15% in expenses—during a time period while they ignore the human implications of actions based on those figures.

A temptation for libraries is to simply go through the budgetary process without thinking about ways of improving operations. This is a particular danger when a line budget is used. When a performance or a zero-base budget is used, this is less likely to occur.

Finally, many things are simply not measurable in monetary terms. Service organizations, such as libraries, that emphasize "intellectual" services have great difficulty in proving the money value of their serivces. The entire question of quality almost becomes a moot point in most budgetary procedures. Managers can measure the quality of production for a toy, for example, by counting the rejects and the total number of toys made; however, quality of service is nearly impossible to rate objectively.

In essence, then, if the budgetary process is to benefit the organization, it should involve everyone who is affected by it. When top management prepares a budget and presents it as fact, this does something *to* people, not *for* them.

THE BUDGETARY PERIOD

The budgetary period is influenced primarily by the supervising or funding agency. Most libraries operate on a 12-month schedule, primarily because governmental units tend to do so, especially those with tax revenues due them. Moreover, the accounting period is normally synchronous with the budgetary period. (Libraries also deal with capital outlay needs by presenting bond issues, but this is exceptional in the life of any library.) A great danger in adopting a straight fiscal-year approach is that it tends to emphasize short-range planning at the expense of the long view.

Budgeting actually does require attention to a 4-to-5-year period. While you spend one budget, you might have details to clean up from the previous year's budget. At the same time, you must be preparing next year's budget for presentation· to the funding authority, which would involve at least some consideration of the year that follows that one. (see Table 14.1.)

TABLE 14.1 Budgeting Sequence[a]

Past fiscal year		Current fiscal year		Coming fiscal year		Future fiscal year		
July	Dec	July	Dec	July	Dec	July	Dec	July
X		$_{****}$X$_{****}$ ++++ $_{oooo}$		X		X		X

[a]Key: $_{****}$, submit coming fiscal year budget.
++++, defend coming fiscal budget.
$_{oooo}$, plan future fiscal year budget.

The fact that government budgets are generally submitted as a package to the legislative body means that you must carefully plan for early submission (seldom later than October, in a 1 July to 30 June fiscal year, and often as early as a year in advance). The budget must be submitted twice—first to the unit that is submitting the general budget of which the library's is a part, and again to the legislative body.

You will have ample opportunity to learn about the budget and how to present it, as it must be reviewed by the library staff and by the governing board (if one exists). These reviews occur before you submit the budget to the executive budget office (which sends its combined request to the legislative body that apportions funds). Almost always, questions will come up as to how this budget compares with last year's and the current year's budgets.

Because a budget is an estimate, people may want to know how accurate your estimates are. They can easily check past years' performance, going several years back if they perceive irregularities. Thus, in preparing a future budget, you work with the current budget, defend the future budget on the basis of past performance, and try to develop budget projections for the next few years. Very few libraries have full-time budget officers; as a result, the work is done by various staff members, from supervisors on up to library directors.

BUDGET PREPARATION

Initial budget preparation should begin with first-line supervisors passing their estimates up the chain of command. Each successive management level combines and coordinates all subunit budgets, and then passes its total on up. Finally, top management assesses all this information and formulates the general budget for all units.

Because libraries compete with other agencies for funds, the librarian needs to be fairly high up the administrative ladder. In an academic situation, the librarian ought to be equal to a dean (not a department head); the public librarian ought to be equal to any department head; and a school librarian also ought to be equal to a department head. If this is not the case, the chances of receiving an adequate hearing and active support for the full budget are quite remote.

Each library—regardless of its size—faces two financial problems. The first involves trying to develop special facilities and services in response to client demand while remaining within the established budget. (The budget is not generally tied to the volume of service.) It simply boils down to the fact that the amount of money available for a particular time period is fixed, regardless of the service demands.

The second problem concerns continually growing collections and staff. Constantly growing collections require more space (= money) and staff time (= money) as they increase in size. Academic libraries often have this problem, whereas public libraries can alleviate it a bit by maintaining a constant collection size or a moderate growth factor. Also, public libraries can eliminate unused or dated items, whereas academic libraries do not always have that option.

Staff growth will also cause a problem in terms of money required to maintain any staff at a constant level (not to mention promotions and regular salary increases). Moreover, there will always be requests for services from special groups with real needs. The problem lies in assigning priorities to these items in the face of limited financial support.

Preplanning is the best means of achieving the broadest possible operating plan. It derives information from two basic sources: the library's objectives and environmental factors. Included are such things as client demands, institutional competitive positions (for funds), and socio-economic trends in the country as a whole. Such plans can be very helpful in preparing a budget, because they provide a realistic framework in which to view the library as a whole.

Usually one person coordinates the budget, and this person normally comes from top management. At this stage, the concern is not so much with details as it is with resolving conflicting interests, recommending adjustments, and giving official sanction to the entire process. Often, a budget committee made up of departmental supervisors will be assigned to assist in this work. Because these persons are responsible for major functions and have full knowledge of their departments' operations, they are in the best overall positions to judge budget requests. This involves active line officers in budget work, which itself (as a political process) helps to determine the library's priorities and constraints.

Once departmental estimates have been coordinated—which usually involves meetings with department heads for adjustments, and so on—they will be ready for presentation to top management in their final form as a unified library budget. The process has gone on all year, not just a month or two, and it has been approached as part of the routine, not as an annual crisis.

DEFENDING THE REQUEST

Preparing a budget request is easier than defending it; this springs from the fact that many agencies are competing for the same monies, and each will seek to prove that its own need is the most urgent of all. Thus, the more care that has gone into the preparation of a budget request, the more likely any agency is to be successful in getting what it sought. Those agencies that do win the battle of the budget are usually the ones that recognize and act on the fact that governmental budgeting is a very political process.

For the past several years, I have conducted an experiment in teaching library management. Several times, I have required classes to read Aaron Wildavsky's *The Politics of the Budgetary Process*.[1] Generally, the effort has not worked well, because students have a hard time accepting Wildavsky's ideas as far as libraries are concerned. They see libraries as cultural havens somehow removed from the ugliness of government and politics, so they also tend to see no connection between the book and reality (as they see it at that time). However, experience seems to alter this view rather quickly. Many former students have contacted me, asking where they can get that "money and politics" book, because it "seemed to have some good ideas."

Indeed, Wildavsky does have some good ideas, and any librarian who has or hopes to have responsibility for a library budget should read his book. The following material is drawn from Wildavsky, but it is *not* a substitute for reading his entire book. Some persons find it hard to translate his emphasis on the United States federal government into local library needs, but so long as a library operates as part of a governmental unit with executive and legislative branches, his analysis will be valuable. Simply substitute the title of chief executive officer, outside of the library, for the word *President* and the title of the appropriate legislative body for the word *Congress*.

Despite all the press given to such concepts as program and planning budgeting systems (PPBS) and zero-base budgeting (ZBS), most governmental budgets are basically line budgets (see next section). Even when efforts have been made to move into one of the newer modes, the end result is the same—an incremental budget (one that is larger than the budget for the previous period). Until very recently, when cuts were made, they were in a particular program or area. Thus, the library could usually assume that its present budget was the base on which to build.

Exceptions to this pattern do take place. If an agency is "under fire," depending on how serious the situation is, the legislative group can use cuts in the budget to show its displeasure. Also, taxpayers have come to demand reduced taxes; such cries will result in real cuts for all governmental agencies. The largest cuts are usually in the "nonessential" services (library, museum, schools, and so on), while health and safety services are usually maintained at existing levels. This is clear evidence that government budgeting is a highly political process. What politician would want to explain to voters why the local fire station was closed instead of the library or the museum? Would you?

The incremental approach is used most often because of the long-term nature of many of the library's commitments (salaries, retirement programs, pension payments, and, in the library, acquisition of serials). Also, if the population increases, the number of patrons will probably increase as well, which will require new staff to handle increased demands for service. In jursidictions with strong collective bargaining units, a workload agreement clause can lead to a significant increase in costs. Annual step increases and cost-of-living increases are difficult to control, because the withholding of cost-of-living increases will be only temporary, and pressure will mount to make up for the losses felt.

It is important to remember the incremental nature of budgets, because almost everyone involved in the process *expects* this to be the case. Unless conditions have changed drastically, last year's budget is the base on which this year's budget will be built. However, if the government's revenues have increased, the library will scramble for its "fair share" of the increase (unless it is operating under the delusion that politics is "beneath the library's dignity"). And scramble it must, if it is to get its "fair share." Most of the ideas presented here regarding building the library's political base (assure maximum funding) apply equally to times of feast and famine.

The library's first effort should be directed at the electors—the library's patrons—who will be as vocal or as silent as the library leads them to believe they should be. A large clientele is fine, but if they are silent during budget crunches, they are not very useful politically. A little extra help extended to patrons—especially to politically influential groups—

can go a long way at budget request time. There is nothing wrong with saying, "Look, we seem to be doing a good job for you, but with a little help and a little more money, we could really show you service!" Patrons who are willing to speak for the library (whether or not they are actually called upon) at budget hearings can have a positive effect on funding agencies. (The "letter to your legislator" approach can be very useful, especially if it occurs year-round and can create a strong positive attitude in legislators' minds before they begin thinking about budgets with the library in mind.)

Letters also can influence legislators' staff members, and they handle a large percentage of daily work. Because they do the digging, provide reports, and make assessments and recommendations, their influence is powerful. Developing a good working relationship with legislative staff members is an excellent idea, especially with the staff of the legislator who heads the committee that first hears the library's budget request. If your relationship is a year-round one, it will be easier to maintain, and your chances of success will be better. Keeping in touch, finding out what will be needed for the hearings (well in advance), identifying possible areas of concern, and offering assistance within reasonable limits are all methods of developing a good working relationship. There is nothing wrong with inviting legislators who are influential in the library's budget hearings to attent library functions at which a number of voters and other influential persons will also be present. They may or may not attend, but they will have the library in mind as something other than a bottomless pit into which money is thrown.

Study the mood of the people and the politicians, and adjust your approach accordingly. During "hold the line on spending" periods, let your request demonstrate how well you are cooperating. Do not try to paint too rosy a picture—play it straight, and do not try to "put one over" on them. You may "fool" people once or twice because of all the other matters they have to consider, but eventually they will catch up to you. And when they do, your good will will be destroyed and the library will probably suffer for a long time to come.

When presenting plans for new programs, be cautious in what you promise. Do not promise more than you *know* you can deliver, even when you *think* you can do much better. As tempting as it may be to make promises in order to get money, resist! Legislative memories are long and detailed when necessary, and failure to deliver on past promises raises serious doubts about current promises.

Does all this sound too political for a library? (This is only a sample from Wildavsky's 271-page book.) It should not because it reflects the unwritten rules by which governments play the budget–politics game.

FORMS OF BUDGETS

An *operating budget* is concerned with the projected relationships between income and expenses. Because the budgeting process usually begins with forecasts of income, the best that one can hope for is that national production and growth statistics will be matched, if not surpassed. The margin for error is large, which only adds to the difficulty; however, once they are set, the operating expenses (OE) define the limits of the library's fiscal activities for the year.

The *materials budget* lists the types and quantities of raw materials, parts, and supplies required to carry out an activity. It must take into account price increases (as fluctuations in the precious metals market have proven so conclusively) and present inventory levels in order to meet output schedules. (For instance, projected price increases may warrant large-volume purchases early on in order to offset those increases.) Libraries must be aware of increase in the cost of paper (books, periodicals, card stock, etc.) as well as increases in the cost of furniture and other supplies. Early purchase can help to beat inflation, if it is planned well.

A *labor budget* specifies the amount of direct labor needed to meet production schedules (usually in work hours). This amount can then be multiplied by the wage rate to obtain a total and per-unit labor cost. This can help in estimating payrolls for future periods and in planning recruitment and training efforts. Alternative plans require separate labor budgets, but this approach could yield the most cost-effective plan.

The *distribution/expense budget* takes into account the estimated costs of services and record keeping. Distribution expenses are generally subdivided in terms of departmental responsibility: for example, public service and branch operations.

An *administrative expense budget*, as the name implies, details those expenses that result from performing general management functions. This might include executive and administrative salaries, travel expenses, professional service fees, and office expenses. Like the other types of budgets, this type tends to reflect only one aspect of an operation when it is not taken in context.

Two other budgets are the *cash budget* and the *capital additions* or *capital outlay* budget. The cash budget, of primary concern to profit-making organizations, is used to prevent cash depletion while keeping people unaware of the true situation. Capital outlay budgets are used primarily for long-term projects, such as new facilities and equipment replacement. Such budgets are highly tentative because they project so far into the future, but they do provide a systematic approach to planning that can save time and money. Short-term capital outlay budgets can be used to acquire new office equipment, and they are often developed from long-term budgets.

LINE BUDGET

Libraries usually are required to use one of two basic budget forms: a *line budget* or a *performance budget* (discussed in the following section). The line budget, the most common type, has two basic categories of funds: the OE (operating expense) and the CE (capital expense or capital outlay). When librarians discuss budgets, they usually talk about their OE, as it covers the following items:

1. Books and materials—20–30%
2. Salaries—60–70%
3. Utilities—4–5% (if included)
4. Maintenance—3–4% (if included)
5. Supplies—3–4%
6. Travel—1%
7. Insurance—1% (if included)

The items listed here represent the majority of a library's expenditures. Note that salaries and materials are the two largest categories. The capital outlay budget is usually small, unless a large-scale construction project or a bookmobile purchase becomes necessary. Because almost 90% of a library's budget is tied up in salaries and materials, personnel work and acquisitions become the major foci of financial control for most library managers. A recent study of academic libraries in the United States found that the average percentage for materials was 29.2%. The average percentage for salaries was 60.3%, and 10.5% was the total for all other expenses.[2]

Capital outlay includes the following items:

Equipment—typewriters, file cabinets, tables, chairs, and books. (Equipment may or may not be a capital outlay item, depending on the rules of the particular jurisdiction that controls the library. Different jurisidictions have different rules regarding what constitutes a capital outlay item.)

Improvements or remodeling—new partitions, doors, and so on.

Major construction—an addition to an existing building, a total renovation, or a new building.

As was noted earlier, the third category is the one that occurs least

TABLE 14.2 Summary of Los Angeles Public Library Budget

LIBRARY

DEPARTMENT

This Department operates and maintains a central library having thirteen specialized reference and circulating book collections and reading rooms, four units in the civic center which offer specialized library service to City government, seven regional branches providing reference and circulating service in their respective regions of the City, fifty-five branches providing neighborhood service and five traveling branches; and controls its own funds.

REVENUE

Receipts 1978-1979	Estimated Receipts 1979-1980		Budget 1980-1981
APPROPRIATIONS			
$ 8,870,399	$ 6,032,393	Mayor-Council Appropriation: Regular..................................	$ 2,006.038
--	--	Reserved in Unappropriated Balance........	500,000
--	--	Property Tax and State Replacement of Property Tax Revenue--One Percent Fund (Schedule 1).............................	5,592,000
7,000,000	11,500,000	Local Assistance Trust Fund (Schedule 6).....	11,500,000
$ 15,870,399	$ 17,532,393	Total Appropriations...................	$ 19,598,038
OTHER REVENUE			
$ 107,437	$ 53,684	Cash Balance, July 1.........................	$ 159,900
553,060	610,000	Fines.......................................	671,000
159,794	182,000	Receipts from Water and Power Department.....	195,000
174,359	160,000	Other Receipts..............................	154,000
--	--	Fire Loss Reimbursement.....................	72,000
$ 994,650	$ 1,005,684	Total Other Revenue....................	$ 1,251,900
$ 16,865,049	$ 18,538,077	Total Revenue..............................	$ 20,849,938

EXPENDITURES

Expenditures 1978-1979	Estimated Expenditures 1979-1980		Budget Appropriation 1980-1981
SALARIES			
$ 13,306,429	$ 14,148,987	General.....................................	$ 16,311,101
(346)	--	Overtime....................................	--
$ 13,306,083	$ 14,148,987	Total Salaries........................	$ 16,311,101
EXPENSE			
$ 6,736	$ 9,300	Office Equipment Expense....................	$ 12,850
99,259	93,000	Printing and Binding........................	75,085
212	1,300	Traveling Expense...........................	5,176
19,849	41,000	Contractual Expense.........................	43,886
52,123	60,000	Transporation Expense.......................	60,200
291,337	300,000	Library Book Reparis........................	360,625
1,285	1,000	Uniforms....................................	3,291
124,103	160,000	Office and Administrative Expense...........	225,532
33,771	40,000	Operating Supplies and Expense..............	71,203
$ 628,675	$ 705,600	Total Expense	$ 857,848

Expenditures 1978-1979	Estimated Expenditures 1979-1980		Budget Appropriation 1980-1981
EQUIPMENT			
$ 41,800	$ 246,000	Furniture, Office and Technical Equipment....	$ 297,221
$ 41,800	$ 246,000	Total Equipment........................	$ 297,221
SPECIAL			
$ 2,373,337	$ 2,968,000	Library Materials...........................	$ 3,382,768
600	--	Unappropriated Balance......................	1,000
$ 2,373,937	$ 2,968,000	Total Special...........................	$ 3,383,768
$ 16,350,495	$ 18,068,587	Total Library..............................	$ 20,849,938

TABLE 14.2   (*Continued*)

SUPPORTING DATA

DISTRIBUTION OF 1980-1981 APPROPRIATIONS BY PROGRAM

Code	Program	Salaries	Expense	Equipment	Special	Budget
DB4101	Public library services	$ 15,087,768 $	789,220 $	285,718 $	3,334,091 $	19,496,797
DB4150	General administration and support.........	1,223,333	68,628	11,503	49,677	1,353,141
		$ 16,311,101 $	857,848 $	297,221 $	3,383,768 $	20,849,938

DISTRIBUTION OF 1980-1981 TOTAL COST OF PROGRAMS

Code	Program	Authorized Regular Positions	Budget	Support Program Allocation	Related Costs	Cost Allocated To Other Budgets	Total Cost of Program
DB4101	Public Library services.....	1,053.50	$ 19,496,797 $	1,353,141 $	8,131,989 $	--	$ 28,981,927
DB4150	General Administration and support......	85.00	1,353,141	(1,353,141)	--	--	--
		1,138.50	$ 20,849,938 $	-- $	8,131,989 $	--	$ 28,981,927

I hereby certify that the foregoing is a true and correct copy of the budget for the Library
Department for fiscal year 1980-81, as finally adopted by the Board of Library Commissioners.

WYMAN JONES, City Librarian

frequently in the history of a library system, even though it might be significantly larger than one year's normal budget when it does occur.

Tables 14.2 and 14.3 illustrate approaches to presenting a line budget showing revenue and expenses. These tables show the relative position of the library vis à vis other City of Los Angeles departments. They serve as a reminder that government budgets and governments are tied to the political process. Note that "Municipal Arts" is deleted from the proposed 1980/1981 budget.

Line budgets are most often calculated on the basis of a formula. For a public library, this is quite frequently a per capita figure based in part on a tax levy for library service. The formula is set by a local tax board in a manner similar to setting school taxes.

Academic libraries use a number of formulas. A common formula is to set aside in arbitrary percentage of the total institutional budget for library service (5% has been suggested as an ideal figure). One of the most common methods is to calculate a budget on a per student FTE (full-time equivalent) basis: the library receives a certain amount of money for each full-time-equivalent student attending the institution. Although this method is responsive in terms of student-body size, it ignores unequal library use among students. When increases in enrollments are greater in the social sciences and humanities than in the sciences, library use may be much heavier. Also, some part-time students will use the library more than some full-time students.

TABLE 14.3 **SUMMARY OF LOS ANGELES CITY BUDGET**

COMPARATIVE STATEMENT OF BUDGET APPROPRIATIONS

1979–1980 BUDGET, 1979–1980 BUDGET AS REVISED 10/10/79*, AND 1980–1981 PROPOSED BUDGET

(Including Estimated Expenditures and Departmental Requests)

	1979-1980 Budget	1979-1980 Revised 10/10/79	Estimated Expenditures	1980-1981 Department Request	1980-1981 Proposed Budget	Increase (Decrease) from 10/10/79 Revised Budget Amount	Increase (Decrease) from 10/10/79 Revised Budget Percent
Animal Regulation	$ 3,762,482	$ 3,653,291	$ 3,750,000	$ 4,804,445	$ 4,289,365	$ 636,074	17.4%
Building and Safety	19,303,355	19,303,355	19,440,458	21,516,672	20,817,978	1,514,623	7.8
City Administrative Officer	4,591,260	4,566,260	4,429,272	4,806,291	4,962,726	396,466	8.7
City Attorney	14,124,900	13,711,992	20,285,915	15,946,396	15,029,673	1,317,681	9.6
City Clerk	5,822,838	5,712,770	6,434,514	8,828,917	8,660,665	2,947,895	51.6
Commission on Status of Women	64,786	64,876	61,948	81,037	78,479	13,693	21.1
Community Development	12,728,653	12,688,634	12,168,954	15,349,613	14,385,103	1,696,469	13.4
Controller	2,103,521	2,051,603	2,165,932	2,165,140	2,131,325	79,722	3.9
Council	5,787,241	5,787,241	7,737,241	7,737,241	7,737,241	1,950,000	33.7
Cultural Affairs	—	—	—	—	1,784,458	1,784,458	NA
Data Services	11,031,433	10,935,394	10,948,394	16,216,055	12,869,859	1,934,465	17.7
Employee Relations	88,231	88,231	84,400	93,265	92,465	4,234	4.8
Fire	100,272,152	100,261,975	106,388,880	108,425,064	110,906,165	10,644,190	10.6
General Service	70,857,259	66,370,438	64,567,115	79,174,024	82,953,834	16,583,396	25.0
Mayor	1,776,744	1,776,744	2,621,675	1,967,969	1,967,969	191,225	10.8
Municipal Arts	1,284,069	1,271,488	1,259,109	1,817,648	—	(1,271,488)	(100.0)
Municipal Auditorium	8,245,443	8,245,443	8,162,083	9,276,743	8,722,129	476,686	5.8
Personnel	50,785,347	50,262,467	53,063,851	57,324,214	56,831,057	6,568,590	13.1
Planning	5,221,785	5,153,850	5,389,216	5,636,545	5,514,283	360,433	7.0
Police	242,424,123	241,118,493	243,206,000	252,509,646	250,173,403	9,054,910	3.8
Public Works:							
Board Office	1,538,866	1,510,196	1,489,076	1,998,784	1,958,515	448,319	29.7
Accounting	926,824	919,999	889,999	1,008,681	1,004,746	84,747	9.2
Contract Administration	4,724,818	4,571,251	4,564,000	5,894,081	4,770,008	198,757	4.3
Engineering	28,734,545	28,536,064	28,398,246	30,933,035	28,455,605	(80,459)	(.3)
Management-Employee Services	597,243	588,564	541,864	622,419	504,018	(84,546)	(14.4)
Sanitation	37,109,089	37,054,508	37,799,840	46,246,720	38,330,246	1,275,738	3.4
Street Lighting	5,525,067	5,415,647	5,830,400	5,618,492	5,543,104	127,457	2.4
Street Maintenance	41,170,180	40,639,195	39,452,023	48,578,835	43,735,369	3,096,174	7.6
Social Service	399,202	377,658	341,116	409,462	393,168	15,510	4.1
Transportation	17,426,911	17,269,176	13,225,486	23,401,925	14,998,339	(2,270,837)	(13.1)
Treasurer	1,007,502	982,477	913,304	996,871	982,613	136	—
Subtotal Budgetary Departments	$ 699,435,869	$ 690,889,190	$ 705,610,311	$ 779,389,230	$ 750,583,908	$ 59,694,718	8.6%

COMPARATIVE STATEMENT OF BUDGET APPROPRIATIONS   (Continued)

	1979-1980			1980-1981		Increase (Decrease) from 10/10/79 Revised Budget	
	Budget	Revised 10/10/79	Estimated Expenditures	Department Request	Proposed Budget	Amount	Percent
Liberty Fund	$ 16,831,136	$ 16,642,136	$ 17,532,393	$ 20,321,411	$ 17,751,250	$ 1,109,114	6.7%
Recreation and Parks Fund	29,858,515	29,140,956	29,890,956	35,483,681	30,800,380	1,659,424	5.7
City Employees' Retirement Fund	60,969,748	60,517,027	60,754,315	59,374,474	59,374,474	(1,142,553)	(1.9)
Fire and Police Pension Fund	160,804,761	160,284,809	162,798,946	176,213,314	165,427,766	5,142,957	3.2
Total--Departmental	967,900,029	957,474,118	976,586,921	1,070,782,110	1,023,937,778	66,463,660	6.9%
Community Redevelopment	12,000	12,000	12,000	12,000	12,000	--	--
General City Purposes	10,561,604	10,462,875	8,618,978	10,214,403	10,183,728	(279,147)	(2.7)
Water and Electricity	20,630,000	20,630,000	21,529,000	22,040,256	24,940,000	4,310,000	20.9
Unappropriated Balance	23,513,387	22,767,288	10,000	82,050,000	82,050,000	59,282,712	260.4
Capital Improvement Expenditure Program	44,378,386	44,103,386	48,246,000	120,109,404	45,680,602	1,577,216	3.6
Community Development Trust	40,669,834	40,669,834	27,246,390	47,014,194	47,014,194	6,344,360	15.6
Police Department Emergency Command Control Communications System Trust Fund	14,716,351	14,716,351	10,504,938	21,227,418	21,277,418	6,561,067	44.6
Bicycle License	48,000	48,000	199,011	48,000	48,000	--	--
Public Facilities Trust	4,700,000	4,700,000	4,700,000	--	--	(4,700,000)	(100.0)
Engineering/Transportation Training-Travel	6,000	6,000	5,800	6,000	6,000	--	--
Special Parking Revenue Fund	3,075,848	3,075,848	2,345,160	4,078,307	2,620,000	(455,848)	(14.8)
Sewer Construction and Maintenance Fund	7,632,352	7,632,352	7,632,352	8,520,000	8,520,000	887,648	11.6
Greater Los Angeles Visitors and Convention Bureau Trust Fund	--	--	--	--	349,000	349,000	NA
Special Purpose Funds	--	--	85,217	--	--	--	--
Bond Redemption & Interest	16,318,577	16,318,577	16,318,577	15,171,839	15,171,839	(1,146,738)	(7.0)
Total--Nondepartmental	186,262,339	185,142,511	147,453,423	330,541,821	257,872,781	72,730,270	39.3%
Total	$1,154,162,368	$1,142,616,629	$1,124,040,344	$1,401,323,931	$1,281,810,559	$ 139,193,930	12.2%

*The adopted budget was revised to reflect (1) the passage of State legislation that resulted in a reduction of $18,600,000 in revenues anticipated from the State; and (2) that the Council did not approve a Refuse Collection Charge anticipated to generate receipts of $15,321,000.

A third technique—one used in all types of libraries—is the comparative method. If it is not part of the formal budget presentation, it may well have entered into the picture during preparation. Yet, libraries hesitate to use this method, because it can be dangerous. It involves selecting libraries that are very similar in size and situation to the one preparing its budget, obtaining their budget figures, and using these to justify increased requests in the budget. The danger lies in the fact that the funding agency can do its own comparisons; it might conclude that too much money had been spent in the past.

PERFORMANCE BUDGET

The performance budget has been a widely discussed tool for fiscal control and is an important form of budgeting in some public and academic libraries. It is also called the program planning budgeting system or PPBS. When applied to libraries and other public agencies, PPBS involves the introduction of three major operational concepts:

Developing an analytical ability for examining in depth both agency objectives and the programs designed to meet them.

Forming a 5-year programming process plan combined with a sophisticated management-information system.

Creating a budgeting mechanism that can take broad program decisions, translate them into refined budgetary decisions, and present the results for action.

The following steps are used to accomplish this task of identifying economically efficient operational programs that meet broad goals:

1. Identify library objectives.
2. Relate broad objectives to specific service programs.
3. Relate programs to resource requirements.
4. Relate resource inputs to budget dollars.

These steps not only provide a quick overview of how the program performance budget works but they also indicate the degree to which all management activities are interrelated.

Performance budgeting is based on functions, activities, and projects. It does not simply detail the objects of disbursement, as does the line budget. Because if is a plan that is prepared, analyzed, and interpreted in terms of services and activities, it emphasizes process, purpose, and achievement. It turns away somewhat from the means of attainment toward the objects themselves. Naturally, then, performance budgeting can be applied to libraries, because their objective is to provide service. "Profit" is seen as the degree to which services are utilized and patrons are satisfied. Thus, a performance budget that explains expenditures in terms of accomplishments and results is oriented toward the library's real goals.

The application of a performance budget requires great detail, especially with regard to unit costs. To institute PPBS, the library's objectives must be as clear as possible. Next, a workable plan must be formulated to achieve those objectives.

The next step in actual budget formulation is to determine *work programs*—groups of related activities that produce complete tasks and products. Each program is then assigned a cost (by determining unit costs), which services as the basis for the estimation of the program's financial requirements.

Each work unit has a program justification, which states that unit's general objectives and its scope of activities. Once the entire budget is set, an allotment system can assure that funds can be redirected if work programs change. Budget review will also be necessary for evaluation.

Theoretically, any activity within a library can be assigned a time factor and a cost factor (work hours, in the former; the combination of the cost of a series of operations, in the latter). These factors are combined in work measurement to tell how much time and money it will take to do the parts of a job as well as the whole job. Work measurement depends on work that is related specifically to time *and* on the correct identification of the right unit of work with the appropriate unit of time.

To determine staff needs, multiply the number of units of work by the time factor per work unit (usually, work hours) and then divide this by the number of hours one person works per year. That is the number of persons needed to do the job. The cost is found by dividing the work-hour cost of producing a measure of work by the annual number of work units; then multiply the cost unit by the number of work units anticipated for the coming year.

This quantitative emphasis presents problems, though. First, how do you determine work-unit measurements? Is cataloging measured by titles done or by volumes? It cannot be both. Also, there is the problem of applying standards where they are amorphous, or nonexistent. A related problem is that measuring public service activities quantitatively is impossible. If unit production drops but quality of service increases, how is that measured? How do you measure the quality of the materials being circulated? What is the relative use of materials within the library, and how is this measured? These problems underline the necessity of clearly stated objectives at the outset of attempting to measure service.

The ultimate objective of unit costing and work measurement is to develop a standard cost and performance for various functions, activities, and subactivities. The standard is simply an average, based on past performance, that is adjusted as new data become available. It can be used to measure effectiveness and to figure average cost per work unit. If a work-measurement reporting system (based on the work program) is set up, new information will provide justification for expanding, changing, or eliminating services (or ways or performing them). It will allow feedback for better planning, and it will provide the means of budgetary control.

Such a system also allows spotting of deviations from the budget, which can then be measured by the work program (by activity, subactivity, or cost center, if need be). This final step of utilizing the performance budget is *control of operations.* Of course, control is necessary in any budget, but the layout of the performance budget makes it easier to spot areas of deviation; this increases the possibility of fast and easy control.

Table 14.4 presents a PPBS summary table, showing areas of control in the library.

The advantage to the performance budget is that it allows the library's service mission to be reflected specifically in the budget. That way the funding authority can see why money is being requested, what it is being used for, and where sensible cutbacks might be made without destroying whole programs. It is also useful as a means of implementing budgetary control and as a planning device.

TABLE 14.4   PPBS Summary Table

Activities	Programs[a]				
	1	2	3	4	Totals
Totals	$30,500	$28,500	$20,500	$20,500[b]	=$100,000
Acquisition	15,500	5,500	2,500	6,000	29,500
Cataloging	5,000	20,000	500	500	26,000
Reference	5,000	1,500	15,000	4,000	25,500
Public Service	5,000	1,500	2,500	10,000	18,000

[a]1, recreational; 2, educational; 3, informational; 4, special services.
[b]$5000.00 state library for cooperative activities.

The primary weakness of the performance budget lies, as noted, in its emphasis on the quantification of service activities. Comparative evaluations will still involve qualitative judgments, which cannot really be reflected. (Consider reference service and readers' advisory services.) So again, the problem of true costs looms large. Also, it is difficult to implement performance budgets in small libraries where positions do not usually duplicate and tasks are often not repetitive enough to form a routine.

In summary, then, program budgeting is *not* the following:

It is not revolutionary, except in its arragement.

It is not a substitute for good judgment, opinion, experience, or knowledge.

It is not an attempt to computerize decision making.

It is not just another way to save money and cut expenses.

It is not the answer to every problem involving every financial issue.

Performance budgeting is no more than a way to force budget managers to think very carefully about their situations, services, priorities, and expenditures.

ZERO-BASE BUDGET

The wave of the future during the 1960s and early 1970s was thought to be PPBS; however, problems in measuring service and the amount of time it took to gather information have reduced the wave to a ripple. The current candidate for new wave is zero-base budgeting (ZBB). How long it will last in that status is another thing. It has been said to be a possible replacement for line, PPBS, and combinations of the two. When taxpayers are increasingly concerned about their burden, ZBB has rather widespread appeal.

Developed by Peter Phyor as a means of achieving more effective planning and fiscal control, the basic concept of ZBB has become somewhat confused in the minds of the general public. The term *zero base* is derived from the first steps in the process—the development of a hierarchy of functions based on the assumption that the unit or agency is starting operations for the first time (point zero). Thus, the focus of the planning and development of the ZBB is on the unit's purpose and on the function(s) it should perform in order to meet the reasons for its existence. In theory, a government or an organization that uses this budgeting system would become more cost effective by continuously reviewing its purposes and attempting to remove unneeded activities. From a taxpayer's point of view, if governments would put ZBB theory into practice, the existing tax base would produce the maximum level of service. However, as was evidenced by the Carter administration's effort to impose ZBB on the federal government, theory and practice often are very far apart.

Several phases of ZBB are necessary in the implementation of the entire system: construction, planning, budgeting, and control. The time-consuming part of the process, and the one that assures a more cost-effective use of the monies available, is the construction phase. It is during the construction phase that the budget maker assumes that the unit is engaging in zero activity. This is the phase that is most frequently omitted (as was the case with the federal attempt at ZBB). Without this phase, one is not really using the ZBB process.

During the construction phase, the person who is responsible for budget preparation in the unit creates a series of function statements and function outcomes in terms of the basic purpose of the unit. For example, assume that you are the head of an academic library reference department. You might identify two functions (there would be more, but only two will be illustrated): "to ensure that patrons receive accurate answers to their reference questions" and "to ensure that patrons are properly educated in the use of the library." The outcome statements would be: "accurate answers to reference questions" and "patrons educated in the use of the library."

Each function is divided into a series of subfunctions, thereby creating a hierarchy of activities. Under the function "educated . . . patrons," one might list a set of the subfunctions, such as "to ensure that the proper library-use skills are identified" (outcome—identified skill), "to ensure that patrons who need to be educated are identified" (outcome—patrons identified), and "to ensure that patrons learn library-use skills" (outcome—knowledgeable patrons). You could go further and subdivide each subfunction. For example, the "identified skills" subfunction might have subdivisions such as "to ensure that patrons know how to use the public catalog," "to ensure that patrons know how to use periodical indexes," and "to ensure that patrons can use online services."

It is apparent that the construction phase can be long and complex, if it is done properly. For each outcome, you must establish a quantitative value and calculate the financial resources required to achieve that outcome. Normally the quantitative figure and total cost are calculated on the basis of annual output rather than unit cost. The costing activities are very similar to those of PPBS.

During the planning phase of ZBB, one questions the "packages" (functions, subfunctions and sub-subfunctions): "Do we need this output at this cost?" "Can we reduce the unit cost in any way (new equipment, more self-services)?" "If we increase our capability, how will that affect our unit cost?" As a result of the questioning process, several alternative plans are developed and ranked by the unit head. Often, the planner is told to develop a minimum of three plans: one to cut total expenditures, one to maintain current levels of spending (with improved productivity), and one to increase the level of spending. Each function or package is prepared and then ranked against the others.

The ranking is repeated at several levels, because each step in the process requires the balancing of more factors. Thus, the process that began in departments and units in the library is repeated by the budget officer or the library director, who may decide to change rankings. The funding agency then reviews the rankings; it may well change them. Thus, a final budget is established—one that should more cost effective and reflective of the purposes and services of all the agencies involved.

The ranking process has been widely discussed, and the idea of a budget for reduced spending has received considerable attention. What has not had much attention is the construction phase of ZBB. Because the construction phase is time-consuming, it cannot be done on an annual basis.

SITE BUDGETING

In the not too distant future, government agencies that operate numerous service points—public libraries, school libraries, and multiple-campus academic libraries—may be required to do site budgeting (SB). Site budgeting ensures that everyone who is to be served will have access to equal services. Originally, it came out of school funding issues, when it was noted that some districts would have better schools because their tax bases were larger than those of other districts. The goal of SB was equal per-student funding, and the more recent extension of the idea has been to ensure equitable distribution within (not only among) districts. Naturally, school libraries will be affected, but there is reason to think that the concept will be applied to public libraries and multiple-campus academic libraries, too.

The first step in SB is to estimate as accurately as possible how much money the system as a whole will be able to take in. From that amount, deduct all the costs for central services and costs not easily assigned a particular location (centralized technical services, for example, which could count as a central cost or be apportioned to locations on the basis of usage). After the central-services deduction has been made, the remaining funds are allocated by formula to the outlying sites. For libraries, this might be done on a per-capita-served basis. Each site is informed of the amount it will receive. Then the head librarian and the staff figure out how they will allocate the money.

An interesting twist at the site level is that patrons need to be involved in deciding how funds will be expanded, if the ideal is to be achieved. (School districts that use the system require parent, student, and teacher involvement in the budget-decision process.) The head librarian cannot give up responsibility for ultimate decisions (that person is accountable for the consequences of any decision that is implemented), but active participation by staff and patrons is a goal here. A budget proposal must be presented to such a group as a topic for *discussion;* it is essential that the participants understand that they are giving advice and are not actually making the final decisions. The librarian's job is to incorporate the discussion into a revision of the proposal, and then submit that revision to the central authority. The central authority will then pass it along the chain to the funding authority for hearings.

Site budgeting has two important advantages: patron participation and equitable funding within a system; however, it depends on a set amount of money from the funding authority. If that figure changes by very much, the entire process will have to be repeated. Also, "average" salaries will be used for planning, but the real salaries, when plugged in, might cause major adjustments to be made.

The more you know about budgeting, the better you will be able to do your job. New forms of budgeting will undoubtedly occur, each with its own pros and cons. By studying the various forms available and learning their strengths and weaknesses, you can be more effective in pointing out the positive aspects of those forms that could aid library service. Of course, you will have no choice as to the system used to report the library's activity to its funding agency; but, internally, you should be given fairly free rein. Remember, budgeting is a year-round activity, and, although it is time-consuming, it cannot be left for tomorrow.

BIBLIOGRAPHY

1. A. Wildavsky, *The Politics of the Budgetary Process* 3rd ed. (Boston: Little, Brown, 1979).
2. J. Cohen, and K. W. Leeson, "Sources and Uses of Funds of Academic Libraries," *Library Trends* 28 (1979): 25–46.

FURTHER READING

Anthony, R. N. "Zero-base Budgeting: A Useful Fraud?" *Government Accountants Journal* 26 (1977): 7–10.

Austin, L. A., and Cheek, L. M. *Zero-base Budgeting: A Decision Package Manual.* New York: AMACOM, 1979.

Baumol, W. J., and Marcus, M. *Economics of Academic Libraries.* Washington, D.C.: American Council on Education, 1973.

Beasley, K. "Governmental and Financial Problems of Urban Areas: Their Relationship to Libraries." *Library Quarterly* 38 (1968): 13–25.

Berger, P. W. "Investigation of the Relationship Between Public Relation Activities and Budget Allocation in Public Libraries." *Information Processing and Management* 15 (1979): 179–193.

"Beyond Zero-Base Budgeting." *Public Administration Review* 36 (1978): 528–529.

Bloomfiend, M. "Cost Characteristics of Library Service." *Special Libraries* 58 (1967): 686–691.

Bundy, A. M. "Defense of a Library Budget." *Catholic Library World* 50 (1978): 69–71.

Burroughs, K. E. "Implementing Zero-base Budgeting." *Financial Executive* 46 (1978): 53–55.

Carlon, B. J. "The Contribution of Behavioral Science to Management Accounting." *Australian Accountant* 49 (1979): 378–380+.

Chen, C. *Zero-Base Budgeting in Library Management.* Phoenix; Oryx Press, 1980.

Collins, F. "The Interaction of Budget Characteristics and Personality Variables with Budgetary Response Attitudes." *Accounting Review* 53 (1978): 324–355.

Contemporary Approaches to Public Budgeting. Cambridge, Mass.: Winthrop Pub., 1979.

Copeland, R. M., and Dascher, P. E. *Managerial Accounting.* 2d ed. New York: Wiley, 1978.

Dino, R. N., and L. W. "A Sure-fire Method to Improve Budget Cycling." *Management Accounting* 61 (1980): 34–41.

Galvin, T. J. "Zero-base Budgeting in Libraries and Information Centers." *Library Acquisitions* 2 (1978): 7–14.

Gardner, W. D. *Government Finance; National, State, and Local.* Englewood Cliffs, N.J.: Prentice-Hall, 1978.

Gelfand, M. "Budget Preparation and Presentation." *American Libraries* 3 (1972): 495–500.

Getz, M. *An Econimic View of Public Libraries.* Nashville: Vanderbilt University, 1979.

Glass, T. E. "Developing the District Budget Through Direct Citizen Participation." *School Business Affairs* 45 (1979): 12–14, 39–40.

Gross, M. J. "Nonprofit Accounting: The Continuing Revolution." *Journal of Accountancy* 143 (1977): 66–68+.

Hamill, H. L. "Numbers Games: Performance Budgeting." *Library Journal* 90 (1965): 3563–3567.

Hayes, R. M. "The Management of Library Resources: The Balance Between Capital and Staff in Providing Services." *Library Research* 1 (1979): 119–142.

Horngren, C. T., and Curry, D. W. *Cost Accounting: A Managerial Emphasis. Student Guide.* 4th ed. Englewood Cliffs, N.J.: Prentice-Hall, 1977.

Horton, F. W. "Budgeting and Accounting for Information." *Government Accounts Journal* 28 (1979): 21–31.

Hovey, H. A. *The Planning-Programming-Budgeting Approach to Government Decisionmaking.* New York: Praeger, 1968.

Howard, R. "Toward PPBS in the Public Library." *American Libraries* 2 (1979): 386–393.

Jacobs, W. C. "Changing Goals and Competition For Tax Dollars: Libraries Adopt Business Management Techniques." *Library Scene* 6 (1977): 27–28.

Jones, R. L., and Trentin, H. G. *Budgeting: Key to Planning and Control*. Rev. ed. New York: AMACOM, 1980.

Jügensen, K. H. "Haushaltsrecht und Rechnungslegung." In *Beiträge zum Bibliotheksrecht*. Berlin: Deutscher Bibliotheksverband, 1978 (pp. 27–48).

Keller, J. E. "Program Budgeting and Cost Benefits Analysis in Libraries." *College and Research Libraries* 30 (1969): 156–160.

Kowalski, T. J. "Attitudes of School Principles toward Decentralized Budgeting." *Journal of Educational Finance* 6 (1980): 68–76.

Lee, S. H., ed. *Library Budgeting: Critical Challenge for the Future*. Ann Arbor: Pierian, 1977.

Leonard, W. P. "The Aftermath of Retrenchment: An Optimistic View." *Journal of Academic Librarianship* 5 (1979): 30–32.

Levine, C. H. "More on Cutback Management: Hard Questions for Hard Times." *Public Administrative Review* 39 (1979): 179–184.

Levine, C. H. "Organizational Decline and Cutback Management." *Public Administration Review* 38 (1978): 315–358.

Lynch, T. D. *Public Budgeting in America*. Englewood Cliffs, N.J.: Prentice-Hall, 1979.

McCarthy, L. *Citizens' Guide to Local Government Budgeting*. Sacramento, Calif.: Calif. Taxpayer's Assoc., 1977.

MacDonald, A. H. "Constraints of Restraint—Doing More With Less." *Atlantic Provinces Library Association Bulletin* 41 (1978): 55–58, 87–89.

Marchand, D. A., and Tyer, C. B. "Budgeting Information Resources: Some Alternative Approaches." *International Journal of Public Administration* 1 (1979): 237–259.

Martin, M. S. *Budgetary Control in Academic Libraries*. Greenwich, Conn.: JAI Press, 1978.

Mishan, E. J. *Cost-benefit Analysis*. Rev. ed. New York: Praeger, 1976.

Molz, K. R. *Federal Policy and Library Support*. Cambridge Mass.: MIT Press, 1976.

Musgrave, R. A., and Musgrave, P. B. *Public Finance in Theory and Practice*. 3rd ed. New York: McGraw-Hill, 1980.

Otley, D. T. "Budget Use and Managerial Performance." *Journal of Accounting Research* 16 (1978): 122–149.

Parker, C. C. "User Evaluation by Budgetary Games." *Aslib Proceedings* 31 (1979): 191–201.

Phyrr, P. A. "Zero-Base Budgeting: Where to Use It and How to Begin." *SAM Advanced Management Journal* 41 (1976): 4–14.

Pinxter, P. "Budgeting for a Main Library and Several Departmental Libraries." In *International Association of Technological University Libraries, 1977*. Louvain, Belgium: IATUL, 1978 (pp. 149–151).

Powell, Ray M. *Accounting Procedures for Institutions*. Notre Dame: Univ. of Notre Dame Press, 1978.

Prentice, A. E. *Pbulic Library Finance*. Chicago: American Library Association, 1977.

Price, P. P. "Budgeting and Budget Control in Public Libraries." *Library Trends* 11 (1963): 402–414.

Readings in Governmental and Non-profit Accounting. Belmont, Calif.: Wadsworth, 1977.

Rehfuss, J. "Zero-base Budgeting: The Experience to Date." *Public Personnel Management* 6 (1977): 181–187.

Sarndal, A. G. "Zero Base Budgeting." *Special Libraries* 70 (1979): 527–532.

Schmiedicke, R. E., and Nagy, C. F. *Principles of Cost Accounting*. 6th ed. Cincinnati, Southwestern Pub., 1978.

"School-site Budgeting and Why It Could be THE Answer to Your Problems." *Executive Educator* 1 (1978): 37–39.

Snyder, J. C. *Fiscal Management and Planning in Local Government*. Lexington, Mass.: D.C. Heath, 1977.

Steele, C., ed. *Steady-State, Zero Growth and the Academic Library.* Hamden, Conn.: Linnet Books, 1978.

Tudor, D. "The Special Library Budget." *Special Library* 63 (1972): 517–527.

Vatter, W. J. "State-of-the-Art:—Non-business Accounting." *Accounting Review* 54 (1979): 574–584.

White, H. S. "Library Management in the Tight Budget Seventies: Problems, Challenges, and Opportunities." *Medical Libarry Association Bulletin* 65 (1977): 6–12.

Wildavsky, A. *Politics of the Budgetary Process.* 3rd ed. Boston: Little, Brown, 1979.

15. Work Analysis

The close connection between budgetary cost-control procedures and work analysis has been mentioned previously. Be learning and applying work analysis techiques, any superviser can make the work environment much more pleasant for everyone concerned. The result can be a more efficient unit in which problems can be dealt with readily. Work analysis can help in solving layout problems in physical space, choosing a sequence for doing work, and finding ways of performing tasks more efficiently. This can either save the library money, or allow money to be spent on other services. The relationship between work analysis and budgeting becomes clear when you consider that most work analysis techniques relate in one way or another to time or money; as a result, they provide a great deal of data used in budgeting and planning.

In addition to work analysis techniques, this chapter will touch briefly on sampling methods, operations research, and systems analysis and evaluation of library services. The diversity of topics is only superficial, because each topic has a bearing on producing a work environment that is comfortable, productive, and rewarding. Because these topics help in understanding work analysis techniques, they will be discussed first to provide background to the coverage of the techniques themselves.

WORK SAMPLING

An important part of statistics, sampling is also a part of any good work analysis project. This is not the place to discuss statistics in full, but there are several good books on the topic for those who have no background in this area. One book that illustrates the way in which statistics fits into library and information science is *Research Methods In Librarianship*, by Busha and Harter (Academic Press, 1980).

To better illustrate the problem, imagine that you are the head of an acquisitions department. You may "feel" that too much time is spent in bibliographic searching. You have six persons in the department; they process an average of 1250 requests per week. This effort keeps the work up-to-date, but you wonder if there might not be a Parkinson's Law in effect here-work expands to fill the time available. Also, a grant to acquire large quantities of material in new areas will probably increase the work in acquisitions by 25–30%. The problem for you as head is to determine whether new personnel are needed, or whether output can be improved in a reasonable manner without adding more staff. This is the time to utilize work analysis techniques, because they will help you to determine what needs to be done.

The present work load represents (in statistical terms) the *universe*, or population, that you wish to study. If you wish to know with almost complete certainty what is being done, you would study all steps in the searching process for all requests for one year. Yet, even then, you could not be absolutely sure that some unusual characteristics of that year's work made it atypical. Fortunately, in the case of most studies, this volume of work is not required. A reasonably small, properly selected sample will provide results that will give you almost as much confidence as you would have if you had studied the entire year's production.

Sampling techniques are based on certain assumptions regarding the nature of the phenomena under study. A basic assumption is that the form of a *distribution pattern* of natural phenomena will resemble a *normal distribution* (bell-shaped curve). Normal distributions are ones in which the characteristics under study cluster around a central point. As you move away from the central point, there are fewer instances of those characteristics (see Figure 15.1).

A random sample drawn from a normal population will probably display a pattern that is similar (although not identical) to the pattern displayed in the population from which it was drawn. Repeated samples from the same population would eventually duplicate the actual pattern.

In the example given here, the actual times for processing might range from 5 minutes to 9 hours, with most of the requests being finished in 127 minutes. The other variable here is the skill of the staff, which will vary; therefore, you should sample both the requests and the staff.

When random samples are drawn from a population, every member of the group has an equal chance of being selected. For instance, to draw a random sample from the requests for new materials, you might consider putting each request into a large container, and then drawing out the

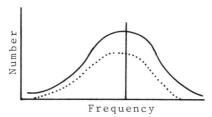

Figure 15.1   Normal distribution curve; Population pattern (—), sample pattern (····).

number of requests that you wish to study. This would not be truly random, however, because the slips on the bottom and the sides would have less of a chance for selection. A way to ensure a truly random selection would be to assign each request a number as it arrived; you could then use a random number table to select the sample you need.

Random number tables are found in almost all statistics books, in mathematical tables books, and in volumes devoted solely to such tables. Using these tables is easy. Table 15.1 is an example of a random number table.

For our purposes, our universe has a maximum of four digits in the series (1250 requests). To select the sample, assuming that you decide to read down the columns (you can read up, or across, or right to left—so long as you are consistent), you would start with line 101 and column 1, and you would use the first four digits in each number in each column. The purpose is to select your sample (for example, 100 requests) from the 1250 requests taken in. Thus, any number between 0001 and 1250 is suitable for inclusion in the sample. So, the numbers in column 1 and lines 101, 102, and 103 are not acceptable (they are 1328, 2122, and 9905). Line 104 is acceptable (0019); the number of the first request to be drawn for the sample is 19. The next acceptable number occurs in line 110 (1075). Simply continue in this fashion until you have 100 numbers. Should you hit a number that has already been selected, skip it and go on, until 100 numbers have been chosen.

Sampling is necessary in work analysis as well as in research. This presentation is a bare minimum background; however, it may help to emphasize the amount of time needed for work analysis. If you do not acquire the statistical background yourself, you should have the help of someone who has such a background.

TYPES OF WORK ANALYSIS

The *block diagram* represents the most elementary form of work analysis. It provides a simple overview of the relationships among various units

TABLE 15.1　Random Number Table
"Random Decimal Digits"[a]

Line	(1)	(2)	Column (3)	(4)	(5)	(6)
101	13284	16834	74151	92027	24670	36665
102	21224	00370	30420	03883	94648	89428
103	99052	47887	81085	64933	66279	80432
104	00199	50993	98603	38452	87890	94624
105	60578	06483	28733	37867	07936	98710
106	91240	18312	17441	01929	18163	69201
107	97458	14229	12063	59611	32249	90466
108	35249	38646	34475	72417	60514	69257
109	38980	46600	11759	11900	46743	27860
110	10750	52745	38749	87365	58959	53731
111	36247	27850	73958	20673	37800	63835
112	70994	66986	99744	72438	01174	42159
113	99638	94702	11463	18148	81386	80431
114	72055	15774	43857	99805	10419	76939
115	24038	65541	85788	55835	38835	59399
116	74976	14631	35908	28221	39470	91548
117	35553	71628	70189	26436	63407	91178
118	35676	12797	51434	82976	42010	26344
119	74815	67523	72985	23183	02446	63594
120	45246	88048	65173	50989	91060	89894
121	76509	47069	86378	41797	11910	49672
122	19689	90332	04315	21358	97248	11188
123	42751	35318	97513	61537	54955	08159
124	11946	22681	45045	13964	57517	59419
125	96518	48688	20996	11090	48396	57177
126	35726	58643	76869	84622	39098	36083
127	39737	42750	48968	70536	84864	64952
128	97025	66492	56177	04049	80312	48028
129	62814	08075	09788	56350	76787	51591
130	25578	22950	15227	83291	41737	79599
131	68763	69576	88991	49662	46704	63362
132	17900	00813	64361	60725	88974	61005
133	71944	60227	63551	71109	05624	43836
134	54684	93691	85132	64399	29182	44324
135	25946	27623	11258	65204	52832	50880

TABLE 15.1 (*Continued*)

Line	(1)	(2)	(3)	(4)	(5)	(6)
			Column			
136	01353	39318	44961	44972	91766	90262
137	99083	88191	27662	99113	57174	35571
138	52021	45406	37945	75234	24327	86978
139	78755	47744	43776	83098	03225	14281
140	25282	69106	59180	16257	22810	43609
141	11959	94202	02743	86847	79725	51811
142	11644	13792	98190	01424	30078	28197
143	06307	97912	68110	59812	95448	43244
144	76285	75714	89585	99296	52640	46518
145	55322	07598	39600	60866	63007	20007
146	78017	90928	90220	92503	83375	26986
147	44768	43342	20696	26331	43140	69744
148	25100	19336	14605	86603	51680	97678
149	83612	46623	62876	85197	07824	91392
150	41347	81666	82961	60413	71020	83658

[a]Source: L. Lipkin, I. K. Feinstein, and L. Derrick, *Accountant's Handbook of Formulas and Tables* 2nd ed. (Prentice-Hall, Inc., Englewood Cliffs, N.J., 1963) © 1963, 1973: p. 444.

or activities within an organization. As is shown in Figure 15.2, a block diagram can look, at first glance, like an organization chart—except that it includes elements outside the actual organizational structure (patrons, jobbers, etc.).

Another technique, the *flow diagram*, brings a finer level of analysis into play, as it gives a graphic view of both the work area and the movement of personnel and materials within that area. The best representation is a scale drawing of the facility, with all activities clearly identified. Figures 15.3 represents a flow diagram for an acquisitions department as it existed prior to analysis, with a line drawn each time a person left a desk (most lines converge on the bibliography shelf outside the door).

Along with the information derived from the diagram, two things were recorded in tabular form: the distance of one trip from desk to bibliography area for each person, and the time required to make such a trip. As a result of this analysis, a new physical layout was designed (see Figure 15.4). Alternatives would be possible, with the final choice probably hinging on the costs (including remodeling as well as personnel time).

Collection Development

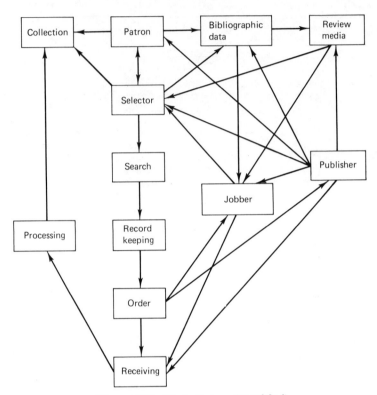

Figure 15.2   Block diagram (simplified).

Old

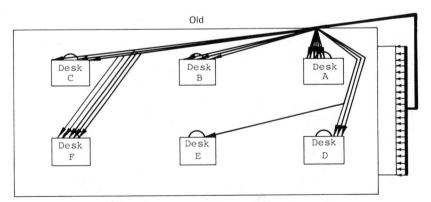

Figure 15.3   Flow diagram (before analysis).

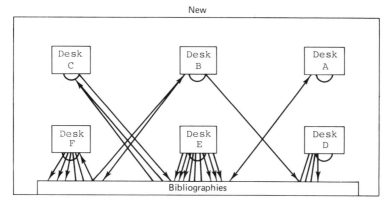

Figure 15.4 Flow diagram (after analysis).

Diagrams cannot make decisions, but they have been of great help in the decision-making process.

A *flow process chart* can indicate the movement of an object of study, but it cannot relate the movement to a physical space. You can choose from among a great many symbols to create a flow process chart (these are found in any numbers of books on systems analysis, operations research, and information science). Figure 15.5 is a simplified flow chart from a public services area.

The decision flow chart—typically used in systems analysis for computer application—is a means whereby you can analyze a work flow in which numerous decisions are made. The symbols used to represent these decisions are great in number also, and they can be found in several sources. Figure 15.6 is a simplified decision flow chart.

Operations analysis is the study of the motions of the hands, eyes, and feet of an individual who is working on a particular activity in one location. It is most effective when it is used sparingly and on jobs that involve a lot of repetition. This is where the classical time-and-motion study has become very important. The goal is always the best, most effective arrangement, and the most effective sequence of activities within that arrangement. Library activities that lend themselves to this type of study include collating order slips for mailing, sorting overdue charge cards, alphabetizing, and even photoduplicating (among other machine-related activities).

Another type of analysis that could be of great use in libraries is *form analysis*. Forms and files in libraries multiply rather like rabbits, and a unit can easily lose control of them and create a great deal of unnecessary work. Each form that is used in a unit should be reviewed annually

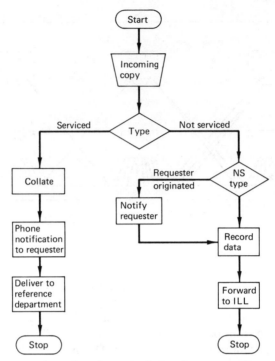

Figure 15.5 Flow process chart for a circulation department. (From *Telefacsimiles in Libraries,* Institute of Library Research, University of California, 1968.)

in order to determine whether it still serves a function and does so efficiently. Naturally, the first question to ask is whether the form is actually necessary at all. What does it do that is not already done? Can some forms be combined? Do all items on the form need to be there? Could a less expensive form be used toward the same end? And how long must the forms be retained before they may be disposed of?

The answer to the last question will vary, and you may have no control over that answer. Governments often set certain mimimum time limits for retaining records, especially fiscal and personnel records. This could range from a few months to indefinitely, although personnel records are now commonly microfilmed and transferred to special storage units. If you *do* have discretion over the use of forms, you can and should control them.

If forms are to be used outside the unit, you should double check them to make certain that they are understandable to nonlibrary personnel. This problem might be found most frequently on acquistions request forms, in the space in which the library requests the imprint data. If it

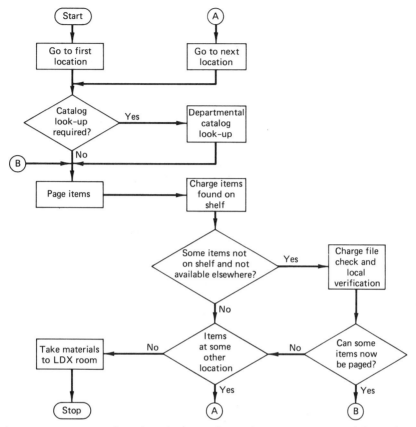

Figure 15.6 Decision flow chart for a circulation department. (From *Telefacsimiles in Libraries,* Institute of Library Research, University of California, 1968.)

says "date" or "year," rather than "imprint date," a very large number of people will fill in the date of their request.

Man – machine charts allow studies to be made of the relationship between people and machines. In a unit that contains a lot of equipment (photoduplication, data processing, microfilming, and so on), man–machine charts can be very valuable. If people or machines are idle for long periods, of time, perhaps this can be altered so that machines and people function effectively in their broadest possible applications. Of course, too much idle time might mean that the function could be better and more inexpensively performed by an outside service. The goal is efficiency in the use of library equipment and personnel. Inefficiency can begin to erode morale if it is not corrected.

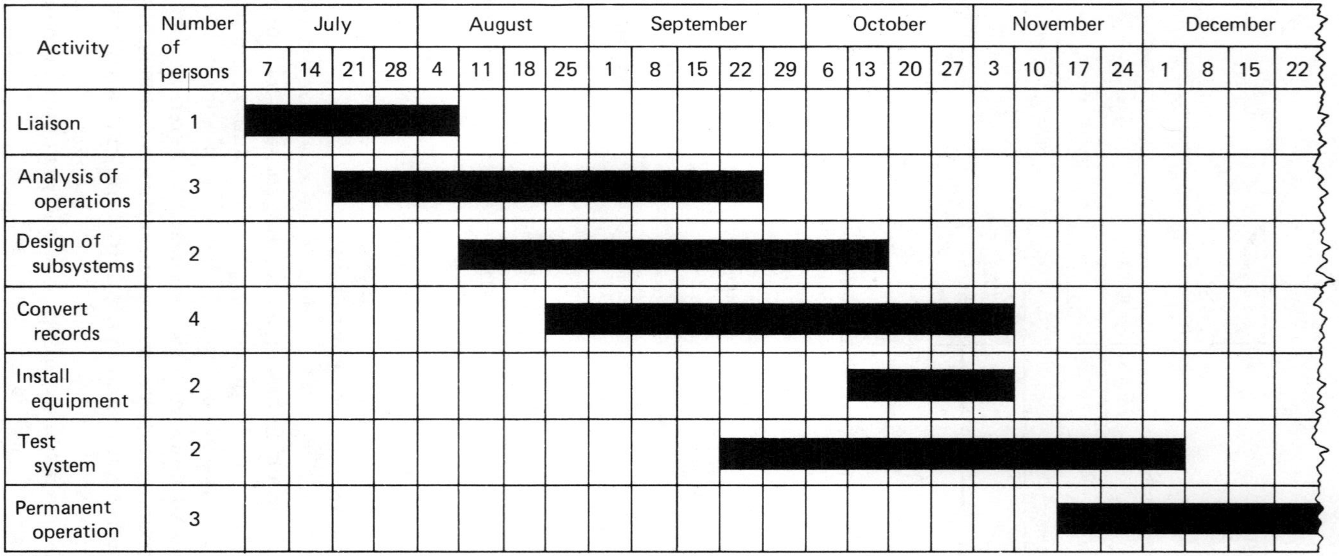

Activity	Number of persons	July				August				September				October				November				December		
		7	14	21	28	4	11	18	25	1	8	15	22	29	6	13	20	27	3	10	17	24	1	8	15	22
Liaison	1																									
Analysis of operations	3																									
Design of subsystems	2																									
Convert records	4																									
Install equipment	2																									
Test system	2																									
Permanent operation	3																									

Figure 15.7 Gantt chart (simplified).

SCHEDULING: GANTT CHARTS

Scheduling—the assignment of a specific time period for each component of work and for the total project—gives vitality and practical meaning to a plan.

We can see the relationships between work and time by using the charts developed by an early prominent management specialist, Henry Gantt. Departments or activities are listed along the left-hand side of the form, along with the number of employees and their weekly capability. Each main column represents one week (the numbers at the top of each column represent the ending day for that week). Many adaptations of the Gantt chart are used today (even though they are not identified as such); they all emphasize the importance of time values and scheduling. Whenever a library needs to develop a complex schedule, a Gantt chart can help to prepare it and plan the workload in terms of overall objectives. Figure 15.7 represents a simplified Gantt chart used in scheduling the development of an automated circulation system.

PERT

The Program Evaluation and Review Technique (PERT) approach is a device developed by the United States Navy Special Projects Office in 1958 to better utilize *timing* in a series of activities. Dupont's Critical Path Method (CPM) and the United States Air Force's Program Evaluation Procedure (PEP) are related to the PERT approach in that all three present analogue models of activities that are plotted against time to reach an objective. Figure 15.8 (and the accompanying key in Table 15.2) represents a simplified PERT chart.

The first phase of such an analysis involved laying out the steps of a sequence in their proper order and assigning each step a time value. Because an overemphasis on time can allow costs to get out of control, however, the original concept has been modified to include both time *and* costs. Thus, both total time and total cost can be computed relatvely easily at any stage in the operation. This goes beyond normal budgetary control sequences in that a distinct cost is associated with each step along the way, and a standard for those costs is set; as a result, the analyst can see whether costs are running ahead of accomplishments.

The drawback here might be obvious—it is difficult to keep track of costs at every step, and equally difficult to budget for them. Even when relatively minor steps are combined for this purpose, it is difficult. PERT usually deals with relatively new activities for which no standard figures

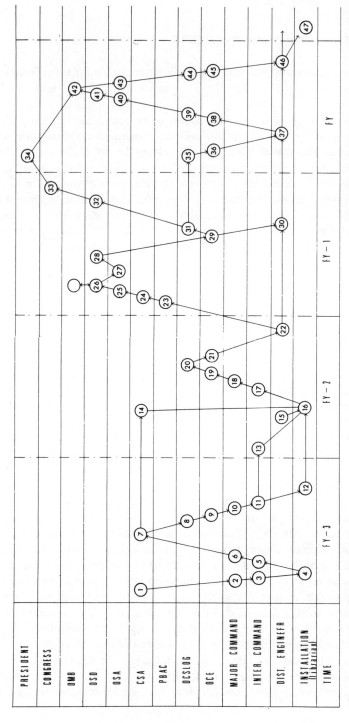

Figure 15.8 A simplified PERT chart. Military construction approval cycle for post library (see Table 15.2 for key.) (From G. E. Evans, *Library Environmental Design: Physical Facilities and Equipment.* TISA Project Report No. 33. Los Angeles: University of California/Institute of Library Research, 1971.)

TABLE 15.2 KEY TO PERT CHART

MCA CYCLE
Explanation of Abbreviations and Terms

OMB —Office of Management and Budget
OSD —Office of the Secretary of Defense
OSA —Office of the Secretary of the Army
CSA —Chief of Staff, U.S. Army
PBAC —Program Budget Advisory Committee
DCS LOG —Deputy Chief of Staff, Logistics
OCE —Office of the Chief of Engineers
FY —Refers to the Fiscal Year in which the program is to be appropriated.
MAJOR COMMAND —Planning Review Board whose composition and function reflects the features of the Planning Review Board at the intermediate command level described below.
INTERMEDIATE COMMAND —Planning Review Board, composed of the Chief of Staff and the principal members of each staff section, to provide information to installations within the command concerning assignment and transfer of missions, activation and deactivation of units, and military and civilian strengths to be used as a basis for developing the Master Plan.
INSTALLATION —Commanders of permanent installations establish Installation Planning Boards for development and maintenance of approved Master Plans. Voting members are normally a senior representative of the installation commander, the post engineer, a representative of the division engineer, and representatives of each independent activity that is a tenant on the installation and for which the installation is responsible for the reporting of real military property (i.e., the librarian).

STEP NUMBER DESCRIPTION OF ACTION

1. Mission and strength guidance issued in stationing plan.
2. Mission and strength guidance received.
3. Mission and strength guidance received.
4. Development of Master Plan.
5. Contribute to Master Plan by establishing Installation Planning Review Board.
6. Review and revision by Command Planning Review Board, forward to HQDA.
7. Approval and issuance of program guidance of the Short Range Construction Program and Intermediate Range Construction Program to installation via the major and intermediate commands.
8. Program Guidance received.
9. Program Guidance received.
10. Program Guidance received.
11. Program Guidance received.
12. First Program Guidance received.
13. Additional intercommand preliminary guidance supplied.
14. DA staff supplies more specific guidance.
15. Contributes as member of Installation Planning Review Board.
16. Projects that will best meet their plans; projects are

(continued)

TABLE 15.2 (Continued)

aligned in priority sequence. Post engineer prepares a DD Form 1390 for each project (cost estimates, etc.) A ten paragraph justification is prepared for each short range project, after this a DD Form 1391 is prepared (a composite listing).

17. Examines program; puts it in a composite with others submitted.

18. Major command considerations, policies and requirements are applied, and priorities realign intermediate packages into an overall construction program.

19. Reviewed for accuracy, completeness and technical sufficiency, incorporated into a total construction plan.

20. Submitted to construction requirements review committee (composed of representatives of the principal staff sections of the DA and OCE) to formulate annual target budget year program. Program is then reviewed and approved by the DCS Log.

21. Last minute refinements in justification arguments and final updated cost analysis.

22. Commence concept designs.

23. Reviews DCS Log package.

24. Review and approval.

25. Review and approval; and submission as part of proposed Army budget.

26. Review, jointly with OMB. A list of requirements is generated by OSD and the approved version of the new construction plan is developed.

27. Handed down for inclusion in the final OSD-approved Army budget for the target year, or for reclamation if desired (on those projects disapproved that the Army feels should be included).

28. Final review.

29. Final smoothup.

30. Commence final design action on OSD-approved projects.

31. Submits OCE prepared program.

32. Forwards OCE prepared program.

33. Committee (House and Senate Armed Service Committees) project authorization deliberations. A 200-word summary ("boilerplate") is prepared on each DD Form 1391 to familiarize committees on projects. Submitted to Appropriations Committees next. Completion of hearings, passage of a bill.

34. Signature and enactment.

35. Prepares MCA program execution circular (based on information from Congressional committee staffs indicating the characteristics and magnitude of final program).

36. Forwards circular to District Engineer to be used as a guide for scheduling.

37. Prepares construction n, and contract schedules in anticipation of forthcoming authorization and funding.

38. Preparation of apportionment request.

39. Apportionment request forwarded to OMB via OSA and OSD

40. Submits apportionment request to OSD.

41. Submits apportionment request to OMB.

42. Funds apportioned in consonance with Congressional appropriation via OSA, DCS LOG, COA (Comptroller of the Army) and OCE.

43. Forward notice of apportioned funds.

44. Forward notice of apportioned funds.

45. Forward notice of apportioned funds.

46. Program execution commenced.

47. Occupancy.

are available, so estimation is difficult. Moreover, because PERT stresses joint contributions, allocation of overhead costs is complicated.

Often, new concepts are used inappropriately or indiscriminately—and such has been the case with PERT. For a library, PERT should be used to plan and control the cost of long-term complex projects (new buildings or elaborate service plans). Remember the effort that needs to be put forth, and remember the limitattions of PERT and other te^hniques.

OTHER USEFUL CONCEPTS

The use of many of the following techniques requires a mathematical background. If you do not have such a background, however, you should learn about the types of techniques that are available so that you can choose one for your situation. Then, you can find someone who has the training needed to gather and interpret the necessary data. *Linear programming* can help to determine the "best" use of scarce resources to achieve a specified goal. It can help in (1) improving the use of all organizational work resources, (2) keeping the costs of an operation or activity to a minimum, (3) determining volume—cost relationships, and (4) selecting the optimum mix of public services.

Queuing theory deals with waiting lines and can provide models for operations. The concept can be applied to people and things. It is especially effective in determining the optimum number of service points for a library. We have all gone to a bank, a store, or a library and stood in line for one of a few service points. Many of us think that we have a knack for always choosing the slowest line; some antagonism and frustration sets in at this point.

Libraries have a surprising number of waiting lines for patrons: lines for checking out books, security checks at entrances, waiting lists for popular materials, reserve service waiting lists, in-person reference service, and telephone reference, to name a few. Library materials spend a great deal of time in line for processing of one sort or another—everything from ordering to shelving. Naturally, this waiting involves costs. There are actually two types of cost present—the cost of additional service points, and the cost to the institution in terms of patron frustration. The trick is to achieve a balance of the two.

Other theories that might be of some use to libraries include the *game theory* (for the allocation of resources between competing demands), the *search theory* (for the optimum means of locating information), and the *Monte Carlo method* (for accounting for chance occurences). These are the most prominent techniques for among the many available. The appropriate application of these and other techniques can make the work load easier and more pleasant for your staff while improving service to patrons. It also will help to enhance the library's image as an effective cost-conscious institution.

COST ACCOUNTING

Throughout the preceding material, references have been made to costs and to work activities. The results of work analysis can be used in an activity called *cost accounting*—the process of comparing costs (expenses) with results (products or services) in order to ascertain the actual cost of a product or service (catalog a book, or answer one telephone reference question, for example). When it is done properly, cost accounting can be a powerful took in preparing a budget, determining staffing needs, planning new services, or arranging new service locations. It can help you decide whether to use an outside service for a particular library function (for example, technical processing or online data-base searching).

A common way of cost accounting is to divide costs into three categories: labor, supplies, and overhead. Supplies such as pens, paper, forms, books, library materials of all kinds, and typewriter ribbon are easy to identify. But what about the actual typewriter and its maintenance. Supplies or overhead? Do you depreciate its cost over a fixed period of time and use only a given year's cost? Or do you use the price paid? Or the cost of a new typewriter? There are various methods and rationales used to decide these things. If you overlook these factors, you will ignore some real costs.

Labor costs would seem relatively easy to calculate, but it all depends on how accurate you want to be. It might not be as simple as the number of persons and the total of their salaries. Persons who work in more than one area present a problem, because the percentage of their time spent performing an activity affects the cost of that activity. Also, do you count vacation time toward the cost of producing a unit, even though the vacationer has nothing to do with production at that moment? Consider also the cost of employee benefits—they certainly do cost the organization. The point here is that the type of data you seek should depend on what you want to do. Simple figures might be adequate for internal planning in a unit; however, library-wide or system-wide planning require that a great deal more be taken into account.

Overhead costs are costs that are *not* directly attributable to the production of a particular product or service. Administrative salaries, building maintenance, utilities, travel expenses, and insurance are commonly considered overhead items. Because publicly funded activities usually take place in public buildings that are tax free and rent free, some writers suggest that cost figures that do not take these factors into account are unrealistic. They suggest treating the building as a private one for accounting, but this would require a great deal of time, effort, and money. Would it be worth it?

Of course, an expert should set up your library's detailed cost accounting system; however, for your own purposes, rough cost accounting isn't that difficult. Use staff salaries as labor costs, the annual supplies budget as supplies cost, and your salary as overhead; this will give you the total to divide by the number of units of service or products produced in a year by your unit. The figure will probably be surprisingly high for unit costs. As you use more cost data, those costs will increase.

SYSTEMS APPROACH

A system is any set of interacting variables. Each system is part of a larger system. For instance, a department's variables will include people, equipment, organization, and procedures. If changes are made with respect to one variable, consequences will be felt within the other variables. Changes within one department can easily affect an entire organization. Remember, too, that the library is part of a larger social system and is greatly influenced by that system as well as by internal changes.

Systems approaches, then, consider the effects of any change on the entire process or organization rather than the effects of change on a variable. System analysis, then, may be considered merely an analysis of an operation in order to identify the controllable and the uncontrollable variables and to determine exactly how the system works. It is a part of operations research, and it may produce either flow diagrams or block diagrams that could lead to improvements.

The starting point is a set of objectives. The whole design remains the focus (*not* the design of subsystems). The results achieved by a team of 11 football players is greater than that achieved by 11 individuals performing without any integrated effort. The analogy for organizations seem clear.

Basic to understanding the systems approach and the design of management information systems is the concept of *information feedback,* which explains the goal-seeking and self-correcting interplay that occurs between parts of a system. The feedback concept is concerned with the use of information for control. It has been applied in engineering, biology, and other areas; however, its use in organizational settings is relatively recent.

A vital development for systems approaches was the notion of *programming decisions* by means of rules. Things such as payrolls, inventory control, and customer billing result from programmed decisions—rules and policies have been programmed into the organization; they need only be followed. The problem here, as always, is how to handle the unquanitifiable factors.

Of course, the absolutely essential element in being able to perform most of these analyses has been the development of the *electronic digital computer*. Without it, the vast amounts of data now processed could never be handled; the mathematical computations needed for these operations would impossible to perform in a lifetime. Nevertheless, *the computer is only the tool of those who see it*. The human element in any system comes before all else, even if it seems to lag behind technology at times.

The computer can read, solve mathematical problems, make simple logical choices, and print—but not in a human manner. An electronic data processing (EDP) system is made up of components that can be categorized as follows: (1) information input or reading devices, (2) memory and information-storage instruments, (3) arithmetical and logical facilities, (4) information output or writing devices, and (5) operator control panels or consoles. These components may be integrated or separated, but they all need to be present in a complete system.

Basically, computers can only add and subtract (they multiply and divide by means of repeated addition and substruction at high speed). This is done by a flow of electrical current through electronic on-and-off switches. The difference between computers and desk calculators is one of speed. A computer can complete thousands of computations in less than a second.

If they are given adequate instructions, computers can make logical choices automatically. They can choose the appropriate reaction to the comparison of two numbers (conditions). For instance, if two numbers are equal, the difference between them is zero. In this case, the computer would be programmed to select a certain sequence of operations: if A is greater than B, another sequence would be initiated; and if B is greater than A, then a third sequence would begin. The computer does not know what the numbers represent; it can only assess logical relationships under the conditions that are given to it. Humans then translate the results to fit their particular terms and uses.

Impact typewriters have simply proved to be too slow for many purposes. Recording information on paper or magnetic tape, and then feeding that tape into printing devices, can produce much greater efficiency. Because speed is of the essence here, research constantly strives to increase speeds, with some devices printing up to 100,000 lines per minute.

The first step in deciding whether to use computers is to figure out where they could be used more effectively than existing procedures. The various computer companies have an abundance of literature on technical and cost alternatives, and they are naturally thrilled to share it with potential customers. Nevertheless, the library itself must determine its need (or lack of need) for computer assistance.

Costs in this area cannot be neglected. Because no true consensus exists as to the various aspects of computer application (even among manufacturers, universities, and professional association members), knowing what training techniques and requirements to set up is difficult for the unitiated. Again, the organization's requirements are the only guideline here, so they must be as specific as possible.

The number of unanticipated difficulties associated with a newly installed EDP system will probably cause most of the people involved with it to wonder why they ever chose the system. One of the major problems is in coverting manual record keeping into a form that is adaptable to computer use. Moreover, there will probably be shutdowns, "dumps" (rejections of the program by the computer because of an error in instructions), and other assorted headaches. However, if the need has been assessed correctly, and the computer is truly needed, then these headaches must be borne.

The introduction of the computer will affect morale, especially among the accounting, production, and control personnel. Managers may be affected, as well as subordinates, because this new factor is surrounded by a mystique. Personnel changes will be inevitable, as even the part-time shelver could tell without knowing much about the operation of the entire system.

Given the introduction of a full-time computer system, a library's organizational patterns are bound to change. Planners must recognize this fact, allow for it in their planning, and be prepared to make adjustments along the way. The computer can be a double-edged tool, but it is one of the most valuable of the basic management tools when it is used well and wisely toward solid organization objectives.

EVALUATING THE LIBRARY

A few years ago, Daniel Gore published an article in *Library Journal* (May 1, 1978; 933–937) entitled "Mischief in Management" in which he commented on the dangers of measuring library performance. At several points in this book, comments are made regarding the need to have sound, objective standards of performance. Yet, how does one measure the value or effectiveness of an answer to a reference question, a book read, or a document used? What is good reference service? Although these questions are difficult, librarians must answer then, along with similar questions regarding the ways in which the library functions. If librarians do not answer these questions, others will—like the International City Management Association, in *Measuring the Effectiveness of Basic Municipal Servoces.*[1] The section on libraries follows, in its entirety. Table 15.3 summarizes the measures of effectiveness for library service.

LIBRARIES SERVICES

Libraries provide reading and audio-visual materials for entertainment, education and information. This section focuses on how satisfactory this service is but not on its impact on other objectives such as community educational development.

The objectives and measures suggested here rely heavily on citizen evaluation. Library users are asked to rate such factors as availability of information, helpfulness of staff and comfort of the library. Non-users are asked about their reasons for non-use.

Other useful measurements include counts of total users and participation rates (the percent of different households using library services) and availabilty of library holdings.

Procedures for measuring opportunities are suggested. They focus on such factors as service hours, accessibility and variety. Some rely on citizen feedback while others draw on objective, internal library measurements.

These data collection procedures also permit evaluation of how well various population groups are served, such as those living in various neighborhoods, and various age, sex, and income groups.

The objectives and measures listed here are for evaluating the overall library system, but the measurement procedures can also provide some information on specific units, such as reference, circulation or branch operations. To evaluate special programs, such as mobile or outreach programs or libraries for lawyers or schools, some measures will have to be modified. For example, the measure on "Diversity and Currentness of Book Holdings" will probably have to be modified for special libraries and the measurement procedures for "Physical Accessibility" would need to be modified somewhat for mobile or outreach programs. However, many measures, such as "Overall Citizen Satisfaction" and "Helpfulness–Attitude of the Staff," apply special operations as well as to the overall system.

Effectiveness data can be used in different ways. For example, if the measurement process finds that citizens fail to use their library because they cannot get to it, outreach programs would seem warranted. If the citizens report that hours are inconvenient, it may be possible to extend or shift hours of operation. If there is a lack of knowledge as to library offerings, new information programs can be devised and tested.

Certainly, more thought needs to go into the development of realistic measures. Would you want your library to be assessed on the bases presented in Table 15.3? For example, measure 8 fails to address the question of relevance of library titles to *your* particular patrons. Some

TABLE 15.3 SUMMARY OF PRINCIPAL MEASURES OF EFFECTIVENESS FOR LIBRARY SERVICE

Overall Objective: Provide to the satisfaction of all citizens a comprehensive, timely, reliable, and readily available body of information in an attractive and easily accessible location.[d]

Objective	Quality characteristic	Specific measure	Data collection procedure[a]
Overall citizen satisfaction	Citizen satisfaction	1. Percentage of households rating library as satisfactory/unsatisfactory.	General citizen survey of a representative set of city households.[b]
	User satisfaction	2. Percentage of households using city libraries that rate them as satisfactory/unsatisfactory.	Library survey of a representative set of user households or general citizen survey.[b]
	Usage—household	3. Percentage of households using/not using a public library four or more times over the period of a year, with reasons for nonuse grouped as relatively controllable and noncontrollable.	General citizen survey of a representative set of city households. (See Questions 15 and 17, Chapter IV.)[b]
	Usage—registration	4. Percentage of households with/without a valid registration card.	Statistics from public library or general citizen survey of a representative set of city households. (See Question 14, Chapter IV.)[b]
	Usage—visitation	5. Number of visits to library facilities per capita.	Some libraries count number of users. Sample counts can be made by those not recording this information on a routine basis. Population estimates made by most city planning departments.
	Usage—circulation	6. Circulation per capita by type of material—e.g., fiction, nonfiction, records, and film—divided between internal and external use.	External circulation figures are kept by most public libraries. Internal figures can be estimated from a periodic sampling.[c]

(continued)

Table 15.3 (*Continued*)

Objective	Quality characteristic	Specific measure	Data collection procedure[a]
	Helpfulness—attitude of staff	7. Percentage of user households rating helpfulness–attitude of staff as satisfactory/unsatisfactory.	Library survey of a representative set of user households or general citizen survey.[b]
	Diversity and Current-ness of Book Holdings.	8. Probability of owning books published during given time period (e.g., last 5 years)	Draw random sample of books published from the Book Publishing Record (BPR) and compare with library holdings.[c]
Comprehensiveness/ timeliness	Diversity and current-ness of book holdings	9. Probability of owning periodicals published during given time period (e.g., last 5 years).	Draw random sample of citations published in one of common periodical indexes (e.g., Readers Guide, Art Index, Education Index) and compare with library holdings.[c]
	Size of holdings	10. Holdings per capita by type of media—e.g., books, periodicals, films, and phonograph records.	Holding statistics kept by most public librar-ies. Population estimates made by most city planning departments.
Reliability/availability	Availability of book holdings	11. Probability that a user would obtain any book owned by the library.	Draw random sample of books held and check shelf for each title.[c]
	Availability of periodic holdings	12. Probability that a user would obtain any periodical owned by the library.	Draw random sample of periodicals held and check shelf for each.[c]
	Quality of reference service	13. Percentage of households using city ref-erence services that rate them as satis-factory/unsatisfactory.	Library survey of a representative set of user households or general citizen survey.[b]
	Speed of service	14. Percentage of households using library that rate speed of service (e.g, book re-trieval and checkout) as satisfactory/ unsatisfactory.	Same as above.

Physical attractiveness	User satisfaction with comfort, crowdedness, noise, etc.	15. Percentage of user households rating comfort, crowdedness, noise, cleanliness, and temperature/ventilation as satisfactory/unsatisfactory.	Library survey of a representative set of user households or general citizen survey.[b]
	Nonuser satisfaction	16. Percentage of nonuser households that give crowdedness and noise as a reason for nonuse of facilities.	General citizen survey of a representative set of city households. (See Questions 16–9, and 16–10, Chapter IV.)[b]
Accessibility	Physical accessibility	17. Percentage of citizens who live within 15–30 minutes travel time (by transport mode) of a city library.	Counts from mapping latest census tract population figures against location of facilities with appropriate travel time radius drawn around each facility.
		18. Percentage of nonuser households that give poor physical accessibility as a reason for nonuse.	General citizen survey of a representative set of city households. (Set Question 16–8, Chapter IV.)[b]
	Hours of operation	19. Percentage of user households rating hours of operation as satisfactory/unsatisfactory.	Library survey of a representative set of user households or general citizen survey.[b]
		20. Percentage of nonuser households giving poor operating hours as a reason for nonuse.	General citizen survey of a representative set of city households. (See Question 16-7, Chapter IV.)[b]

[a]Except for measures obtained from the general citizen survey, measures can readily be obtained for individual library branches. Even in the cases of the general citizen survey measures, information by individual libraries could be obtained if questions are included regarding specific branches.

[b]An annual multiservice citizen survey that might be used to collect this data is described in Chapter IV of this report.

[c]For specific measures and procedures, see E. R. DeProspo et al., *Performance Measures for Public Libraries*, Chicago: American Library Association, 1973. Another, and more direct procedure is to ask a sample of library users whether materials they wanted were available at the public library when they attempted to obtain them. A user sample survey is currently under development.

[d]Reprinted with permission of the publisher.

points (15–20) relate to the level of funding, not to the service given. Despite these serious problems, the system is used. Some people continue to believe that a poor something is better than nothing.

Several years ago, I was involved in a study of criteria of library effectiveness. Despite the passage of 8 years, the basic message remains the same. The following edited reprint of an article reporting the results of that study sums up the issues involved in measuring library effectiveness.

Many measures have been employed in attempts to evaluate library performance, as we discovered in our review of over five hundred articles, books, and abstracts. Obviously, not all of these measures were unique; they were in fact slight modifications of one another. In order to make sense of the extensive list which we had accumulated, we grouped them in accordance with the aspect of the system that was being evaluated. These we called "criterion concepts"—for an example, accessibility of materials, cost, and user satisfaction are some of the important concepts in evaluating library effectiveness. The specific techniques or data used to measure these concepts we called "criterion measures." We believe that this distinction between concepts and measures is meaningful and that it eliminates a good deal of confusion in the literature on library evaluation. In addition, the list enabled us to organize and classify the various evaluation procedures we came across in our review of the literature, for most of the reported measures turned out to be slight modifications of one of six basic criteria. The complete list that follows indicates the criterion concepts (Roman numerals) and the various specific criterion measures (Arabic numerals) that fall into the basic categories:

I   Accessibilty
   1. Number of services and degree of services provided various classes of users.
   2. Ratio of services requested to services available.
   3. Ratio of holdings to total user population (actual and potential).
II   Cost
   1. Staff size.
   2. Staff skill and characteristics.
   3. Unit cost.
   4. Ratio of book budget to users.
III   User Satsifaction
   1. User satisfaction with services rendered.
   2. Number of user activities in library.
   3. Percentage of items in collection as listed in a checklist.
   4. Percentage of items in collection by type of materials (books, serials, reports, etc.).
   5. Percentage of items in collection by type of material compared to various classes of users.
   6. Quality-value of items in collection based on expert opinion.
   7. Ratio of documents used to materials requested.

IV Response Time
   1. Speed of services.
   2. Ratio of number of services offered to average response time for all services.
   3. Ratio of response time (secure document) to total time document is of value.
   4. Ratio of holdings to response time.
 V Cost/Benefit Ratio
   1. Ratio of services provided to total cost.
   2. Ratio of total service expenditures to users (actual and/or potential).
   3. Ratio of item cost to item value or utility.
   4. Ratio of a given service (including overhead cost) to response time cost.
VI Use
   1. Gross use of services (reference questions answered, bibliographies completed, etc.).
   2. Ratio of actual users to potential users.
   3. Total library use (attendance figures, circulation, etc.).
   4. Ratio of a given service to toal number of users.
   5. Ratio of total use for all services to total number of services provided.
   6. Percentage of materials used by type and by class of users (student, teacher, researcher, etc.).
   7. Ratio of documents circulated to various classes of users.
   8. Ratio of documents circulated to number of users.
   9. Ratio of total use to total holdings.
   10. Item-use-day (a measure based on the number of items used in a twenty-four-hour period).

BACKGROUND COMMENTS

Perhaps the most surprising aspect of the literature review was the lack of concern with the how and why of the evaluation process. It would seen to be self-evident that any evaluation of library performance should include a discussion of the purpose, the method of evaluation, and the reasons for the evaluation. There are a surprising number of reports and studies on the subject of evaluation that fail to make it clear just what the purpose is. Consequently, confusion arises over the interpretation of the results. Of the studies surveyed very few identified the goals or the importance of a given service to the achievement of those goals. . . .

Even those few studies dealing with the full range of services failed to consider one of the most basic of all library functions, conservation. Dissemination, the library's best-known function, has been carefully considered; however, conservation for later dissemination has been consistently ignored. None of the studies examined concerned itself with the question of conservation. While it may be true that only the large teaching-research-regional medical library must be greatly concerned with conservation, all libraries need to consider the question to some extent. Many methods of evaluation place a high premium on the performance of a service (circulation) that is or may be detrimental to the conservation of materials—an equally important library function. When evaluating library effectiveness, the total program of library services and functions must be taken into account. . . .

Our literature search indicates that in measuring library performance, a great many variations of a few basic approaches have been tried. Most of the studies concentrate on one or two services. The literature in general reflects the lack of consideration of (a) the total service program, and (b) the importance of using multiple criteria for evaluating service functions. Without such consideration it seems to be impossible to arrive at valid measures of library performance.

As a further complication, one must consider whether all the measures, even the six "basic" criterion concepts, are equally important for measuring all services. If not, these should be weighted to reflect their relative importance both for the evaluation of a specific service and for the total library program. Research that would provide an empirical basis for deciding these issues would seem to be of primary importance. Libraries perform multiple services, and therefore it seems unlikely that any single criterion can be considered as the sole valid measure of library performance. When it is possible to apply several different criteria, the question of weighting each one becomes critical. In order to determine what the weighting factor should be, one needs to know the relative importance of each element in achieving a specific library function.

In light of these considerations, it is suggested that research should be directed to the development of a technique to aid in establishing for each individual library a list of its services, ascribing to each service its relative importance to the total library program. A second phase of this problem would be to determine which criteria were appropriate to measure the performance of these services and the weight that should be assigned to each. For example, does it seem valid to give the same weight to response time for two such different services as translation and information–reference? While response time would be a valid criterion in both cases it seems likely that most people would rather see a slower response time (less weight) and more accessibility (more weight) when evaluating a translation service. However, these differentiations have not yet been made.

Considering total library performance, conservation is another area that needs to be investigated. No studies were encountered in the literature search that even discussed conservation as an aspect of library performance. A library may incur conservation losses when user services are increased, and some techniques should be developed for counterbalancing these functions. From an overall point of view, it would seem that less effort should be devoted to developing modifications of existing measures of performance evaluation and more effort should be directed toward developing precise operational procedures for—

(a) defining the variables involved in the measurement of each criterion concept;

(b) specifying the statistical data and formulas needed to calculate the criterion measures;

(c) suggesting a procedure that will enable one to combine these individual criterion measures so as to evaluate total library performance;

(d) developing a procedure to weight the individual criterion measure in accordance with each library's estimation of the importance of services being provided; and

(e) eventually arriving at a procedure whereby meaningful comparisons can be made of libraries.[2]

As may be inferred, each major topic in this chapter has been the subject of countless books, articles, and discussions. Anyone who is serious about a career in management must be familiar to some degree with all these subjects, (and in greater depth than is appropriate in a general text of this type).

The great interrelationship between work analysis and budgeting cannot be emphasized too strongly. These two elements in turn provide the basic means of controlling both the direction and the operation of the library. Connected with that is the fact that budget requests are assessed in terms of the achievement of the library's goals. The process of assessing how well this is done draws on the measures of library effectiveness, with the goal always remaining the best possible service to the patron.

BIBLIOGRAPHY

1. International City Management Association, *Measuring the Effectiveness of Basic Municipal Services* (Washington, D.C.: ICMA, 1974), pp. L–1 to L–4.
2. G. E. Evans, H. Borko and P. Ferguson, "Review of Criteria Used to Measure Library Effectiveness," *Bulletin of the Medical Library Association* 60 (1972): 102–110.

FURTHER READING

Baily, R. O. "Let's Make Word Processing Really Work." *Computer Decisions* 11 (1979): 37–38+.

Becker, J. "System Analysis: Prelude to Library Data Processing." *ALA Bulletin* 59 (1965): 293–296.

Beeler, M. G. F. *Measuring the Quality of Library Services.* Metuchen, N.J.: Scarecrow, 1974.

Berg, I. *Managers and Work Reform: A Limited Engagement.* New York: Free Press, 1978.

Bliss, E. E. "ABCs of Time Management." *Supervisory Management* 23 (1978): 28–33.

Bolles, S. W. "Use of Flow Charts in the Analysis of Library Operations." *Special Libraries* 58 (1967): 95–99.

Bommer, M. "Operations Research in Libraries: A Critical Assessment." *Journal of the American Society for Information Science* 26 (1975): 137–139.

Bonus, H. "How to Operate a Non-profit Organization Effectively: Principles of Cost–benefit Analysis." In *International Association of Technological University Libraries, 1977.* Louvain, Belgium: IATUL, 1978.

Budnick, F. *Principles of Operations Research for Management.* Homewood, Ill.: Irwin, 1977.

Buhler, W. B. *Controlling Paperwork—Yours and the Government's.* New York: AMACOM, 1979.

Burkett, J. "Time Factor in Library and Information Management." *Journal of Librarianship* 8 (1976): 21–32.

Connolly, T., and Deutsch, S. J. "Performance Measurement: Some Conceptual Issues." *Evaluation and Program Planning* 3 (1980): 35–43.

Daft, R. L., and MacIntosh, N. B. "A New Approach to Design and Use of Management Information." *California Management Review* 21 (1978): 82–92.

Davidson, J. *Effective Time Management; A Practical Workbook.* New York: Human Sciences Press, 1978.

De Prospo, E. R., Altman, E., and Beasley, K. E. *Performance Measures for Public Libraries.* Chicago: American Library Association, 1973.

DeProspo, E. R. "The Use of Community Analysis in the Measurement Process." *Library Trends* 24 (1976): 557–567.

Dougherty, R. M., and Heinritz, F. J. *Scientific Management of Library Operations.* New York: Scarecrow, 1966.

Drott, M. C. "Random Sampling: A Tool for Library Research." *College and Research Libraries* 30 (1969): 199–225.

Duckworth, W. E. *A Guide to Operational Research.* London: Chapman & Hall, 1977.

DuMont, R. R. "A Conceptual Basis for Library Effectiveness." *College and Research Libraries* 41 (1980): 103–111.

Duyvis, F. D. "Standardization as a Tool of Scientific Management." *Library Trends* 2 (1954): 410–427.

Euster, J. R. "Washington Library Network as a Management Information System." *Pacific Northwest Library Association Quarterly* 42 (1978): 4–8.

Evaluation Research Methods: A Basic Guide. Beverly Hills, Calif.: Sage Pubs., 1977.

Franklin, J. L., and Thraser, J. H. *An Introduction to Program Evaluation.* New York: Wiley, 1976.

Gabriel, R. A. *Program Evaluation: A Social Science Approach.* New York: MSS Information Corp., 1975.

Gilmour, R. W. *Business Systems Handbook; Analysis, Design, and Documentation Standards.* Englewood Cliffs, N.J.: Prentice-Hall, 1979.

Goldberg, R. L. *A Systems Approach to Library Program Development.* Metuchen, N.J.: Scarecrow, 1976.

Goodell, J. S. *Libraries and Work Sampling.* Littleton, Colo.: Libraries Unlimited, 1975.

Gottheimer, D. "Manager as Forms Designer—A Cost/Efficency Approach." *Administrative Management* 37 (1977): 64–65.

Gull, C. D. "Logical Flow Charts and Other New Techniques for Administration of Libraries and Information Centers." *Library Resources and Technical Services* 12 (1968): 47–64.

Hawgood, J. "Participative Assessment of Library Benefits." *Drexel Library Quarterly* 13 (1977): 68–83.

Hayes, R. M., and Becker, J. *Handbook of Data Processing for Libraries.* 2d ed. Los Angeles: Melville Publishing, 1974.

Hellwig, K. D. "Ten Steps toward Successful Work Measurement." *Management World* 5 (1976): 3–6.

Herzlinger, R. "Why Data Systems in Nonprofit Organizations Fail." *Harvard Business Review* 55 (1977): 81–86.

Hirsch, H. "Implementing Word Processing With a View toward Success." *Administrative Management* 40 (1979): 53–54+.

Housley, T. *Data Communications and Teleprocessing Systems.* Englewood Cliffs, N.J.: Prentice-Hall, 1979.

Hu, T., Booms, B. H., and Kaltreider, L. W. A. *Benefit-Cost Analysis of Alternative Library Delivery Systems.* Westport, Conn.: Greenwood Press, 1975.

Johnson, R. H., and Winn, P. R. *Quantitative Methods for Management.* Boston: Houghton, 1976.

Kantor, P. B. "A Review of Library Operations Research." *Library Research* 1 (1979): 295–345.

Kaser, D. "Evaluation of Administrative Services." *Library Trends* 22 (1974): 257–264.

Kozumplik, W. A. "Time and Motion Study of Library Operations." *Special Libraries* 58 (1967): 585–588.

Ladendorf, J. "Information Service Evlauation." *Special Libraries* 64 (1973): 273–279.

Lancaster, F. W. *The Measurement and Evaluation of Library Services.* Washington, D.C.: Information Resources Press, 1977.

McCormick, E. J. *Job Analysis: Methods and Applications.* New York: AMACOM, 1979.

McCrossan, J. A. "Planning and Evaluation of Library Programs throughout the States." *Library Trends* 27 (1978): 127–148.

Mansfield, J. W. "Human Factors of Queuing: A Library Circulation Model." *Journal of Academic Librarianship* 6 (1981): 342–344.

Mason, R. O., and Swanson, E. B. "Measurement for Management Decision: A Perspective." *California Management Review* 21 (1979): 79–81.

Mitchell, B. J. *Cost Analysis of Library Functions: A Total Systems Approach.* Greenwich, Conn.: JAI Press, 1978.

Mundel, M. E. *Motion and Time Study; Improving Productivity.* 5th ed. Englewood Cliffs, N.J.: Prentice-Hall, 1978.

Myers, G. "Forms Management. Pt. 3. Forms Construction and Printing." *Journal of Systems Management* 27 (1976): 6–13.

Pederson, K. M. "A Proposed Model for Evaluation Studies." *Administrative Science Quarterly* 22 (1977): 306–317.

Pflug, G. "Effects of Automation on Library Administration." *IFLA Journal* 4 (1975): 267–275.

Poister, T. H. *Public Program Analysis; Applied Research Methods.* Baltimore: Univ. Park Press, 1978.

Program Evaluation in the Public Sector. New York: Praeger, 1979.

Reynolds, H., and Tramel, M. E. *Executive Time Management; Getting 12 Hours' Work Out of an 8-Hour Day.* Englewood Cliffs, N.J.: Prentice-Hall, 1979.

Rouse, W. B. "Tutorial: Mathematical Modeling of Library Systems." *American Society of Information Science Journal* 30 (1979): 181–192.

Sassone, P. G., and Schaffer, W. A. *Cost-benefit Analysis; A Handbook.* New York: Academic Press, 1978.

Schlacter, G., and Belli, D. "Program Evaluation—An Alternative to Divine Guidance." *California Librarian* 37 (1976): 26–31.

Schwartz, J. H. "Factors Affecting Comparison of Special Libraries." *Special Libraries* 71 (1980): 1–4.

Shatzkin, L. "The Fallacies of Unit Cost Accounting." *Publishers' Weekly* (Oct. 8, 1979): 36–37.

Soumelis, C. G. *Project Evaluation Methodologies and Techniques.* Paris: UNESCO, 1977.

Steers, R. M. *Organizational Effectiveness: A Behavioral View.* Santa Monica, Calif.: Goodyear Pub. Co., 1977.

Talbert, T. L., and Carroll, K. I. "Measuring Clerical Job Performance." *Personnel Journal* 55 (1976): 573–575.

Turner, A. M. "Why Do Department Heads Take Longer Coffee Breaks? A Public Library Evaluates Itself." *American Libraries* 9 (1978): 213–215.

U.S. Office of Management and Budget. Evaluation and Program Implementation Division. *Problems in Evaluation Design; A Background Paper.* Washington, D.C.: Government Printing Office, 1976.

U.S. Small Business Administration. *Techniques of Time Management.* Washington, D.C.: Government Printing Office, 1979.

Urban Institute. *Measuring the Effectiveness of Basic Municipal Services.* Washington, D.C.: International City Management Association, 1974.

Voos, H. "Standard Times for Certain Clerical Activities in Technical Processing." *Library Resources and Technical Services* 10 (1966): 223–227.

White, G. T. "Quantitative Measures of Library Effectiveness." *Journal of Academic Librarianship* 3 (1977): 128–136.

Zemke, R. "Task Analysis: Figuring Out What People Need to Learn." *Training* 14 (1977): 16–20.

16. Changing Environments

Prophecies usually have a way of coming back to haunt the prophet. Certainly, no long-range predictions about the future of library management will be made in this chapter; but some observable trends that I feel may be long-term are presented for brief consideration.

TRENDS

First, it is obvious that the "knowledge explosion" will continue. It may take place less frequently in the print forms, but whatever the vehicle, people will continue to want information. Perhaps not too many years from now, collections of books and serials will be considered museum pieces; most people will secure needed information by electronic means in their homes or places of work. Even if this happens, the need will remain for persons to compile collections of material and organize it for use. Managers will still exist, and the basic skills needed to manage will remain almost unchanged.

Until that time, libraries must recognize the impact of expanding knowledge on the whole of society. Growth is change, and it must be reckoned with as it happens. In societies that place great faith in knowledge (especially scientific knowledge), the uncertainties generated by "breakthroughs' in various fields have a disturbing effect on people. Indeed, some people have suggested that the knowledge explosion has increased social instability; taking a broad view, that may be true to an extent. The morning or evening news can indeed leave a person with a sense of unease.

As part of the government to which people tend to turn in times of uncertainty, libraries have unwittingly contributed a bit to this unease. In fact, by taking advantage of generous government spending designed to solve social problems, libraries have grown tremendously. This growth, in turn, has both benefited from the knowledge explosion (more materials are available) and contributed to it (more materials are needed).

Library staff members are as susceptible to uneasiness as anyone else. Knowing as we do that people prefer the status quo to the unknown, no one should be surprised that library staff are often reluctant to undertake any type of change in their daily environment. Both at home and at work, they constantly face the full impact of the knowledge explosion and increased knowledge of the world's problems.

Neither of these factors—change and people's resistance to it—seems likely to disappear. Consequently, managers will need to spend more and more time in planning and implementing change so as to keep anxiety at a minimum. Participatory management does not seem to be the answer, because staff resent spending as much time as it requires away from the "real work." Managers must seek methods of balancing participation and "real work" if they are to truly allay fears of change.

Uncertainty about the future is likely to increase rather than decrease. The pace of technological development is difficult for many people to adjust to, and applications are just beginning to be made of new methods in areas such as technical services. Moreover, even newer methods may be just down the road. Perhaps older staff who have used other methods will feel most uncomfortable with changes, while younger staff will find it easier to adjust. The manager's role in such cases is to recognize these feelings genuine and to help the staff adjust to new systems. In this sense, the manager is a buffer between staff and technology.

Also, in the future managers will have to increasingly accept paradoxes as part of institutional life. Paradoxes have always been with us, but their number seems to increase along with social complexity. The library currently faces one such paradox. On the one hand, people expect more and more services (more service points, bigger collections, longer hours, and so on), and they will continue to do so. At the same time nations are becoming aware of the finite nature of the resources that they must use in order to satisfy ever-growing demands. Some of the current catch phrases are "steady state," "zero growth," "stable services," "small is beautiful," "era of limits," and "limits to growth." They simple reflect the attitude we can do little more than we are already doing, and perhaps we might be better off doing less. Of course, managers are in the middle on this one, as they always have been. It is difficult to reconcile the fact that the patron who constantly demands more and better service from the library is actively participating in a local "Limit Government Spending" committee.

A final example of the type of paradox that you will face is what George Gordon identifies as multiple meanings of the terms *representation* and *representative*.

> Throughout our discussion we have referred to the calls for "representativeness" as meaning inclusion in decision-making processes of those whose interests are affected by decisions made, especially those previously excluded. An older, more traditional meaning of "representation" refers to "overhead democracy"—that is, majority control through political representatives, "wherein administrative officers are primarily responsible and loyal to their superiors for carrying out the directions of the elected representatives." Old and new meanings of representation have collided in theory and practice during the past two decades, and no slackening of the conflict between them is in sight. Ultimately, it is a conflict between concepts stressing respectively *majoritarian* and *minoritarian* political representation—that is, generalized majority rule versus systematic inclusion of social, political, and economic minorities.[1]

Libraries encounter the minoritarian situation in staffing need requirements in many areas. The future will probably see this reflected in terms of library governing boards as well.

More and more graduate librarians will have course work in both a type of library (public, school, academic, special) and in general management techniques. These persons will not be forced to learn on the job; as a result, they may be better able to cope with the problems that they encounter. Further in the future, students may simply graduate with a specialty in management, much as one can graduate with a specialty in cataloging today. Sound programs could lead to a marked improvement in library management. A 2-year course would assure full attention to the subject. This might produce better results than those found in the current situation, which reflects a combination of several classes, on-the-job learning, and independent study.

The next trend is that of collective bargaining. Library managers can expect to do a lot more of it, and with much more aggressive bargaining agents on the other side of the table. Demands for better working conditions will need to be balanced against funding limitations. Also, staffing patterns will have to include more minority representation, which could become a union issue very soon.

The future manager must consider the library in a systems approach, acknowledging that the library is (1) integrative (more than the sum of its parts), (2) interdisciplinary, (3) empirical, (4) organistic, (5) decision oriented, and (6) informational. The manager must operate with these facts in mind.

The manager will need to be a synthesizer—a person who is deeply involved in integrating the library into a total system, both internally and externally. The past practice has been to consider only the parts; however, the relationship between people and physical objects as an entire system cannot be ignored.

In the future, managers will operate in an interdisciplinary environment. They will be required to draw on mathematics and the physical sciences as well as on the social sciences. Thought will be in terms of human response to situations, which will require compatible interaction of factors from a multitude of areas of knowledge.

Empirical information will become increasingly important for the manager. Past experience will yield more and more to collectible, collatable data in attempts to rationalize decision making. Imaginative analysis will continue to be important, but there will be more data on which to draw in order to make such analysis.

The organistic approach simply means that the manager treats the entire organization as a living organism. Things are not done in a rough-shod manner that is reminiscent of a factory at its worst. Rather, the organizational environment is structured to encourage interaction of employees in problem-solving groups that need less face-to-face leadership than they did previously. This is also a holistic approach, recognizing the unity and interaction of all parts of the organization.

Rational decision making will certainly come more and more to the fore. Because decisions will become more numerous, top management will be more and more involved in establishing policies and strategies, as well as the design of the system to implement these plans. Thus, more operational decisions will be automated to permit time to be spent on planning.

Finally, information will be the means, and the information systems will be the structure, for implementing the systems approach for the manager of tomorrow. Because knowledge will continue to increase, logical, effective information systems *must* be developed and put into practice by managers whose approach to management differs from the one used today.

All of this will probably make the future an exciting environment in which to work. Despite an increased emphasis on scientific management and hard data, I am certain that the service orientation of libraries will not be lost in the shuffle. The most successful librarians will be those who combine management knowledge with a true interest in people and their needs.

BIBLIOGRAPHY

1. G. Gordon, *Public Administration in America* (New York: St. Martin's, 1978), pp. 426–27. Internal quotation from E. Redford, *Democracy in the Administrative State* (New York: Oxford Univ. Press, 1969), p. 70.

FURTHER READING

Boaz, M. T. "Crisis of Librarianship: What Can We Do About It? Where Can We Go? What are the Futures?" *California Librarian* 38 (1977): 6–10.

Christopher, W. F. *Management for the 1980's.* New York: AMACOM, 1980.

Dickson, P. *The Future of the Work Place: The Coming Revolution In Jobs.* New York: Weybright & Talley, 1976.

Dunlap, C. R. "Challenge of the Future." *Southeast Librarian* 29 (1979): 9–14.

Fox, W. H. "Uncertain Future of Public Management." *Public Personnel Management* 5 (1976): 250–254.

Galvin, T. J. "Beyond Survival: Library Management for the Future." *Library Journal* 101 (1976): 1833–1835.

Heisel, W. D. "The Personnel Revolution: An Optimist's View." *Public Personnel Management* 5 (1976): 234–238.

Lancaster, F. W. "Whither Libraries? or, Wither Libraries." *College and Research Libraries* 39 (1978): 345–357.

"Letters-comments." *College and Research Libraries* 40 (1979): 267–268.

Leach, J. J. "Merging the Two Faces Of Personnel: A Challenge for the 1980a." *Personnel* 57 (1980): 52–57.

MacKenzie, A. G. "Library Management in the Eighties." Presented at a conference of the Library Association of Australia, Mobart, Australia, 1977. "Libraries in Society," Library Association of Australia, pp. 395–401.

Odiorne, G. S. "Personnel Management for the 80's." *Personnel Administrator* 24 (1979): 77–80.

Swanson, D. R. "Libraries and the Growth of Knowledge." *Library Quarterly* 49 (1979): 3–25.

Wilson, L. "Last Thirty Years as the Seedbed of the Future." *ASLIB Proceedings* 31 (1979): 2–15.

Index